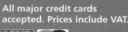

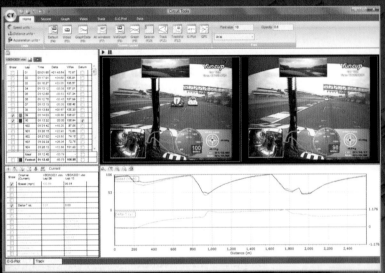

Contents

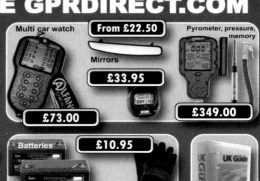

Introduction

For the driving enthusiast it's almost impossible to match the buzz of driving on track, and for trackday fans there is nowhere better to live than the UK. Nowhere else in the world has such a profusion and variety of circuits in such close proximity, while the spectacular thrills of Spa-Francorchamps and the Nürburgring are little more than a Channel hop away. You'll find guides to those two legendary circuits within this special **evo** magbook, along with all the major UK venues.

I have been fortunate enough to have raced and driven at circuits all over the world, but it all began with trackdays. After attending a handful of events, I bought myself a Caterham, went to as many days as I could, learnt a lot, met a bunch of new mates and had an absolute blast. In 2002 I started **evo**'s own trackday programme alongside my usual journalistic duties. In effect this book is a download of all that experience, along with tests and features written by my **evo** colleagues and respected track experts Mark Hales, John Barker and Richard Meaden.

Inside you'll find tips and information for both novices and experts alike, from the kit you'll need through to the mindset required for track driving. We've also included the very best **evo** Track Car of the Year tests from the past decade. So if you want to discover what it's like to drive a Westfield or a McLaren F1 (or anything in between) you'll find it here.

I hope you enjoy this **evo** magbook. But don't just read about it – get out there and have a go. You'll never look back.

Roger Green, editor

MAGAZINE

The evo Guide to Trackdays
From the publishers of **evo** magazine
www.evo.co.uk

EDITORIAL
5 Tower Court, Irchester Road, Wollaston,
Northants NN29 7PJ, United Kingdom
Email eds@evo.co.uk Tel 020 7907 6310

Production editor Peter Tomalin
Sub editor Ian Eveleigh
Art director Paul Lang
Senior designer Adam Shorrock
Staff writer Stephen Dobie

Contributing writers
John Barker, Henry Catchpole, Roger Green,
Mark Hales, Ralph Hosier, Richard Meaden

Contributing photographers
Gus Gregory, Matt Howell, Andy Morgan,
Kenny P, Chris Rutter, Matt Vosper

ADVERTISING
30 Cleveland Street, London W1T 4JD
email ads.evo@dennis.co.uk

Advertising manager Rob Schulp
Group advertising director Des Flynn
(020 7907 6742)
Advertising director Sarah Perks
(020 7907 6744)
Deputy advertising manager Tim Deeks
(020 7907 6773)

MANAGEMENT
Bookazine manager Dharmesh Mistry
Operations director Robin Ryan
Digital production manager Nicky Baker
Managing director of Advertising
Julian Lloyd-Evans
Newstrade director Martin Belson
Chief operating officer Brett Reynolds
Group finance director Ian Leggett
Chief executive James Tye
Chairman Felix Dennis

MAG**BOOK** The MagBook brand is
a trademark of Dennis
Publishing Ltd.
30 Cleveland St, London W1T 4JD. Company
registered in England. All material © Dennis
Publishing Ltd, licensed by Felden 2010, and may
not be reproduced in whole or in part without the
consent of the publishers.
The evo Guide to Trackdays
ISBN: 1-907232-33-8

LICENSING
To license this product, please contact Ornella
Roccoletti on +44 (0) 20 7907 6134 or email
ornella_roccoletti@dennis.co.uk

LIABILITY
While every care was taken during the
production of this MagBook, the publishers
cannot be held responsible for the accuracy of
the information or any consequence arising from
it. Dennis Publishing takes no responsibility for
the companies advertising in this MagBook.
The paper used within this MagBook is produced
from sustainable fibre, manufactured by mills with
a valid chain of custody.
Printed at BGP

Everything you always wanted to know about

TRACKDAYS

With another trackday season fast approaching, experienced circuit drivers are already planning their trips to Snetterton and Brands. It's a different story for those who haven't tried it before. Your first laps on track will certainly be thrilling but, equally, they'll be a bit scary and potentially intimidating. It's a leap into the unknown, a new adventure; your heart will be pounding, adrenalin will be coursing through your veins, and your stomach will be battling with a whole swarm of butterflies.

It won't even be particularly enjoyable at first. We've all been there, but we also know that the fear quickly dissipates and driving on track rapidly develops into one of the most exciting, rewarding and pleasurable things you can spend your money on. However, that first hurdle is a big one; there are plenty of questions to be answered and experience takes time to accumulate. So we've compiled a list of the most commonly asked questions – and profiled three drivers who are just starting out...

Can I get insurance?
Yes. Your current insurance company may even cover you on your existing policy, although this is increasingly becoming less common. They may extend the cover for the day for an additional fee and they will probably increase the excess. If they won't cover you at all – or you would rather not risk your no claims bonus – there are a number of companies who specialise in trackday cover.

How much will it cost and what will it cover?
There are a large number of variables, but the biggest factors here are the car you're driving and the type of cover you require. The cheapest cover is that provided by your road insurance (see above). If you go down the specialist route, you don't have to insure the full value of the car. However you should be realistic and we advise that you take out enough cover to provide for most bumps and scrapes; we suggest at least half the value of the car.

Standard road cars on road tyres are the cheapest to insure as a percentage of their total value, but an expensive road car is still going to command a chunky sum from a specialist broker. Ex-racecars or modified trackday cars are seen as a higher risk by these brokers, but on the plus side they are cheaper to repair than road cars and generally their total value is less, so they can be more cost-effective. This example is a real quote from Motorsport Insurance Services (01943 884555 email: info@raceinsurance.co.uk) for a thirty-year-old driver with a good record: Radical Clubsport, sum insured £8000, excess £850, premium £95 (excluding damage to the engine and gearbox).

Finally, the trackday organiser also has a bearing on insurance cost; there can be a 5 per cent weighting on your premium if you go on circuit with a company with a poor track record.

What happens if someone else drives into me and they're not insured?
Nothing. You are responsible for your own car, which is another reason to ensure you're covered for this eventuality. With strict track driving rules, however, this is a very rare occurrence.

How will track driving affect my warranty?
Good question, and a tricky one to answer, especially since in recent months some manufacturers appear unsure themselves! Most will honour any mechanical failure as long as these components have not been 'abused'. The definition

K146 LPN

Above: a cheap old rear-drive saloon can serve up plenty of entertainment. Below: a modified Golf is another route to trackday fun

DRIVER PROFILE:
STEPHEN HALL

If you thought trackdays were the preserve of the rich, think again. Of course you'll see 360s and 911 Turbos at full chat, but those drivers are unlikely to be having any more fun than guys like Stephen Hall. A few months ago, Hall splashed out on a new trackday toy and it cost him a paltry £400. 'To be honest, I probably paid over the odds,' he grins. 'I've since seen Senators for much less…'

Not many people would choose a large and very tired Luton saloon for their circuit kicks, but that doesn't worry Hall. 'I did my first trackday at Cadwell in an old Senator that I'd had a while. It was on its last legs but I figured that if it broke I'd just throw it away and get another. I got completely bitten by the circuit driving bug, had an absolute ball and had more fun than ever before. I did another three track-days last year, one in an E36 325i, but to be honest I had more fun in the Senator, so I carried on using that.

'It is a surprisingly well-balanced car and soaks up all the stick I give it, so I've bought another one now, a 2.6-litre auto. I've made some brake ducts to channel more air to the discs, but that's all I'm doing because the less I spend on the car, the more days I can afford.'

DRIVER PROFILE:
DUNCAN CLARKE

Even the evo advertising team aren't immune from the lure of track driving. Take Duncan Clarke, former evo ad executive, pictured with his modified Mk 1 Golf GTi.

'I've always been a Vee-Dub fan,' says Duncan. 'I think this one is my seventh. I've had other cars, but they always seem to break when I drive them. The Golf doesn't and it's what I term a no-bullshit car – it does exactly what it's supposed to do, it's not flash and it's not stuffed full of gizmos and airbags. As far as I am concerned, the Mk 1 is the ideal car to turn into a trackday machine.'

It's taken Clarke over two years to bring his Golf up to scratch, making the odd modification when funds have allowed. Including the initial purchase price, he reckons it's cost him around £6500. 'I wanted more pace but I didn't want a highly-tuned engine with all the added running costs that come with it, so I fitted a standard 16-valve Mk 2 lump and set about lightening the rest of the car. The interior has been stripped out and I've fitted polycarbonate windows. I've also replaced the standard suspension with Koni adjustable dampers and Eibach springs to improve the handling, along with two-piece split-rim wheels and Avon ACB10 track tyres.

'Now the car's finished, I'll be taking it to a few more circuits.'

You don't have to own a 911 or an M3 to have fun on track, as Stephen Hall and Duncan Clarke (left) prove

'Your car will be driven harder for longer than it has ever been before'

of abuse is, it seems, open to interpretation. Check the warranty small print and contact them if you need further clarification.

Can I take my standard road car on track?
Absolutely. There are no minimum requirements, and our advice is to keep the car standard to begin with. After a few trackdays you'll start to get a feel for what changes, if any, will make it even more fun.

Which are the best affordable (i.e. cheap) road cars to drive on track?
Hot hatches are effective, small roadsters are entertaining, Caterhams are quick, coupes are compelling and big saloons can be amusing. The bottom line is that, whatever you drive, it's going to be fun. Among those to consider are Golfs, Minis, 968 Porsches, E36 and E46 M3s, MX-5s, Elises, MR2s, Renaultsport Clios and SEAT Cupras.

How much will it cost to take, say, a hot hatch on an average trackday – petrol, tyre and brake wear, etc?
Not as much as you might think – if you drive with a degree of mechanical sympathy. Hammering round for lap after lap, stamping on the pedals, will destroy brakes and tyres very quickly. However, if you drive smoothly they can last well. Don't brake at the last possible moment, be progressive, especially if braking from high speed to a slow corner. If you start to feel some brake fade or the tyres getting hot, back off and give them time to cool down. Always do a cooling-down lap anyway, don't stay out for more than ten laps at a time and

don't apply the handbrake once parked. Reckon on a couple of tankfuls of fuel.

What basic preparations should I make?
Your car needs to be in top order – it will be driven harder for longer than it has ever been before. Ensure the wheelnuts are correctly torqued and that there is plenty of meat on the brake pads. Check that all the fluid levels are are up to the mark. Your oil level should be at the top mark without being over-filled, and you should check it regularly through the day. Tyres should be pumped up to the manufacturer's recommended pressures.

Is it a good idea to have a spare set of wheels and tyres for trackdays?
It's not necessary, especially to start with. Experienced trackday drivers may do this to allow them to use sticky, special compound rubber.

Should I uprate the brakes?

This is a good idea, particularly the pads. This is quite cost effective (usually less than £100) and you will gain an increase in stopping power as well as a greater resistance to fade.

What can I do to turn my standard road car into a trackday weapon?
After the brakes and tyres, take a look at the suspension. This is not recommended for beginners, but experienced drivers looking to move the game on will gain from adjustable platforms. Again the specifics depend on the car of choice but, in general terms, lowering and stiffening the springs, uprating the dampers and fitting firmer anti-roll bars will improve your cornering capabilities. However it will have an adverse effect on the ride quality on the road. (For more details, see pages 172-175.)

Don't upgrade the engine until you have looked at every other aspect of the car first – it's the least cost-effective modification, so ignore the temptation to spend your money here.

Cars like Skyline are a blast on track but can be heavy on tyres and brakes. Radical takes lightweight philosophy to extremes

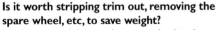

instructors (see p20-23) for more info. Days that run 'sessions' are also better for beginners as novices will all be on track together and the more experienced drivers in faster cars will not be driving at the same time.

What can I expect when I get to the track – how does it actually work?
The day begins with the signing of an indemnity form and the allocation of wristbands. No-one is allowed out on track without one. Then there will be a briefing where the rules will be explained along with meaning of the flags and safety procedures.
Any circuit familiarisation will then take place before the circuit opens and track time begins. Overtaking rules are strictly enforced (usually only on the left and never in the braking zones or corners) and dangerous driving will see you sent home. The track is usually open from 9am to 5pm with a break for lunch between 1pm and 2pm.

Which circuits are best for novices?
Those with wide, open corners which provide clear sight-lines. Donington, Silverstone and Snetterton are good choices.

Are airfield trackdays any good?
Depends what you want from the day. If it's a cheap, wide stretch of tarmac to thrash around on, then they can be good. They don't provide the thrills that a real circuit can provide, being flat and featureless. It's like comparing playing golf on a championship course to hitting balls on a driving range.

Where can I get tuition for driving on track, and are there any good books about it?
The best trackday companies will have fully licensed instructors available. You will learn much more from them than spending all day lapping on your own (see p20-23 for more). There are tips from Mark Hales at evo.co.uk, while *Track Day Driver's Guide* by Art Markus is also a good read.

Is it worth stripping trim out, removing the spare wheel, etc, to save weight?
It's always worth leaving the spare wheel in the pit garage, but unless you are turning your car into a trackday special, leave the trim alone.

How do I make my car safe? Do I need a rollcage, fire extinguisher, etc?
Safety items are always recommended, although a rollcage is an extreme modification and not necessary. An extinguisher is a good idea, and before getting a cage we would suggest a good race seat with a race harness. This can also help you feel more 'connected' with the car.

Do I need to buy a helmet and race-suit?
Not necessarily. At many trackdays you can borrow a helmet (the minimum requirement), which could

be a good idea for a first-time circuit driver.
However if you start to attend regularly we suggest you buy your own, and you should buy the best you can afford (see p84-85 for more details). Driving boots and gloves are a good idea as they increase your feel for the controls. A racesuit is not necessary, although you should wear comfortable clothing (cotton preferably) and your arms and legs should be covered.

What should I take with me – tyre pump, basic tools, glass cleaner, sticky tape?
Yes to all of those.

Will I feel out of my depth first time out?
Depends which organiser you use. The best ones will ensure that novices are looked after and are given extra instruction by ARDS qualified racing

---

DRIVER PROFILE:
BRUCE TURNER
Along with Caterhams, Porsches are among the most popular trackday cars, and it need not cost you a second mortgage to run one. The 968 Clubsport has always been a favourite of ours. It excels on track and good ones can still be bought for around £10,000. In fact these cars are so accomplished that many are bought by enthusiasts with access to much more expensive equipment.

Bruce Turner took up track driving last year and although he has a 996 Turbo to play with, prefers the Club Sport for track work. 'It communicates with you so much more clearly,' he says. 'The Turbo is a great car and it compliments the driver, but it does too much for you and ultimately isn't as satisfying. I did ten trackdays in my first year and had an instructor with me for every one. I realised that the best way to go faster was to get my driving up to standard, and I estimate that I'm

as much as ten seconds quicker than I was when I started.
'The only upgrades I made to the car were to fit trackday brakepads, which resist fade much better than the road items – although they do squeak a bit – and a new set of wheels and tyres. The tyres are sticky Michelin Pilot Sports and with the wheels cost about £1000. In total the running costs for the year were about £3500. I'm now looking at a Radical SR3, but the 968 CS has been a brilliant car to learn in.'

NOT THE SOUND OF SILENCE

ABARTHCARS.CO.UK

ABARTH PUNTO EVO

EVEN MORE POWER, EVEN MORE SAFETY, EVEN MORE ABARTH.
1.4 TURBO MULTIAIR 165 BHP,
PEAK TORQUE 250 NM (25.5 KGM) AT 2250 RPM,
0 – 60 MPH IN 7.6 SEC,
FUEL CONSUMPTION AND CO2 EMISSIONS REDUCED BY 10%*,
AERODYNAMIC DESIGN,
7 AIRBAGS, TTC TORQUE TRANSFER CONTROL & ESP AS STANDARD.

MORE POWER TO YOUR SENSES

**FOR MORE INFORMATION OR
TO BOOK YOUR TEST DRIVE VISIT**
www.abarth-puntoevo.co.uk

**A WORLD OF
EMPOWERMENT**

Fuel Cons mpg (l/100km): urban 35.3 (8.0) / extra-urban 56.5 (5.0) / combined 46.3 (6.1) / CO2 emissions: 142g/km.
*10% reduction compared against the Abarth Grande Punto.

Circuit Guide: Silverstone

As the home of the British Grand Prix, at Silverstone you can retrace the tyre tracks of countless Formula 1 heroes

Until a couple of years ago Silverstone's future was uncertain. That has all changed now, as with a long Formula 1 commitment more money is being invested here than at any other time in the circuit's history. The new Arena Grand Prix layout is part of this, as is a new pit complex, due to open in 2011.

HISTORY

Lying half in Northamptonshire, half in Buckinghamshire, Silverstone started out as a wartime airfield in March 1943 and remained active throughout the hostilities.

In 1948 the Royal Automobile Club was looking for a site to run a British Grand Prix – the first since 1927. As there were no suitable permanent venues, no facility to close roads and, in the aftermath of war, no money to build a new circuit, the huge numbers of concrete runways that dotted the country soon became the obvious focus of the club's attention.

Silverstone emerged as favourite, and on October 2, 1948, a 3.7-mile circuit marked out with oil drums and straw bales became home to the first post-war Grand Prix, won by Italian Luigi Villoresi in a Maserati.

Today there are no fewer than four layouts in regular use for racing. However, it is still the Bridge circuit that is mostly used for trackdays and so this is the one detailed on the following pages – although the other variants use most of these corners too.

GENERAL INFORMATION

Website: www.silverstone.co.uk
Phone number: 0844 3728 200
Address: Silverstone Circuit, Towcester, Northamptonshire, NN12 8TN
Circuit length: 3.19 miles (Bridge layout)
Noise limit: 105 dB static (102 dB evenings)
Directions: Situated halfway along the A43 between the M40 (J10) and the M1 (J15a), Silverstone is both easily accessible and well signposted.

ABBEY

CLUB

STOWE

WOODCOTE

LUFFIELD

BROOKLANDS

BRIDGE

PRIORY

COPSE

MAGGOTTS

BECKETTS

ARENA CIRCUIT

The latest part of Silverstone's ongoing development and not pictured in the main image is the Arena Circuit. New for the 2010 British GP, this leaves the old circuit at Abbey, throws in a handful of new corners and finishes with a long, 185mph straight before rejoining at Brooklands.

ABBEY

BROOKLANDS

CHAPEL

Google

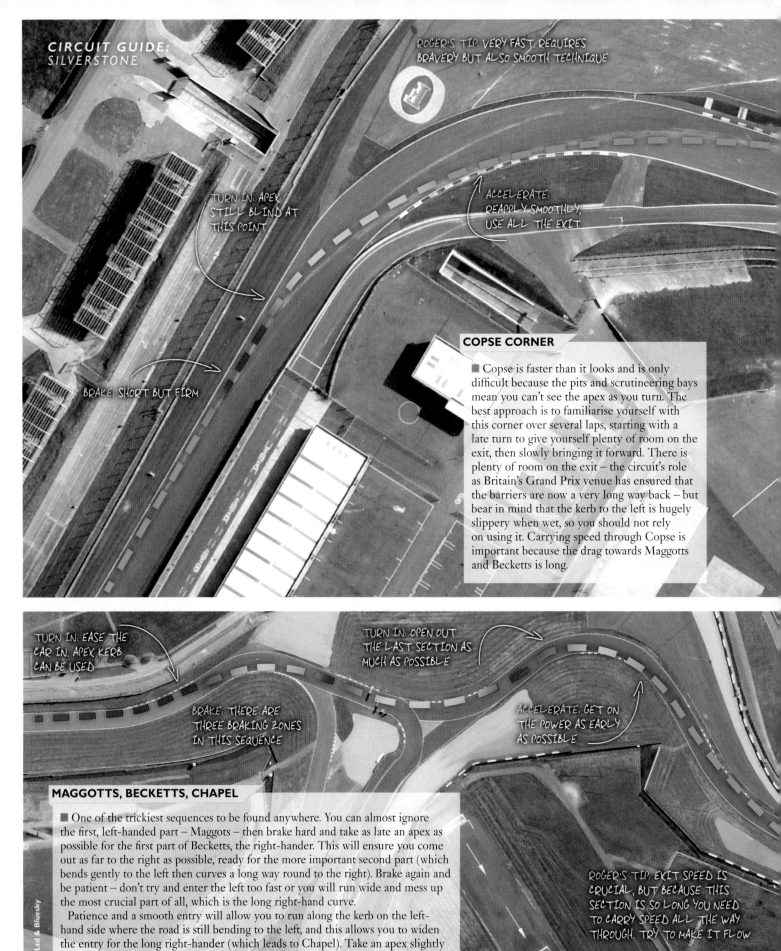

ROGER'S TIP: VERY FAST. REQUIRES
BRAVERY BUT ALSO SMOOTH TECHNIQUE

TURN IN: APEX
STILL BLIND AT
THIS POINT

ACCELERATE:
REAPPLY SMOOTHLY,
USE ALL THE EXIT

BRAKE: SHORT BUT FIRM

COPSE CORNER

■ Copse is faster than it looks and is only
difficult because the pits and scrutineering bays
mean you can't see the apex as you turn. The
best approach is to familiarise yourself with
this corner over several laps, starting with a
late turn to give yourself plenty of room on the
exit, then slowly bringing it forward. There is
plenty of room on the exit – the circuit's role
as Britain's Grand Prix venue has ensured that
the barriers are now a very long way back – but
bear in mind that the kerb to the left is hugely
slippery when wet, so you should not rely
on using it. Carrying speed through Copse is
important because the drag towards Maggotts
and Becketts is long.

TURN IN: EASE THE
CAR IN. APEX KERB
CAN BE USED

TURN IN: OPEN OUT
THE LAST SECTION AS
MUCH AS POSSIBLE

BRAKE: THERE ARE
THREE BRAKING ZONES
IN THIS SEQUENCE

ACCELERATE: GET ON
THE POWER AS EARLY
AS POSSIBLE

MAGGOTTS, BECKETTS, CHAPEL

■ One of the trickiest sequences to be found anywhere. You can almost ignore
the first, left-handed part – Maggots – then brake hard and take as late an apex as
possible for the first part of Becketts, the right-hander. This will ensure you come
out as far to the right as possible, ready for the more important second part (which
bends gently to the left then curves a long way round to the right). Brake again and
be patient – don't try and enter the left too fast or you will run wide and mess up
the most crucial part of all, which is the long right-hand curve.

Patience and a smooth entry will allow you to run along the kerb on the left-
hand side where the road is still bending to the left, and this allows you to widen
the entry for the long right-hander (which leads to Chapel). Take an apex slightly
after the middle of the right-hander's radius and start to pour on the power. The
earlier you can accelerate without upsetting the car, the better, all the time trying
to avoid the need to lift through Chapel's gentle left-hander. Stay flat from there all
the way down the long Hangar straight.

ROGER'S TIP: EXIT SPEED IS
CRUCIAL, BUT BECAUSE THIS
SECTION IS SO LONG YOU NEED
TO CARRY SPEED ALL THE WAY
THROUGH. TRY TO MAKE IT FLOW

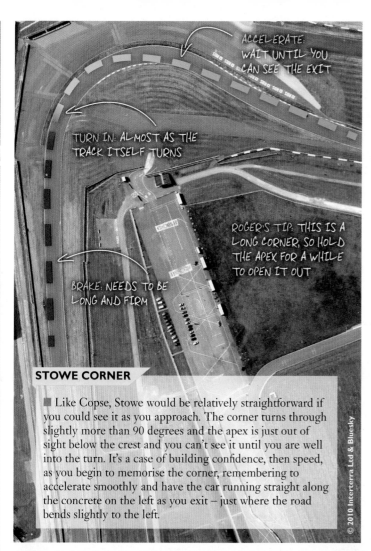

ACCELERATE: WAIT UNTIL YOU CAN SEE THE EXIT

TURN IN: ALMOST AS THE TRACK ITSELF TURNS

ROGER'S TIP: THIS IS A LONG CORNER, SO HOLD THE APEX FOR A WHILE TO OPEN IT OUT

BRAKE: NEEDS TO BE LONG AND FIRM

STOWE CORNER

■ Like Copse, Stowe would be relatively straightforward if you could see it as you approach. The corner turns through slightly more than 90 degrees and the apex is just out of sight below the crest and you can't see it until you are well into the turn. It's a case of building confidence, then speed, as you begin to memorise the corner, remembering to accelerate smoothly and have the car running straight along the concrete on the left as you exit – just where the road bends slightly to the left.

TURN IN: VERY LATE. COMPROMISE THIS LEFT TO OPEN UP THE RIGHT

BRAKE: VERY HARD. WATCH FOR LOCKING BRAKES

ACCELERATE TRY TO STAY ON THE POWER ALL THE WAY TO THE EXIT

CLUB CORNER

■ This corner has changed in the last year in readiness for the new pit complex. The section between the right-handers has been elongated and a large run-off area has been added to the exit. Don't try and brake too late for the left, but turn-in late so that you can run along the left-hand kerb until the road begins to open out to the right. For a change, you're then looking for a fairly early apex, added to which the road also falls away slightly at this point, so the car will naturally want to run wide towards the middle of the road. Try not to let it get quite this far and gently pull it back towards a second apex – which is still just before the mid-point of the sweep. The road now opens up and you should be hard on the gas.

ROGER'S TIP: TAKE THE FINAL PART FLAT-OUT, AS THERE'S LOTS OF SPACE ON THE EXIT

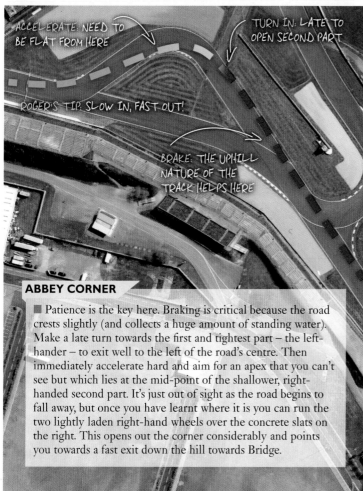

ACCELERATE: NEED TO BE FLAT FROM HERE

TURN IN: LATE TO OPEN SECOND PART

ROGER'S TIP: SLOW IN, FAST OUT!

BRAKE: THE UPHILL NATURE OF THE TRACK HELPS HERE

ABBEY CORNER

■ Patience is the key here. Braking is critical because the road crests slightly (and collects a huge amount of standing water). Make a late turn towards the first and tightest part – the left-hander – to exit well to the left of the road's centre. Then immediately accelerate hard and aim for an apex that you can't see but which lies at the mid-point of the shallower, right-handed second part. It's just out of sight as the road begins to fall away, but once you have learnt where it is you can run the two lightly laden right-hand wheels over the concrete slats on the right. This opens out the corner considerably and points you towards a fast exit down the hill towards Bridge.

BRIDGE CORNER

■ The camber and the dip here both add grip and help you through the downhill plunge. The turn-in point is difficult to judge because the bridge hides the apex; it also makes a difference whether you're in a car which needs to brake first or not. Ideally the turn starts late, but the road is dirty here and most people turn slightly earlier and take an earlier apex, coming out left of the road's middle then wrestling the car back over to the right, ready for Priory. In a car which needs to brake, the dirty part is even less inviting, so you turn earlier still, but if you're able to make a later turn in a nimble car, you can apex later in the dip then exit in the middle of the road, ready to ease right and brake in a straight line for Priory.

ACCELERATE: NO NEED TO USE FULL WIDTH ON EXIT

BRAKE: LITTLE OR NO BRAKING

TURN IN UNDER BRIDGE

ACCELERATE: ONLY A SHORT
RUN TO BROOKLANDS, BUT
OVERTAKING IS POSSIBLE

ROGER'S TIP: USE THE
APEX KERB TO OPEN
OUT THE CORNER

TURN IN: CAN USE
ACCESS ROAD FOR
EXTRA WIDTH

BRAKE
TRAVELLING
DIAGONALLY
FROM BRIDGE

© 2010 Interterra Ltd & Bluesky

PRIORY

■ If you exit Bridge in optimum fashion, not only will you be able to brake in a straight line, but you will also more easily be able to open out Priory's radius – and most importantly, be able to accelerate much earlier. The road is already wide on the entry, but if you don't make use of it, the car will simply wash out as the road turns and narrows and you'll have to lift. Priory is faster than it looks but a lot of good laps are wasted here. Beware, too, the kerb on the exit: it's high and grippy and will launch the car while pulling it to the right and onto the grass.

ACCELERATE: WAIT UNTIL
EXIT IS VISIBLE BEFORE
GETTING HARD ON THE GAS

ROGER'S TIP: PATIENCE IS
THE KEY. ALL CARS WILL
UNDERSTEER HERE

BROOKLANDS AND LUFFIELD

■ Brooklands simply requires discipline. Brake too late, or enter too fast, and you will wash wide and have to lift, or worse, end up in the gravel trap beyond the kerb. The apex at Brooklands is almost always later than you thought and the kerb on the left is high enough to upset some suspensions. Ideally, you should exit parallel with the exit kerb on the right then move immediately left to the middle of the road for Luffield.

Opinions are many and varied about the ideal line for Luffield, but most people turn relatively early and hug the inside kerb all the way round before finally letting the car open out on the exit and head for the exit concrete to the left. In a more powerful car it's sometimes worth trying a later apex, but because most people don't, the road is dirty and you tend to lose whatever you might have gained.

TURN IN: NO NEED
TO RUN OUT TO THE
EDGE OF THE TRACK

BRAKE: HARD BRAKING
AND VERY LATE TURN-IN

© 2010 Interterra Ltd & Bluesky

Where can I gain the most lap-time?

Brain Power is the new Horse Power

With the availability of affordable, focussed training aids that record video and GPS, driver training is becoming more popular. In a series of articles we discuss track driving technique with various professional coaches to help you extract every last ounce of performance from yourself as well as your car.

In this article we discuss Slow Corners and Hairpins with accomplished race driver and personal coach, Nigel Greensall. Here's an extract...

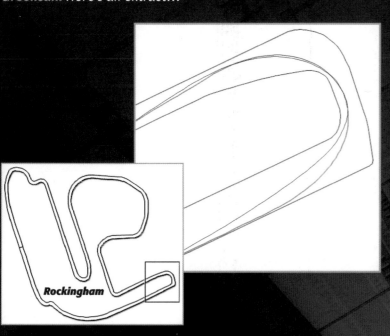

Rockingham

Nigel Greensall — "You spend more time in slow corners than in fast corners, so you can often gain most lap-time by concentrating in these areas. Exit speed is important, but equally as important is minimising the time spent in the corner. You often see drivers taking a big wide entry into hairpins to gain a fast exit speed, but due to the slow speeds involved, this sacrifices huge amounts of lap-time, in order to gain a few tenths down the straight."

"The hairpin at Rockingham is a great example to examine in more detail. Take these two lines taken in the same car at the same race meeting — The blue line was taken by my team-mate taking a wide entry, and the red line is my preferred approach, which is braking at a diagonal towards the first apex. The red line is 14m shorter than the blue line, meaning I spend 0.45s less time in the corner. The blue line does gain 2mph down the straight, The blue line does gain 2mph down the straight, but this is only worth 0.15s, so the gain from taking the shorter line is 0.3s."

"Looking at the screenshots from the in-car video, right, you can see my tighter entry. This means I have to go slightly slower, but I'm gaining time by travelling less distance."

To get the whole article and others in the series, please visit our website and click on 'Driver Training Articles:

www.VideoVBOX.co.uk

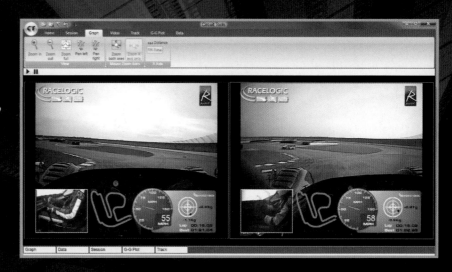

Circuit training

*One-to-one driver training could make the difference between enjoying a trackday and finishing up in a gravel trap. And it needn't cost the earth, as **Stephen Dobie** explains*

Your first trackday can be a daunting experience. A spirited road drive is one thing, but the idea of cranking up your speed while sharing tarmac with two dozen strangers can be outside of many people's comfort zone.

Yet gaining some appropriate training is easier – and quite probably cheaper – than you'd imagine. There's a wide range of advanced driving tuition available to lift your confidence and improve your technique for trackdays, with prices starting from less than the cost of half a tank of fuel.

Even handier, you can organise your training as part of your trackday: all reputable trackday companies offer on-the-day training and have a clutch of instructors on hand ready to help, which means you can usually book a session on the day. These normally last around 20 minutes and involve the trainer – usually a former or current racing driver – sitting in the passenger seat, instructing you as you drive. To give you some idea, a session at a MotorSport Vision (MSV) event costs around £25.

Left: our man Dobie is shown the lines around Cadwell. Above: in his ex-long-term Clio 200 at Oulton Park

MSV's James Auld is one such instructor. 'Any instructor worth anything can work with a novice and within 20 minutes give them the information they need to get to a high standard,' he reckons. 'This is basically how to do it right in terms of your stages of braking, steering and when to get on the power out of corners. If you see it on TV or YouTube, you'll see that's all experienced racing drivers are effectively doing.

'Basically I look at what someone is doing for the first lap, bring in any technique improvements for a few laps after that, then

Pictures Matt Howell

spend the rest of the run getting the driver to cement these techniques, particularly trail-braking. Then the driver can spend the rest of forever perfecting them, which of course is the big trick – even top F1 drivers never feel they've done the 'perfect' lap!'

James is insistent that such sessions aren't just for novices though – he's confident that no matter how high a client's experience level, he can teach them something new.

And even if you aren't a beginner or seeking any technical training, such sessions can be a great idea at the start of any trackday in order to learn a new circuit or refresh yourself on cornering lines if you're revisiting. A smoother, more consistent driving style will do wonders for your car's wear and tear costs, too.

You may want to prepare more heavily for your first trackday, though, and there's an impressive range of companies and individuals who offer suitable tuition. A favourite of evo is CAT Driver Training (www.catdrivertraining. co.uk). Its chief instructor, Colin Hoad, answers our 'Ask the Expert' questions on driving techniques, and has provided several of our team with training, myself included. Many of the skills I honed with CAT proved very effective on my first trackday, despite six months separating the two.

Using Millbrook Proving Ground provides both a range of great facilities and a controlled environment, allowing one-to-one training and lots of breathing space. Colin teaches a number of helpful techniques, including threshold braking (heavy braking without triggering ABS), single-input steering (maintaining one constant steering angle through a corner or sequence of corners) and high-speed lane-change manoeuvres, as well as pushing ahead your vision to improve anticipation and awareness, a skill that's handy (and to the huge benefit of safety) on both road and track. And, once again, wear and tear is kept in mind as much as corner speed.

As well as trackday virgins, Colin finds his clients include those who've tried trackdays and had a bad experience: 'We get at least two people a month who've had a bad track

Above: Colin Hoad (centre) of CAT Driver Training passes on some of his hard-won knowledge to evo's Adam Shorrock and Stephen Dobie. Right: many trackday companies employ race drivers like Phil Bennett (race-suited) to provide on-the-day training

experience – a crash or a spin onto gravel. It's from situations where road driving doesn't correlate with the track. They've never been told to threshold brake, for instance, so they'll gradually build on the brakes like they would on the road rather than being assertive on them. Learning how to brake and then structuring the corner is key. Training gives you a structure to go out, have fun and be safe.'

CAT's courses range from half-day experiences (£435) and four-hour trackday introductions (from £540) to Nürburgring training (from £540) and drift training (from £240 per person). Most courses are on a one-to-one basis. If trackdays are to become a regular hobby, investing in extra training like this is certainly a good idea, most notably to cement the differences between fast road driving and circuit driving, and get you honing skills relevant for the latter.

If you're really serious about trackdays, or want to learn the art of controlling a high-end performance car at its limits, there are even more comprehensive courses available. The Drivers Club (www.thedriversclub.co.uk) is part of the Jota Group, a motor racing organisation which runs race teams all over the world, including at the Le Mans 24 Hours.

The club offers the chance to learn from some of Jota's racing drivers and tutors – including Williams F1 test driver Jonathan Kennard and Ben 'Stig' Collins – and provides one-to-one training at UK and overseas circuits. A varied fleet of cars, including a Renault Mégane R26.R and a Radical SR3, means there's something for everyone. A full

'We get at least two people a month who've had a bad track experience – a crash or a spin into gravel'

range of experience levels are catered for, and if you have the time and ambition, the training to prepare you for full-on motorsport is available.

While everything is private and bespoke, you do share circuit space, though your tuition will only be booked during trackdays run by companies that The Drivers Club trusts, and only then on their higher experience days.

Sam Hancock is a Le Mans veteran and founder of The Drivers Club: 'We get guys just dipping a toe in the water of trackdays and motorsport, as well as those on long-term bespoke programmes – one of our clients is in year three of a four-year course, which started with his first ever trackday and ends next year when he races at the Le Mans 24 Hours. We also have many clients who own supercars and aren't established with car control at high speeds.' He reckons the ratio of novices to professionals who seek their tuition is 50:50.

Such personal training costs, though it does

include mechanical support, insurance, a pit garage, any required racewear and a disc of your onboard video footage to take home and analyse. A UK day in the Mégane costs £1962 plus VAT, the Radical £3605 plus VAT, while the club also offers drift control days (from around £1000) and karting days (£980 plus VAT). Sam takes pride in the latter, insisting skills learnt in an 80mph racing kart are very relevant to those used in a 180mph sports car.

So with your inaugural trackday approaching, what's my advice? Pick a novice-level event, pre-book the first instructor session of the day and hunt out your strengths and weaknesses. Decide whether practice and further sessions will be enough, or if a pricier, more professional course is needed. A few hundred pounds spent on training could save you a lot of financial heartache later on. But as your first taster of circuit life, that extra £25 goes a long way.

Circuit Guide:
Donington Park

Donington is a fast, flowing circuit that has some of the most dramatic sweeps in UK motorsport. **Roger Green** *is your guide*

For a short while it looked like we might have lost Donington for good, as the failed attempt by the former leaseholders to host the British Grand Prix left the place looking like a building site. Thankfully it's now back to its former glory, for this is one of the best circuits in the UK. It flows like no other and rewards drivers who have good technique in maintaining momentum. The downhill twists of Craner Curves are one of the most exciting sequences to be found anywhere.

HISTORY

Despite losing out on the British GP, Donington has held Grands Prix before, most notably the European GP of 1993. This race was won in fantastic style by Ayrton Senna, with arguably the most brilliant opening lap ever when he worked his McLaren into the lead despite finding himself in fifth place at the first corner.

During the 1930s there were the Donington Grands Prix, the parkland circuit witnessing battles between the mighty Mercedes and Auto Unions right up to the start of WWII. After that Donington began to fall into decline until it was acquired by Tom Wheatcroft in the 1970s. Since then it has grown back into one of the UK's premier venues. It also houses one of the best motor racing museums in the country.

GENERAL INFORMATION

Website: www.donington-park.co.uk
Phone number: 01332 810048
Address: Donington Park, Castle Donington, Derby, DE74 2RP
Circuit length: 1.95 miles (National Circuit)
Noise limit: 98 dB drive-by
Directions: Donington can be approached from either the M1 or M42. From the M1 take J23A or J24 and follow the A453.

OLD HAIRPIN

CRANER CURVES

HOLLYWOOD

REDGATE

McLEANS

SCHWANTZ CURVE

COPPICE

STARKEYS BRIDGE

THE ESSES

Google

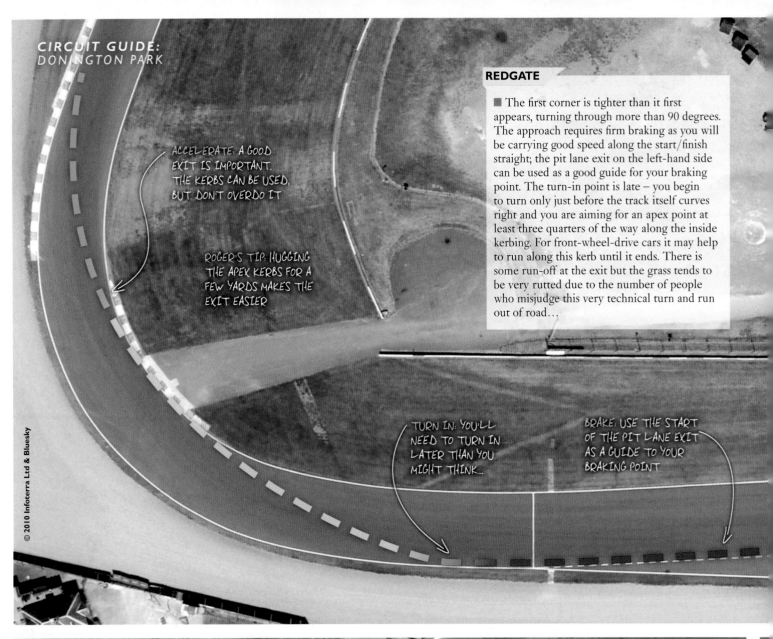

ACCELERATE. A GOOD
EXIT IS IMPORTANT.
THE KERBS CAN BE USED,
BUT DON'T OVERDO IT

ROGER'S TIP: HUGGING
THE APEX KERBS FOR A
FEW YARDS MAKES THE
EXIT EASIER

REDGATE

■ The first corner is tighter than it first
appears, turning through more than 90 degrees.
The approach requires firm braking as you will
be carrying good speed along the start/finish
straight; the pit lane exit on the left-hand side
can be used as a good guide for your braking
point. The turn-in point is late – you begin
to turn only just before the track itself curves
right and you are aiming for an apex point at
least three quarters of the way along the inside
kerbing. For front-wheel-drive cars it may help
to run along this kerb until it ends. There is
some run-off at the exit but the grass tends to
be very rutted due to the number of people
who misjudge this very technical turn and run
out of road…

TURN IN: YOU'LL
NEED TO TURN IN
LATER THAN YOU
MIGHT THINK…

BRAKE: USE THE START
OF THE PIT LANE EXIT
AS A GUIDE TO YOUR
BRAKING POINT

HOLLYWOOD

■ The gentle right-hander that
follows Redgate should be used to
position the car on the correct part
of the track for the critical Craner
Curves that follow. You should be
in the middle of the track here,
gradually bringing the car over to
the right in preparation for the left
that comes next.

ROGER'S TIP:
THIS GENTLE CURVE WOULD BE EASY IF
YOU COULD SEE YOUR WAY THOUGH, BUT THE
DROP HIDES THE ROAD. EASE THE CAR TO
THE RIGHT AS YOU GO OVER THE BROW

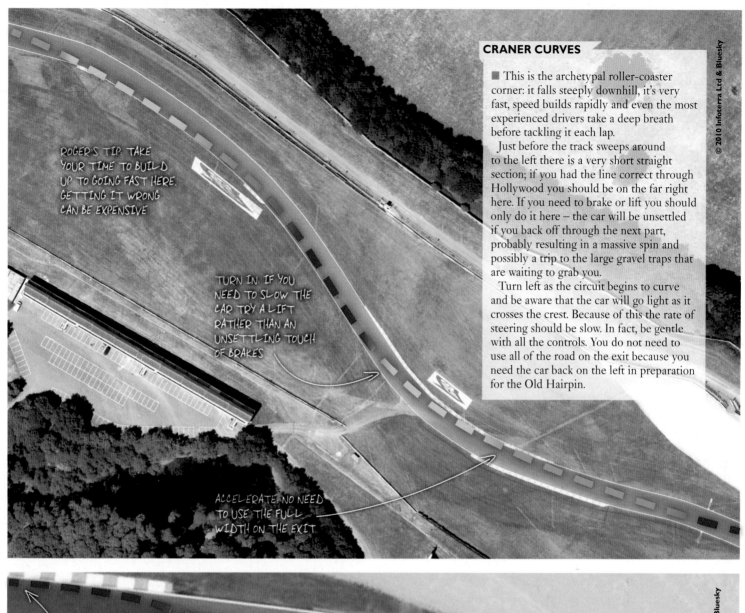

CRANER CURVES

■ This is the archetypal roller-coaster corner: it falls steeply downhill, it's very fast, speed builds rapidly and even the most experienced drivers take a deep breath before tackling it each lap.

Just before the track sweeps around to the left there is a very short straight section; if you had the line correct through Hollywood you should be on the far right here. If you need to brake or lift you should only do it here – the car will be unsettled if you back off through the next part, probably resulting in a massive spin and possibly a trip to the large gravel traps that are waiting to grab you.

Turn left as the circuit begins to curve and be aware that the car will go light as it crosses the crest. Because of this the rate of steering should be slow. In fact, be gentle with all the controls. You do not need to use all of the road on the exit because you need the car back on the left in preparation for the Old Hairpin.

ROGER'S TIP: TAKE YOUR TIME TO BUILD UP TO GOING FAST HERE. GETTING IT WRONG CAN BE EXPENSIVE

TURN IN: IF YOU NEED TO SLOW THE CAR TRY A LIFT RATHER THAN AN UNSETTLING TOUCH OF BRAKES

ACCELERATE. NO NEED TO USE THE FULL WIDTH ON THE EXIT

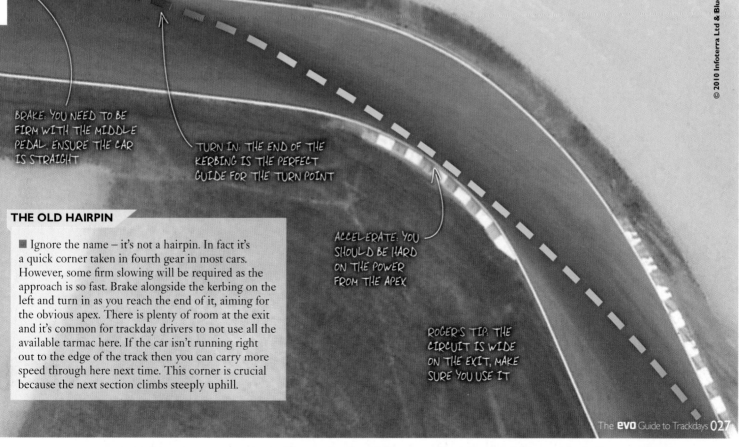

BRAKE. YOU NEED TO BE FIRM WITH THE MIDDLE PEDAL. ENSURE THE CAR IS STRAIGHT

TURN IN: THE END OF THE KERBING IS THE PERFECT GUIDE FOR THE TURN POINT

ACCELERATE: YOU SHOULD BE HARD ON THE POWER FROM THE APEX

ROGER'S TIP: THE CIRCUIT IS WIDE ON THE EXIT, MAKE SURE YOU USE IT

THE OLD HAIRPIN

■ Ignore the name – it's not a hairpin. In fact it's a quick corner taken in fourth gear in most cars. However, some firm slowing will be required as the approach is so fast. Brake alongside the kerbing on the left and turn in as you reach the end of it, aiming for the obvious apex. There is plenty of room at the exit and it's common for trackday drivers to not use all the available tarmac here. If the car isn't running right out to the edge of the track then you can carry more speed through here next time. This corner is crucial because the next section climbs steeply uphill.

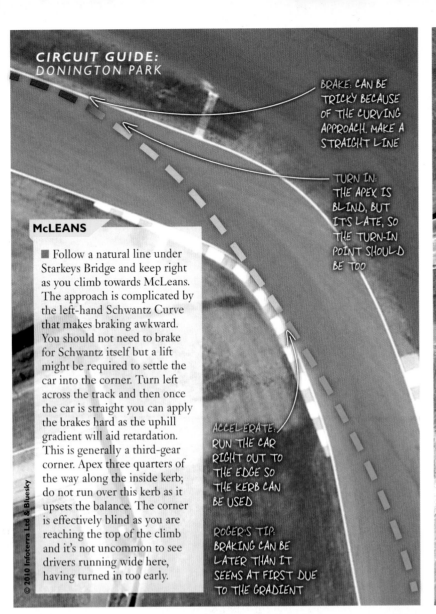

BRAKE: CAN BE TRICKY BECAUSE OF THE CURVING APPROACH. MAKE A STRAIGHT LINE

TURN IN: THE APEX IS BLIND, BUT ITS LATE, SO THE TURN-IN POINT SHOULD BE TOO

McLEANS

■ Follow a natural line under Starkeys Bridge and keep right as you climb towards McLeans. The approach is complicated by the left-hand Schwantz Curve that makes braking awkward. You should not need to brake for Schwantz itself but a lift might be required to settle the car into the corner. Turn left across the track and then once the car is straight you can apply the brakes hard as the uphill gradient will aid retardation. This is generally a third-gear corner. Apex three quarters of the way along the inside kerb; do not run over this kerb as it upsets the balance. The corner is effectively blind as you are reaching the top of the climb and it's not uncommon to see drivers running wide here, having turned in too early.

ACCELERATE: RUN THE CAR RIGHT OUT TO THE EDGE SO THE KERB CAN BE USED

ROGER'S TIP: BRAKING CAN BE LATER THAN IT SEEMS AT FIRST DUE TO THE GRADIENT

© 2010 Infoterra Ltd & Bluesky

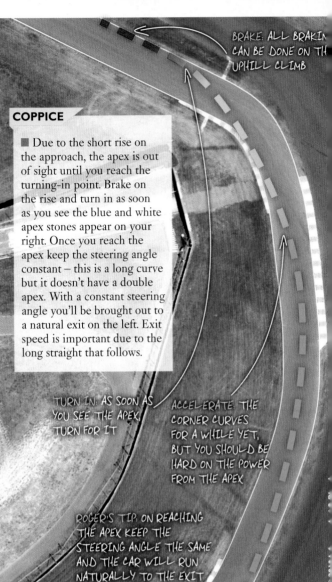

BRAKE: ALL BRAKIN CAN BE DONE ON TH UPHILL CLIMB

COPPICE

■ Due to the short rise on the approach, the apex is out of sight until you reach the turning-in point. Brake on the rise and turn in as soon as you see the blue and white apex stones appear on your right. Once you reach the apex keep the steering angle constant – this is a long curve but it doesn't have a double apex. With a constant steering angle you'll be brought out to a natural exit on the left. Exit speed is important due to the long straight that follows.

TURN IN: AS SOON AS YOU SEE THE APEX, TURN FOR IT

ACCELERATE: THE CORNER CURVES FOR A WHILE YET, BUT YOU SHOULD BE HARD ON THE POWER FROM THE APEX

ROGER'S TIP: ON REACHING THE APEX KEEP THE STEERING ANGLE THE SAME AND THE CAR WILL RUN NATURALLY TO THE EXIT

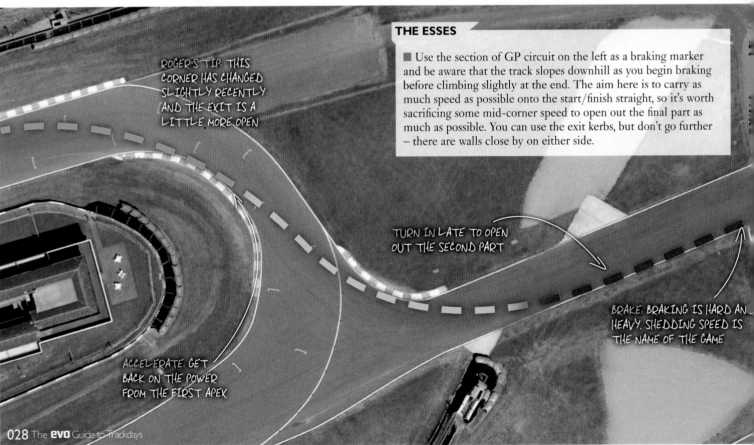

THE ESSES

■ Use the section of GP circuit on the left as a braking marker and be aware that the track slopes downhill as you begin braking before climbing slightly at the end. The aim here is to carry as much speed as possible onto the start/finish straight, so it's worth sacrificing some mid-corner speed to open out the final part as much as possible. You can use the exit kerbs, but don't go further – there are walls close by on either side.

ROGER'S TIP: THIS CORNER HAS CHANGED SLIGHTLY RECENTLY AND THE EXIT IS A LITTLE MORE OPEN

TURN IN LATE TO OPEN OUT THE SECOND PART

BRAKE: BRAKING IS HARD AN HEAVY. SHEDDING SPEED IS THE NAME OF THE GAME

ACCELERATE: GET BACK ON THE POWER FROM THE FIRST APEX

Member laps with Sabine Schmitz on the Nordschleife. Scan to see video.

Scan this Polaroid to our Gallery area.

Scan this Polaroid to see our Events.

Driving Tours | Track Days | Driver Training | Social Events | Hospitality

This Ad is interactive! Scan the Polaroid of Sabine to see the video of her losing it on our Nordschleife Grantour!

Introducing the *Gentleman Drivers Club*, a members club created by enthusiasts for enthisiasts. We have an unrivalled selection of members events that run throughout the year. **From** our private booking of the *Nordschleife*, ice-driving inside the *Arctic Circle* to our *New York Grantour* at the *Monticello Motor Club.*

Our members are a group of like-minded individuals that simply enjoy driving. Our *Supercar Sunday* breakfast events are also a great opportunity to meet fellow members, whilst admiring the cars over a coffee and bite to eat – take a look at the website *gallery* to see what you're missing (scan the above left Polaroid).

If you like the sound of what we do, why not become a *Gentleman Drivers Club* member? Visit our website to see a full list of benefits and events. This ad is also interactive, so download the *Clic2C* App on your mobile phone, then simply scan the Polaroids above to see video, galleries or a list of upcoming events...

12 Months Membership is £129.00 < All Members receive the membership box with members black card and grille badge.

Join us now at www.gentlemandriversclub.com

Gentleman Drivers Club Limited is Registered in England. No. 07029591. Telephone: +44 (0) 1525 288 134. Email: membership@gentlemandriversclub.com

TRUTH ABOUT TRACKDAY
NOISE LIMITS
CIRCUITS HIT BY 'NOISE NUISANCE' COMPLAINTS. BY OLLIE MARRIAGE

Trackdays are a blast. The ability to drive as hard as you want, to get the adrenalin pumping, epitomises the thrill of driving. But there's a downside: noise. Those few seconds when you have your car decibel-tested can be the most nerve-wracking of the entire day – fail and it's likely you won't be allowed near the track at all.

But how is it that race tracks, of all places, have come to have noise limits? There are four main parties involved, book-ended by the trackday attendees and the people who live nearby. In between lie the track itself and the local council. The council has a responsibility to its residents, but also needs to be mindful of the benefits the circuit brings to the local economy, so most lay down guidelines that stipulate not only noise limits but how often and at what times the track can be used. If the track breaks these rules – which are often monitored remotely by the local authority – it can face being shut down.

It's a balancing act for all concerned. By and large, councils follow guidelines laid down by the MSA (Motor Sports Association), the basics of which are a 105 dB static reading, measured at three-quarters of maximum revs, half a metre from the exhaust at a 45-degree angle, but stricter rules can be implemented.

Bedford Autodrome, evo's home circuit, has some of the toughest regulations in the country – a 101 dB static limit and a 87.5 dB drive-by

reading (measured at a distance of 20 metres) – and this is despite spending a fortune building noise defences. 'Well over half of our development costs go into fighting noise,' chief instructor Phil Ellis told us. 'Besides building huge earth walls, we've fitted extra silencers to our single-seaters, and our racing Clios use rallycross tyres because they're quieter.'

'A NOISY CIRCUIT CAN FACE BEING SHUT DOWN'

Bedford is not alone. During the recent restructuring of Anglesey Circuit, the hairpin was moved away from nearby houses, banks built and trees planted. A similar scheme is also underway at Bruntingthorpe, with 5000 lorry-loads of material being used to restrict sound-waves travelling towards a particular village.

But it's the Croft situation that has sent shockwaves through the industry. 'We were served with an injunction last year,' circuit manager Tracey Morley told us. 'A local resident has

been against us for over 13 years and had tried various ways of closing us down, finally bringing a private noise nuisance case. This went to court and the judge found in his favour.' Croft had to cancel all trackdays and very nearly went bankrupt before agreeing to restrictive new regulations. The new quiet drive-by limit is just 70 dB averaged over an hour.

Some circuits can help if your car fails the decibel tests. For instance, at Castle Combe a firm called Merlin Motorsport can fit a temporary additional silencer to your car's exhaust. 'A foot-long pipe out the back may not be pretty,' explained Rodney Gooch, sales and marketing director of Castle Combe, 'but it'll make the difference between taking part and going home bitterly disappointed.'

However, the easiest way to ensure your car passes the noise test is to keep it on its standard exhaust. 'If we have trouble, it's almost always something with a sports exhaust,' said Phil Ellis. 'With the exception of one or two Ferraris there are very, very few standard road cars that break the sound limits.'

So is it likely that noise regulations will get even tighter? 'We don't believe so,' said Ellis, and most people we spoke to seemed to agree that a successful compromise has been reached. 'Ultimately local residents are our neighbours,' Ellis continued. 'We don't want to upset them, but neither do we want to compromise our business and the people who come here to enjoy driving their cars.'

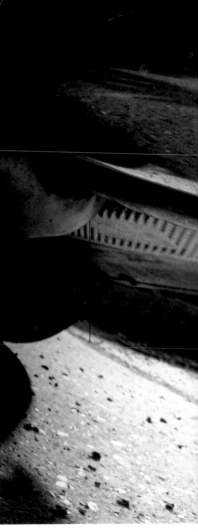

The situation abroad

Even Ferrari's test track in Maranello, Italy, is subject to limits

Noise limits are not unique to UK circuits. Spa had its licence suspended recently due to complaints, and although F1 is exempt from this due to the economic benefits it brings to the area, trackdays (which run a 105 dB limit) have now been restricted. The Nürburgring, meanwhile, randomly tests for a 95 dB limit.

Perhaps most shocking is that Ferrari's Fiorano test track has restrictions placed upon it, too. It may be the home of the supercar, but no running is allowed in the early morning, late evening or over lunch, and regulations stipulate a drive-by limit of 72 dB averaged over a set period of time.

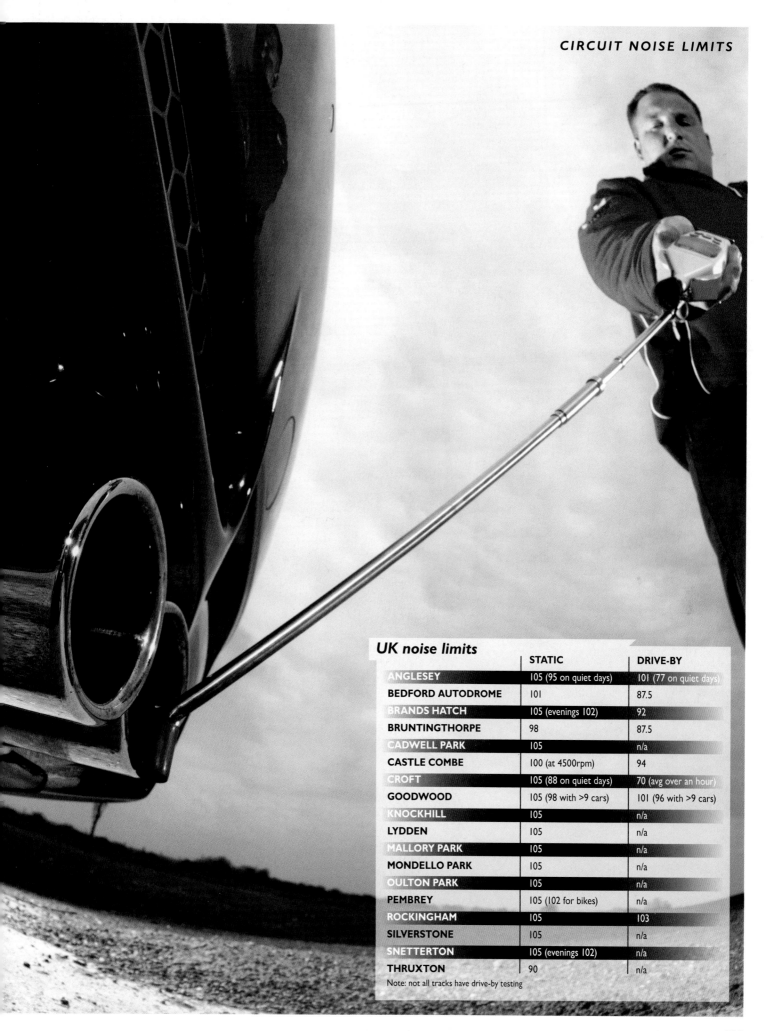

UK noise limits

	STATIC	DRIVE-BY
ANGLESEY	105 (95 on quiet days)	101 (77 on quiet days)
BEDFORD AUTODROME	101	87.5
BRANDS HATCH	105 (evenings 102)	92
BRUNTINGTHORPE	98	87.5
CADWELL PARK	105	n/a
CASTLE COMBE	100 (at 4500rpm)	94
CROFT	105 (88 on quiet days)	70 (avg over an hour)
GOODWOOD	105 (98 with >9 cars)	101 (96 with >9 cars)
KNOCKHILL	105	n/a
LYDDEN	105	n/a
MALLORY PARK	105	n/a
MONDELLO PARK	105	n/a
OULTON PARK	105	n/a
PEMBREY	105 (102 for bikes)	n/a
ROCKINGHAM	105	103
SILVERSTONE	105	n/a
SNETTERTON	105 (evenings 102)	n/a
THRUXTON	90	n/a

Note: not all tracks have drive-by testing

Circuit Guide:
Brands Hatch Indy

One of the most popular trackday venues in the south-east, Brands has the advantage of location but also, in Paddock Hill bend, one of the greatest corners too. **Roger Green** *explains*

N o doubt about it, the Indy circuit at Brands Hatch is a great place to drive. It's the sweeps and dips that are absent from most airfield circuits in the UK that make the main difference, and with some complex sequences and almost no straights on the short 1.2-mile Indy circuit (so named after the American CART IndyCars made a visit there in the '80s), you have a blueprint for a busy and entertaining day. Almost too busy, it has to be said – at some trackdays you never get anything even approaching a clear lap.

HISTORY

Motorsport activity at Brands dates back to 1926 when a group of cyclists stopped to investigate a mushroom field and decided it would be a good place to hold competitive events. The farmer who owned the land was duly persuaded and grass-track motorcycle events began to take place in the natural amphitheatre.

In 1950 a kidney-shaped mile of tarmac was laid and on April 16 a race was staged for 500cc single-seaters. In 1954 the section up to Druids was added to make the current 1.2-mile Indy layout, then known as the Club circuit, and in 1960 the 2.3-mile Grand Prix track was created using most of the Indy layout.

Brands Hatch shared the hosting of the British GP with Silverstone until 1986, and today hosts a number of international race meetings including DTM and World Touring Cars.

GENERAL INFORMATION

Website: www.motorsportvision.co.uk
Phone number: 01474 872331
Address: Brands Hatch Circuit, Fawkham, Longfield, Kent, DA3 8NG
Circuit length: 2.3 miles (GP), 1.2 miles (Indy)
Noise limit: 105 dB static (evenings 102 dB)
Directions: Brands is on the A20 near West Kingsdown, just 3 miles from junction 3 (Swanley) of the M25. The A20 can also be accessed from the M20 and M26 motorways

DRUIDS

GRAHAM HILL

PADDOCK HILL

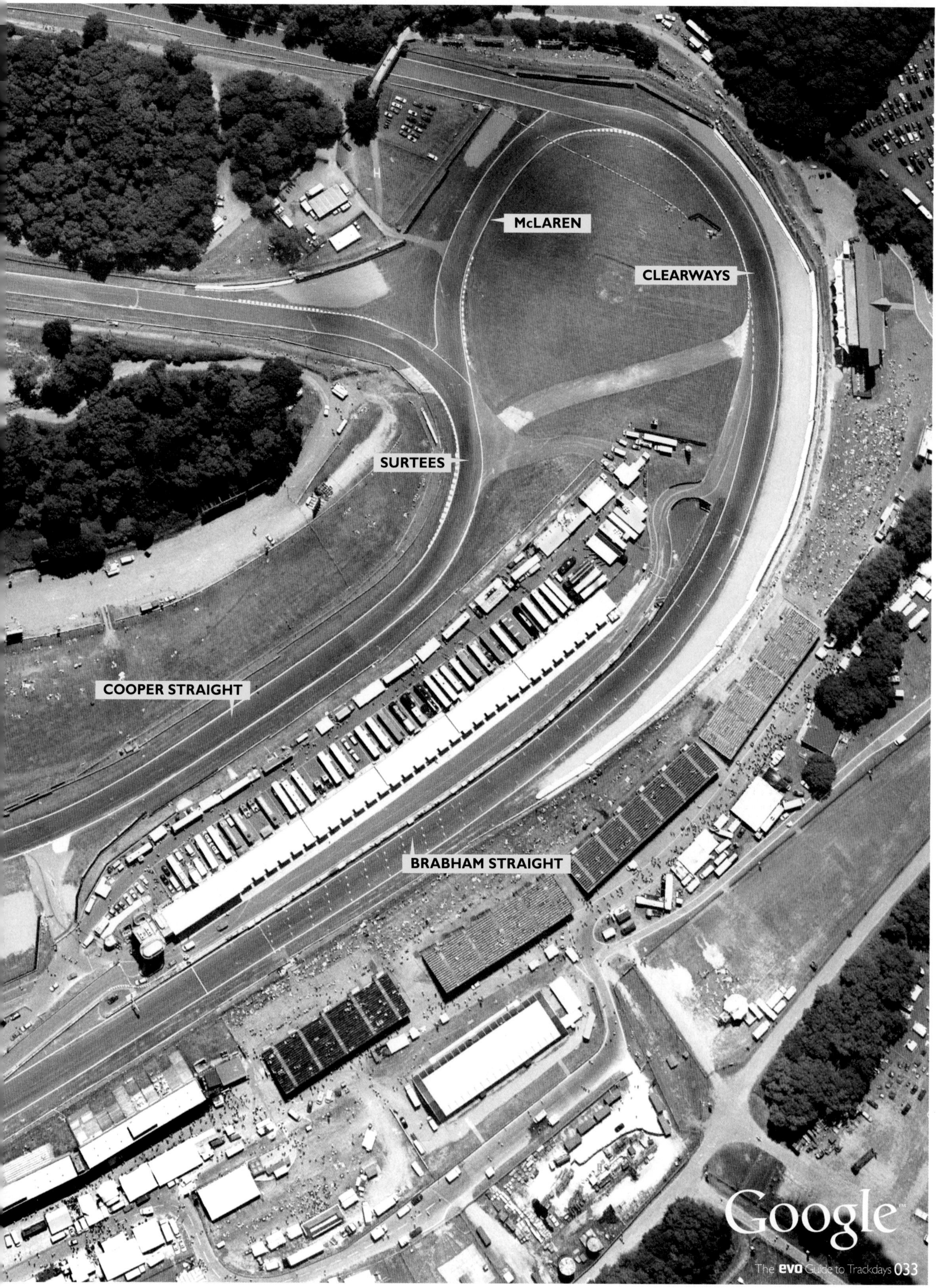

McLAREN

CLEARWAYS

SURTEES

COOPER STRAIGHT

BRABHAM STRAIGHT

Google

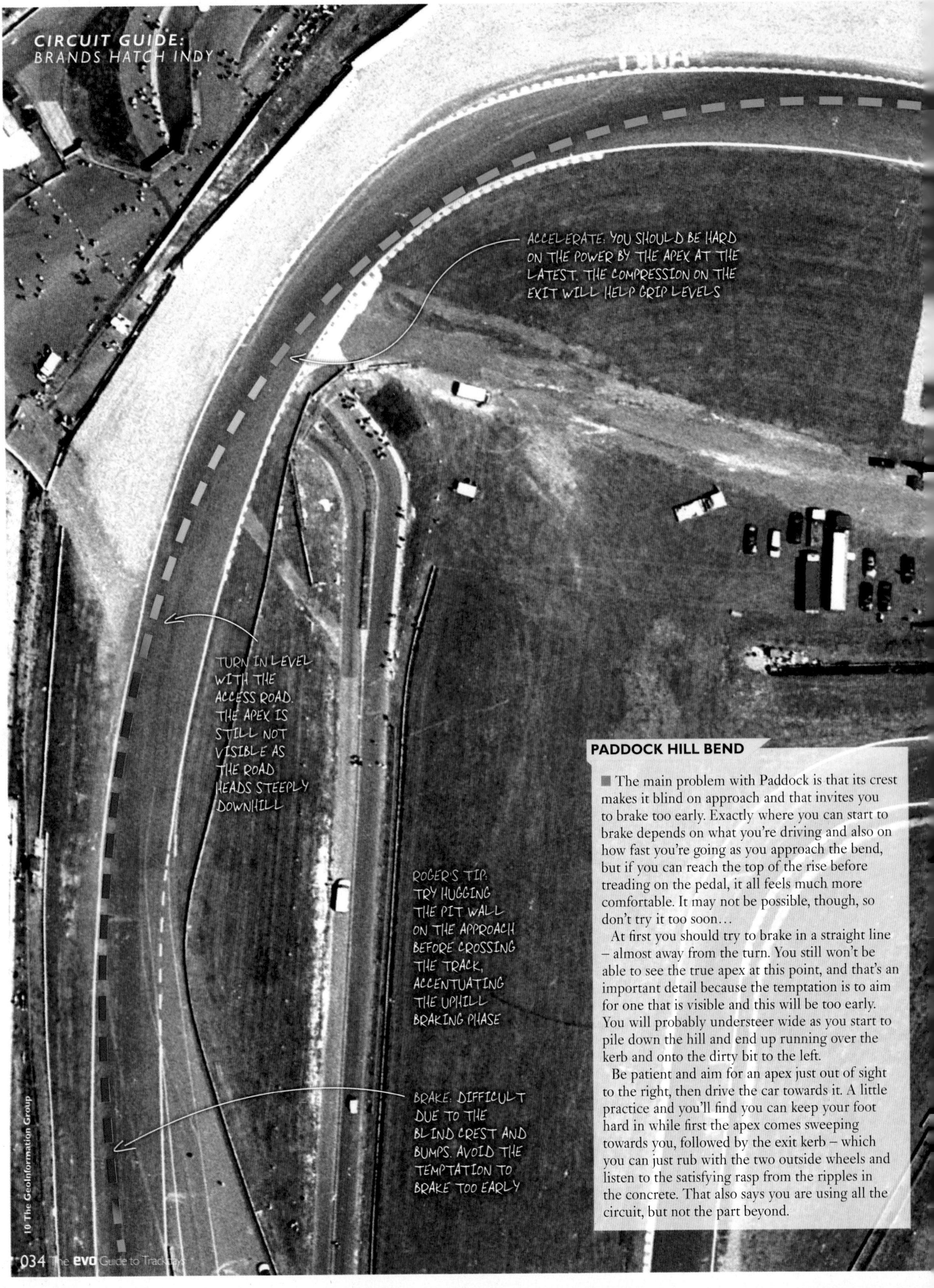

ACCELERATE. YOU SHOULD BE HARD
ON THE POWER BY THE APEX AT THE
LATEST. THE COMPRESSION ON THE
EXIT WILL HELP GRIP LEVELS

TURN IN LEVEL
WITH THE
ACCESS ROAD.
THE APEX IS
STILL NOT
VISIBLE AS
THE ROAD
HEADS STEEPLY
DOWNHILL

ROGER'S TIP:
TRY HUGGING
THE PIT WALL
ON THE APPROACH
BEFORE CROSSING
THE TRACK,
ACCENTUATING
THE UPHILL
BRAKING PHASE

BRAKE. DIFFICULT
DUE TO THE
BLIND CREST AND
BUMPS. AVOID THE
TEMPTATION TO
BRAKE TOO EARLY

PADDOCK HILL BEND

■ The main problem with Paddock is that its crest
makes it blind on approach and that invites you
to brake too early. Exactly where you can start to
brake depends on what you're driving and also on
how fast you're going as you approach the bend,
but if you can reach the top of the rise before
treading on the pedal, it all feels much more
comfortable. It may not be possible, though, so
don't try it too soon…

At first you should try to brake in a straight line
– almost away from the turn. You still won't be
able to see the true apex at this point, and that's an
important detail because the temptation is to aim
for one that is visible and this will be too early.
You will probably understeer wide as you start to
pile down the hill and end up running over the
kerb and onto the dirty bit to the left.

Be patient and aim for an apex just out of sight
to the right, then drive the car towards it. A little
practice and you'll find you can keep your foot
hard in while first the apex comes sweeping
towards you, followed by the exit kerb – which
you can just rub with the two outside wheels and
listen to the satisfying rasp from the ripples in
the concrete. That also says you are using all the
circuit, but not the part beyond.

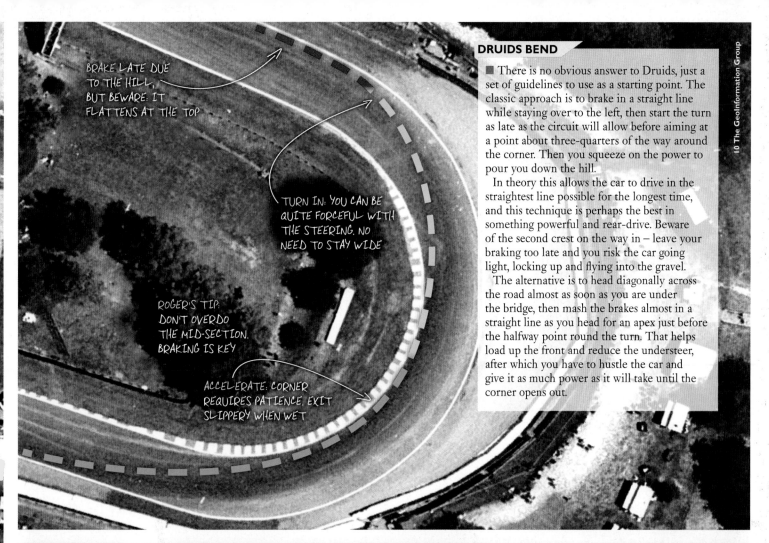

BRAKE LATE DUE TO THE HILL, BUT BEWARE: IT FLATTENS AT THE TOP

TURN IN: YOU CAN BE QUITE FORCEFUL WITH THE STEERING. NO NEED TO STAY WIDE

ROGER'S TIP: DON'T OVERDO THE MID-SECTION. BRAKING IS KEY

ACCELERATE: CORNER REQUIRES PATIENCE. EXIT SLIPPERY WHEN WET

DRUIDS BEND

■ There is no obvious answer to Druids, just a set of guidelines to use as a starting point. The classic approach is to brake in a straight line while staying over to the left, then start the turn as late as the circuit will allow before aiming at a point about three-quarters of the way around the corner. Then you squeeze on the power to pour you down the hill.

In theory this allows the car to drive in the straightest line possible for the longest time, and this technique is perhaps the best in something powerful and rear-drive. Beware of the second crest on the way in – leave your braking too late and you risk the car going light, locking up and flying into the gravel.

The alternative is to head diagonally across the road almost as soon as you are under the bridge, then mash the brakes almost in a straight line as you head for an apex just before the halfway point round the turn. That helps load up the front and reduce the understeer, after which you have to hustle the car and give it as much power as it will take until the corner opens out.

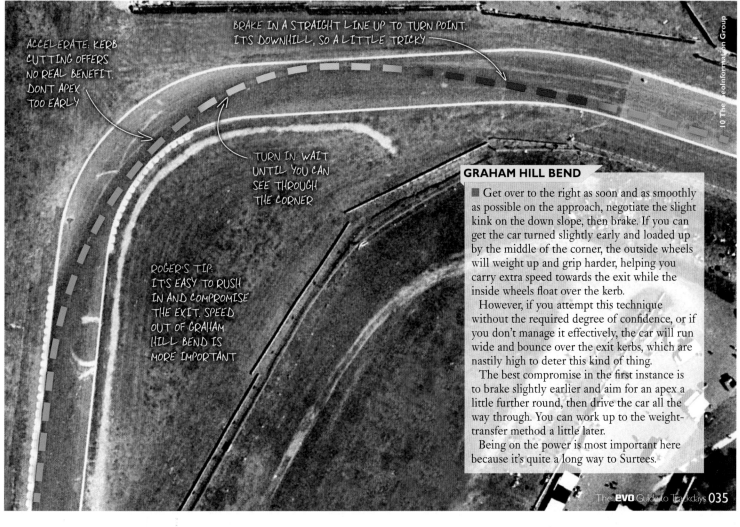

ACCELERATE: KERB CUTTING OFFERS NO REAL BENEFIT. DON'T APEX TOO EARLY

BRAKE IN A STRAIGHT LINE UP TO TURN POINT. IT'S DOWNHILL, SO A LITTLE TRICKY

TURN IN: WAIT UNTIL YOU CAN SEE THROUGH THE CORNER

ROGER'S TIP: IT'S EASY TO RUSH IN AND COMPROMISE THE EXIT. SPEED OUT OF GRAHAM HILL BEND IS MORE IMPORTANT

GRAHAM HILL BEND

■ Get over to the right as soon and as smoothly as possible on the approach, negotiate the slight kink on the down slope, then brake. If you can get the car turned slightly early and loaded up by the middle of the corner, the outside wheels will weight up and grip harder, helping you carry extra speed towards the exit while the inside wheels float over the kerb.

However, if you attempt this technique without the required degree of confidence, or if you don't manage it effectively, the car will run wide and bounce over the exit kerbs, which are nastily high to deter this kind of thing.

The best compromise in the first instance is to brake slightly earlier and aim for an apex a little further round, then drive the car all the way through. You can work up to the weight-transfer method a little later.

Being on the power is most important here because it's quite a long way to Surtees.

SURTEES, McLAREN & CLEARWAYS

■ As a trio, these three corners pave the way for a critical part of the track – the long run up to Paddock Hill Bend. The most important part of the sequence is Clearways (the tightest part of the long right-hand section), and that's what you need to focus on, even if it means compromising another part of the series.

A lot of people make the mistake of making a late entry into Surtees (the left-hander that starts the sequence) and shedding a lot more speed than they need to. This is an early turn where you aim to put both left-hand wheels onto the shallow outer part of the kerb – and preferably not the rougher inside part, at least not until you know if your car will cope with it, as this can so easily launch the car and hop you wide onto the grass opposite, setting you up for a spin into the barriers on the left. Aim too early, though, and you'll find yourself running out of road while the road is still bending left, so somewhere in between is the optimum.

McLaren (the start of the long turn right) is where you make the real compromise; you don't turn so much as ease right on the exit of Surtees then brake in a straight line aiming at a point 90 degrees or even more away from the track you are about to occupy to the right.

Turn right for the first part of Clearways with the car settled, aiming to apex just beyond the piece of tarmac that forms the point where the Grand Prix circuit joins. At first this will seem far too soon, but be patient…

You apex early because the track soon opens out generously to the left where you can let the car run wide and use all the available road, which also falls away. Just relax on the wheel and don't be tempted to hold the car to the right. Let it run all the way to the left in a big, gentle arc until you just clip the kerb on the outside, after which you keep the steering where it is for a couple of moments longer. The main point to remember is that making the line as open as possible allows you to stay hard on the power for a very long time, which is something a lot of people forget to do, even if they remember to use all the road.

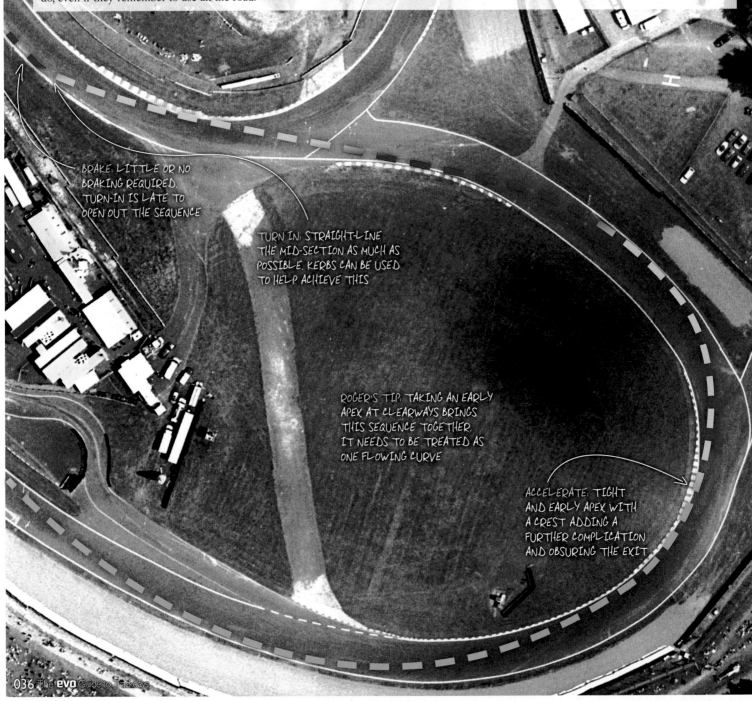

BRAKE: LITTLE OR NO BRAKING REQUIRED. TURN-IN IS LATE TO OPEN OUT THE SEQUENCE

TURN IN: STRAIGHT-LINE THE MID-SECTION AS MUCH AS POSSIBLE. KERBS CAN BE USED TO HELP ACHIEVE THIS

ROGER'S TIP: TAKING AN EARLY APEX AT CLEARWAYS BRINGS THIS SEQUENCE TOGETHER. IT NEEDS TO BE TREATED AS ONE FLOWING CURVE

ACCELERATE: TIGHT AND EARLY APEX WITH A CREST ADDING A FURTHER COMPLICATION AND OBSURING THE EXIT

CLUBMSV
YOUR CAR. YOUR BIKE. OUR CIRCUITS.

WHAT IS CLUB MSV?

Club MSV is the in-house trackday arm of MotorSport Vision. We organise trackdays, driver training and race licence tests across the MSV group of circuits which include Brands Hatch, Oulton Park, Cadwell Park, the new Snetterton 300 and Bedford Autodrome.

WHAT WE OFFER

Trackdays

Club MSV organise trackdays for all levels of driving ability from complete novices through to seasoned trackday drivers. Our Taster Sessions are a great place to start, where you can get 20 minutes of track time for just £25.

Driver Training

Club MSV offer a range of driver training events specifically tailored to help you get the most out of your car. We can help you become a better driver and improve the performance of every car you ever drive.

Go Racing

If you are ready to race then Club MSV can help you every step of the way including taking your ARDS National B race licence test at any MSV circuit. Get started by buying your Go Racing pack today for just £65.

For more details call: 0843 453 3000
or visit www.clubmsv.co.uk

Brands Hatch

Oulton Park

NEW LAYOUT
Snetterton

Cadwell Park

Bedford Autodrome

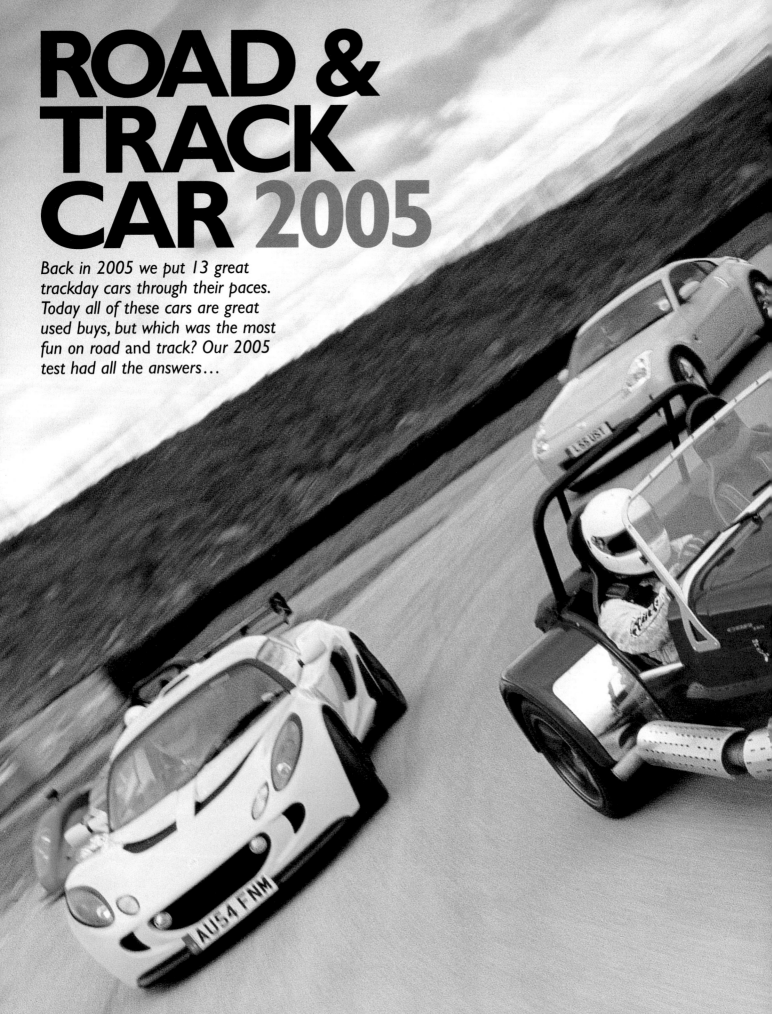

ROAD & TRACK CAR 2005

Back in 2005 we put 13 great trackday cars through their paces. Today all of these cars are great used buys, but which was the most fun on road and track? Our 2005 test had all the answers…

Words: John Barker Pictures: Andy Morgan, Kenny P & Owen Brown

GN05 KTL

THE TEST TEAM

RICHARD MEADEN
Editor at large
'What election?' said pasty-faced, hobbit-sized Meaden when we finally lured him away from the PS2. Only the promise of driving lots of real cars on a real track broke his 58-day giga-pixel GT4 marathon.

JETHRO BOVINGDON
Road test editor
As well as annoying evo's wrinklies with his burgeoning driving skills, Bovingdon is also a bit of a magician with the household budget; just this week he turned a brand new fitted kitchen into a BMW M3 trackday project.

JOHN BARKER
Motoring editor
Despite strong lobbying, Barker wasn't allowed to enter his project Capri V8 for this test. Firstly because it cost twice as much as anything else here, and secondly because after three years it's still not bloody finished.

MARK HALES
Contributor
Former Tuscan champion, historic racer, and Beard of the Year '96, Hales' ability to describe a car's dynamics using only his arms, facial expressions and sound effects is mesmerising. Shame he's a writer.

ROGER GREEN
evoactive mgr.
Roger would like to thank his Brian James Trailer-load of sponsors, but frankly he's too Dunlop-tyred-out to remember who they all are. So, in a refreshingly Radical approach, he won't mention any of 'em.

JOHN HAYMAN
Road test ass.
evo road test assistant, car racer, bike racer and hard-tabbin' man of steel (as airport x-ray machines will testify), Hayman has a hitherto unrevealed soft side. He is also a world-class breeder of chipmunks.

TIM SMITH
Reader
A reformed biker, evo reader Smith's pride and joy is his beloved 135bhp Caterham Supersport. Admits a craving for more power now his confidence and experience have grown. Should find it here.

Welcome to Road and Track Car 2005, a contest for sports cars that's designed, as the title cunningly suggests, to find the best drivers' car for both road and track work. Today there's a wide choice of series-production cars that deliver an inspiring drive whatever the road throws at them and which can raise their game when pushed to the limit on a circuit. There are also rawer, more track-focused specialist cars that, despite appearances, are remarkably accomplished, engaging and usable day-to-day. Our aim is to find which is the best all-round sporting car.

In this contest no fewer than 13 cars do battle, from pure road cars like the Nissan 350Z and Porsche Boxster S, through a phalanx of crossover cars including the potent TVR Sagaris and the brand new Caterham CSR 260, to the positively track-oriented Ariel Atom and Radical SR4. Horsepower ratings range from a humble 65bhp in the Westfield XI up to a colossal 425bhp in the twin-turbo Noble M400, but this test isn't a game of Top Trumps; what matters is how each car uses what it's got.

Over the best part of a week, our contenders will be put to the test on the stimulating roads of north Wales and around the curves and crests of the Ty Croes race track on Anglesey. This short, technical circuit overlooking the Irish Sea is a challenge for both driver and car but with only one heavy braking point it's among the UK's more road-car-friendly tracks. Each car will carry our VBOX data-logger to determine lap times and allow us to analyse how it made its speed, but it's how capable and entertaining each proves to be, on both road and track, that will ultimately determine our 2005 champion.

Recognising that our own criteria may differ from yours, road and track ability will be marked separately, so you'll be able to judge which car best suits your needs, whether you're a committed trackday nerd or someone who simply wants a sporty road car that will be fun for the odd track foray without wrecking its brakes, tyres and your bank balance.

TVR Sagaris leads Nissan 350Z GT4 down one of the fabulous roads of north Wales – you can see why we make the effort to go there. These two, plus Atom (right), Noble (below) and many others, are soon to meet again at the Anglesey race circuit

MORGAN
ROADSTER

- Layout: Front-engined, rear-wheel drive
- Engine: V6, 2967cc
- Max power: 223bhp @ 6150rpm
- Max torque: 206lb ft @ 4600rpm
- Weight: 920kg
- Power/weight: 246bhp per ton
- 0-60mph: 4.9sec (claimed)
- Max speed: 134mph (claimed)
- Tyres: 205/60 R15, Yokohama 032 R
- Price: £34,950 (2005 prices)

PORSCHE
BOXSTER S

- Layout: Mid-engined, rear-wheel drive
- Engine: Flat-six, 3179cc
- Max power: 276bhp @ 6200rpm
- Max torque: 236lb ft @ 4700rpm
- Weight: 1345kg
- Power/weight: 208bhp per ton
- 0-60mph: 5.4sec (claimed)
- Max speed: 166mph (claimed)
- Tyres: 235/35 ZR19 fr, 265/35 ZR19 rear. Michelin Pilot Sport
- Price: £38,720

NOBLE
M12 M400

- Layout: Mid-engined, rear-wheel drive
- Engine: V6, 2968cc, turbo
- Max power: 425bhp @ 6500rpm
- Max torque: 390lb ft @ 5000rpm
- Weight: 1060kg
- Power/weight: 407bhp per ton
- 0-60mph: 3.5sec (claimed)
- Max speed: 185mph (claimed)
- Tyres: 225/40 ZR18 fr, 265/35 ZR18 rear. Pirelli P Zero Corsa
- Price: £55,995

PERFORMANCE 5
MAZDA MX-5

- Layout: Front-engined, rear-wheel drive
- Engine: In-line 4cyl, 1839cc. s/c
- Max power: 230bhp @ 7000rpm
- Max torque: 190lb ft @ 5000rpm
- Weight: 1174kg
- Power/weight: 199bhp per ton
- 0-60mph: sub-5sec (est)
- Max speed: 130mph-plus
- Tyres: 205/40 R17 Goodyear Eagle F1
- Price: c£20,000 (see text)

WESTFIELD
XI

- Layout: Front-engined, rear-wheel drive
- Engine: In-line 4cyl, 1275cc
- Max power: 65bhp @ 6000rpm
- Max torque: 72lb ft @ 3000rpm
- Weight: 498kg
- Power/weight: 132bhp per ton
- 0-60mph: 8.5sec (claimed)
- Max speed: 120mph (claimed)
- Tyres: 165 R13 82T, Comac NC80
- Price: £17,750

CATERHAM
CSR 260

- Layout: Front-engined, rear-wheel drive
- Engine: In-line 4cyl, 2261cc
- Max power: 256bhp @ 7500rpm
- Max torque: 200lb ft @ 6200rpm
- Weight: 575kg
- Power/weight: 452bhp per ton
- 0-60mph: 3.1sec (claimed)
- Max speed: 155mph (claimed)
- Tyres: 195/45 R15 fr, 245/40 R15 rear, Avon CR500
- Price: £39,790

THE CARS

Our contenders represent a broad definition of the term 'sports car' and a microcosm of a trackday paddock. What they have in common is that they are all road-legal and, coincidentally, rear-drive. Naturally, our gathering presents some interesting in-fights – Caterham CSR versus Westfield S2000S, Boxster versus Sagaris versus M400, and Atom versus Grinnall.

Least powerful and least expensive is the Westfield XI, a replica of the sleek, Colin Chapman-designed Lotus XI of the '50s. It launched West Midlands-based Westfield as a kit car company 23 years ago and although it went out of production in 1986, there has been a steady trickle of enquiries ever since. Last year Westfield considered there was sufficient interest to put it back into production and since remaking the body moulds it has sold 40 kits.

It's a handsome little car and, although it borrows heavily from a donor MG Midget, weighing in at just 498kg and being so small and aerodynamic means that 65bhp, a live rear axle, a four-speed 'box and drum brakes endow it with more ability than you might imagine.

Next step up the power ladder is the Lotus Exige, a car we know well and which, if we were bookies, we'd give short odds on. The harder,

hardtop version of the Elise is also light enough to make its 189bhp Toyota engine highly effective, and with lightly treaded 'trackday' tyres and a beautifully sorted chassis, it has the credentials for a podium finish.

It might look pretty standard but Performance 5's tweaked Mazda MX-5 packs 230bhp thanks to the addition of a belt-driven supercharger and air-to-air intercooler. It's not just an engine job, though; the Performance 5 kit adds firmer springs and dampers and harder brake-pads to give the MX-5 the composure and durability for trackdays. This demo car is running on non-standard wheels and tyres but a brand new, basic MX-5 1.8i with the £4000 conversion represents a sub-£20K investment, which looks mighty tempting given what a hoot the standard 146bhp MX-5 is around a track.

When Morgan re-engineered the Plus 8 to take the sonorous Ford 3-litre 24-valve V6 and renamed it the Roadster, it also created the Roadster Lightweight, a pared-back single-seat race version that's eligible for Morgan's one-make series. We were expecting that model but in fact got a more roadable version with two seats and a hardtop but no roll-cage. The 223bhp engine is unchanged but this car is 20kg lighter. There are over-riders where once there were full metal bumpers, the facia is carbonfibre rather than timber, the suspension has been firmed-up and

the classic Plus 8 alloys are shod with Yokohama trackday rubber.

It's a stark contrast with the Ariel Atom, powered here by a state-of-the-art Honda 2.0 VTEC tuned to 245bhp which drives through a close-ratio six-speed 'box. This skeletal car has been around for longer than you'd imagine but still looks striking and fresh, while its handling has improved with almost every new version.

It hasn't quite shaken up the sports car and trackday scene in the same way that Radical has, though. The SR4, 2004's **evo** Trackday champion, is somewhat marginal as a road car and we include it mainly as a reference for the others – anything that gets close to the pace of this £32K diminutive sports-racer-alike with its 250bhp Suzuki motorbike-based 1500cc engine, is really going some.

There was a time when Caterham and Westfield wouldn't be seen together in the same test and this is certainly the first time I can recall having their similar models go head-to-head. On paper the CSR 260 and Sport 2000S are remarkably alike, both boasting around 250bhp from Ford-based four-cylinder engines. But while the wide-body Caterham has been honed with road performance firmly to the fore, the stripped-out Westfield is fully equipped for the track, with a sequential gearbox, adjustable suspension and trackday rubber. There is, however, a £7K price

WESTFIELD
SPORT 2000S

- Layout: Front-engined, rear-wheel drive
- Engine: In-line 4cyl, 1999cc
- Max power: 250bhp @ 7500rpm
- Max torque: 192lb ft @ 6000rpm
- Weight: 550kg
- Power/weight: 463bhp per ton
- 0-60mph: 3.2sec (claimed)
- Max speed: 148mph (claimed)
- Tyres: 205/50 R15 front and rear, Toyo Proxes R888
- Price: £32,312 (2005 prices)

NISSAN
350Z ANNIVERSARY

- Layout: Front-engined, rear-wheel drive
- Engine: V6, 3498cc
- Max power: 296bhp @ 6400rpm
- Max torque: 260lb ft @ 4800rpm
- Weight: 1525kg
- Power/weight: 197bhp per ton
- 0-60mph: 5.8sec (claimed)
- Max speed: 155mph (claimed)
- Tyres: 225/45 R18 fr, 245/45 R18 rear, Bridgestone Potenza RE040
- Price: £29,500

ARIEL
ATOM 245

- Layout: Rear-engined, rear-wheel drive
- Engine: In-line 4cyl, 1998cc, s/c
- Max power: 245bhp @ 8200rpm
- Max torque: 151lb ft @ 6100rpm
- Weight: 505kg
- Power/weight: 490bhp per ton
- 0-60mph: 3.4sec (claimed)
- Max speed: 143mph (claimed)
- Tyres: 195/50 R15 fr, 225/45 R15 rear, Avon ZZ-R
- Price: c£28,000

LOTUS
EXIGE S2

- Layout: Mid-engined, rear-wheel drive
- Engine: In-line 4cyl, 1796cc
- Max power: 189bhp @ 7800rpm
- Max torque: 133lb ft @ 6800rpm
- Weight: 875kg
- Power/weight: 219bhp per ton
- 0-60mph: 3.9sec (claimed)
- Max speed: 147mph (claimed)
- Tyres: 195/50 R16 fr, 225/45 R17 rear, Yokohama Advan A048
- Price: £29,995

GRINNALL
SCORPION IV

- Layout: Rear-engined, rear-wheel drive
- Engine: In-line 4cyl, 1781cc, t/c
- Max power: 365bhp @ ????rpm
- Max torque: ???lb ft @ ????rpm
- Weight: 690kg
- Power/weight: 536bhp per ton
- 0-60mph: 3.9sec (claimed)
- Max speed: 150mph (claimed)
- Tyres: 215/45 R17 fr, 245/45 R17 rear, Toyo Proxes T1R
- Price: £27,000

TVR
SAGARIS

- Layout: Front-mid-engined, rear-wheel drive
- Engine: In-line six, 3996cc
- Max power: 406bhp @ 7500rpm
- Max torque: 349lb ft @ 5000rpm
- Weight: 1078kg
- Power/weight: 383bhp per ton
- 0-60mph: 3.7sec (claimed)
- Max speed: 185mph+ (claimed)
- Tyres: 255/35 ZR18 front and rear. Dunlop SP SuperSport Race
- Price: £49,995

difference in the Westfield's favour.

The Boxster S and 350Z are the only cars in this group that have no obvious pretensions to be track stars. They stand or fall on their ability to maintain the poise and adjustability they demonstrate on the road when they venture onto the circuit. We have high hopes they'll perform at Ty Croes because both have previously proved themselves on track. The versatile and accomplished Boxster is out-gunned by the 350Z here because this is one of the 35th Anniversary editions (also known as the GT4) with an uprated engine giving 296bhp.

We've tried the Grinnall before and a year on we're keen to see if it has improved to allow its staggering power to be fully exploited. The VAG-sourced 1.8-litre turbo engine tucked in the tail of the Scorpion IV gives 300bhp, or 350bhp if you twist the boost knob to the stop.

That gives it a superior power-to-weight ratio to even the big-hitting Noble M400 and Sagaris, both of which boast more than 400bhp. Both are designed as road cars that can take trackdays in their stride, and this example of the aggressively styled TVR rides on Dunlop SP SuperSport Race tyres (rather than Goodyear F1s) though they have a lot more tread than the M400's Pirelli P-Zero Corsas. The front-engined TVR costs £6K less than the mid-engined Noble and its straight-six develops 406bhp, within 20bhp of the M400's twin-turbo V6.

DAY ONE

I'm feeling pretty smug because I've bagged the job of collecting our most expensive car, the £56K Noble, from the factory north of Hinckley.

I can imagine the **evo** crew back at the office arguing over who's going to drive, say, the Atom first, all of them worried that if they accept the job they'll be in it for the whole four-hour schlep to Anglesey. Right now the weather's fine but, this being England in April, the chances of a downpour are good. Buzzing along in a car that lacks weather equipment, a heater, a windscreen even – not to mention anti-lock brakes, luggage space and tread on its tyres – with one eye on the clouds is an adventure, though not a particularly enticing one.

Northants to north Wales is an awfully long way to go to hoon around a race track, but the idea is that the journey will provide the chance to swap cars periodically and appraise their ability on the road. So my Noble-fuelled smugness was always destined to be short-lived.

It's enjoyable while it lasts, though. There's a

long-legged potency about the M400 and it effortlessly devours the motorway run to our first meeting point. If anything, it feels even more ferociously fast than when we drove it last year. The stint doesn't reveal the mild tweaks that Noble has made since then, designed to give better chassis balance, but there'll be plenty of time to interrogate the car on Welsh roads.

Bovingdon calls before I arrive at Hilton Park services on the M6 to say that there are some no-shows at the office, Atom and SR4 among them; they're making their way to Anglesey on trailers. Can't say I'm surprised. I know the Westfield XI will be at the services because I spot its distinctive, tiny shape trundling along the inside lane of the motorway at about 60mph. It looks worryingly low and vulnerable, barely as tall as the wheel-nuts of adjacent trucks.

Why, then, do I volunteer to take it for the next

Westfield 2000S (above) and Caterham CSR (left) are closely matched in terms of performance but quite different to drive

'IF ANYTHING, THE NOBLE FEELS EVEN MORE FEROCIOUSLY FAST THAN WHEN WE DROVE IT LAST'

leg? Partly for the amusement of switching from the most to the least powerful car, but mainly because the next stretch is very short – just a couple of junctions down the M54 to collect the Grinnall – so I'll be able to get out of it pretty quickly. Devious, huh?

Only it doesn't work out like that. The little Westfield is a real charmer, an honest, simple car with terrific steering feel, a wonderfully tactile gearshift and more pace than you'd think. It nips up to a brisk motorway cruise with little effort and it's a credit to Lotus's grasp of aerodynamics that there's still appreciable urge when you put your foot down at an indicated 90mph. You feel

snug, gripped by the short-backed bucket seat and helmeted just in case a stone comes at you over the wrap-around polycarbonate screen.

The Grinnall is late and Bovingdon and I hang around with the XI, intending to catch up with the rest of the party. Eventually Mark Grinnall hoves into view and off-loads the bright red Scorpion IV, saying he's glad we've introduced a road element because he's worked hard on the ride quality of his car. The broad-tracked Grinnall looks like a huge slipper and rollerskate merged and makes a startling contrast with the Westfield, but I'm not ready to step forward 40 years and up almost 300bhp just yet.

I had intended to stop for a swap with Bovingdon before we got to Wales but having punted the Westfield along the M54 and the straight stretches of the A5, I'm keen to see how it feels on twistier roads. Involving is the answer. On its 165/80 section tyres it moves around nicely and you drive it with momentum conservation in mind, though another reason for carrying speed into bends is the brakes. They have little power and awful pedal feel – squishy with firm patches, like standing on a dead animal.

Bovingdon gets bored and blasts by a few miles before Betws-y-Coed. He looks wired when I catch up. 'I'm sure it would be fun if you could feel what was happening at the back end,' he says. I soon know what he means, though there's plenty more to get used to before reaching under the steering column and winding up the boost.

It's the pedals rather than the seats of the Grinnall that adjust, which is fine, but I find the fat-rimmed steering wheel a slight stretch away. The open-sided cockpit feels very exposed but, more concerning once I get rolling, is the total lack of side-support from the simple seat and the fact that the windscreen is at exactly the wrong height – I can't see through it or over it.

It's an uncomfortable combination and I don't feel at ease with the car even after a few miles. The front-end is very darty and when the engine comes on boost it's terrifically fast but I feel more like a passenger as the A5 twists and bucks its way through Snowdonia. Even so, curiosity gets the better of me and I turn the boost up to 11, just to see. The change is dramatic. The exhaust

Time to saddle-up at the start of day two (above). Grinnall has straight-line pace to catch Exige (right), but despite the appeal of its power it's too much of a handful for most. Noble (left) the most costly of our gathering, yet justifies £56K price. Radical (below right) marginal as road car

note becomes an angry snort and an explosion of torque arrives at the rear wheels, making it even harder to flow with the road. Once, and only once, the boost arrives when the front wheels aren't quite straight and I spend a few tense moments on opposite lock.

At the bridge over into Anglesey, the dual carriageway funnels down to one lane. The beauty of driving something odd is that you can go right down the outside to the front of the queue and get let in, though with heavy raindrops bouncing off our crash helmets, Bovingdon and I are probably on the receiving end of some sympathy, too. I'm relieved to arrive at Ty Croes and park the Grinnall under cover with the other roofless wonders.

Back at the house where we'll be staying for the next few days, the hunt for a take-away leaflet has turned up one for a curry house a few miles away in Llangefni. There are a few extra provisions to be hunter-gathered too and a quick scan of the contenders reveals only one car capable of taking a modest weekly shop and curry for 15 – the Boxster. Mark Hales has just arrived in it, and he's impressed. 'That is so accomplished,' he says.

He's right. The first aspects of the Porsche that impress are its major controls – the quality of feel of its steering action, the precision of its pedals, the slickness and positivity of its gearshift. When those features are so right, you just know that the ride and handling are going to be spot-on too. Kenny P in the passenger seat says what I'm thinking: 'This is bloody good, isn't it?'

In the take-away, Kenny (a Mancunian) spots the distinctly non-Anglesey accents and asks where they're from. Bradford is the reply. 'We're in for a good curry then,' says Mr P cheerily as we load endless boxes and bags into the commodious front boot of the Boxster. 'Mind,' he adds, 'I'd have been even more impressed if they'd said Keighley.'

DAY TWO

Day two doesn't so much dawn as get marginally less dark. It looks like we've used up all our good luck in finding the best curry house in Wales. Low, black clouds scudding in from the Irish Sea jostle to dump their rain on our parade. By mid-morning, however, the skies are clear and a few cars are slip-sliding around the track in an attempt to hasten the appearance of a dry line. The setting of lap times has fallen to Meaden and we agree a simple running order of least to most powerful. Killing two birds with one stone, I volunteer to take the cars that are low on fuel to

the nearest Optimax station so that they're primed for him.

First up is the Exige, which is Meaden's own and which graces evo's Fast Fleet pages. I've driven a few but not one with the optional, firmer Ohlins suspension and a fruitier Lotus Sport exhaust. You certainly notice the louder pipe, which creates a much more resonant, intrusive bark in the mid-range and, more appealingly, creates muffled pops and bangs on the overrun.

The ride may be a fraction firmer but one of the reasons you could consider the Exige as a daily driver and trackday tool is that the nuggety ride quality doesn't disrupt the natural flow of this lightweight, compact coupe on the road. And despite the lightly treaded Yokohama Advans, rain doesn't stop play either. In fact, the tenacity of the A048s is a real surprise; it took two laps of a big, deserted wet roundabout before I got the front to push wide. You have to be pretty quick but calm if you want to play with the rear, though, winding on the lock briskly but accurately and working the throttle gently to prevent things getting snappy.

The half-hour route I've devised features a number of surfaces and a good mix of sweeping sections and tighter, undulating switchbacks. The chassis of the Lotus remains poised and communicative for its entirety, steering weight modulating delightfully, traction unfeasibly strong now that the dampness has evaporated. It's a hard car to keep on the boil, though, the gearing being over-long – third is good for around 90mph – and the manic, VTEC-like zone

RADICAL
SR4 TRACKSPORT

- Layout: Mid-engined, rear-wheel drive
- Engine: In-line 4-cyl, 1500cc
- Max power: 250bhp @ 9000rpm
- Max torque: 130lb ft @ 8000rpm
- Weight: 462kg
- Power/weight: 550bhp per ton
- 0-60mph: 3.5sec (claimed)
- Max speed: 160mph (claimed)
- Tyres: 185/530 13 fr, 210/560 13 rr, Matador
- Price: £33,000 (2005 prices)

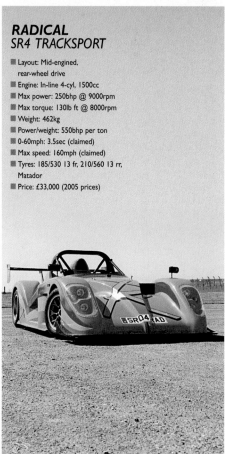

of the Toyota engine being even more obvious thanks to a distinct pop from the exhaust as the cam timing changes and an even louder blare to the redline.

'I know I'm a bit biased with this one,' says Meaden, 'but I really enjoy the added edge and focus the suspension brings to the car. Yes, it's hard – 30 per cent stiffer than the standard car – but as I increasingly use the car for weekend blats or long road drives with a circuit as the destination, sacrificing some on-road compliance for on-track incisiveness is the right way to go.'

'It's fantastic on the road – fast, grippy and a real hoot!' says John Hayman, before adding a couple of provisos. 'The engine's a pain, though. It really needs to be worked at its max all of the time, and I find the initial dead travel on the brake pedal unacceptable in such a focused drivers' car.'

The Performance 5-modified Mazda MX-5 presents quite a contrast and also shows why the forthcoming Exige 240R with the supercharged Toyota engine will improve this aspect of the Lotus. The Eaton-style BRP 'charger fitted to the otherwise standard Mazda 1.8 is whining and boosting from 2000rpm; you really feel its effect from 3000rpm and from there on it gets ever stronger, in a natural, progressive sort of way.

This MX-5 flies, yet the curious thing about this conversion is that it seems to drive like the standard car, playfully and with what feels like similar degrees of roll and pitch and squat. The suspension has been uprated, with firmer springs and dampers, but they seem to match the pace the 230bhp delivers as ideally as the standard car's softer suspension matches the stock 146bhp engine. Only the more noticeable body-flex gives the game away. Still, point-to-point, I reckon the Mazda would have the edge over the Exige, thanks to its closely stacked pack of short gear ratios and instant and generous performance.

Hales wonders if all the claimed power is there but concedes that it might just be the competence of the chassis and the linearity of the delivery that makes it feel less potent. Caterham-owning reader Tim Smith is impressed. 'Fantastic fun,' he says. 'Its understated appearance hides the enormous overtaking grunt, and I enjoyed the neutral handling. Given the cost of the conversion this has got to be close to top of anyone's list of practical cars that can actually be driven every day on the road and on trackdays.'

Not John Hayman's. 'If this engine or something very similar was standard fitment, would that give the MX-5 some cred or what! But it's a bit hairdressery, the interior is very shiny

plastic and it's not an event to be in, so I couldn't ever be passionate about it.'

The 350Z has us wondering if there's more to the GT4 spec than just a bit more power. As ever, there's a lovely, beefy, heavy feel to the Nissan that suggests durability, yet dynamically this example feels more polished with tighter body control and crisp steering. No chassis changes are claimed beyond the new-style Rays alloys, but it does feel like there's better wheel control. Maybe they're a bit lighter.

Whatever, the Nissan is mighty impressive. 'As an overall package it's great,' says Hales. 'Involving enough to be fun and quick enough to be exciting, all in a slightly vintage way.' Green agrees: 'There's a brawny feel to the controls but the feedback is detailed and accurate and it's lighter on its feet than it first appears.' It's carrying a lot more weight than the majority of the cars here but it's composed and responsive even through the sinuous sections of the road route, and gutsy too, with plenty of torque readily available to adjust the balance and trim a line. Add in great seats, a precise, meaty gearshift and strong brakes, and the 350Z could be the sleeper of this test.

'When you factor in the price, it's difficult to see any competition anywhere,' adds Hales. 'I'm not in the market for such things, but I could actually see myself buying a 350Z. Not in metallic yellow with that number plate though…' Just then Bovingdon returns from the track in the Grinnall. He hops out, takes off his helmet and bends down to inspect the front end. I'm sure he'll explain the incident in his track review but there are some witness marks on the nose-cone showing that it has been wiped lightly along a tyre barrier somewhere…

I make sure the roads are totally dry before I give the Grinnall another shot but it's no better. I just don't feel comfortable. Later I see Hales stepping out of it and wander over to see what he makes of it. He looks thoughtful. 'Not because I want to find for the underdog, but this isn't actually as bad as some people are making out,' he says. 'It could be quite good fun. The turbo engine seems well sorted and you can leave black lines and waltz the tail from side to side. It is hard to balance it on the power though, something you need to do when the engine is in the rear and the chassis isn't fully sorted. I think a bit of investigation and development could make a huge difference.'

Green is less enthused. 'If there was ever a car where you need to hold on, then this is it. Shame, then, that there's literally nothing to hold onto. After a while you can get into a rhythm on the road, but what the hell must it be like for a passenger? You'll never catch me sitting there…'

'I never felt fully in control,' says Tim Smith, 'and that's something I consider key when driving a vehicle whose power delivery has all the subtlety of indoor nuclear weapons.'

The contrast with the 65bhp Westfield XI couldn't be clearer. It seems that everyone loves its involving, playful nature. Green again: 'It's got a brilliantly delicate ride – in fact, everything feels delicate. The steering is a delight and, although the brakes are poor, it's not an issue.'

Meaden reckons the cockpit ambience and wraparound screen are worth the purchase price alone. The only downside, he says, is that after the other more powerful stuff in the test it feels

New Caterham CSR (right) turns the Seven into an extraordinarily polished road car. Boxster S (left) initially felt a little sterile in the company of such hardcore rivals, yet the more you drove it the more accomplished it seemed. After a day with hurricanes in their hair, our intrepid testers relax with a game of pool and a great Welsh curry (below)

odd that your progress relies on light traffic: 'You wouldn't want to try overtaking anything doing more than 50mph unless you get a run on it!' Hayman points out that any number of classics for the same money could be just as much fun: 'You really need the build experience to be part of the desire to buy one.'

In a reversal of the previous day, I ease myself into the Noble's enveloping Sparco seat. I reckon that after any of the cars here, the M400 would feel fast. Yes, there's the rush of the twin turbos, but this engine is on boost from such low revs you're never hanging around waiting for it to come on the boil, and although the torque is staggering, it ramps up smoothly.

'I don't think I have ever driven anything that can overtake like the M400,' says Green. 'Short straight, half a dozen cars bumbling along in front of you – they're dispatched with a single wave of monster turbocharged torque. After a while you go looking for people to overtake.'

You don't have to work it hard to storm along though, while the chassis is tightly controlled but not agitated and the steering is keen but not over-bright. Track work will show for sure, but there does seem to be more poise, less nervousness, when you're pushing on. A neat touch is the dual belt arrangement – harness plus lap and diagonal are provided – and this does feel like a car that will be as happy on the ring road as the Nürburgring.

Hales is impressed. 'Good spring and damping balance to the chassis – probably second best after the Porsche – and especially so when you look at the performance it has to deal with. It has a reassuring, nicely planted sensation and great steering, too – lots of feedback and lots of point without any sense that it might set off the back just when you didn't want it.'

I'm a big fan, though like all of us I'm less taken with the interior. The glamorous cockpit and beautifully engineered pedals of the Sagaris show what a low-volume specialist can do, given the will. The TVR looks stunning and seriously fast pounding around the track, and it's an event fastening yourself in. Not just for the interior ambience; sat low you can see the saw-tooth front wings and, in the mirror, the perspex spoiler and its aluminium spars. Turn the key and you feel like you're in a rawer, edgier car than the Noble, the straight-six idling with a deep, classy, slightly hesitant rumble, the gear lever needing a positive shove to engage first, and yet, once you're rolling, the ride of the Sagaris proves firm but finely damped.

It's massively, gloriously, loudly fast, and it's a proper drivers' car – you get as much out as you put in. Blip the throttle on downshifts and the gears engage sweetly; measure your steering and throttle inputs and you enhance the poise and balance of the car through the corners. The high-speed damping is perhaps a fraction sharp but resolutely resists float and wallow, while the steering is weighty and chatty and the brakes feel strong. What's unforgivable, though, especially considering that this is TVR's trackday weapon, is that you feel as if you're

PN05 OUL

Sagaris (above) a menacing spectacle to have looming in your rear-view mirror. Morgan Roadster (above, right) drives as you might expect – as if from a bygone era. Ariel Atom (below Morgan) requires a resilient spirit to punt it quickly down a wet road sitting *on* the seat rather than in it.

Twice Tuscan champion Hales reckons this car has been tinkered with and softened since he last drove it. 'There's now a slight woolliness to the front end and a sort of lost motion in the tail's response, which have made the car slightly remote to the touch. Put the front end back as it was but tame the tail and it'd be special again.'

Green also reckons that the steering lacks a little feel and the front end a little bite: 'You wait for it to hook up before squeezing the throttle. A slow in/fast out approach is required on the road as well as the racetrack. Mind you,' he adds, 'it sounds the business, looks the dog's and really gets you involved with the drive. It feels more old-fashioned muscle-car than modern GT.'

Can a car be too polished, so competent that it's, well, a bit dull? Straight after the TVR and Noble, the Boxster feels muted, over-refined and a lot heavier. However, give yourself a couple of miles to dial into its feedback, then tackle a difficult road and you appreciate that there's a chassis of rare ability beneath you. Bumps that upset other cars slip unnoticed beneath its wheels, yet when you start working its copious grip, its poise and measured responses are deeply impressive. It's as if Porsche's engineers have anticipated – and fixed – anything about which you might wish to complain.

'It oozes quality everywhere,' says Green. Hales loves the damping and the drivetrain. 'The engine gets going at about 2500 and then winds the needle further and further round that big dial, seemingly pulling for ever while that donkey-on-drugs Porsche noise grows more strident. Wonderful.' Any criticisms at all? He ponders a moment. 'Just possibly, the steering could be a little sharper – though it is mid-engined – and this is possibly one area where the Nissan has a slight edge on the road.'

Given Caterham's, ahem, track record in producing thrilling road cars that are equally at home on a circuit, the new CSR has to be fancied for the top slot. Caterham's objective with the CSR was to make a Seven that would be more capable on the road, less troubled by bumps and more measured in its responses, and it certainly feels that way. Indeed, when its 256bhp Cosworth engine comes on song it's shockingly loud and fast, almost out of character with the impressively calm, relaxed way this wider, more supple Seven traverses tricky tarmac.

Since I first drove the new CSR the seat has been lowered further and the steering wheel swapped for a smaller diameter item. I still have an issue with the driving position and the steering, though. The slower-geared rack and new front-end geometry reduce bump and camber distraction and bring a linear weighting, but the downside is the nose isn't as alert on turn-in – you feel like you're steering into corners rather than jinking it in with a flick of the wrists. And although this is the wider-bodied Seven, paradoxically I found that there wasn't enough elbow room for me to work the wheel with the freedom I'd like.

'There's plenty of knee-room for me and my six-foot frame and I liked the new dash treatment which makes the chassis tubes part of the furniture,' says Hales. Caterham-owning Smith concurs, saying the interior is much improved over his car and gives an impression of real quality. Hales has an idea what CSR stands for,

'THE ARIEL ATOM FEELS LIKE A BALL OF PENT-UP MANIC ENERGY'

too – Completely Sorted for the Road. 'It's very composed and stable, staying level and showing no signs of pitch or yaw. It feels like a more intimate version of a bigger GT. However, the 'bigness' extends to the steering, which has lost some of the R300's delightful intimacy and involvement.'

Hayman owns an R300 and Green has just returned from a trip to the Nürburgring in our long-term R300, so what do they make of it? 'Really good on the road,' says Hayman, 'but I was surprised that on the inside it didn't feel any bigger than my R300.' Green is also impressed by its road manners. 'You can see where the work has gone,' he says. 'It feels considerably more grown-up. That said, it lacks the razor-sharp steering and dartiness of our long-term R300.' Final word to Smith: 'The engine is fantastic, but overall it feels like a much larger car than my Seven without the same feedback and adjustability.'

The lightly furnished cockpit of the Westfield

Sport 2000S, with its minimal instrumentation, painted metal transmission tunnel and exposed tubular chassis rigging, shouts track car. And if that doesn't get the message across, there's a sequential gearbox with screaming straight-cut gears. You only have to lift the throttle a fraction to make wonderfully snappy upshifts but you have to work quite hard to make smooth progress when you're not going for it, using the clutch to smooth things out, and you have to remember to downshift all the way when you come to a halt.

Like the CSR, the 2000S has a powerful Ford Duratec engine, a 2-litre in this instance tuned to 250bhp by Dunnell. While it may lack a little of the Caterham's torque, it powers a lighter car (550kg versus 575) and so the 2000S feels every bit as potent. With trackday tyres and firm suspension, it fidgets around more on the bumps but, oddly, in the twisties its steering is light and there isn't as much feel as you might expect.

Meaden drove it from Betws-y-Coed to Anglesey and thought it was a blast. 'I enjoyed it

Left: rain does not stop play, though you need to be hardy to enjoy driving the Westfield or Atom in such conditions. Performance 5-modified MX-5 (right) is a cracker, with enough pace and chassis ability to mix it with Exige

more than any Seven-style Westfield I've driven previously. The transmission is ruthlessly effective but right on the borderline of what you'd be prepared to live with in regular road use. The chassis works well in the dry but I suspect it doesn't engage you quite enough to make it a comfortable, confident partner in the wet. Overall, it's well-sorted, more realistically priced than most Caterhams, but the fit, finish and detailing dents its owner appeal.'

'It's quite hard work on the road,' chips in Green. 'The gearbox clunks, thunks and whines, while the front end feels a little light and not quite as connected to the tarmac as I'd like. But it ain't slow.'

Wearing a private number plate, the Morgan could pass for a Plus 8 from the '60s. Drive it and it feels like a car from an even earlier decade. It's an undeniably handsome thing, though the trackday tyres look incongruous, like your grandad wearing Nikes.

The cockpit is wonderfully traditional too, with classic dials and a fat-rimmed Mota-Lita wheel, yet there's a sliver of modernity in here too, with a genuine carbonfibre dash panel where you'd expect machine-turned aluminium. Meanwhile some of the kit you might expect – roll hoop, harnesses – is strangely absent.

It's a wonderful view down the long, vented bonnet and over the flowing wings, and when you turn the key, the new 3-litre 24-valve Ford V6 even has a classic six-cylinder rumble. With 223bhp and oodles of torque, the creamy smooth engine gives the Roadster a decent turn of speed and is allied to a lovely gearshift.

All that said, I couldn't draw much pleasure from its dynamics. The Morgan revealed bumps on the road route that hadn't registered in any other car. The front was reasonably well tied-down but the rear was in turmoil, finding and amplifying undulations.

The steering, meanwhile, went from vague and finger-light in a straight line to weighty and writhing in a decent corner, so that while there is a fair amount of grip on offer, you don't feel much inspired to exploit it.

Hales recognises these characteristics but does feel inspired. 'All these things are part of being Morgan and it is certainly intimate and involving in a physical way that is hard to find these days. If you don't like that kind of thing, you will never like a traditional Morgan.

'The seats are surprisingly supportive, lots of torsal support without a bucket, there's a surprising amount of grip and it tracks round a corner with little or no understeer and the tail is very stable even when you try to provoke it.' Not for everyone, then, but not without appeal.

Last up is the Ariel Atom which is, in its own unique way, as challenging as the Morgan. It always amazes me that the Atom qualifies as a road car because there's so little of it. It's like driving a ghosted illustration of a car where the bodywork has been airbrushed out to reveal all its mechanical and structural parts.

Like the Grinnall it thrums and fizzes to the tune of the engine, in this instance a highly tuned Honda VTEC developing a crazy 245bhp. It seems impossible to drive the Atom slowly yet it's

'THIS MX-5 FLIES. IF ONLY THIS WAS THE STANDARD ENGINE...'

darned tricky to drive it as fast as its engine will allow too. The car feels like a ball of pent-up manic energy, the nose light and agitated, the fat tyres grabbing at bumps and cambers. You have to hang on grimly when the engine hits the VTEC zone, and when you take a hand off the small steering wheel to grab the next gear, the car weaves half a lane. Mad, bad and dangerous to know, though maybe I'm getting too old for this lark.

Green reckons it was a hoot, 'so long as you can get over the draught and ignore everyone staring at you. I really enjoyed it on the road; it kind of makes you tingle – although that could be the vibration through the chassis. Good steering, an excellent snick-snick box and lots of rasping VTEC power.'

Smith liked it too. 'Excellent fun,' he declares. 'Really good turn-in and steering feel, and the air intake by your head sounds fantastic as the VTEC kicks in. I suspect it can be better set-up to dial some of the twitchiness out, though.'

THE HALF-TIME SCORE

So, how do they stand after the road section of the test? The weather was almost too kind to us, being mostly sunny and dry for two days, allowing the more extreme cars, and those wearing near-bald trackday-style tyres, to shine. Even so, when it came to scoring, the judges also remembered the trip up to Anglesey...

You won't be surprised to learn that the Grinnall and Morgan are to be found at the very bottom of all our judges' listings. However, there is one car we haven't mentioned which doesn't score any points at all – the Radical SR4. Why? Because we couldn't get it over the speed humps leading from the track to the public road.

Heading the points table after round 1 is the Boxster, an incredibly well-polished, entertaining and satisfying car. Not to mention versatile; it's a convertible and has at least twice as much load space as you'd expect a mid-engined car to have.

Not far behind is the Noble M400, another highly accomplished mid-engined car that's

ultimately more thrilling but rather less habitable and less good value. The Nissan 350Z is a surprising equal third. This GT4 version seems to have raised the beefy 350Z's game subtly but tellingly and it holds station with the outrageously handsome and characterful Sagaris.

So, that's first qualifying over, with the Boxster on provisional pole, but second qualifying, the track session with its more specific demands, is sure to mix the order up, big style...

Scores after road section: Boxster 92; Noble 90; 350Z 87; Sagaris 87; Exige 85; Caterham 83; Westfield XI 83; MX-5 80; Westfield S2000 79; Ariel Atom 77; Morgan 65; Grinnall IV 61.

Exige is our Mr Meaden's very own car (above). Everyone admires the chassis, but the Toyota engine elicits mixed responses

'I'M LEFT CONFUSED AND COVERED IN MUD, THE GRINNALL RESTING NOSE-FIRST IN THE TYRE WALL'

on't let the photos fool you. Although we were incredibly lucky with the weather in Anglesey, it wasn't exclusively dry and sunny. The very first morning of track-testing was held in wet-but-drying conditions: in other words, the very worst, most unpredictable conditions possible. In hindsight the manic, monster-turbocharged Grinnall probably wasn't the best car in which to start the day…

Turn One, okay, take it steady… umm, not too bad, maybe it's not quite as slippery as it looks. Turn Two, gentle power, the mid-mounted 1.8 Audi turbo engine starts whooshing and gnashing menacingly and suddenly the Grinnall spits sideways; bit of opposite lock, feather the throttle… and the turbo shuts down instantly, the corrective lock suddenly becomes too generous and the scarlet Grinnall snaps back and sends me rallycrossing across the dirt.

You might think that I should have learnt something from this, like 'send someone else out in the 680kg, 350bhp Grinnall first' or simply 'park it in the pits until its dries out'. But that's assuming that a) I'm a rational human being and b) that I can make it back to the pits without incident…

Three corners later, I'm left confused, covered in mud and with the Grinnall resting nose-first into a tyre wall. Thankfully there's no real contact and the unnaturally powerful Grinnall lives to fight another day. Me? I think I'll have a cup of coffee and wait for the sun to burn off the water and slime that's turned the track into a virtual ice-rink.

And then I get back to the pits and park next to the bright yellow Porsche Boxster S. Suddenly ABS, PSM, doors and a luxuriously insulated hood seem like the greatest inventions of all time. About 30 seconds later I'm back on track; two minutes after that the PSM is disabled. I'm

Above left: the gang lines up for a group photo on the Ty Croes circuit, with the Irish Sea in the background. Above: from the driver's seat of the Westfield 2000S looking across to its arch rival, the new Caterham CSR 260. Boxster S (right) proves remarkably capable on the track

having fun, the Boxster sliding gracefully through the turns, utterly obedient, brilliantly controlled and lapping quicker than all the semi-slick-shod lightweights. The Boxster may not win this contest but it's already proved itself as a worthy contender, and if you really want a roofless/doorless trackday special then maybe we've found the perfect tow car…

The real point of the Grinnall/Boxster contrast is that this 13-car line-up is blessed with at least one car for every track occasion. Dry and sunny, empty track and with your qualifying head on? The Radical SR4 should do nicely. Or maybe you fancy a bit of crowd-pleasing sideways action? Okay, take your pick from the brilliantly forgiving Nissan 350Z or exploitable but ferocious TVR Sagaris. Somewhere in the middle there's the screaming Atom, searing Caterham CSR… the list goes on. But if you must have just one (and let's face it, most of us would have to settle for just the one), which one gives the biggest thrill, won't bankrupt you after a 20-minute session and will go on rewarding even when you know every facet of its character? Two days at Anglesey's fabulously flowing, cresting Ty Croes circuit should reveal all…

Richard Meaden is our nominated hot-head, or is that hotshoe? Anyway, while we're all enjoying ourselves and showing off for the cameras he'll be in race driver mode, trying for the absolute optimum lap. Mark Hales, seasoned racer and the man rich people call when they want to see their priceless historic racers at the pointy end of the grid, will be going similarly flat-out (he only

has one speed) but just for fun, along with myself, evo active trackday manager and Radical SR8 racer Roger Green, road test regular and part-time racer Smokin' John Hayman and trackday regular and friend of evo Tim Smith.

With the track drying out, the lightweights become more appealing but it seems logical to tackle the cars in various groups. The Porsche Boxster and Nissan 350Z are very clearly compromised towards road driving, as is the one modified car we've included in this test, the intriguing 230bhp supercharged MX-5, fettled by Mazda specialist Performance 5. The Noble, TVR, Exige and Morgan tread the middle ground: all developed as road cars but with a heavy trackday bias, they could almost have been designed with this test in mind.

Then there are the lightweights, which operate on a sliding scale of roadability from the newly civilised Caterham CSR, through the hardcore Westfield 2000S, exposed Atom, unhinged Grinnall and racecar-that-can't-even-be-bothered-to-pretend-it's-not Radical SR4. The endearing Westfield XI has no obvious rivals, unless you can think of another 65bhp trackday special that we've forgotten.

First up the Nissan 350Z GT4. It looks handsome and cool in the paddock. It may not pack the visual head-butt of the Sagaris but it looks hunkered down, wheel-at-each-corner nimble and with a snarly V6 up front and rear-wheel drive you just know it'll want to play.

We'll get to that in a minute, but it's the polish of this 350Z that surprises. Usually the brawny

Nissan feels a little clunky, and pulses to a surprisingly coarse engine note. This GT4/Anniversary car seems to have had the rough edges buffed out and the result is that the chassis' composure and adjustability shine even brighter. As you might expect of a heavy road car, the 350Z will understeer unless provoked with the throttle or brakes to lose grip at the rear, but it's easy to keep things very neutral and tidy and the 350Z carries really good speed through the faster turns.

And it's a showboater's (for which read road tester's) dream, happy to sit at ludicrous angles for an age and easy to provoke, hold and recover. Perhaps more impressive is that the brakes show no signs of fading in the five-lap bursts we're driving. Fortunately for all of the heavier cars, the ever-challenging Anglesey circuit tests everything but brakes to the absolute limit. There's only one big stop (into the hairpin) and plenty of cooling time until you summon the brakes again. Even so, the 350Z puts up an excellent show. Meaden hops out after his balls-out laps with a big grin: 'I really expected it to wilt, but the brakes were fine, the engine's smooth and the wide powerband makes it easy to build a rhythm. Surprisingly good in every area,' he concludes.

'THE BOXSTER IS A PRECISION TOOL WITH BEAUTIFULLY JUDGED STEERING'

It's an early bullseye for the everyday practical road cars and the Boxster S continues the trend. With the track now completely dry, the Porsche is lapping almost constantly. It's a precision tool with beautifully judged steering, a fine gearbox and an exquisite balance. Again, the Boxster will understeer but after a couple of laps it's the most natural thing in the world to turn-in just snagging the brakes to get the rear steering the front tyres into the apex. From there you can keep things tidy and get that delicious flat-six hooked-up and away or use slightly exaggerated steering and throttle inputs to drift the car all the way to the exit. Surely mid-engined cars aren't meant to be quite so forgiving?

Green is effusive. 'The Boxster really is brilliant. Obviously it feels heavy and soft after

something like the Westfield 2000S, but within yards you're comfortable and it's so entertaining.' Hales isn't so sure and thinks you'd crave more power. He might be right, and the other killer with the heavier cars like the Boxster S is that you really need to budget for a new set of brake pads after every full trackday, while tyre life will be massively reduced. And much as drifting around in the 350Z feels perfectly safe, most trackday organisers would take a dim view of any car smoking its way through the corners.

Does that rule out the MX-5? Well, it's certainly keen to wag its pert tail, but because it's that bit lighter it seems to dance on its modest 205-section rubber and there's less attention-grabbing blue smoke as it slips effortlessly from one apex to the next with just a hint of opposite

lock. It's a wonderfully fluid little car. Fortunately Performance 5 has resisted the temptation to screw the suspension to the ground looking for good lap times and instead has just tightened things up with slightly stiffer KYB dampers and FM (Flying Miata) springs. It has retained the standard car's incredibly friendly on-limit handling but given it just enough extra grip to handle the horses unleashed by the BRP Eaton-type supercharger.

My feeling is that the conversion isn't quite good for the claimed 230bhp, but as Meaden points out, the track probably disguises the supercharger's real strength – low- and mid-range punch – simply because you're always keeping the sweet little 'four' right on the boil. Even so, the chassis feels perfectly matched to

ROGER GREEN – A SECOND THOUGHT

The two cars that stood out for me couldn't be more different. The cute Westfield XI is an absolute joy, a car in which you can't help but smile as you adjust your line with light, fingertip movements. Meanwhile, the Radical SR4 provides a full-on adrenalin buzz that demands maximum concentration and tempts you into chasing a lap time.

In the Westfield, cornering speed and the desire to knock a tenth off your best time are irrelevant; you

simply enjoy the predictability of the lazy slides and the graceful way it glides over the bumpy Anglesey track. It has hardly any power, poor brakes and minimal grip and yet it does everything so right, and it's embellished with a purity of feedback to savour. And for many that's what trackdays are all about – the ability to enjoy your car at eight-tenths rather than being pressurised into running right to the edge of your talent. The Westfield XI may be old-school, but it adds a welcome freshness to the

trackday scene.

It's probably true to say that the tight, gnarled confines of this circuit helped its cause and the same can be said of last year's winner, the Radical. The SR4 is nimble, darty and enjoys being chucked around.

It's a no-compromise racer without a doubt, but you always feel on top of it, able to ride the limit of adhesion without fear of it throwing you off. It is a brilliant piece of kit; if the XI is your cup of tea, then the SR4 is like a treble-shot espresso.

the power and there's always just a bit more grunt than grip. You'd have an awful lot of fun in this and with good post-2001-facelift MX-5s going for as little as £10,000 and the conversion at just £3995 plus £750 fitting, it's big entertainment on a tight budget.

If you never got to drive something as wild as an Ariel Atom or as nimble as a Caterham, any one of these three would seem to hit the spot as inspirational road and trackday cars. But when you do buckle-up a four-point harness, lower your helmet visor and really attack the racetrack in one of the lightweights, your senses and your sense of reality are forever scrambled. If you can sacrifice those creature comforts, and put up with getting a bit wet occasionally, then a whole new world of sensations and thrills open up to you. It's not for everyone, but wringing out a Radical or taming a Grinnall is about as visceral an experience as you could ever hope for.

Traditionally Caterham has been the master of building beautifully developed, stunningly quick, almost magical trackday-and-weekend-fun road cars. Some people think any Seven-type car is much the same, but our experience suggests that there's only one genuine article. Caterhams have won two of the previous Trackday Car of the Year titles and with the new broader 'Road and Track' format the wider, stiffer and intensely developed CSR was odds-on favourite to sweep out of Wales with yet another title under its belt.

Mutterings in the paddock suggest it won't be quite that simple. Hales has had a few exploratory laps and looks a little crestfallen. 'It doesn't feel like a Caterham. It won't turn-in, it locks its wheels as soon as you get on the brakes and there's no traction to speak of,' he says with mild disbelief. 'Not sure what they've tried to do with this car but it doesn't flow like the brilliant R300,' is his conclusion.

What Caterham has done is not simply develop it as a track car. This CSR, despite its rip-snorting 256bhp 2.3-litre Ford Duratec motor, is Caterham's all-new road offering. It's been painstakingly developed by chassis wizards Multimatic (as chronicled within these pages), and although they've endowed the Seven with a newfound maturity and poise on the road, on the track a narrow-bodied Superlight-R would run rings around it.

Of course, the CSR will be developed into a more track-orientated machine as time goes on (already there's a pure race version that was superb when we tried it around Donington Park, evo 076) but it's a big gamble on Caterham's part to launch with a car that isn't suited to track work. As Meaden points out, 'the rest of the lightweights are compromised on the road so that they shine on the track; with the Caterham it's the other way round.' The question is, will potential owners really think of it as a Boxster rival or just an even faster Seven? If it's the former, Caterham is onto a winner, but if it's the latter (which we suspect it is) then the CSR might be a compromise too far...

Westfield's 2-litre 250bhp Dunnell-tuned Duratec-engined Sport 2000S snarls with almost the same venom as the Cosworth-built CSR motor, and with its race-spec six-speed sequential 'box, barely-treaded Toyo R888 rubber and frill-free interior it shouts its track credentials louder than any other car bar the tarmac-grazing Radical. Within a lap it feels

JOHN HAYMAN – A SECOND THOUGHT

For me, trackdays are about having a laugh, smiling insanely whilst sliding around. Those perfect fast laps I save for racing, as that's where they belong! That said, my competitive side still shows through when a quick car's in front, especially if it's a trick bit of kit – I love giant-slaying! So I suppose my trackday toy requirement is that a car has to be super-fast and a playful laugh at the same time!

The Noble M400 fits that brief rather well; stunningly powerful motor

in a more than capable chassis. It's just a wee bit on the expensive side and consumes rear tyres at an astonishing rate! And if it's not quite my ideal, then neither is the TVR.

The Caterham CSR should be, but on the day this particular one wasn't. The potential is certainly there, but I'm not convinced that it's as good as the original Seven on track and it certainly doesn't warrant its premium price on circuit ability alone.

The Grinnall, on the other hand, utterly lacks any potential – what a

horrid thing! It's an overly powerful contraption and it feels as if the chassis would struggle to cope with a quarter of its current horsepower.

I can't ignore the Westfield XI. What an absolute hoot. I loved it wholeheartedly until discovering it costs as much as a nice E-type.

So I ended up with three faves – Radical, Atom and Exige – and after due deliberation (fun factor, price, running costs, reliability, etc) decided the Atom fulfils just about everything I want in a trackday car.

Sport 2000S (right) is the most cohesive Westfield we've yet tried on the track, and brutally quick. Atom (left) is also fearsomely fast, and amongst the lightweights is the best finished, most exotic in feel. Westfield XI (below right) delightfully playful and entertaining, teaches you the joys of driving with your mind and your fingertips. Exige (bottom left) continues its dynamic excellence on the track

keener than the Caterham to indulge. There's less understeer, a limited-slip diff that translates wheelspin into genuine drive and a keenness to change direction, an appetite for any aggression you might throw its way that the CSR lacks.

Green is a fan. 'This is the best Westfield I've driven. It's more together than previous cars of theirs, and the engine is really strong in the low- and mid-ranges. The 'box works brilliantly on track and it just adds to an already strong package.' The 2000S lacks the killer bite of the CSR at high revs but it can get the power down really nicely and it's quicker across a lap because it rarely flares into wasteful wheelspin.

For me the Westfield still lacks the intimacy, involvement and control of a well-sorted Caterham, but that's due in large part to the wider chassis and body and should take nothing away from the achievement of the 2000S. It's a physical car to hustle with steering that weights up on lock, a stiff set-up and a gearbox that needs positive, measured tugs to slam into gear (pull back for up changes and push away to change down), but it rewards with razor-sharp reactions and faithful, clinical shifts in balance according to your steering, throttle and brake inputs.

Bizarrely, it reminds me of my old Caterham Academy racer; the way it turns-in and then seems to sit in a neutral stasis waiting for your commands is spookily similar. Only the odd driving position (the steering wheel is very close to you and canted slighted to the left, and the low seating position means you bang your elbow on the high side sill) and slightly clumsy construction take away from the Westfield's otherwise bright sheen.

Let's not forget that these tiny, flyweight sports cars are big money and, despite big strides by Caterham with the CSR, only the Ariel Atom has a real, tangible sense of integrity. Okay, so it's got no doors or roof but that exposed Honda iVTEC engine is bulletproof and the beautifully detailed suspension and substantial steel chassis are brilliantly executed. It feels special before it's even turned a wheel.

The problem in the past has been that the Atom hasn't quite gelled out on the track. It's lacked feel through the steering and the way the car lurched into oversteer on turn-in and then couldn't be controlled on the power made it a frustrating experience. The supercharged car we took to our Car of the Year bash (evo 075) was better but perhaps a bit too extreme, so we settled on this 245bhp naturally aspirated version, set up with lessons learnt from Ariel's considerable racing success in the Brit Cup series last year.

It's a blinder. The engine is immense, with good torque and a thrilling top end. As it hits full VTEC mode the big snorkel intake just to the left of your head shakes your eyeballs in their sockets and it feels like your head's about to be sucked into the intake chamber. There's still that turn-in oversteer but now you can pick up the throttle once the nose is on line and steer the

Atom from the rear with confidence.

Perhaps this car is a bit too fast and loose (it pretty much oversteered for the entire lap) and it takes confidence to stay on top of it; but there seems to be more information through the steering to help keep ahead of the chassis now. And the brakes have been transformed from dead but grabby to nicely weighted and easy to modulate. This car normally runs on much stiffer track-only suspension and is apparently much more settled, but for the experienced its current set-up is massive fun.

Hayman, who's driven the car before with its less lively set-up, loves it. 'It's mad. The engine is barking, the 'box is super-quick, and with this set-up you'd never stop laughing. But the beauty is that it's a relatively simple procedure to fit the stiffer set-up if you just want to go fast,' he says. Of course the race set-up would kill any road pretence stone dead.

Hales would probably much prefer it, though. 'It's great fun but only for a short while. You've got to be pretty confident to drive the Atom as it demands, and even if you can hang on to it I'm not sure you'd get through a full session without being black-flagged for reckless driving.' After a few laps Green is grinning but also pondering the merits of this particular set-up: 'It's got turn-in oversteer, lift-off oversteer, power oversteer… it's easy to control and it's fun because it's flawed. It does show the inherent friendliness of the

chassis, though. Superb fun.'

The Radical's only flaw, if you can call it that, is its sheer speed. It's a hugely accomplished and searingly quick track car with great steering, immense grip and a playful side that betrays its Le Mans-prototype-in-miniature looks. It sucks you in, goads you into going quicker and quicker and it just seems to get better with every ounce of commitment you throw at it. The engine screams its approval, the sequential gearbox loves to be hurried, the brakes soak up the punishment and all the time you're pushing at the very edges of your own ability.

After about ten laps of daring myself to carry that bit more speed, braking just a few feet later than I'm comfortable with, I decide it's time to come in before I have an almighty off. I'm exhilarated, but to be pushing that hard on a track with 20 or more other cars circulating would seem a bit mad. Hales, ever the racer, really enjoys the challenge of the Radical and thinks you can enjoy it on many levels: 'It is very quick and I can see why people might think it's too quick, but I think even less experienced drivers would enjoy the fine controls and that feeling that you're in something truly special. And you're always sliding it to get the best out of it. This particular set-up doesn't entirely suit Anglesey's bumps – very bouncy at the front. But it's still pretty fantastic.'

Mr Hales is also relishing the challenge of the Grinnall, but for different reasons. 'You can make this work, but it's a case of managing the boost and driving it as smoothly as you can.' Personally I'm not sure the reward is equal to the effort required. The problem is that even on low boost (a mere 300bhp) the engine drives the chassis to such an extent that you feel like you're simply avoiding a spin at all times. The last thing a lightweight sports car needs is a huge slug of instantly delivered torque, but that's what the

'THE RADICAL SEEMS TO GET BETTER WITH EVERY OUNCE OF COMMITMENT YOU THROW AT IT'

Grinnall gets every time you hit the power and the results are highly unpredictable.

I found it best to turn-in on the brakes to get the tail gently moving and then measure out the boost (generally a gear higher than you'd expect to avoid the really angry part of the delivery) and keep the car as neutral as possible to the exit. With the boost wound up to full and a frantic 360bhp to avoid, it gets trickier still, and even Hales suggested Meaden should leave it on low boost for the timed laps because 'it creates more problems than the time you'd theoretically make up between the corners'.

After OD'ing on adrenalin in the Grinnall and Radical, the tiny Westfield XI should feel like a total anti-climax, but judging by the number of laps it's putting in there must be more to the XI than cute looks. With just 65bhp from an A-series lifted straight out of an MG Midget, your expectations of the Westie are somewhere south of the Radical's chin spoiler, but against the odds it's a hoot. And it's not just an, 'Ahh. That's great for two laps, but I never want to drive it again' type experience. No, you could drive the XI all day and never stop enjoying its keen chassis, gutsy little engine and the delicate balance served up by its Bakelite-spec tyres.

As I strap myself in, Hayman's advice is simple: 'Don't use the brakes. Just turn-in and let it drift.' Essentially he's right, the XI never needing more than a dab of the brakes even into the hairpin. It's got a great interior with tight-fitting little bucket seats, a gorgeous Moto-lita style steering wheel and door-to-door red leather, and you find yourself absorbing every little detail of the experience as it flows around Anglesey.

It rarely requires much steering input, reacting to the soft and fairly hopeless brake pedal obediently and tackling corners in an indescribably satisfying four-wheel drift. The four-speed 'box has a pretty long and

 TIM SMITH – A SECOND THOUGHT

The Porsche Boxster is very impressive on track for a car I'd always thought was owned by those with hairdresser tendencies. Good balance, brakes and engine, though ultimately it does feel like a road car. And looking at the state of the tyres after a day on the track, the running costs could be prohibitive!

The Atom is clearly much more at home at Anglesey but I found it difficult to drive fast as it feels as though grip is switching from front to rear for no apparent reason, resulting in some surprisingly rapid transitions from under- to oversteer. One for the very confident, but it's a real challenge.

The Radical's pace is phenomenal and I was surprised that it does slide around a bit, but it never feels like it's going to spring any nasty surprises. That said, I think you would need considerable track experience to get the most out of it. For different reasons the same is true of the heavier, more road-orientated TVR Sagaris. It's much more confidence-

inspiring than I'd expected of a 400bhp road-racer but still perhaps more for the experienced driver.

As a Caterham owner, I was most looking forward to the CSR and although I love the high quality interior and the fantastic engine, the handling on track was a bit of a disappointment. It has a tendency to understeer and then lose traction at the exit from the corners, and overall it feels like a much larger car than mine and is missing that classic Seven feedback and adjustability.

Hot lapping at Ty Croes

Richard Meaden on how our posse faired
against the stopwatch at Anglesey

Setting lap times is a serious business, especially at a tricky and potentially unforgiving circuit like Anglesey. It's also somewhat at odds with the ethos of trackday driving, where enjoyment should always take priority over extracting the absolute maximum from yourself and your car.

That said, you can't beat Old Father Time as the ultimate barometer of a car's performance relative to its peers, which is why we attached our Racelogic VBox equipment to each car in turn and gave each ten laps in which to achieve a representative time.

As you'd expect, with such a diverse group of cars, you need to employ a wide range of driving styles to get the best from each car. The SR4, despite being the baby of Radical's range, is the most intense experience here by quite some margin, and demands total concentration as a result. The driving environment, sequential 'box, brickwall brakes and banshee engine are all pure racecar, and while the chassis is actually extremely playful, by the end of ten laps you can feel your concentration wilting under the sensory assault.

At the other end of the scale, 'fast' laps in the Westfield XI appear to unfold in slow-motion. It's still an absorbing experience, though, for the lack of power and exquisitely driftable chassis demand you carry as much momentum as possible. Thus you find yourself seeking out the very fringes of the circuit to eke out the last drop of corner speed. You could learn an awful lot about on-limit driving in this car without frightening yourself once.

Another old-timer is the Morgan, but the experience is less satisfying. There's grunt aplenty from the lusty-sounding Jaguar V6, but the ancient chassis design and super-sticky trackday tyres are an unhappy combination. The front-end bucks and skitters in protest on turn-in, while the rear follows suit as you feed in the power. It's

good discipline to hone your technique to achieve a clean lap, but the overall experience is an acquired taste.

Surprisingly, neither the Westfield 2000S nor the Caterham CSR give their lap times as freely as you'd expect, the former bludgeoning its way around with abundant grip and grunt but not much involvement. A less sticky tyre would doubtless make it more fun without sacrificing too much speed. As a track car the latter is a work in progress, currently suffering from a road-biased set-up that creates a lack of front-end bite at track velocities. This forces you to monster it through the corners on the power, fighting it rather than flowing with it. The potential's there, but for now the old-school R300/400/500 are more satisfying track tools.

The Atom is another car you drive on the throttle, despite trying to keep things as neat as possible for the clock. This one feels much more forgiving on its road-biased set-up than last year's example. You'd probably get a bollocking from trackday marshals for hanging the tail out so much, but it really is the car's natural stance; a little too lairy perhaps.

The Grinnall has the makings of a super-Atom, what with its rabid dodgem styling and rampant 350bhp Audi 1.8T engine. Sadly it has many fatal flaws, the main ones being you simply can't see through the fairing-like windscreen or get comfortable behind the wheel, thanks to an odd driving position and seats that offer no lateral support. Trying to get a lap time out of it is horrid; as well as not being able to see properly and feeling like you're going to fall out of the thing, you have to contend with turn-in, lift-off and power oversteer, traits

compounded by the stampede of turbocharged horses. Less power, more attention to fundamental ergonomics please, Mr Grinnall.

Of the more obvious road cars, the 350Z is surprisingly effective and composed, but when driven for speed and not for photography it isn't so much fun. Likewise the MX-5, which posts an identical time and in a broadly similar style, always feels like a sweet-handling road car and lacks the teeth to really attack the circuit. After the lightweights, the Boxster feels big and a little blunt, but posts an impressive time, thanks to its balance, brakes and tractable engine. All three are pretty easy to lap quickly, and if you're the kind of driver who does just the occasional trackday, all should score highly.

The Exige and Noble are similar in execution, majoring on low weight, intimate steering feel, high grip levels and pointy mid-engined poise. The explosive M400 monsters the little Lotus around the undulating Ty Croes circuit, a lap that exposes the Exige's peaky motor and overly tall gearing. At full chat the Noble is epic, with recent chassis revisions releasing the M400's full potential. Raw pace aside, though, both cars demand precision and commitment and reward with terrific corner speed and a smooth, fluid style.

The TVR is less focused than the mid-engined duo, but the brawny motor, tireless brakes and exploitable front-engined, rear-drive chassis make the Sagaris an absorbing car to push hard. A little more front-end response and a set of grippier tyres would improve it further, and help fulfil its billing as TVR's ultimate trackday weapon more convincingly.

LAP TIMES

1.	Radical SR4	47.80sec
2.	Westfield 2000S	48.65sec
3.	Noble M400	49.10sec
4.	Caterham CSR	49.80sec
5.	Ariel Atom	50.05sec
6.	TVR Sagaris	50.15sec
7.	Lotus Exige S2	52.40sec
8.	Porsche Boxster S	52.55sec
9.	Grinnall Scorpion	52.85sec
10.	Morgan Roadster	53.35sec
11.	Mazda MX-5	53.85sec
12.	Nissan 350Z	53.85sec
13.	Westfield XI	57.15sec

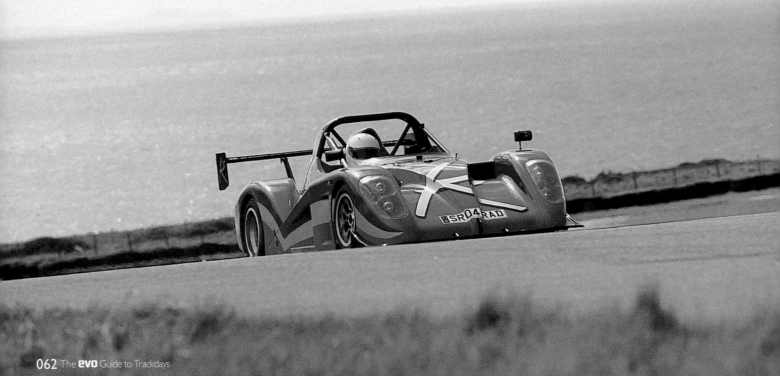

indeterminate throw but it's rarely out of third anyway and you're so wrapped up in maintaining speed and enjoying the sweet chassis flowing underneath you that the spongey brakes and old-school shift barely register. Hales sums it up perfectly when he jumps out and says, simply, 'it's magic'.

The other 'old-timer' in the group is Morgan's Roadster, which is a new model but in fact feels more vintage than the XI. The steering is quite slow and the pedal positioning makes heel-and-toeing almost impossible, but the real problem is suspension that seems to discover bumps you never knew were on the track.

It's plain hard work, and getting the best from the Morgan sometimes feels like you're putting it through real pain. It turns-in with good bite and rarely loses grip at the rear but it's not a fluid handler and super-grippy track tyres seem at odds with the ancient underpinnings. Maybe if it was as easy to set-up for corners as the XI the suspension would make a bit more sense, but on soft-compound rubber it's not as entertaining as you'd hope. Hales, a man who's raced many Morgans, can see past the lack of composure over the bumps and the He-Man controls, but pretty much everyone else loved the looks but couldn't live with the reality.

Which brings us to TVR's burly Sagaris, the lithe Noble M400 and Meaden's Exige, with its new factory-fitted Ohlins adjustable dampers. All fabulous road cars, all perfectly at home mingling with the Atoms and Radicals of this rarefied world.

The perfectly-formed Exige is the most inviting. With a 'Stage 2' Lotus Sport exhaust system it certainly sounds ready to punch above its weight and the stream of information flowing through the steering immediately sets it apart as a truly special experience. Grip is enormous, and the brakes with uprated pads work much better than the standard set-up, although they retain that irksome dead centimetre of travel. But Anglesey's slow and medium speed corners and big gradients don't suit the Exige's revvy Toyota engine and it's tricky to keep it in hot cam mode.

It's a great shame because the fleeting moments of manic, hard-edged acceleration leave you frustrated that you can't access its full potential for more of the lap. Meaden's just returned from the Nürburgring with the Exige and apparently it worked brilliantly on the high-speed transitions that cling to the Eiffel mountains, but here it's not as happy.

Having said that, the Exige is still a unique and addictive flavour, with real precision built into all its controls and such incredible feedback that you feel confident to drive right up to its limits

Trackday-spec Morgan Roadster (top) a very, very acquired taste. Noble M400 (above) completely at home on the circuit; TVR Sagaris (below left) very fast but would benefit from more front-end grip

even in the fast Turn One. That a chassis with this much mechanical grip can have such progression when you breach the limits is almost beyond belief. And there's a real sense of occasion when you're ensconced in the neatly-styled cabin; it's just so intimate and the driving position is perfect. With just a bit more torque this could be the ultimate road and track weapon. Roll on the supercharged 240R.

Torque isn't something the Noble M400 wants for. What a mighty engine! The 3-litre twin-turbo V6 delivers epic punch out of corners and as the revs pile on it just goes into warp drive. With 425bhp and a kerb weight of little more

than a ton, you'd be right to expect fireworks but the scale of the performance still takes your breath away. As does the chassis balance, the sublime damping and the accurate, almost Exige-like steering.

I know Barker enjoyed it on the road because it was one of the few cars he found time to actually lap, and his reaction mirrored everybody else's: 'Unbelievably well sorted. The damping is just incredible. What a car...' Green was more pithy still, managing just an excited 'mega', with Hayman delivering an equally conclusive 'cor... that's lovely, and SO fast'. Hales was a little more considered but equally enthusiastic and Meaden

said it 'made me feel like a proper racing driver'.

The TVR has a lot to live up to, then. And it does a fine job of taking the fight to the M400. It has better brakes, less prone to fade and easier to judge at track speeds (although I still find them a little disconcerting on the road); the 4-litre Speed Six engine doesn't offer the dizzying hit of acceleration that the on-boost M400 does, but in absolute terms it's equally ferocious and sounds even better. The edgy front-end response has been dialled out and the rear tyres have no problem living with front's rate of response, and where you think it'll be intimidating and edgy the Sagaris encourages you to stay committed and exercise that mighty engine to the full. It is without question the best road TVR we've ever driven on a race track.

Which isn't to say the Sagaris is a pussycat. Of course, it'll still bite if you take liberties – it's a 400bhp rear-drive coupe with just 1100kg to haul around, after all. But now it feels like it's on your side rather than simply indulging you before the inevitable stinging retribution. There's just a bit of understeer, which is easily countered with a lift or through judicious use of that long travel throttle, and the quick steering makes catching any slides a natural process.

Hales commented that the gearbox felt a bit old-fashioned and found the damping lacking compared with the Noble, the Sagaris occasionally running out of rear suspension

MARK HALES – A SECOND THOUGHT

Anglesey is an interesting place. Not big, but certainly clever – the lap is less than a mile, but very technical and bumpy. A well-sorted road car handles the bumps better than some of the racers but tends to understeer more through the complex hilly section. Anglesey highlights the difference between cars set up for the track and those configured more for road use, but only if they've been set up to cope with Anglesey's peculiarities.

Our SR4, for instance, had been set-up for the high speed corners of Spa; at Anglesey it pattered and bounced over the bumps and was looser at the tail than it should have been.

Caterhams are normally a reasonable compromise between road and track, but the CSR has been tuned to make a better road car. Which might explain why it wasn't very good on the track. The Nissan 350Z was a proper old-fashioned GT on the road but understeered too much on track. Even the Boxster, a

consummate piece of engineering, felt a touch numb on the circuit.

For me, two things then. However much manufacturers might wish it, there is no such thing as the ultimate dual-purpose car. Caterham, Westfield and occasionally Lotus come close, mainly because they're light. Once you add weight it gets more difficult still. And second, if you make a car go nicely round Anglesey, it will probably be OK most other places. Can't be sure though. It's not an exact science...

Left: despite obvious road-bias, the 350Z proved wildly amusing on the circuit, despite needing a bit more steering feel. Westfield XI (top) was another unexpected hit and was almost constantly out on the track. Grinnall (above) a nightmare in the wet, requires concentration in the dry too

travel. Meaden suggested it could go even further down the trackday-biased route without sacrificing too much of its road composure, but overall the Sagaris was warmly received. It came with non-standard Dunlop SuperSport Race tyres (Goodyear F1s are standard fit), which helped its lap time.

The Noble has super-sticky Pirelli P Zero Corsas as standard, so the lap times are an accurate indication of the two cars' relative performance, but ultimately it's the polish of the Noble that just edged it ahead in all the judge's scores. The M400 is simply one of the best trackday cars we've driven in a long time.

So after two days of almost constant track driving it's time to put a bit of order to the chaos. The Grinnall is still unresolved and we can't recommend it; at the other end of the scale the Nissan 350Z is great for drifting around but doesn't have the speed or depth of ability to challenge the best here. It's hard to dismiss the Caterham having seen just how much effort has been put into its development but it might have paid them to venture out on track before signing off the chassis. Away from the public highway it was one of the biggest disappointments.

Left: Boxster S, Sagaris and Westfield XI all out-pointed the trackday specials, a result none of us would have predicted at the start of our inaugural Road & Track Car test. However, it was the Noble M12 M400 (below) that really blew us away

The Morgan also quickly falls from contention. It's a lovely object but feels all at sea around Anglesey. An Aero 8 would have been more composed, fun and desirable. Performance 5's supercharged MX-5 dished up much more entertainment despite its modest lap time and is perhaps the best value package of all the cars. If you're on a tight budget we can't think of a more practical but fun trackday car.

If you crave speed and purity of response the Radical SR4 is without peer, but we can't help thinking that you'd be better off going racing if you've caught the Radical bug. The Westfield Sport 2000S is a more enticing trackday proposition, blindingly quick but less demanding to enjoy and rewarding even when you're not flat to the boards. We still feel it can't match the delicacy and involvement of a Caterham R300, though. That's where our £30K would be headed if we wanted a Seven-type car.

Porsche's Boxster works well on the track but after a couple of trackdays you'd be looking for lighter, more nimble alternatives. Maybe something like the Exige, a wonderful package only let down here by its uncompromising power delivery. The Sagaris has no such problems but

the added weight blunts its corner speed and the Noble highlights its relative lack of body control.

Which leaves the manic Ariel Atom, serene Westfield XI and ballistic Noble M400; three very different ways to scratch your trackday itch. Each is blessed with a unique character and each appealed universally to our judging panel. A 65bhp classic might not sound like fun, but it really is. Try one. The Atom is very sensitive to set-up but get it right and there's not a more daring, individual or exuberant trackday toy. And the Noble M400 is a true-blue supercar that just happens to be one of the great track experiences. But if you had to drive one of them back home after a long day's track driving…

THE FINAL TALLY

So with the votes for both road and track driving totted-up, and against our expectations, the podium isn't dominated by lightweight would-be racers but big-hitting and clearly road-optimised cars that just happen to have a healthy appetite for being pasted around a track.

The TVR Sagaris was always one of the favourites and worked superbly on the wicked roads that sweep around Anglesey. On the track a number of our judges felt that TVR has dialled out a bit too much front-end response and the suspension couldn't quite keep up with that Speed Six motor, but we're huge fans and are happy to report that despite the upheavals at TVR in recent months the product is getting better and better.

The Boxster is more of an occasional trackday car than a hard-as-nails road-racer, but its polish on the road and surprising competence on the track are enough to put it on the second step of the podium. If you do just a handful of trackdays a year and get most of your thrills on the road it's an unbeatable package.

But here in Wales the Noble M400 struck the almost perfect balance between road-going missile and trackday-junkie and enthralled our test team with every turn of its wheels. On the track it took top honours for its combination of extraordinary engine response, monster grip and a minutely adjustable chassis. Stringing together the perfect lap in the M400 is a rare treat and enough to keep your heart pounding for weeks. On the road it's equally adept, bombastically fast and with damping control to make all but the Porsche weep. Quite simply the M400 blew not only us away but, as it turns out, the competition too.

THE SCORES (out of 100)

	Road	Track	Overall
Noble M400	90	91	**90.5**
Porsche Boxster S	92	84	**88.0**
TVR Sagaris	87	87	**87.0**
Lotus Exige	85	87	**86.0**
Westfield XI	83	88	**85.5**
Ariel Atom 245	77	90	**83.5**
Nissan 350Z	87	80	**83.5**
Caterham CSR	83	82	**82.5**
Westfield 2000S	79	84	**81.5**
Mazda MX-5 s/c	80	81	**80.5**
Morgan Roadster	65	71	**68.0**
Grinnall IV	61	63	**62.0**
Radical SR4	–	90	**–**

Circuit Guide: Croft

It's one of the most technical circuits in the UK, and a real treat for trackday goers. **Roger Green** *explains how to tackle it*

The North East's only major circuit has an excellent mix of high-speed, full-commitment corners, long straights and slow technical turns. To be quick here requires the driver to be highly skilled in track craft, and learning Croft's complex turns is a challenge to be relished.

HISTORY

Originally a Canadian RAF base in World War II, Croft can be described as having had a chequered career as far as motorsport is concerned. It was first opened for racing in 1964 and was very successful for more than a decade and a half, but in 1981 it became a rallycross-only venue. This niche form of motorsport was popular during that period and full tarmac racing didn't return until 1995. Two years later, £1.5million was invested to lengthen the track to its current 2.1-mile length and today's circuit reflects most of the original – in fact its airfield origins can still be seen in the paddock areas.

GENERAL INFORMATION

Website: www.croftcircuit.co.uk
Phone number: 01325 721815
Address: Croft Circuit, West Lane, Dalton On Tees, North Yorkshire, DL2 2PL
Circuit length: 2.1 miles
Noise limit: 105 dB static (88 db on quiet days)
Directions: From the A1(M), take J58 if travelling from the north, J57 if travelling from the south – both are signedposted Darlington. Next follow the A167 towards Northallerton. Croft Circuit is signposted approximately 2 miles south of Croft on Tees.

BARCROFT

JIM CLARK ESSES

COMPLEX

HAIRPIN

TOWER

SUNNY

CLERVAUX

CHICANE

HAWTHORN

Google

TURN IN JUST AFTER THE SECOND MARKER BOARD

BRAKE: BRAKING NEEDS TO BE HARD. MIND THE BUMPS AND ENSURE THE CAR IS STRAIGHT

CLERVAUX

■ The start/finish straight is one of the longest sections at Croft, so it's approached at high speed with cars taking a diagonal line down the straight. Ensure you are fully on the left with the car lined up correctly before you begin braking. Use the painted pit lane exit line as a guide to braking, which is straightforward other than the couple of small bumps you'll pass over. Begin turning-in just after the second marker bollard and head to the obvious apex on the inside kerb. Use the full width of the track on the exit as you need to open out the start of Hawthorn as much as possible.

ACCELERATE: RUN OUT TO THE EDGE. DON'T STAY TIGHT

ROGER'S TIP: THE KERBS HERE ARE QUITE LOW AND CAN BE USED

HAWTHORN BEND

■ A long but tightening right-hander, Hawthorn is bumpy and the outside can be very dirty. The first apex is on the immediate inside kerb and there is usually a tyre barrier positioned here. After passing this point, hug the inside for another ten metres then let the car run wide while increasing speed all the time. The trick now is to get a full-speed run through the chicane. A small lift may be required in a powerful car because the exiting left-hander is tight, so hold the car back a little before you blast off down the bumpy straight towards Tower.

BRAKE: SLOWING IS NEEDED, BUT NOTHING MORE THAN SHORT DAB

TURN IN EARLY TO HIT THE FIRST APEX KERB

ROGER'S TIP: TRY ADJUSTING YOUR LINE IN THE MIDDLE OF THE CORNER TO DISCOVER WHAT WORKS BEST FOR YOUR CAR

ACCELERATE: BUILD PACE THOUGHT THE MID-SECTION FOR A GOOD EXIT

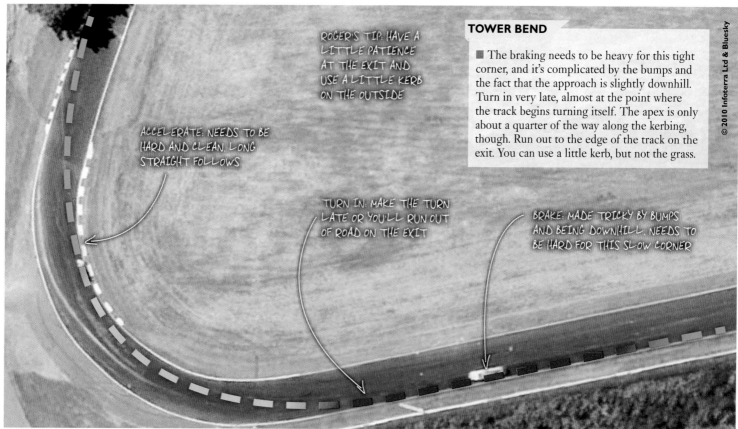

TOWER BEND

■ The braking needs to be heavy for this tight corner, and it's complicated by the bumps and the fact that the approach is slightly downhill. Turn in very late, almost at the point where the track begins turning itself. The apex is only about a quarter of the way along the kerbing, though. Run out to the edge of the track on the exit. You can use a little kerb, but not the grass.

ROGER'S TIP: HAVE A LITTLE PATIENCE AT THE EXIT AND USE A LITTLE KERB ON THE OUTSIDE

ACCELERATE: NEEDS TO BE HARD AND CLEAN. LONG STRAIGHT FOLLOWS

TURN IN: MAKE THE TURN LATE OR YOU'LL RUN OUT OF ROAD ON THE EXIT

BRAKE: MADE TRICKY BY BUMPS AND BEING DOWNHILL. NEEDS TO BE HARD FOR THIS SLOW CORNER

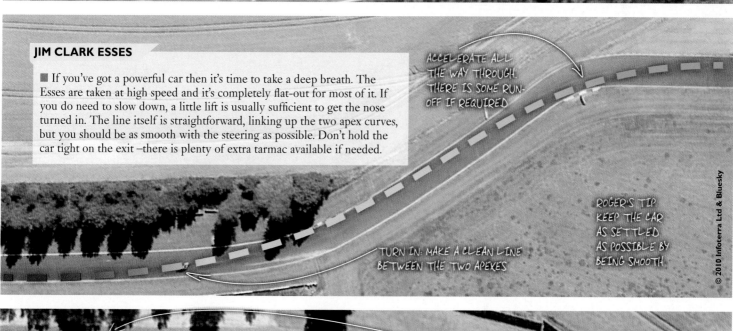

JIM CLARK ESSES

■ If you've got a powerful car then it's time to take a deep breath. The Esses are taken at high speed and it's completely flat-out for most of it. If you do need to slow down, a little lift is usually sufficient to get the nose turned in. The line itself is straightforward, linking up the two apex curves, but you should be as smooth with the steering as possible. Don't hold the car tight on the exit –there is plenty of extra tarmac available if needed.

ACCELERATE ALL THE WAY THROUGH. THERE IS SOME RUN-OFF IF REQUIRED

ROGER'S TIP: KEEP THE CAR AS SETTLED AS POSSIBLE BY BEING SMOOTH

TURN IN: MAKE A CLEAN LINE BETWEEN THE TWO APEXES

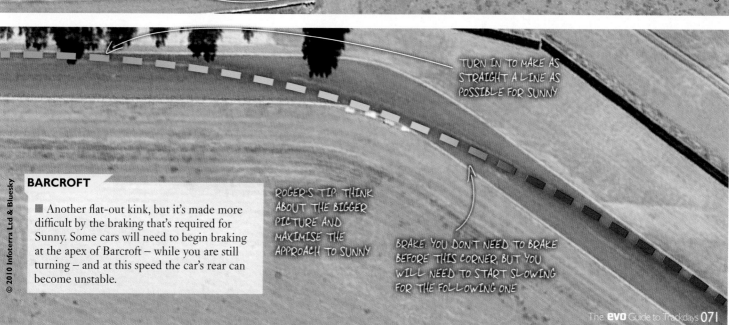

TURN IN TO MAKE AS STRAIGHT A LINE AS POSSIBLE FOR SUNNY

BARCROFT

■ Another flat-out kink, but it's made more difficult by the braking that's required for Sunny. Some cars will need to begin braking at the apex of Barcroft – while you are still turning – and at this speed the car's rear can become unstable.

ROGER'S TIP: THINK ABOUT THE BIGGER PICTURE AND MAXIMISE THE APPROACH TO SUNNY

BRAKE: YOU DON'T NEED TO BRAKE BEFORE THIS CORNER, BUT YOU WILL NEED TO START SLOWING FOR THE FOLLOWING ONE

ACCELERATE: TRY
TO POWER ALL THE
WAY THROUGH THE
SECOND PART

TURN IN: TAKE THESE
TWO CORNERS AS ONE
WITH A LINE THAT
SWEEPS THROUGH BOTH

BRAKE: TRY AND KEEP
THE CAR AS STRAIGHT
AS POSSIBLE

ROGER'S TIP: MISTAKES
ARE EASILY MADE ON THE
FIRST PART, SO DON'T
TRY TOO HARD HERE AS
THE EXIT SECTION IS
MORE IMPORTANT

SUNNY

■ This is two corners – known as Sunny In and Sunny Out – taken as one. It's important to use the full width of the circuit at all points here; there is a temptation to keep things tight but this will only slow you down. The two apexes are easily found and you want to be flat-out – or as close as possible to flat-out – through Sunny Out as a long straight follows.

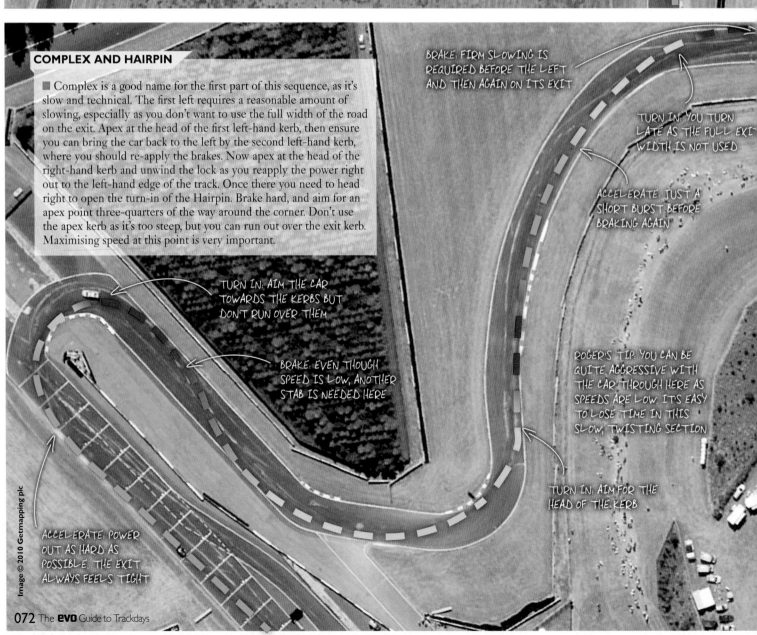

COMPLEX AND HAIRPIN

■ Complex is a good name for the first part of this sequence, as it's slow and technical. The first left requires a reasonable amount of slowing, especially as you don't want to use the full width of the road on the exit. Apex at the head of the first left-hand kerb, then ensure you can bring the car back to the left by the second left-hand kerb, where you should re-apply the brakes. Now apex at the head of the right-hand kerb and unwind the lock as you reapply the power right out to the left-hand edge of the track. Once there you need to head right to open the turn-in of the Hairpin. Brake hard, and aim for an apex point three-quarters of the way around the corner. Don't use the apex kerb as it's too steep, but you can run out over the exit kerb. Maximising speed at this point is very important.

BRAKE: FIRM SLOWING IS
REQUIRED BEFORE THE LEFT
AND THEN AGAIN ON ITS EXIT

TURN IN: YOU TURN
LATE AS THE FULL EXI
WIDTH IS NOT USED

ACCELERATE: JUST A
SHORT BURST BEFORE
BRAKING AGAIN

ROGER'S TIP: YOU CAN BE
QUITE AGGRESSIVE WITH
THE CAR THROUGH HERE AS
SPEEDS ARE LOW. IT'S EASY
TO LOSE TIME IN THIS
SLOW, TWISTING SECTION

TURN IN: AIM THE CAR
TOWARDS THE KERBS BUT
DON'T RUN OVER THEM

BRAKE: EVEN THOUGH
SPEED IS LOW, ANOTHER
STAB IS NEEDED HERE

TURN IN: AIM FOR THE
HEAD OF THE KERB

ACCELERATE: POWER
OUT AS HARD AS
POSSIBLE. THE EXIT
ALWAYS FEELS TIGHT

CLUBGT
Performance & Supercar Club

Experience the greatest circuits and the best roads, all in the finest supercars at CLUBGT

CLUBGT organises a range of trackdays throughout the year at some of the best circuits in Europe where you can experience driving our superb fleet of supercars with expert race tuition. Membership also gives you access to other exclusive events throughout the year from manufacturer days to European road tours, motorsport events, bespoke race level driver training and use of our superbly maintained garage of supercars.

Membership is £50 per year, instructed track sessions from £99

www.clubgt.co.uk | 020 7935 8485 | contact@clubgt.co.uk

Masterclass

By Mark Hales

The art of track driving

Why slowing down and thinking more can make you a better – and faster – track driver

I t's an old one and I've used it many times, but driving on a track is much more a cerebral activity than a genital one. By that I mean you don't need balls. Because, like almost any physical activity, being more aggressive or simply trying harder will not make you faster or better.

You need to employ the mind – consciously or not – and you need to feed that mind with knowledge. And as if to back that up, women invariably make better students of the track driving art because they are willing to listen and they don't usually begin with anything to prove.

The most important thing is the desire to be a better driver. You must want the satisfaction that comes with greater skill and you must learn to recognise what constitutes 'better' because it's not always just about the lap times. I've seen so many people who couldn't be bothered with the information on offer from various sources – all they wanted was the freedom from regulation available on a track, and it is usually horrible to witness. They roar up to a corner, smash the brakes and haul at the wheel – but not before they have rammed it down a gear and made the rear tyres judder and chirrup as the clutch came up. Then the car heels over as they dive far too early for

the corner, front tyres peeling over, howling in protest as the driver winds the wheel ever further in an attempt to combat the understeer they have created.

These are, in the main, hopeless cases. They may not even profess to know it all, but they have no desire to learn. Some years ago I rode in a TVR with someone like this. I was unsure which of brakes, tyres, gearbox or Rover valvetrain would give out before we hit something. I asked him to pull over and let me drive, not something I normally do because it's almost an admission of failure – the student should be doing as much driving as possible. I left it in fourth for most of the lap

and braked early everywhere, gently squeezing on the power towards a late apex and using the TVR's prodigious low-down grunt rather than spinning the wheels in second. It was a six-tenths effort that wouldn't have spilt a cup of tea but it was at least as quick. 'There,' I said, 'don't you think that's better and easier on the car…' The curl to his lip suggested he was unimpressed. 'I bet Ian Flux tries harder than that…' he said.

I felt there was no point in continuing with this one, but I've found that pressure or stress can have a similar effect, even on people who do want to learn. We have all experienced the frozen brain effect when something nasty happens, when you just sit there, mind in neutral and completely unable to think what to do, and then someone says afterwards, why didn't you just…

These are examples of the need to keep spare brain capacity in order to think about what you are doing while you are doing it, and – for the

race driver – to remember it all afterwards. This is all, however, very much easier to say than it is to do, but it does get better with experience, and the familiarity which that breeds appears to free up space in the mind. Experience also enables you to recognise the potential for a situation that has happened before and to know what to do about it, but you can speed up these processes a great deal by learning some basics that will help you teach yourself. I have always found that to be the key to instruction of any kind. Greater knowledge breeds a calm that frees capacity in the brain.

Just remember what it was like when you first learnt to do anything, how busy you were and how focused on the task to the exclusion of anything else. Then, having learnt, you found it became almost routine. Think how you drive for miles then can't remember doing it because your conscious mind was full of what you were going to do when you got to work, or perhaps the row you just had with the beloved.

Driving on a track is made more difficult still because of the potential danger, because it all happens quickly, and because it almost needs to go wrong in order to guide you to do it right next time. You have to recognise a condition in order to apply the correct cure. That said, the same initial caveat applies. Learn more about it and it will all happen more slowly.

Car control begins with keeping a clear head and knowing how the car will react to your inputs

'I braked early everywhere, gently squeezing on the power. It was a six-tenths effort, but it was at least as quick'

Circuit Guide: Goodwood

*If you want to step back in time and experience a racetrack that has barely changed since it was first used just after the war, then head to Goodwood. **Roger Green** shows the way*

The West Sussex circuit has grown in popularity since the reintroduction of racing in 1998 for the annual Revival weekend. Part of its appeal is that it remains virtually the same today as it did when it first opened in 1948. That is, very fast and a rewarding challenge for the trackday driver.

HISTORY

Goodwood's first motorsport event was a hillclimb in the grounds of the House in 1936 hosted by Freddie March, the 9th Duke of Richmond. Twelve years later, on the site of the former RAF airfield at Westhampnett, the circuit opened its gates for racing – Stirling Moss was one of the winners on that famous day in 1948. The close proximity of barriers meant that danger was never far away and Moss himself had a crash at St Mary's corner in 1962 that ended his international racing career.

In its 1950s and '60s heyday, the circuit was famous for its nine-hour endurance races, but all racing came to an end in 1966 because the circuit couldn't meet modern safety requirements. And that would have been that if Charles March (the 9th Duke's grandson) hadn't pledged to return the track to its former glory and reintroduced racing to Goodwood in 1998 in the form of the Revival meeting. This three-day festival takes place every September for cars that would have competed in the circuit's glory years. For the rest of the year the circuit is available for testing and trackdays.

GENERAL INFORMATION

Website: www.goodwood.co.uk
Phone number: 01243 755000
Address: Goodwood Motor Circuit, Chichester, West Sussex, PO18 0PH
Circuit length: 2.38 miles
Noise limit: 105 dB (98 with >9 cars) static
Directions: Well sign-posted, it can be reached via the A27, A286 and A285

MADGWICK

CHICANE

WOODCOTE

Image © 2010 Getmapping plc

FORDWATER

ST MARY'S

LAVANT

LAVANT STRAIGHT

Google

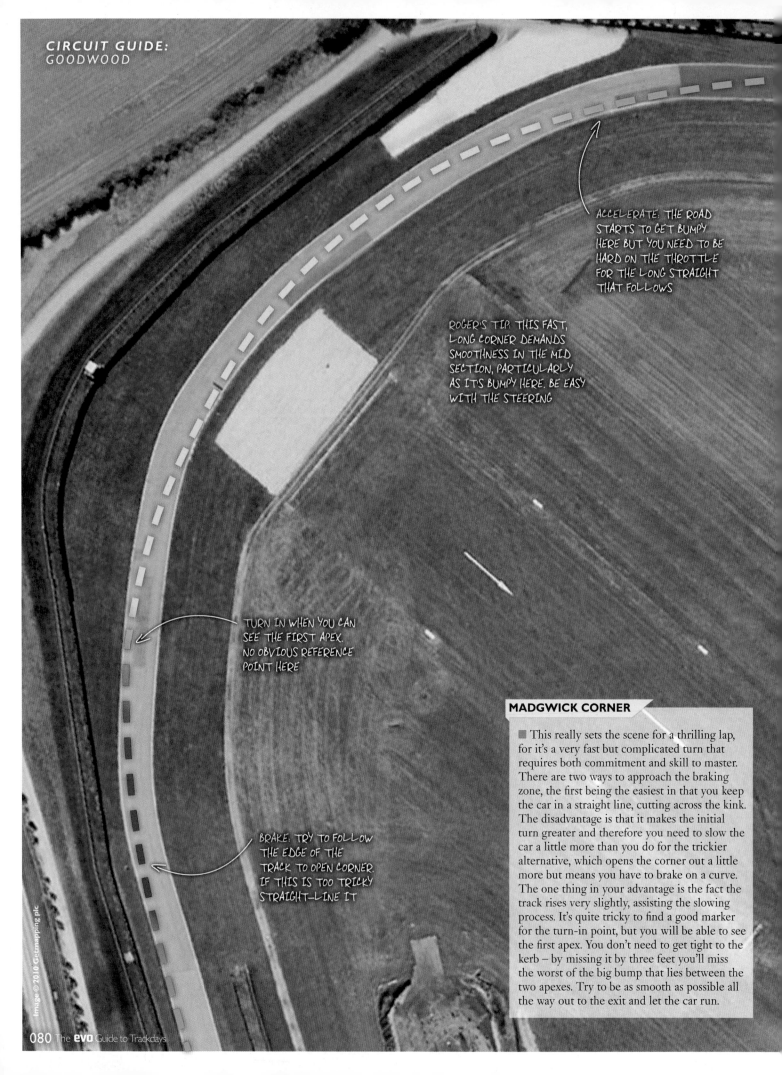

ACCELERATE: THE ROAD
STARTS TO GET BUMPY
HERE BUT YOU NEED TO BE
HARD ON THE THROTTLE
FOR THE LONG STRAIGHT
THAT FOLLOWS

ROGER'S TIP: THIS FAST,
LONG CORNER DEMANDS
SMOOTHNESS IN THE MID
SECTION, PARTICULARLY
AS ITS BUMPY HERE. BE EASY
WITH THE STEERING

TURN IN WHEN YOU CAN
SEE THE FIRST APEX.
NO OBVIOUS REFERENCE
POINT HERE

BRAKE: TRY TO FOLLOW
THE EDGE OF THE
TRACK TO OPEN CORNER.
IF THIS IS TOO TRICKY
STRAIGHT-LINE IT

MADGWICK CORNER

■ This really sets the scene for a thrilling lap,
for it's a very fast but complicated turn that
requires both commitment and skill to master.
There are two ways to approach the braking
zone, the first being the easiest in that you keep
the car in a straight line, cutting across the kink.
The disadvantage is that it makes the initial
turn greater and therefore you need to slow the
car a little more than you do for the trickier
alternative, which opens the corner out a little
more but means you have to brake on a curve.
The one thing in your advantage is the fact the
track rises very slightly, assisting the slowing
process. It's quite tricky to find a good marker
for the turn-in point, but you will be able to see
the first apex. You don't need to get tight to the
kerb – by missing it by three feet you'll miss
the worst of the big bump that lies between the
two apexes. Try to be as smooth as possible all
the way out to the exit and let the car run.

TURN IN JUST AFTER THE SERVICE ROAD, NO BRAKING REQUIRED

FORDWATER

■ This is a very fast kink that is flat-out in most cars, although you may need to build up to this as the track is a little bumpy and the run-off area seems very small when you're going this fast. Begin to turn into the corner at the end of the service road, make the steering input as gentle as possible, aiming to apex next to the kerb just before the brow. The trick here is to allow the car to flow.

ACCELERATE: FLAT-OUT FOR MOST, BUT A LINE NEEDS TO BE TAKEN

ROGER'S TIP: VERY FAST, BUT RATE OF STEERING SHOULD BE SLOW. HUGGING KERB AVOIDS WORST OF THE BUMPS

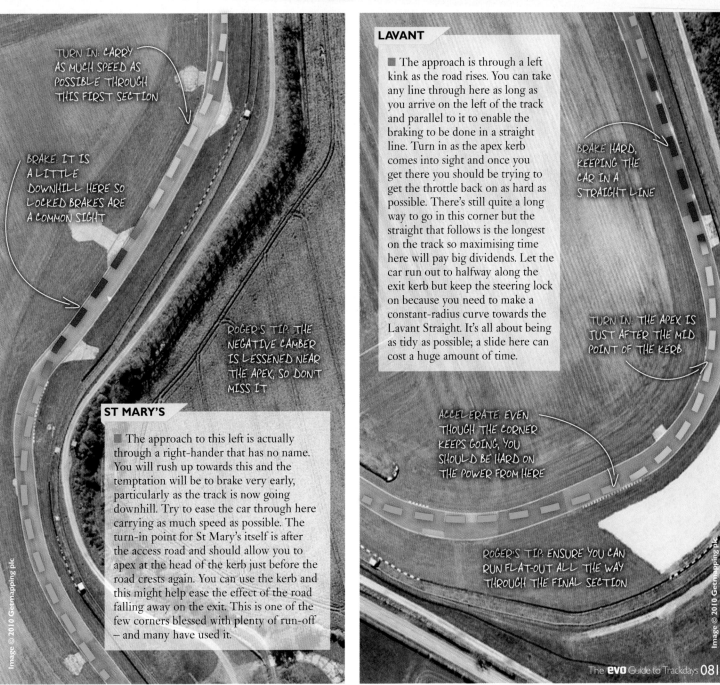

TURN IN: CARRY AS MUCH SPEED AS POSSIBLE THROUGH THIS FIRST SECTION

BRAKE: IT IS A LITTLE DOWNHILL HERE SO LOCKED BRAKES ARE A COMMON SIGHT

ROGER'S TIP: THE NEGATIVE CAMBER IS LESSENED NEAR THE APEX, SO DON'T MISS IT

ST MARY'S

■ The approach to this left is actually through a right-hander that has no name. You will rush up towards this and the temptation will be to brake very early, particularly as the track is now going downhill. Try to ease the car through here carrying as much speed as possible. The turn-in point for St Mary's itself is after the access road and should allow you to apex at the head of the kerb just before the road crests again. You can use the kerb and this might help ease the effect of the road falling away on the exit. This is one of the few corners blessed with plenty of run-off – and many have used it.

LAVANT

■ The approach is through a left kink as the road rises. You can take any line through here as long as you arrive on the left of the track and parallel to it to enable the braking to be done in a straight line. Turn in as the apex kerb comes into sight and once you get there you should be trying to get the throttle back on as hard as possible. There's still quite a long way to go in this corner but the straight that follows is the longest on the track so maximising time here will pay big dividends. Let the car run out to halfway along the exit kerb but keep the steering lock on because you need to make a constant-radius curve towards the Lavant Straight. It's all about being as tidy as possible; a slide here can cost a huge amount of time.

BRAKE HARD, KEEPING THE CAR IN A STRAIGHT LINE

TURN IN: THE APEX IS JUST AFTER THE MID POINT OF THE KERB

ACCELERATE: EVEN THOUGH THE CORNER KEEPS GOING, YOU SHOULD BE HARD ON THE POWER FROM HERE

ROGER'S TIP: ENSURE YOU CAN RUN FLAT-OUT ALL THE WAY THROUGH THE FINAL SECTION

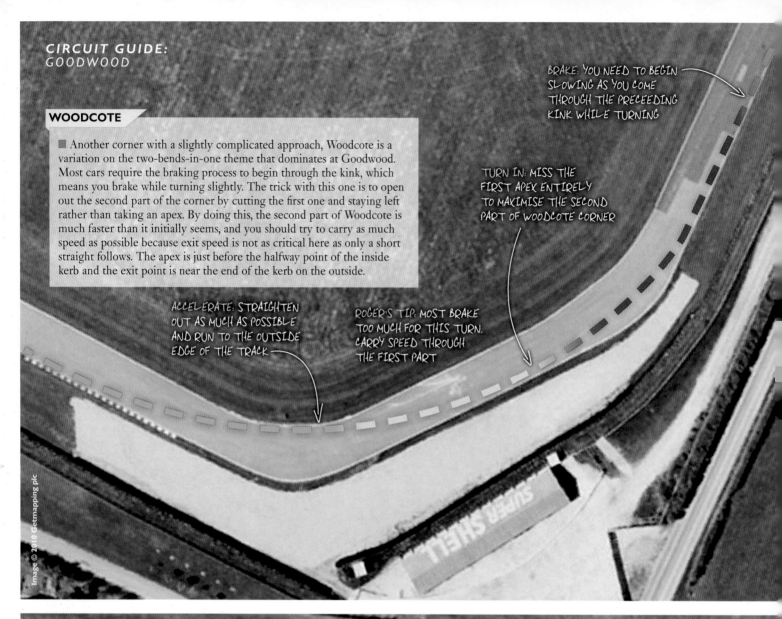

WOODCOTE

■ Another corner with a slightly complicated approach, Woodcote is a variation on the two-bends-in-one theme that dominates at Goodwood. Most cars require the braking process to begin through the kink, which means you brake while turning slightly. The trick with this one is to open out the second part of the corner by cutting the first one and staying left rather than taking an apex. By doing this, the second part of Woodcote is much faster than it initially seems, and you should try to carry as much speed as possible because exit speed is not as critical here as only a short straight follows. The apex is just before the halfway point of the inside kerb and the exit point is near the end of the kerb on the outside.

BRAKE: YOU NEED TO BEGIN SLOWING AS YOU COME THROUGH THE PRECEEDING KINK WHILE TURNING

TURN IN: MISS THE FIRST APEX ENTIRELY TO MAXIMISE THE SECOND PART OF WOODCOTE CORNER

ACCELERATE: STRAIGHTEN OUT AS MUCH AS POSSIBLE AND RUN TO THE OUTSIDE EDGE OF THE TRACK

ROGER'S TIP: MOST BRAKE TOO MUCH FOR THIS TURN. CARRY SPEED THROUGH THE FIRST PART

Image © 2010 Getmapping plc

CHICANE

■ It's quicker than it seems and, as it arrives shortly after the exit of Woodcote, only a short brake will be required. It's a fiddly end to a fast, dramatic lap but you should turn in quite early and smoothly. Try to open out the second part as much as possible but this is difficult because it's tight through here and the wall reduces visibility. Running out of the corner early and taking to the grass is a common mistake here.

ACCELERATE: ANOTHER LENGTHY STRAIGHT FOLLOWS SO A FAST EXIT IS ESSENTIAL

ROGER'S TIP: TRICKY END TO THE LAP. REMEMBER THAT ITS ALL ABOUT MAXIMISING EXIT SPEED

TURN IN: THE OVERWHELMING BIAS SHOULD BE THE EXIT PHASE SO OPEN IT OUT AS MUCH AS POSSIBLE

BRAKE FIRMLY, BUT ITS NOT AS HARD AS YOU MIGHT THINK AS THE RUN FROM WOODCOTE IS SHORT

Image © 2010 Getmapping plc

Get your kit on

Getting the latest helmet, suit, boots and gloves could easily cost well over a grand. Are they really worth it, and why do they cost so much? Roger Green *finds out*

For trackdays the only actual clothing requirement is to have your legs and arms covered and a helmet stuffed on your bonce.

Most trackday companies will hire a lid out to you for around £10 a day, which is fine for your first couple of events, but if this becomes a regular hobby then upgrading to your own kit is a far better idea. It will fit better, it'll be looked after and it won't have had a hundred other drivers sweating in it. But more than that, you wear a helmet and all the other racewear you may wish to purchase (we'll come to suits, boots and gloves later) for a reason, and should you need them to do the job they're designed for, they'd better be up to it. I've been racing for 16 years and there's been the odd crash; I've even experienced the horror of a full car fire. Those circumstances are very rare, but you suddenly realise that race kit isn't for pit lane fashion, it's there to save your life.

For the last six years I have been racing in an Arai GP5 helmet. Why? Because out of the different types this was the best fit and the most comfortable, the level of detail is at least as good as anything else available, and there were a lot of F1 drivers wearing them. Chat to other racers and you'll find they choose other brands (OMP, Bell Simpson, Sparco and Stillo are all recommended) for similar reasons, and price usually comes into the mix too, but importantly they all have the required Snell standard sticker. Why do they cost so much? I paid a visit to Arai's Dutch test centre to find out.

Each GP5 takes 18 hours to produce and it's hot, hard work as the individual layers are set inside moulds as hot as a bread oven. The quality of the outer shell is vital to resist penetration and abrasion and therefore once complete it is subjected to two inspections – if it fails either it is thrown away. The polystyrene inner lining is made from one piece and its job is to act as a safety cell, absorbing the impact of a crash. It does this by compressing and slowing down the impact, which means the density of the polystyrene is absolutely crucial and therefore it varies around different parts of the head. Once the liner has been compressed, it is destroyed and will not be effective a second time.

Finally there are the comfort fittings and the all-important strap with its Double 'D' ring buckle to keep the whole thing secure.

Each design is subjected to rigorous testing and the same goes for race suits, boots and gloves. If you can't afford the suit, then gloves and boots are still a wise purchase as they are your contact points with the car and they go through their own exacting tests.

Perhaps the most important of these for clothing is the flame test, where all raceworthy items are checked to ensure they surpass the FIA requirements for both heat resistance and transmission. Potentially critical, the requirements are very demanding. The transmission test runs at 1000 degrees C; in order to pass, a material has to protect a sensor from climbing 24 degrees in eleven seconds, and afterwards that material has then to be able to withstand five foldings in each direction. For fire resistance the requirement is for the material to withstand a flame (which has a temperature at the tip of 700 degrees C) touching the cloth for ten seconds.

If it's good enough for professional racers, then I reckon it's okay for the likes of us.

'You suddenly realise this gear isn't for pit lane fashion, it's there to save your life'

Circuit Guide: Castle Combe

Before the introduction of a pair of chicanes, Combe was one of the fastest circuits anywhere. It still offers some very fast corners and long flat-out blasts. **Roger Green** *is your guide*

CAMP CORNER

WESTWAY

BOBBIES

TOWER

Nestled near the tiny Wiltshire hamlet of Tiddleywink, Castle Combe is fast, technical and a real buzz for the driver, which is intensified by the proximity of the tyre walls that surround the track. First-timers should therefore ensure they take things easy to begin with, and booking a session with an instructor is doubly worthwhile. Noise limits are a little restrictive (F3 and British GT can no longer run here because of this), but it's a track that's well worth visiting if you can.

HISTORY

Opened in the summer of 1950, Castle Combe is just 18 months younger than Silverstone and until 1999 the layout remained unchanged. In that year two chicanes were added because race speeds had become incredibly high (some average laps were topping 130mph), while run-off was very limited. Those chicanes were well designed, though, so the circuit still retains much of its original character.

The circuit has been owned privately by the same team since 1976 and has continued to flourish, and despite lacking luxuries such as pit garages and gravel traps it continues to be a venue enjoyed by trackday drivers and club racers alike. Barry Sheene, Ayrton Senna, Stirling Moss and Nigel Mansell have all won races here.

GENERAL INFORMATION

Website: www.castlecombecircuit.co.uk
Phone number: 01249 782 417
Address: Castle Combe Circuit, Castle Combe, Chippenham, Wiltshire, SN14 7EY
Circuit length: 1.85 miles
Noise limit: 100 dB static (at 4500rpm)
Directions: Castle Combe Circuit is 5 miles west of Chippenham on the B4039, just half a mile from the village of Castle Combe and 10 minutes from junction 17 of the M4

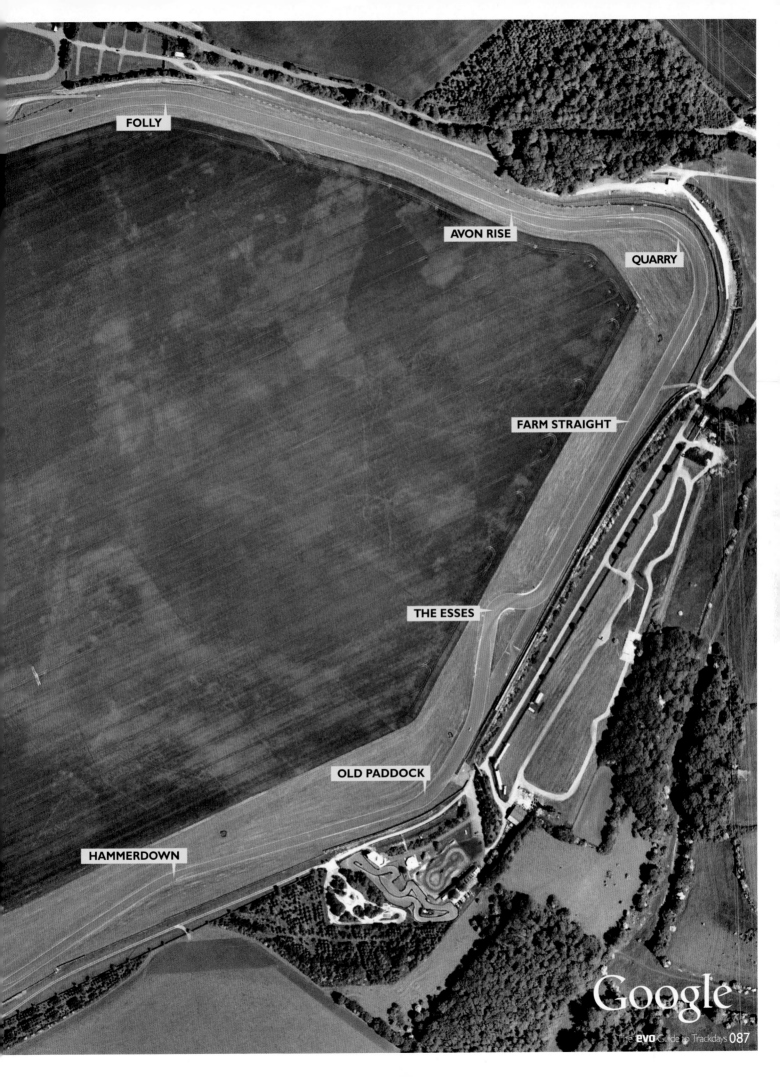

FOLLY

AVON RISE

QUARRY

FARM STRAIGHT

THE ESSES

OLD PADDOCK

HAMMERDOWN

Google

BRAKE. VERY DIFFICULT
BRAKING AS YOU ARE
BOTH TURNING AND
GOING OVER A CREST

ROGER'S TIP: IF YOU CAN, LEAVE
BRAKING UNTIL AFTER THE
CREST. THIS WILL ALLOW THE
SUSPENSION TO SETTLE

TURN IN LATE AS
THE CORNER CURVES
THROUGH MORE THAN
NINETY DEGREES

ACCELERATE FROM THE
VERY LATE APEX. SOME
KERB CAN BE TAKEN
HERE AND AT THE EXIT

QUARRY CORNER

Quarry is one of the most challenging corners of any UK circuit. It's approached at maximum speed through Avon Rise, which curves and crests just where you want to start braking. This gives you a choice: you either brake just before the crest and release the pedal again as you go over the rise, or you squeeze the brake pedal hard and late once the suspension settles after you've crossed it. The decision is dependent on the car and its power and grip levels. Those cars that brake early tend to take the more conventional line into the corner (as shown), while those that brake later will not be able to get all the way over to the left before turning in. The clipping point is late in order to open out the exit and allow you to get back on the power as early as possible.

Image © 2010 Getmapping plc

THE ESSES

You can brake later than it might at first appear because the right-handed first section is faster than the tighter left that follows. In fact many racers don't brake until they start turning right, trail-braking through the first part of the turn. On the exit some cars don't use the full width of the track because they need to open out the following curve as much as possible to ensure it can be taken flat-out. During race meetings plastic posts are positioned just inside the clipping point to prevent corner cutting. Don't use this extra track when they are not there.

ROGER'S TIP: DON'T USE THE FULL WIDTH OF THE TRACK ON THE EXIT TO TAKE THE FOLLOWING CURVE FLAT-OUT

BRAKE LATER THAN YOU THINK. TRAIL-BRAKING IS ALSO POPULAR HERE

TURN IN TO LINK THE TWO CLIPPING POINTS. POSTS STOP CUTTING

ACCELERATE HARD AND EARLY. IT'S BUMPY AS IT CURVES RIGHT. TRY NOT TO LIFT

Image © 2010 Getmapping plc

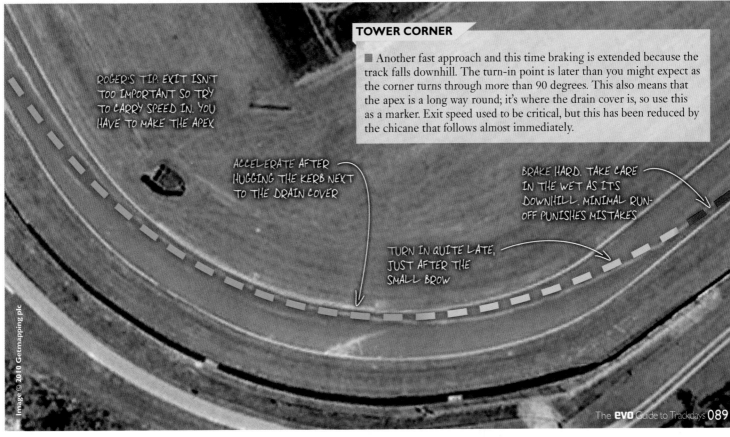

TOWER CORNER

Another fast approach and this time braking is extended because the track falls downhill. The turn-in point is later than you might expect as the corner turns through more than 90 degrees. This also means that the apex is a long way round; it's where the drain cover is, so use this as a marker. Exit speed used to be critical, but this has been reduced by the chicane that follows almost immediately.

ROGER'S TIP: EXIT ISN'T TOO IMPORTANT SO TRY TO CARRY SPEED IN. YOU HAVE TO MAKE THE APEX

ACCELERATE AFTER HUGGING THE KERB NEXT TO THE DRAIN COVER

BRAKE HARD. TAKE CARE IN THE WET AS ITS DOWNHILL. MINIMAL RUN-OFF PUNISHES MISTAKES

TURN IN QUITE LATE, JUST AFTER THE SMALL BROW

Image © 2010 Getmapping plc

ROGER'S TIP: A LONG STRAIGHT FOLLOWS SO ENSURE YOU MAXIMISE THE EXIT. SPEED IN THE MID-SECTION LESS VITAL

ACCELERATE AS SOON AS YOU LEAVE THE SECOND APEX. THERE IS GRASS-CRETE THAT CAN BE USED IF NEEDED

TURN IN: THE APEX KERBS ARE USED HEAVILY HERE BUT THIS CAN UNBALANCE THE CAR

BRAKE FIRMLY HERE. SOME TRAIL-BRAKING MAY BE USEFUL

BOBBIES

■ Most cars tend to be caught between gears as you approach the braking point, so a choice has to made whether to go for a short burst of 4th before braking and shifting down to 3rd again or to just hold onto 3rd. The line through the corner is obvious but the exit is crucial and it's not uncommon for drivers to run wide onto the 'grass-crete' run-off area.

ROGER'S TIP: DON'T BE SUCKED IN BY FIRST APEX. LONG UPHILL RUN FOLLOWS

CAMP CORNER

■ Castle Combe's final turn is fast, bumpy and has a false early apex that often caches out novice drivers. Use the pit lane entrance as a guide to braking and ensure the car is balanced as you turn in. There is a long run from here to Quarry, so time lost is amplified. Use all the tarmac on the exit and the little kerb too. This can be nerve-racking as the pit wall is very close and speeds are high. It's a thrilling end to a fantastic lap.

ACCELERATE WHEN YOU REACH THE LATE APEX THAT'S HIDDEN FROM VIEW ON ENTRY

TURN IN LATER THAN YOU THINK - ALMOST AT THE POINT WHERE THE TRACK TURNS

BRAKE AT THE PIT LANE ENTRY MARKINGS

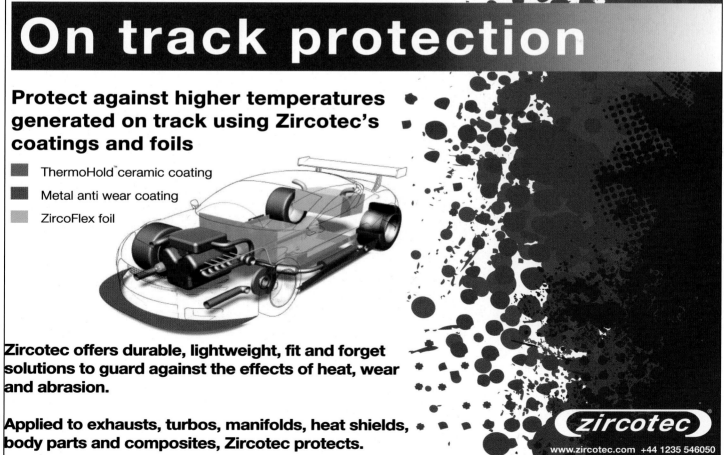

Masterclass
By Mark Hales

Improving your technique

The importance of steering, braking and gearshifting in isolation and, crucially, as a combined process

ow you handle the car is where you start the driving process and there are three main ingredients: steering, braking and gearshifting. What you do with one always has an effect on the other two, so they are all part of an integrated process. To study them, though, we will first have to look at them individually.

Steering is the first and most important and you can conduct a little experiment to prove it to yourself. Find a deserted car park or area of tarmac where there's nothing to hit and no kerbs or bits of broken concrete or the like, and preferably with a wet surface to save the machinery a bit. Drive along at 30mph and knock the car into neutral. Then wind the wheel as fast as you can. It depends on the car but it is almost certain that it will head straight on, losing speed, then after a few yards will reluctantly start to turn. Now repeat the exercise and instead of frantically piling on the lock, just ease the wheel as if you were turning into your drive. The car will dive in

the direction you point it with an alacrity so far removed from the time before that you might have fitted a different set of tyres. The difference is utterly startling

Now, in the cold and analytical armchair of life, this is something that almost every driver with any interest in the process knows only too well. But it is also true that half of them will use the former technique rather than the latter

> ## 'Look ahead up the road or track.
> ## Feed the brain with information…'

and it is because the thought processes are running more slowly than the events unfolding beneath the wheels, and the driver is trying to catch up. So practise easing the wheel rather than jerking it. You should also be looking ahead up the road or track, rather than staring at the piece of tarmac in front of you. This will feed the brain with information as to the nature of the corner and then it won't come as a surprise. It will also feed the tyres with information, which is fantastically important.

Next is braking and this too you can research in the car park. But before you do, consider what happens when you press that middle pedal. The car is travelling forwards (hopefully) so when you retard the wheels, the weight goes forwards. More weight is effectively added to the front and this gives the front tyres more to deal with. But because the actual weight of the car hasn't altered during the manoeuvre – it's

only the distribution – the effective amount that has been added to the front has to come from somewhere and it's the rear. The rear tyres then have less to press them to the road.

If adding weight to the front tyres is a bad thing, then surely reducing weight at the rear is a good one because it gives the tyres less to do. Which is true, but less load also makes them more likely to lock, which is the key thing. Conversely, more load at the front won't necessarily lock the front wheels, but it gives a

'Braking is the most difficult thing to do well. Practise squeezing rather than stamping on them'

tyre more to do when it is about to be asked to steer the car.

Braking is the most difficult thing to do well in any car. Practise squeezing rather than stamping on them. Imagine there's a soft-boiled egg on the pedal which you don't want to burst. Any weight transfer that results from this and the way it makes itself felt via the layout and suspension geometry of the particular car will then happen more progressively and you stand a better chance of dealing with it.

Which leaves gearchanging. Like the braking system, a modern transmission is now so vastly better than it was even 20 years ago that simply preserving it is less of an essential driving skill. Modern shifts are in general very light and positive and most will have a spring bias to

guide the lever. Shift with fingertips and you won't get the wrong hole because the box will do the work for you. Learn to heel-and-toe so the revs will be matched and the tyres won't protest, but if you can't – or the car needs some modification to suit your dainty plates – just be more considered about the shift. The time you take to do all this nicely will be more than compensated by the speed that comes from a settled car and an early application of power.

Now the key is to blend all the elements together seamlessly. So, brake smoothly and progressively, match revs, change into the appropriate gear with smooth, light precision, then ease on the steering lock. Take the time to finesse your technique and you'll find your next track outing so much more satisfying.

Circuit Guide: Thruxton

*Noise restrictions are a problem for Thruxton, but if you can get on, it's one of the most adrenalin-fuelled trackday experiences out there. **Roger Green** shows you round*

If you're addicted to speed then this is where you need to head, for Thruxton has the highest average lap speed of any circuit in the UK, and yet the loop has precious few straight bits. If you like adrenalin, it'll be flowing here. However, events are limited due to heavy noise restrictions placed on the venue by the local council, so check the website for dates and book early – it's one not to be missed.

HISTORY

In common with most UK tracks, Thruxton was formed from the perimeter roads of a World War II airbase, and it still has active runways running across the middle today. The airfield was built in 1941 and used by both the RAF and USAF during the war, including a role in the D-Day landings. Immediately after the war it fell silent, but motorsport first arrived in 1950 in the form of motorbike racing, with car races added two years later. The layout we see today was built in 1968 and it hasn't changed since despite some calls for it to be slowed down. This would be a travesty, and fortunately the British Automobile Racing Club agree that Thruxton should be left in all its glory as one of the biggest tests of nerve and skill you'll find anywhere

GENERAL INFORMATION

Website: www.barc.net/venues/thruxton
Phone number: 01264 882200
Address: Thruxton Circuit, Andover, Hampshire, SP11 8PN
Circuit length: 2.36 miles
Noise limit: 90 dB static
Directions: Just off the A303 south of Andover

SEGRAVE

COBB

CAMPBELL

ALLARD

CLUB

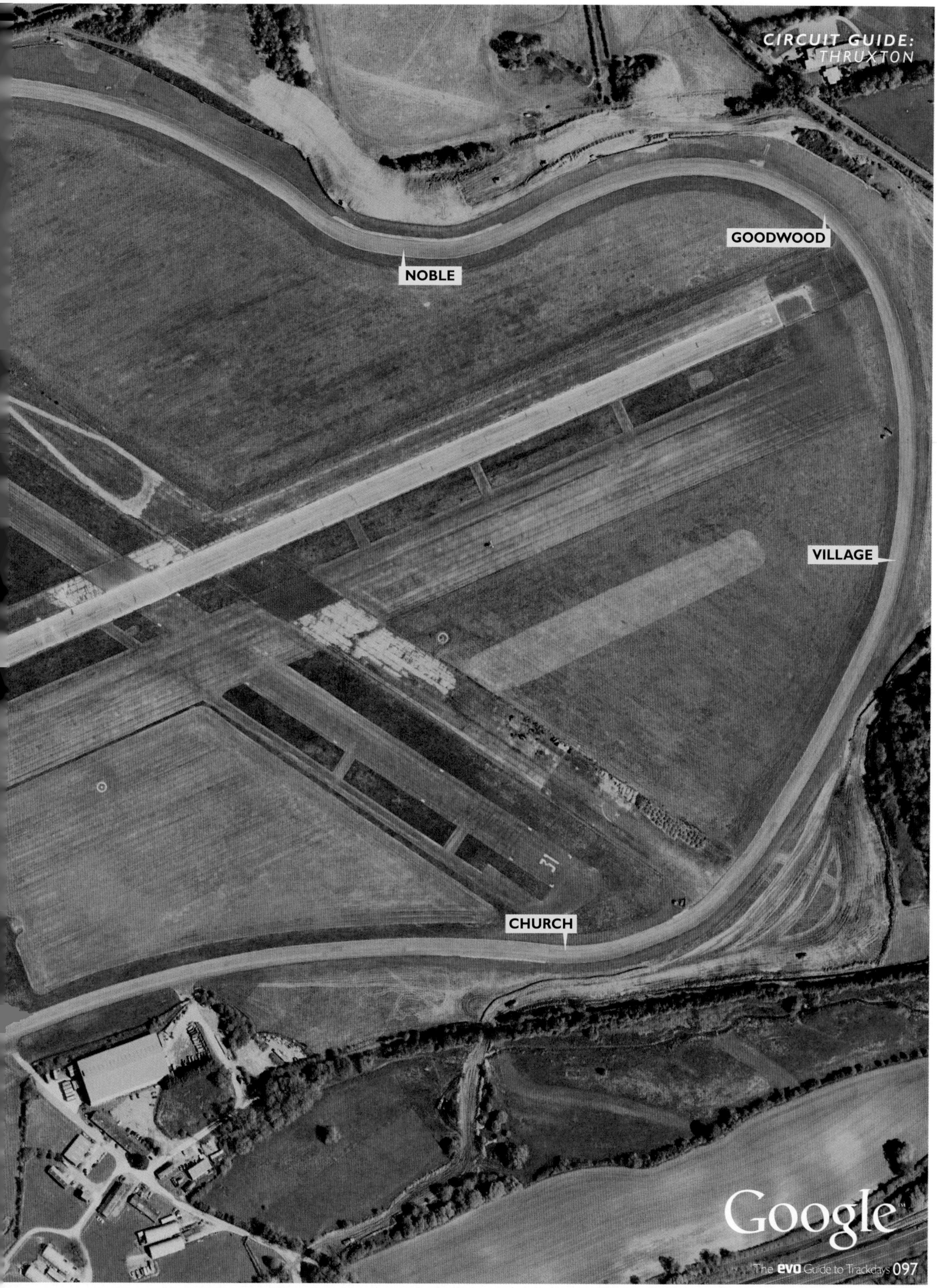
GOODWOOD
NOBLE
VILLAGE
31
CHURCH
Google

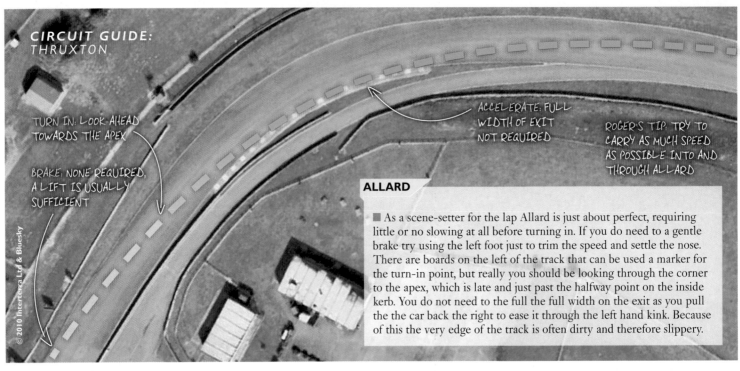

TURN IN: LOOK AHEAD
TOWARDS THE APEX

BRAKE: NONE REQUIRED,
A LIFT IS USUALLY
SUFFICIENT

ACCELERATE: FULL
WIDTH OF EXIT
NOT REQUIRED

ROGER'S TIP: TRY TO
CARRY AS MUCH SPEED
AS POSSIBLE INTO AND
THROUGH ALLARD

© 2010 Interterra Ltd & Bluesky

ALLARD

■ As a scene-setter for the lap Allard is just about perfect, requiring little or no slowing at all before turning in. If you do need to a gentle brake try using the left foot just to trim the speed and settle the nose. There are boards on the left of the track that can be used a marker for the turn-in point, but really you should be looking through the corner to the apex, which is late and just past the halfway point on the inside kerb. You do not need to the full the full width on the exit as you pull the the car back the right to ease it through the left hand kink. Because of this the very edge of the track is often dirty and therefore slippery.

ROGER'S TIP: TRY TO KEEP
THE THROTTLE PINNED
ALL THE WAY FROM COBB

TURN IN: A LATE TURN
AS YOU NEED TO OPEN
OUT THE NEXT SECTION

ACCELERATE:
POWER SHOULD BE
HARD ON ALL THE
WAY THROUGH THE
FINAL PART

BRAKE HARD FROM
HIGH SPEED FOR THIS
SLOW FIRST PART

© 2010 Interterra Ltd & Bluesky

CAMPBELL/COBB/SEGRAVE

■ Three corners taken as one complex. Keep left as you come through the kink on the approach and brake when the car settles after passing a small brow. Braking will be late and hard and the tarmac is usually covered in tyre marks, particularly down the inside where many racers attempt a late overtake. As the exit is crucial, the entry should be very late to hit a late apex in Campbell and a tight exit that keeps the car over to the right in readiness for Cobb. For some cars this is the most important part as they can stay hard on the power from the apex of Cobb, but most will need another settling lift before Segrave. Again don't use the full width on the exit of Cobb, but equally don't hold the car too tight – a common cause of spins. Don't run the kerb at Segrave. Be aware there's a large bump here, but not severe enough to cause you to back off.

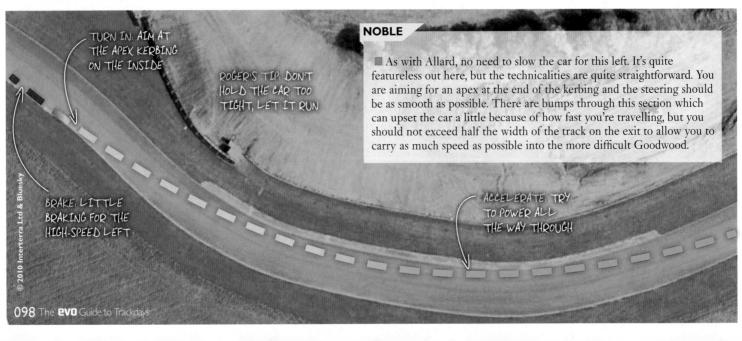

TURN IN: AIM AT
THE APEX KERBING
ON THE INSIDE

ROGER'S TIP: DON'T
HOLD THE CAR TOO
TIGHT, LET IT RUN

BRAKE: LITTLE
BRAKING FOR THE
HIGH-SPEED LEFT

ACCELERATE: TRY
TO POWER ALL
THE WAY THROUGH

© 2010 Interterra Ltd & Bluesky

NOBLE

■ As with Allard, no need to slow the car for this left. It's quite featureless out here, but the technicalities are quite straightforward. You are aiming for an apex at the end of the kerbing and the steering should be as smooth as possible. There are bumps through this section which can upset the car a little because of how fast you're travelling, but you should not exceed half the width of the track on the exit to allow you to carry as much speed as possible into the more difficult Goodwood.

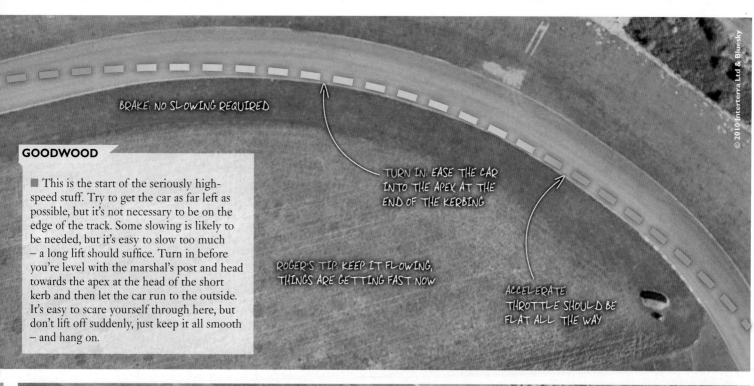

BRAKE: NO SLOWING REQUIRED

TURN IN: EASE THE CAR INTO THE APEX AT THE END OF THE KERBING

ROGER'S TIP: KEEP IT FLOWING, THINGS ARE GETTING FAST NOW

ACCELERATE: THROTTLE SHOULD BE FLAT ALL THE WAY

© 2010 Interterra Ltd & Bluesky

GOODWOOD

■ This is the start of the seriously high-speed stuff. Try to get the car as far left as possible, but it's not necessary to be on the edge of the track. Some slowing is likely to be needed, but it's easy to slow too much – a long lift should suffice. Turn in before you're level with the marshal's post and head towards the apex at the head of the short kerb and then let the car run to the outside. It's easy to scare yourself through here, but don't lift off suddenly, just keep it all smooth – and hang on.

© 2010 Infoterra Ltd & Bluesky

CHURCH

■ Little more than a continuation of the curve of Goodwood. The power should be hard on, so take a deep breath and ready yourself for Church, the hairiest corner of the lot.

Cars with reasonable levels of downforce or a surfeit of grip over power may be able to take this flat, but for most a lift or short brake will be required. The apex for this is early on the kerb and to get there you need to begin the turn where the road dips and begins to climb. The camber works against you here, so make sure you don't miss the apex as the effect gets worse the wider you are. Don't use the apex kerb, though, as it will upset the car; instead let the car rush towards the exit kerb. It is possible to use this, but most don't, unless the car drifts there.

BRAKE: SOME MAY NEED TO A DAB OF THE BRAKES: TRY A LONG LIFT

ROGER'S TIP: REMEMBER TO BREATHE!

TURN IN FOR AN APEX THAT ARRIVES EARLY ON THE KERBING

ACCELERATE: RUN RIGHT OUT THE EDGE. THE KERBS CAN BE USED BUT TRY NOT TO

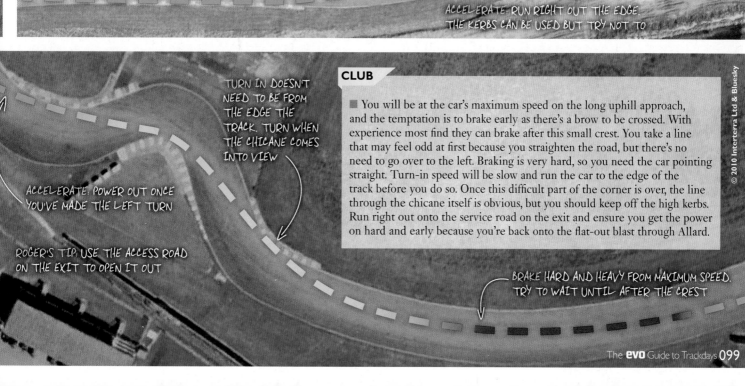

TURN IN DOESN'T NEED TO BE FROM THE EDGE THE TRACK. TURN WHEN THE CHICANE COMES INTO VIEW

ACCELERATE: POWER OUT ONCE YOU'VE MADE THE LEFT TURN

ROGER'S TIP: USE THE ACCESS ROAD ON THE EXIT TO OPEN IT OUT

© 2010 Interterra Ltd & Bluesky

CLUB

■ You will be at the car's maximum speed on the long uphill approach, and the temptation is to brake early as there's a brow to be crossed. With experience most find they can brake after this small crest. You take a line that may feel odd at first because you straighten the road, but there's no need to go over to the left. Braking is very hard, so you need the car pointing straight. Turn-in speed will be slow and run the car to the edge of the track before you do so. Once this difficult part of the corner is over, the line through the chicane itself is obvious, but you should keep off the high kerbs. Run right out onto the service road on the exit and ensure you get the power on hard and early because you're back onto the flat-out blast through Allard.

BRAKE HARD AND HEAVY FROM MAXIMUM SPEED. TRY TO WAIT UNTIL AFTER THE CREST

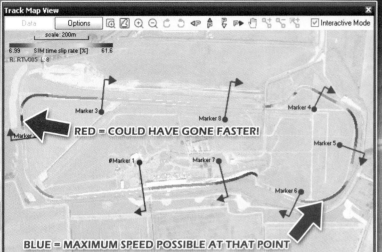
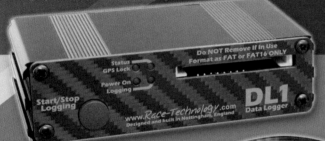

ROAD & TRACK CAR OF THE YEAR 2007

Back in 2007 we gathered together 16 of the finest performance cars and headed for Cadwell Park and the surrounding roads

INCLUDING: Porsche 911 GT3 RS, Aston N24, Lotus Exige S, Renaultsport Mégane R26, Hi-Tech GT40 Continuation, Subaru Impreza RB320, Caterham R400, Morgan Aero 8, Lingenfelter Corvette Z06, BMW M Coupe, Nissan 350Z GT-S, SEAT Leon Cupra, Aston V8 Vantage Roadster

We've lined up some corking roads for our 16 cars, and the most spectacular circuit in the UK in the shape of Cadwell Park. Cars range from £8K self-build Westy (left) to £100K GT40 replica

Welcome to the second running of our Road and Track Car of the Year competition (RaTCoty for short), the test designed to discover the best all-round performance car on sale today. For many of us the thrill of driving is confined to rare moments when a favourite stretch of road is miraculously free of traffic, which is why we seek guaranteed excitement in trackdays. Other luckier souls inhabit areas where the roads are lightly populated and endlessly entertaining, making a trackday a special treat. The best cars can satisfy the needs of both drivers, and to help us decide which they are, this year's contest uses the fabulous and largely undiscovered roads of Lincolnshire and the uniquely rewarding race track you'll find there: Cadwell Park.

As before, RaTCoty is a test of two halves. First we'll assess each car's credentials as an engaging, exploitable everyday road car, then we'll put them around the track to discover how capable and thrilling they are at the limit. The overall winner will be the car with the highest combined score.

The last time we ran the contest, the Noble M12 M400 beat a dozen others, led by the Porsche Boxster S. Two years on, the M400 would still be a strong contender but Noble has given up on the M12 as it strives to bring the M15 to market, while TVR, which last time fielded the third-placed Sagaris, is in limbo. However, there's no shortage of big-hitting sports cars here, with both Porsche and Aston Martin represented.

The sense of déjà vu that pervades any contest including a 911 seems well founded when the car in question is the GT3 RS, except that Aston might have something to say about that – on its first attempt at making a road racer, the team at Gaydon has moved straight to 'RSR'. The V8 Vantage-based N24 is fully caged, stripped of 250kg of fripperies and retains only enough standard componentry to satisfy 'production' racing regulations. The virtually ready-to-race N24 makes the RS look half-hearted.

Of course not everyone who can afford the best part of £100K would feel comfortable sliding it a few feet from an Armco barrier. Fun on a race-track can be greatly enhanced by a modest fiscal risk, hence the entry-level car of this year's test is the Westfield 1600, the model that uses Mazda MX-5 running gear and can cost as little as £8K to build.

This year we've grouped the 16 contenders into three categories. The first is for hot tin-tops; the genuinely everyday cars with mod cons such as anti-lock brakes, air bags, traction control and air conditioning. Fast hatches are represented by the Renault Mégane R26, which has already showed us its road and track credentials (**evo** 102), plus the newly landed and even more potent SEAT Leon Cupra. They're joined by a pair of compact coupes, the character-rich BMW M Coupe and supercharged Nissan 350Z GT-S, along with the Subaru Impreza RB320, the most hard-edged UK-spec Impreza yet.

Our second category is for traditional sports cars, open cars that range from stripped-out lightweights to leather-trimmed roadsters. As well as the Westfield we have two new Caterhams, the modest Roadsport 125 and immodest R400, the latest incarnation of the Ariel Atom, and a pair of hi-po V8s, the revised Morgan Aero 8 and new Aston V8 Roadster.

Joining the 911 GT3 RS and Aston N24 in the road-racer category are David Yu's Lingenfelter-enhanced Corvette Z06, the effortlessly deft Lotus Exige S and the rather wonderful Hi-Tech 'GT40 Continuation' in evocative Gulf livery.

May the best car win…

THE ROADS: LINCOLNSHIRE WOLDS

Contrary to popular opinion, Lincolnshire isn't all flat and featureless. The A153 that runs north from Sleaford to Cadwell Park and the town of Louth beyond initially takes an Etch-a-Sketch path over the plains, with long straights punctuated by abrupt turns around the dyked fields. In summer it can be busy, when the heat triggers the great migration of caravans to the abundant pitches at Skegness and Ingoldmells, but pre-Easter it's fine.

Beyond Coningsby the character of the A153 changes, becoming more sinuous, and from Horncastle it climbs, gently, up on to the Wolds. Now it becomes more demanding, offering a similar mix of challenges to Cadwell Park itself; frequent elevation changes, plenty of sweeps and dips and the occasional tight-knit sequence of falling and rising bends.

It's a road that can produce definitive moments; one sequence of bends can galvanise your respect and admiration for a car and set it in the pantheon of greats inside your head. Equally it can relentlessly pick at a car's dynamics until your respect and enthusiasm are left tattered.

No less appealing is the road that helps triangulate our road route to and from Cadwell. The B1225, 'the Caistor road' from Horncastle,

flows smooth-surfaced across the highest part of the Wolds. You get into a rythm with its long curves but you shouldn't relax and enjoy the views because it also conceals several sets of corkscrew bends to keep you and the car focused.

THE CIRCUIT: **CADWELL PARK**

Of all Britain's race circuits, Cadwell Park is undoubtedly the most challenging and spectacular. Narrow, twisty and characterised by severe gradients, its 'Mini-Nürburgring' nickname is well deserved.

Set in the heart of the beautiful Lincolnshire Wolds, the track was established by a Mr Mansfield Wilkinson from Louth, creating the circuit from a rudimentary course made by his sons for racing each other on their motorbikes. In 1953 the original track was extended to 1.3 miles, and in a break from the exclusively two-wheeled action hosted its first car race (for 500cc F3 cars) at the revised circuit's inaugural meeting.

Some years later the circuit was extended once more to form the 2.173-mile lap we know today, with Mansfield, Charlies and Chris Curve bearing the names of the Wilkinson family. While top-flight car championships such as British F3 and the British Saloon Car Championship (now BTCC) have steered clear of Cadwell's unforgiving corners for years, the British Superbike Championship continues to visit.

Cadwell remains a favourite venue for club-level races, everything from Minis to Radicals attacking its rollercoaster contours. Indeed when the Radicals came to Cadwell they left with the outright lap record in tatters, Shaun Balfe's SR8 lapping in a faintly disturbing 1.22.50.

In common with evo's road test practice, all timed laps were conducted with a full tank of fuel and the same driver and passenger combination, in this instance Richard Meaden and the valiant Henry Catchpole. Weather conditions were consistently dry during all the timed laps.

For more information on race and trackday dates at Cadwell Park, log-on to: www.motorsportvision.co.uk

THE TEST TEAM

Barker profiles the test team. The bribes weren't big enough, obviously

Jethro Bovingdon
Deputy editor
Initially a strong candidate for fast lapping duties, young, carefree Bov was passed over on the grounds that marriage and impending fatherhood have just caught up with him

John Barker
Motoring editor
Lincolnshire-born Barker adores Cadwell, his home circuit. Was put in charge of the road section. Didn't mind that everyone else was having fun on track, oh no. The bastards

Richard Meaden
Editor-at-large
Set the lap times at Cadwell, describing it as a 'real rollercoaster of a circuit', which shows great imagination because he's too short for all the big rides at Alton Towers

John Hayman
Road tester Hayman leapt at the chance to go to Cadwell despite the fact that years ago he had a spectacular bike crash at the Gooseneck and has a ward in Louth General named after him

Roger Green
Road tester
Testers with vast experience in a huge array of machinery, who can be relied on as a 'safe pair of hands', are rare as hen's teeth. And they don't come cheap. That's why we use Green

Henry Catchpole
Staff writer
As the only person in the office who knows how to work the new VBox data logger, Catchpole was Meaden's sack of spuds for the fast laps. King Edwards, obviously

Peter Tomalin
Associate ed
The quiet man at evo would never boast about his prowess on track, and with some justification. No point adding any more jokes, because he'll sub them out anyway

THE TIN-TOPS

The sensible option. The ones you could live with day-to-day, but take them to a trackday and they can still entertain without feeling out of their depth. But which is the best all-rounder?

Pictures Gus Gregory & Andy Morgan

Words John Barker (Road) & Richard Meaden (Track)

The tin-tops make up our most accessible group, and the most varied, with one 4wd saloon, two hot hatchbacks and two front-engine, rear-drive coupes – one, the Nissan 350Z GT-S, a manufacturer-modified one-off

Subaru Impreza RB320

Specification Layout: Front engine, four-wheel drive Engine: Flat-four, 2457cc, turbo Max power: 316bhp @ 6000rpm Max torque: 332lb ft @ 3750rpm Power/weight: 215bhp/ton 0-62mph: 4.8sec Max speed: 155mph Basic price: £29,995

Nissan 350Z GT-S

Specification Layout: Front engine, rear drive Engine: V6, 3498cc, supercharger Max power: 378bhp @ 6850rpm Max torque: 313lb ft @ 5130rpm Power/weight: 252bhp/ton 0-62mph: 4.8sec Max speed: 155mph Basic price: £36,500 (est)

Renault Mégane R26

Specification Layout: Front engine, front drive Engine: In-line 4-cyl, 1998cc, turbo Max power: 227bhp @ 5500rpm Max torque: 229lb ft @ 3000rpm Power/weight: 171bhp/ton 0-62mph: 6.5sec Max speed: 147mph Basic price: £19,570

SEAT Leon Cupra

Specification Layout: Front engine, front drive Engine: In-line 4-cyl, 1984cc, turbo Max power: 237bhp @ 5700rpm Max torque: 221lb ft @ 2200rpm Power/weight: 175bhp/ton 0-62mph: 6.4sec Max speed: 153mph Basic price: £19,595

BMW Z4 M Coupe

Specification Layout: Front engine, rear drive Engine: In-line 6-cyl, 3246cc Max power: 338bhp @ 7900rpm Max torque: 269lb ft @ 4900rpm Power/weight: 241bhp/ton 0-62mph: 5.0sec Max speed: 155mph Price: £41,285 (all 2007 prices)

The first five contenders in RaTCoty 2007 take to the road route. Leon Cupra combines 237bhp with Golf GTI-like surefootedness. Mégane R26 (right) can't quite match its straight-line pace, but its limited-slip diff makes it much keener in the corners

All the cars in this category have their practical side, an everyday usefulness and level of habitability that is discarded, along with the trim and creature comforts, by most of the lightweights in this test. However, when the road twists and falls into a fold in the countryside and plots an equally interesting course up the other side, you want to enjoy it; you want confirmation of why you opted for the performance version. After all, this is the sort of road you imagined driving when you signed on the line.

Initially the new SEAT Leon Cupra feels like it isn't going to deliver. Right away you can feel the extra power its 237bhp version of the light-pressure-turbo 2-litre FSI unit has over that used by its cousin, the Golf GTI, but it feels like a bigger, less wieldy hatch. Partly this is psychological; its one-box shape looks ungainly despite the big alloys and gaping gills, and from the driver's seat the fat screen pillars reach way forward, MPV-style. There's a tactile reason too, though: in the first couple of corners the steering feels a bit slow, a bit dull.

Happily, the chassis soon wins you over, demonstrating that satisfying sensation of all the weight being slung low between the wheels that makes the Golf feel so sure-footed when the road dips and writhes. There's lots of grip, lots of absorbency, and although the rear is rather immobile, the accuracy with which you can pick and hold lines means that you wouldn't describe it as inert.

John Hayman, who drove the Leon up to Cadwell from London, was eventually won over, too. 'On start-up the engine sounds like a diesel, but it's really punchy in the low and mid ranges and there aren't traction or torque-steer issues. It's quick, comfy and capable.' Overall, however, the Leon was deemed a little one-dimensional in this company, the dreaded word 'dull' appearing in a couple of assessments.

Like the Leon, the Mégane R26 ticks the right boxes when you test-drive the cockpit, with even huggier seats and a less extravagantly sculpted but smaller diameter steering wheel. That said, it's undeniable that you're in a lower quality environment; the materials look less costly, the gearshift has a looser action and the pedals feel less substantially engineered.

All these concerns shift rapidly to the back of your mind once you're steering the R26 along the road route. The Mégane feels every bit as punchy and rapid as the Leon, and, thanks to its limited-slip differential, the drive its front wheels find out of corners is simply astonishing. There's so much traction available so early that you have to adjust your expectation of when you can get back on the power, and in some corners the diff actually drags the nose hard into the apex.

The downside is that there's less feel through the wheel, presumably because some of the steer effect induced by the diff has been damped out, and with it has gone some of the detail steering information. Also, the Mégane is clearly a more firmly set-up hatch than the Leon. Over the less smooth sections it has a jumpier ride that seems to match the grabby character of the steering. There's never a dull moment at speed in the Renault…

'You sense that the engineers have had more influence over the R26 than the marketing department,' says staff writer Catchpole, 'but I still think it should let the driver in on the fun more than it does.' Hayman singled out the Mégane's excellent Brembo brakes for praise and felt that, steering feel apart, he couldn't criticise its on-road ability, though he reckoned that ultimately it lacked the sense of fun of the Clio Trophy. Personally, I'd be disappointed if its borderline acceptable ride quality didn't pay dividends on track.

As in the Mégane, the sense of value for money you derive from the Impreza RB320 comes from what it does rather than how it looks, inside and out, though the all-black exterior with its spoilers, multi-spoke Prodrive alloys and

'With the supercharger boosting, it feels like
a bung has been pulled out, the 350Z's V6 now
rampant, and a match for the BMW's straight-six'

smattering of orange RB320 logos looks faintly
menacing.

There's no denying that the Impreza is
sensationally effective, nor that it has spirit and
vitality. In this era of the light-pressure turbo,
it's refreshing to feel the wallop of an old-school
fizz-bang turbo, the Impreza having no need to
smooth its kick because it has four-wheel drive
– proper four-wheel drive, not some on-demand
system that feeds power to the other axle when
the first is overwhelmed.

When the boost is up, the RB320 snaps forward
in a manner that suggests both big power from
the throbby flat-four and a lightness of build, and
the handling is configured to exploit drive at both
axles. Sure, there's not an abundance of steering
feel, but this is a very obedient chassis. Turn-in
is very keen, traction absolute, allowing you to
nail the throttle early and feel the front tyres
nibbling at the apex as they do in the Mégane,
only here the chassis is deploying an even greater
torrent of torque that can conclude with a whiff
of oversteer at the end of third-gear turns.

The further you drive this tautly damped and
firmly sprung Impreza, the more you feel that
its handling is actually keener, sharper and more

accurate than the steering can convey. That's
more an observation than a criticism, but the
high-backed seat's lack of lateral thigh support
and insufficient rake adjustment to prevent the
feeling you're forever falling forward certainly is.

'Feels much more sorted than any current STI
I've driven,' concludes Catchpole. 'It's at its best
at speed,' says Roger Green, who adds that it
can feel over-firm at other times. He's right; the
earlier RB5 which celebrated Richard Burns'
WRC successes was a more supple car but no less
entertaining, and it worked superbly on track too.
Still, the RB320 is an outstanding Impreza.

After a trio of essentially ordinary cars
engineered to do extraordinary things, your
notion of what makes an entertaining, everyday
road car gets knocked sideways when you take
the wheel of the BMW M Coupe. The seduction
starts before you've dropped into the low-slung
driver's seat. Resist, by all means, Chris Bangle's
challenging 'flame surfacing' and discordant
detailing, but you can't deny the intrinsic appeal
of the classic long-nosed, Kamm-tailed coupe
proportions.

Equally, you may find the interior a little
over-designed, though it's still quite tasteful, and

when the legendary M Power 3.2-litre straight-
six fires up, the BMW is already streets ahead
of the others here on character. Then, within
a few hundred yards, you're in thrall to the
slack-free relationship that the throttle pedal has
with a big-capacity, normally aspirated engine;
you press harder and instantly the push in the
back gets more insistent and the blare from the
tailpipes crackles louder. And the gearshift has an
even more direct feel, the lever's knuckly action
bringing you within inches of the meshing gears.

One-off supercharged GT-S shows what Nissan's already appealing 350Z could be like with some extra horsepower – another 82bhp in this case. Other changes mean it requires more effort to drive, though

Ah, yes. But can it deliver dynamically? Well, the low-speed ride is supple, and, being rear-drive, there's another joy denied the previous combatants, namely unfettered steering. And it's pretty chatty at the fat rim, describing every verge-side scallop and hump, and the general quality of the surface.

This is a fast car, too, when you stretch your right leg and take the six to 7500rpm, yet it's not a car you feel was designed to beat corners into submission. You feed the car into turns, feel when the nose is hooked up, and then pick up the throttle to balance it and adjust the line. When you're pushing-on the DSC intervenes, especially over bumps, and at speed on choppy roads the M Coupe's tail gets rather unsettled. It can muster a pace to match the Mégane and Leon, but it's busier, more demanding of its driver, giving away a little in the corners and clawing it back on the straights.

'I don't understand why this coupe has such a traction issue,' says Hayman. 'Just a sprightly junction exit has the rears spinning, but traction aside, the engine is lovely and it's a cool looking car, if a bit classic.' Green likes it too, and also reckons it's more satisfying when it

isn't driven at its limits.

The Nissan 350Z has the same innate appeal as the BMW, but is an altogether chunkier proposition. That's how the standard cars compare, but with the GT-S the hefty demeanour of the 350Z is taken to another level. The output of its lazy-sounding V6 is boosted from 296bhp to an M Coupe-beating 378bhp by a selectable Novidem supercharger, but with it comes a thigh-testing clutch and a stickier, less snappy gearshift.

Frankly, it's a mystery why the supercharger is switchable, because without it the 350Z feels leaden and unresponsive, physically and dynamically. Turn-in is almost reluctant, the nose feeling inertia-laden, while the effort needed at the wheel is so high you wonder if the steering is assisted. This doesn't change when the supercharger is boosting, but the instantly more sparky and willing delivery makes all the difference to the car's demeanour. It feels like the bung has been pulled out, the V6 now rampant and a match for the M Coupe's straight-six.

The Nissan is a slow-burner, and as the miles rack up, the heftiness of its controls becomes less of an issue. What is revealed is a chassis with fine

balance and adjustability, and more consistent poise and steering response than the BMW, as well as much better high-speed composure.

The GT-S's visual changes have a certain appeal and more power is just what the car needs, but it's hard to say, hand on heart, that the beefier clutch and gearshift (not to mention the extra outlay) are a price worth paying for it, especially as there's a revised regular 350Z with 313bhp due any time now.

Scores: road

1st	Impreza RB320	87.0
2nd	350Z GT-S	86.8
3rd	Mégane R26	86.7
4th	M Coupe	84.0
5th	Leon Cupra	83.4

'The M Coupe's zinging straight-six is a firecracker of an engine, pulling with increasing enthusiasm to the lofty red line'

Owning a dedicated trackday car is a dream for many of us, but the financial pressures of reality often force us to find weekend fun in our workday wheels. Choose well and it's a compromise that needn't spoil your fun.

Visit any trackday paddock and amongst the Porsche 911s and BMW M3s you're guaranteed to find a smattering of hot hatches. They might not have the same kerbside kudos, but as we all know, a determinedly driven hatch can often hold its own amongst the more potent machinery. Two such giant-slayers are SEAT's grunty Leon Cupra and Renault's tightly focused Mégane R26.

The Leon's an intriguing package, for the bold but boxy body hides that bruising 237bhp turbo four, a six-speed gearbox and impressive-looking brakes. Inside it's overtly sporty, with a chunky, ergonomic steering wheel and gearknob, and sculpted seats. Promising stuff.

The circuit's dry so we disable the traction/stability control and head out of the pits into Hall Bends (see p136-140 for a circuit map). After a sighting lap the SEAT feels ready to go, powering out of the crucial Barn corner and into a flying lap. It pulls hard, with plenty of low and mid-range urge blending into a smooth top-end, and we're touching 107mph before peeling into the uphill sweep of Coppice. The Leon doesn't turn-in keenly, but once you learn to compensate

On to Cadwell's twisting tarmac and Z4 M Coupe proves less grippy than 350Z, but more adjustable. This particular Coupe feels better balanced than earlier example we tried

for the gentle but insistent in-built understeer, you can hold a tight enough line to set yourself up nicely for the uphill-downhill double-apex Charlies.

Once again the Leon lacks the incisive front-end response you crave, and you find yourself waiting too long for the front tyres to regain their grip to really get a good slingshot onto the straight. Once again the strong, free-spinning engine works hard to hurl us towards Park. Braking hard for the tightish right-hander, the Leon squirms a little but doesn't need correcting. However, the nose-led stance and the tail's refusal to come into play means Park feels clumsier than it should.

Accelerating hard through the endless Chris Curve reveals the Leon's benign nature, as does the perilous right-left at the Gooseneck. The downhill approach to Mansfield works the brakes hard but they still feel potent, though the wheelspin is frustrating, both here and through the even tighter left-right into The Mountain, which has you crying out for a limited-slip diff.

Knowing that the tail isn't going to bite you means the Leon can be chucked through Hall Bends with abandon, but the Hairpin and Barn require patience if you're to minimise wheelspin and understeer. Tidy and brisk, the Leon's composure is perfect for learning a circuit, but not exciting enough to keep you lapping.

We expected the LSD-equipped Mégane to feel more aggressive, but the difference in steering response is startling. Gone is the

woolly turn-in, replaced by immediate direction changes and tenacious traction. It almost feels jumpy at first, but once you learn to calm your steering inputs, the Renault slices through Cadwell's corners with minimal inputs and maximum forward motion.

It's not got the SEAT's poke, though, for despite carrying more speed onto every straight it can't quite match the Leon's peak velocity. After an early surge you can feel the Mégane's power tail off where the Leon continues to pull hard, which is a shame as it largely squanders the hard-won advantage scored by the diff. There's no arguing with the VBOX, though; the R26's best lap is 1.6sec quicker than the Leon's.

An objective victory then, but subjectively the Renault (like the SEAT) could do with being a little edgier. Not wayward like an old Pug 205 GTI, but agile and biddable like the Clio Trophy. As it stands, the Mégane has all the grip

in the world, but manages to make the process of attacking Cadwell feel a little clinical. As Jethro says after his stint in the Frenchie, 'It's a very quick way around Cadwell for very little effort, but is that a good thing?'

Next up is the menacing Prodrive-tweaked Impreza RB320. As Subaru's iconic saloon has evolved, so it has become more suited to circuit work. Stiffer, more aggressive, and happy to cut loose with the right provocation, the Impreza is no longer all about grip and traction.

As we discovered last month, the RB320 is the fiercest and most focused official UK Impreza ever. It's something the boys at Prodrive have wanted to do for years and, quite frankly, it's something we wish they'd done years ago. Predictably, with 316bhp to play with, the RB320 feels explosive after the hatchbacks, but with the adjustable rear anti-roll bar set to stiff it also knocks spots off the hatches for throttle adjustability.

Contrary to the stereotypical view of four-wheel-drive cars like the Impreza, it's not an easy or intuitive car to drive at the limit on a

track. It feels almost hyper-alert, ready to dart this way and that on your command, but because the steering is light either side of straight-ahead it's easy to over-steer, which makes the car feel nervous. It's not, but to fully exploit the Subaru's abundant potential you have to analyse your driving style and adapt to its needs.

Once the technique clicks, the RB320 is a devastating partner, especially somewhere as narrow and gnarly as Cadwell. Whether it's clawing its way up and over The Mountain, piling into Coppice, tip-toeing around Chris Curve or tumbling through the Gooseneck, the Impreza's unique combination of grip, grunt, stonking brakes and near-infinitely adjustable balance means it can tackle anything Cadwell can throw at it. A searing 1:44.9 lap is the evidence.

Front- and four-wheel drive have their place on track, but for the purist nothing feels more effective or appropriate than a front-engined, rear-wheel-drive car. Two of the best everyday exponents of this traditional layout are the BMW M Coupe and Nissan's enduring 350Z.

Both add an enticing edge of muscle and menace to our tin-top group, none more so than our old friend 'Darth Vader', Nissan's satanic supercharged 350Z GT-S. In truth this is something of a rematch, for Darth did battle against the M Coupe in issue 097, on both Belgium's roads and the Spa-Francorchamps GP circuit. Actually both got nailed by the silky-smooth Cayman S on that occasion, but the rough-hewn charm of the Beemer and Zed compelled us to bring them to Cadwell.

Though blessed with brilliant weather for most of the test (and for all the timed laps) the Zed

and M Coupe are two of the few cars that were driven in both wet and dry conditions. With its foursquare stance and generous rubber, the Nissan proved unshakable in all weathers, which is testament to the inherent soundness of the chassis, especially given this one-off's claimed 378bhp and 313lb ft of torque.

While the chassis' poise and the meaty steering feel completely appropriate on track, the all-pervading sense of weight is less inspiring. The engine doesn't rev freely and actually feels a bit rough when extended. It doesn't feel like it's kicking out close-on 400bhp either, but the big Zed compensates with tireless brakes and a willingness to be hustled.

Through the long, fast corners – such as Chris Curve – it remains utterly planted, and even through the more inviting Mansfield and Barn the 350Z's tail continues to dig for traction unless you provoke it with a sharp lift on turn-in. It's quick enough (1:46.8) and supremely effective, and would be a great car to take to the Nordschleife, but there's also the sense that it should be a bit more of a buzz.

The M Coupe doesn't share the Nissan's liking for the rain, snapping between understeer and oversteer with little warning or progression. In the dry, however, this particular car feels much better than the car we tested in Belgium. The balance feels closer to neutral, and the brakes –

RB320 not an easy car to drive to its limits, Prodrive's tweaks having made it highly sensitive to the driver's inputs. But with 316bhp, four-wheel drive and powerful brakes, once mastered, it's devastatingly fast – the fastest of our tin-top group, in fact

though still lacking stamina – are up to a handful of maximum-attack timed laps.

As ever, the zinging straight-six is a firecracker of an engine, pulling with increasing enthusiasm through the to the lofty red line. It also gives the M Coupe a couple of mph advantage over the allegedly more powerful Nissan at the end of the straight (117.5 plays 115.6), which is impressive.

While generating less outright grip, you can adjust the M Coupe's trajectory with subtle changes in throttle and steering, which makes it feel more delicate than the stable but more stubborn Nissan. At Cadwell this also makes it the quicker car by almost 1.5sec, although the tables would doubtless be turned in the rain. On balance, the Nissan is better equipped for track work, but the M Coupe has moments of blissful clarity that hint at tremendous untapped potential. A trip to a BMW tuning specialist such as Birds for some brakes and chassis tuning would surely make it a cracker.

Scores: track

1st	Impreza RB320	89.0
2nd	350Z GT-S	86.7
3rd	M Coupe	86.0
4th	Mégane R26	84.5
5th	Leon Cupra	77.5

'The Impreza RB320 is almost hyper-alert, ready to dart this way or that on your command'

THE
SPORTS
CARS

Six of the best, from an MX-5-based kit car to a luxurious, prestige-brand drop-top, via an iconic design and a mad, modern, stripped-to-the-skeleton trackday special – something for every taste and every budget

Pictures Gus Gregory & Andy Morgan

Words John Barker (Road) & Richard Meaden (Track)

Morgan Aero 8

Specification Layout: Front engine, rear drive Engine:
V8, 4398cc Max power: 333bhp @ 6100rpm Max torque:
330lb ft @ 3600rpm Power/weight: 295bhp/ton 0-62mph:
4.5sec Max: 160mph Basic price: £62,500 (all 2007 prices)

Westfield 1600

Specification Layout: Front engine, rear drive Engine: In-line
4-cyl, 1597cc Max power: 109bhp @ 6300rpm Max torque:
99lb ft @ 5500rpm Power/weight: 221bhp/ton 0-60mph:
5.7sec Max speed: 120mph Basic price: £8000 (approx, incl
kit and MX-5 donor)

Caterham R400

Specification Layout: Front engine, rear drive Engine:
In-line 4-cyl, 1999cc Max power: 210bhp @ 7800rpm
Max torque: 152lb ft @ 5750rpm Power/weight:
406bhp/ton 0-60mph: 3.8sec Max speed: 140mph Basic
price: £25,995

Ariel Atom 300

Specification Layout: Rear engine, rear drive Engine:
In-line 4-cyl, 1998cc, supercharger Max power: 300bhp @
8200rpm Max torque: 162lb ft @ 7200rpm Power/weight:
554bhp/ton 0-60mph: 3.3sec Max speed: 155mph
Basic price: £34,500

Caterham R'sport

Specification Layout: Front engine, rear drive Engine:
In-line 4-cyl, 1595cc Max power: 125bhp @ 6100rpm Max
torque: 120lb ft @ 5350rpm Power/weight: 235bhp/ton
0-60mph: 5.9sec Max speed: 112mph Basic price: £18,495

Aston Roadster

Specification Layout: Front engine, rear drive Engine:
V8, 4280cc Max power: 380bhp @ 7000rpm Max torque:
302lb ft @ 5000rpm Power/weight: 234bhp/ton 0-60mph:
4.9sec Max: 175mph Basic price: £91,000

Less is more. It's a maxim that certainly applies to the lightweights in this group. They offer motoring stripped to its bare essentials – even further in the case of the Ariel Atom – but the return is a raw and intoxicating level of interaction, connectedness and intimacy. They also make a little go a long way; with a kerb weight of half that of the average hot hatch, you get more from the same horsepower.

Following that train of thought, if you take the running gear from a Mazda MX-5 and install it in a car weighing only 500kg, you should get twice the performance on the straights and half the inertia when you jink it into the corners. Say hello to the Westfield 1600, a Seven-alike that conceals many of the MX-5's vitals, including its snappy five-speed 'box and peppy 1.6-litre twin-cam four.

For some it will be a disappointment that the car looks just like the previous, Ford Sierra-based entry-level Westfield, but this is key to that budget self-build price of around £8K. That includes a scrap MX-5 ('89-'95) – there are plenty in breakers' yards, so don't worry that a useable Mazda has died to make it. Instead celebrate the recycling of some quality Japanese engineering with plenty of life left in it.

The cockpit is a disappointment; the facia is rather shapeless, the switchgear shoddily installed, and the small, chunky steering wheel obscures important chunks of the speedo and tacho in the neat MX-5 instrument pack. Still, the plump seat is comfy and the sweet little 1.6 engine sounds fruity.

It's good fun, too, with zesty performance, that trademark MX-5 snickety gearshift and a gentle, supple ride that soaks up all manner of surfaces and only runs out of travel in severe compressions. It's not quite as sharp as you might hope of a lightweight, though, the steering being a little woolly and the brakes mushy, but it grips reasonably well on its modest tyres and at the limit of grip it is soft and benign.

'The engine sounds great, the gearshift is wonderfully swift and although it feels quite soft it's well balanced,' says Catchpole. Tomalin echoes his thoughts and reckons that it has 'more than adequate performance for "my first sports car".' However, he concludes, 'What ruins its chances, after you've sat in the Caterham, is the crude shape and charmless interior. A missed opportunity.'

The Caterham in question is the Dartford company's new entry-level Roadsport 125, powered by the 1.6-litre Ford 'Sigma' engine. This year marks the Seven's 50th anniversary, and in that time it has spawned numerous imitators, yet there's no mistaking the original. You can spot a genuine one coming towards you at 100 metres. There's a rightness about the view from the wheel too; the neat, simple facia, the vented aluminium bonnet and the backs of the chromed headlamp bowls giving fisheye reflections.

There's not a great deal of difference between the straight-line pace of the Caterham and the Westfield, the Ford engine perhaps sparkier at the top end, yet the Seven gets so much more from the same, modestly sized 185/60 HR14 tyres. Its suspension is firmer, though still comfortable enough, and when you tack into corners there's no slack, no hesitation. Indeed it's so wonderfully direct that understeer never happens; turn harder mid-corner and the nose responds and the rear edges out. It's all so natural, so fluid and responsive, so well communicated and absorbing, and it all happens at reasonable speeds.

'Love this to bits,' says Tomalin. 'You realise all over again just what a uniquely pure and wonderful thing these little Sevens are. There's

Westfield 1600 (blue car) and Caterham R400 (green) represent the two ends of the spectrum of Seven-style cars. The former has just over 100bhp and can be built at home for around eight grand, the latter costs £26K fully built, and stuns with its 210bhp. Morgan and Aston (below left) have their own unique takes on the sports car theme

a real sense of precision and quality shot right through it.' Catchpole's smitten, too: 'What a great car. The way it moves around through every corner is intoxicating. And you don't feel guilty after you've been for a good drive in it, like you do in the Ariel…'

Or, perhaps, the R400. Same shape but a dramatically more intense experience. This one has the optional lowered floor, so when you slide down into the shiny carbon/Kevlar shell of a seat and pull the full harness belts tight, you know you're in for a different experience. There's a carbonfibre dashboard with a Stack digital display and, under the hood, a very strong 2-litre engine that idles with a bigger, hungrier noise.

Despite the seat's lack of padding, the R400 feels comfortable, the ride surprisingly smooth and compliant. Initially it feels like someone at the factory has made a mistake and duplicated some of the ratios in the gearbox, so short and closely stacked are they – in sixth at 90mph the engine is

spinning at 5000rpm. Even when you're hanging on to the higher gears and stroking along on the engine's torque, the R400 feels significantly faster than the Roadsport 125, and there's a real wild side waiting to be unleashed.

Pummel the throttle and snap through the ratios and the R400 is breathtakingly rapid. Yet the beauty of it is that, even when you're attacking a road, the handling is so poised and instinctive, the weight feeling low-slung and the grip so strong yet progressive, that you still feel absolutely in control. Tricky stretches of road simply flow beneath you despite the intense pace, and you know that there's very little else that could live with it, be it four- or two-wheeled. Some testers reckon the previous K-series-powered R400 had a crisper throttle response; Bovingdon agrees, but reckons that's nit-picking. 'It's a fantastic car,' he says.

Cars like the Westfield and Caterhams ask that you make sacrifices for your fun – they come with fiddly hoods that make getting in awkward, offer

cockpits that feel two sizes too small for anyone of above average build, and have limited boot space. That said, if you're keen enough you could use one all-year round. Not so the Atom. Its weather equipment is what you choose to wear, and that will always include a crash helmet. But what an incredible buzz it is when the sun is shining.

Although wider and more substantial-feeling than the Seven-type cars, you feel exposed in the Atom's cockpit, while the supercharged Honda engine bolted to the chassis behind you agitates the whole car as it works through the rev range. As always, the nose feels very light and the tail heavy, but the spring and damper rates of this example are the best we've tried, bringing more-workable front-end grip and better traction. The brakes are strong too, with fine feel and progression.

You're mighty glad of this when you press the throttle to the stop, because when the supercharger shrieks, the acceleration is utterly stupendous. The Atom gobbles up its six close ratios even faster than the R400, and the riotous force shoving you forward seems immune to aerodynamic drag. Even on short straights you're soon hooking sixth and seeing 130mph on the speedo. It's nuts.

The chassis is improved, but there's still a tension to the balance, a taut springiness that doesn't allow you to relax into the drive and work the grip like you can in the Caterhams. You're always

'Half an hour at the wheel of the Ariel leaves you wired, your whole body tingling, your bloodstream awash with adrenalin'

Caterham Roadsport
has similar performance
to Westfield (left).
Powered by a 125bhp,
1.6-litre Ford unit,
it captivates with its
precision and unfiltered
feedback. Atom's on
another planet

a little wary of pushing the front too hard on the entry to a turn, and concerned about the effect of mid-corner bumps or a slug of power, or both. Half an hour at the wheel leaves you wired, your whole body tingling, your bloodstream awash with adrenalin. 'Brilliant in its execution of automotive insanity,' says Catchpole. Amen.

It takes a while longer to get the measure of the Morgan. It feels like a classic car at first, the cream leather interior cosy, the view beyond the machine-turned facia an evocative vista of rolling front wings and tapering bonnet. At idle the BMW V8 sounds like traditional American type, a soft, lazy beat *phat-phat*-ing from the optional side-exit pipes. There's little effort involved at town speeds, the variable rate steering having an easy weight, the gearshift almost finger-light, though the low biting-point of the clutch and the lost motion at the top of the brake travel are irksome.

Stretch you right leg and you're immediately aware that the Aero 8 is a very light car for its size. It surges forwards, the curiously stereophonic exhausts blatting somewhat flatulently like some twin-prop aeroplane, and then falling curiously silent on a steady throttle. The rear suspension is calm beneath you, but the distant-feeling front suspension is rather fidgety and sends back the odd shudder, almost as if it is stiffer than the structure it's attached to.

So far, so curious, and then at some point I wasn't quite aware of, everything clicked into place. The Morgan is a seriously quick car without ever seeming to try too hard; you drive it on the V8's torque, rarely venturing beyond 5000rpm, the rear end delivering remarkable traction despite the lack of a limited-slip diff. And the busy front end? Well, as in a 911, you just loosen your grip on the wheel a little and let it do its own thing on a bumpy road, experience reassuring you that it has a firm grip on the road. That's when the Morgan really starts to fly, cornering keenly and wonderfully all-of-a-piece, and gets right under your skin.

'This is the first Morgan I've driven where I've thought "I could make a real case for owning and living with this",' says Tomalin. 'The pedals are a nonsense, the overlapping doors would drive me to distraction and the suspension occasionally runs out of answers, but when you're travelling very, very quickly across country behind that long bonnet and you feel like Biggles flying a Spitfire or something, then it's pretty bloody marvellous.'

After any of the other cars in this group – or this test for that matter – the Aston Martin V8 Roadster feels like a lot of metal in motion. It even looks heavy from the inside, the cockpit high-waisted and clad in black leather. Like the clean, handsome bodywork, it's all beautifully finished, but the feeling of mass and inertia is acute through

the first few corners; turn-in feels reluctant, over crests the car feels floaty, and the crooning V8 seems to produce more noise than go.

By the end of our road route, however, you're dialled into it and enjoying it much more. This is a thoroughly sorted chassis with fine damping and good steering feedback, and although it never quite throws off its hefty feel, the well-judged power steering and responsive brakes help you to work the grip and feel its balance and composure.

'Hugely desirable and accomplished,' says Henry. 'Just lacks a bit of thrill in the driving experience.'

Scores: road

1st	Caterham R400	92.6
2nd	Caterham R'sport 125	90.2
3rd	Morgan Aero 8	90.0
4th	Aston Roadster	86.2
4th	Ariel Atom	84.6
5th	Westfield 1600	82.4

Flyweight four-cylinder sports cars are stalwarts of the trackday scene, none more so than Caterham and Westfield. Inevitably it's the ballistic range-toppers that tend to grab the headlines, but with both companies releasing new entry-level machines we've taken the opportunity to try them. OK, so we've also brought along a Caterham R400 and the ever-improving supercharged Atom, not to mention a pair of luscious V8-engined bruisers for those who like a bit more metal around them, but hopefully you'll forgive our weakness…

As ever, it makes sense to start with the least powerful car, which in this group means the Westfield. If the pretty Minilite-alike wheels look vaguely familiar then they should, for this is the ingenious MX-5-based model. It's a neat idea, but the end product doesn't look very nice, and though this shouldn't deter you, the clunky detailing and rudimentary execution doesn't exude the promise of the concept.

Climb in and the driving position feels awkward and the seats lack lateral support, but start it up and the engine has that sweet, eager character that made the original MX-5 such a hoot. Though the front-end isn't a carry-over from the Mazda, the Westfield retains the MX-5's soft and friendly feel, which is fine on the road but not controlled enough on track.

Modest power and grip make the Wazdafield amusingly wayward, but the way the soggy tail falls into oversteer soon becomes frustrating. On the positive side, the underpinnings feel robust and there's no doubt you could complete lots of harmlessly amusing laps without signs of car fatigue, but you can't help thinking that it would make more sense – and a more satisfying car – if you ploughed £8K into buying and fettling an old MX-5 into shape, or even buying a race car to do a few of the MaX-5 one-make races.

The new Ford Sigma-engined Caterham Roadsport 125 is similarly modest in power output and aspiration, but delivers a much sweeter experience. The Seven looks so much better for starters, and clearly benefits from higher-grade components and decades of detail development. The driving position is spot-on, and you sit right *in* the car rather than on it.

Caterhams revel in Cadwell's curves, and the baby Seven is a vivid reminder that so long as

You get a different perspective on Cadwell in the Ariel Atom – the only car to go into low orbit as it hits The Mountain

a chassis has poise and polish, mild grunt and moderate grip delivers more pure fun than any amount of brow-furrowing power and teeth-gritting grip.

The new Ford engine is soft-edged but willing, with a broad spread of power and torque, and you're soon immersed in what amounts to one of the great driving sensations: extracting 110 per cent from a well-sorted Seven.

With so much forgiving mid-corner adjustability you're soon buoyed with the sense that there's nothing you can't do with this wonderful little car. The 125 puts its heart and soul into entertaining you. No matter that it doesn't breach 100mph at

any point in the lap, this humble-spec Caterham casts a spell that's hard to resist. 'Sweet as could be,' says Bovingdon, 'and easily more exciting than should be possible for a car with so little power'. A 1:48.3 lap has never felt so good.

Climbing out of the 125 and dropping into the R400 is to enter a fast-forward world of wheelspin, snap gearshifts, nudges of understeer and stabs of oversteer. It's a frantic, fabulous assault on your senses that has your heart pounding on neat adrenalin.

Where the laid-back 125 is soft and harmless, the R400 demands respect and a firm hand, but it rewards you with blistering pace and jaw-

Top: Aero 8 amazingly quick on track thanks to its light weight, sorted chassis and 333bhp V8. Above right: unusually, Aston's V8 Vantage Roadster has a stiffer set-up than the coupe, which should make it better suited to track work than the hard-top

dropping doggedness. The truly special thing about the R400 is that, despite being almost 9sec quicker around Cadwell than its baby brother, once you've got dialled-in to its responses you find you can take just as many liberties. That's unique in so fast a car, and what continues to make the quickest Sevens so desirable.

That's not to say this one's perfect. Though potent, the Ford Cosworth engine lacks the fizz and fine throttle response of the old roller-barrel-throttled K-series, which can make the R400 feel clumsy when you want part throttle to balance the car. It's not so much of a problem in the dry, for the Avon CR500s find enough traction to allow full throttle most of the time, but in the wet this binary delivery would be more irksome. The six-speed gearbox also threw more than its fair share of missed upshifts from second to third, which ruined a few fast laps, but it otherwise delivered whip-crack changes. Jethro reckons the super-stubby gearlever is to blame. He may have a point.

While annoying at the time, those minor

glitches are soon forgotten when you get back to the pits, switch off the engine and let the experience soak in. The way you can attack your own limits and those of the car make the R400 totally enthralling. It eggs you on, tempts you to turn-in that little bit harder and faster, lures you to take risks. Think about it for too long and you conclude that the R400 is a bad influence, but the next time you drive it you go at it hammer and tongs once more.

The Ariel should also come with a health warning, for it too is capable of over-revving your adrenal gland and bypassing your common sense. With a lot more power than the Caterham but no more weight, the Atom is an explosive device. It used to be virtually undriveable too, but with constant detail development and some new Bilstein dampers and Eibach springs, the Atom is now the car it always promised to be.

Early cars always felt tense and horribly edgy. Their reluctance to yield to track contours and cornering forces made it impossible to read. It would grip, grip, grip then let go completely. It

was also very easy to lock a front brake, and you were always aware that the engine was slung behind you. Now the Atom is a car transformed: supple, fluid and genuinely feelsome, you can push to its prodigious limits safe in the knowledge that it'll give some warning before letting go.

That's not to say you get in and give it death as you can the R400. In fact it's a serious enough machine to warrant half a lap of tyre-warming zig-zags before you feel like lighting it up. Despite the improvements, old habits die hard.

However, once you summon the nerve to uncork it, the Atom is truly manic. The buzz-saw whine of the blower, the head-bobbing 126mph slipstream on the approach to Park, and the slingshot traction and mouth-parching opposite-lock through the heart of the Gooseneck all combine to leave you breathless and tingling. The

R400 was the first car of the test to break the 1:40 barrier (by two tenths), the Atom knocks a further second off that. Amazing stuff.

There can be few greater culture shocks than swapping the Ariel for a Morgan Aero 8, but such is the joy of this year's RaTCoty. After the almost total exposure of the Atom's cockpit the Morgan feels a little too snug. The steering wheel is in your chest and the windscreen is so close you might as well be wearing it like a pair of spectacles. This is bygone motoring and no mistake.

Turn the ignition key, finger the starter button, and the 4.4-litre BMW V8 punches into life with a burst of machine-gun fire from the side-exit exhausts. Blip the throttle and the lightweight alloy Aero 8 shimmies on its springs. Mother of God, what is this thing all about?

Extraordinary fun, that's what. It takes a couple of laps to begin to relax into the Morgan's style, not to mention getting used to the bludgeoning straight-line snort of the thing, but once you take a breath and loosen your white-knuckle grip on the vertical wheel, something extraordinary happens: the Morgan absolutely flies. It's quicker than the hatches, quicker than the Nissan and M Coupe. It even slaps the gaping grin off the Impreza's chops.

The secret is finding the confidence to let the car find its own way through the corner. All you need to do is nudge it towards the apex and sit in wonder as the Aero drifts through the corner with minimal fuss and loss of forward momentum. Then, as the corner begins to open out, you get back on the trigger – sorry, throttle – and thunder off towards the next leap of faith. It's how you imagine a well-sorted classic racer to be.

The action of the pedals feels a bit odd at first, and the clutch seems to take-up very early, but the brakes bite hard and the chassis feels more than a match for all that Bavarian brawn. Just as well, for the men from Malvern are about to drop the 4.8iS motor into a hotter Aero. Now *that* will be something to behold.

Such blood and thunder leaves Aston's new Roadster with an unexpectedly tough act to follow. John Simister came away from the launch well impressed by the new soft-top's hard edge (evo 104), and it takes but a few corners at Cadwell to see why. Though you feel a stage removed from the action compared with the visceral Morgan, the Aston has a creamy delivery and more mainstream style. The exhaust note is more musical, the steering feel and response calmer and more linear, the dynamics more conventional.

The result is a more exploitable car, making for a more committed lap. In fact, of all the cars here the Aston is amongst the most composed and consistent. Yet despite feeling like I'd wrung all I could from it in the braking areas and through the corners, the Vantage Roadster remains two tenths shy of the Morgan's best time, which seems bizarre.

Weight is the culprit. Coming in at 1650kg, the Aston is more than 500kg heavier than the Morgan. That the Aston's 4.3-litre V8 never feels like a 380bhp motor while the Morgan's 4.4-litre V8 feels good for every one of its claimed 333bhp could also play a part. It certainly doesn't make the Roadster a bad car, far from it in fact, for experience suggests that its stiffer suspension settings make it a more accomplished car on track than its coupe brother. Still, you can't help but shake your head with incredulity that the unlikely-looking Morgan is the quicker car at Cadwell. If I hadn't been doing the driving, I wouldn't have believed it.

Scores: track

1st	Ariel Atom	94.0
2nd	Caterham R400	93.5
3rd	Caterham R'sport 125	90.4
4th	Morgan Aero 8	90.0
4th	Aston Roadster	85.5
5th	Westfield 1600	80.5

THE ROAD RACERS

Whether it's a musclebound coupe, a faster, lighter version of a favourite, a recreation of a '60s classic, or just a road-registered race car, if you're after the ultimate trackday toy, you'll find it in this bunch

Pictures Gus Gregory & Andy Morgan

Words John Barker (Road) & Richard Meaden (Track)

Lotus Exige S

Specification Layout: Mid engine, rear drive Engine: In-line 4-cyl, 1796cc, supercharger Max power: 218bhp @ 7800rpm Max torque: 159lb ft @ 5500rpm Power/weight: 237bhp/ton 0-62mph: 4.3sec Max speed: 148mph Basic price: £34,945

Porsche 911 GT3 RS

Specification Layout: Rear engine, rear drive Engine: Flat-six, 3600cc Max power: 409bhp @ 6000rpm Max torque: 298lb ft @ 5500rpm Power/weight: 302bhp/ton 0-62mph: 4.2sec Max speed: 193mph Basic price: £94,280 (all 2007 prices)

Aston V8 Vantage N24

Specification Layout: Front engine, rear drive Engine: V8, 4281cc Max power: 409bhp @ 7500rpm Max torque: 313lb ft @ 5000rpm Power/weight: 312bhp/ton 0-60mph: 4.2sec Max speed: 175mph Basic price: £82,000

Lingenfelter Z06

Specification Layout: Front engine, rear drive Engine: V8, 7011cc Max power: 570bhp @ 6250rpm Max torque: 535lb ft @ 4800rpm Power/weight: 408bhp/ton 0-60mph: 3.8sec Max speed: 200mph (est) Basic price: £68,195

Hi-Tech GT40

Specification Layout: Mid engine, rear drive Engine: V8, 5600cc Max power: 430bhp @ 5800rpm Max torque; 430lb ft @ n/a rpm Power/weight: 406bhp/ton 0-60mph: 4.2sec (est) Max speed: 200mph (est) Basic price: £99,875

Exige S impressed in our 2006 Car of the Year (evo 099), so we already know it can put in a strong performance on the road, but it faces some stiff, expensive competition from the other cars in this group

n a group that includes a couple of race-inspired road cars, a highly authentic race replica and a pukka race car with number-plates, it seems wisest to start with a pure road car. Mind, the Lotus Exige S fits right in here with its miniature GT styling, roof scoop, venturi-style rear undertray and scantily treaded Yokohamas. Inside you'll find lots of exposed aluminium chassis, a skinny seat and a rear-view mirror that shows only the rear bulkhead. It's a good place to be, almost like a scaled-down Ford GT40, with its fat sills and the raised front-wing edges visible through the near panoramic windscreen.

Less alluring is the plain, zizzy four-cylinder note of the Toyota engine, which is little improved when the revs are up and the supercharger is swelling its output, the dry rasp sounding like chunks of tree going through a sawmill. It's undeniably effective, though, the engine's strong, consistent delivery managing surprisingly long gearing and firing the lightweight Exige down the road at a pace to match its looks.

Feelsome steering, a supple ride and copious grip suggest that the chassis would be little troubled by another 50bhp, the rear barely acknowledging full power even out of tight turns. As in the Atom, though, you do feel you're cajoling the front end into quicker turns, the unassisted steering being much heavier than it is at moderate speeds. It's a car that demands to be driven neatly and positively, rather than one that you take by the scruff.

Catchpole is a big fan: 'I love it in spite of the engine, which I know should feel and sound so much better. Phenomenal grip and so little

mass – you feel it's going harder at the road than just about anything else. It's amazing how high it can hold its head in this group given its price.' Bovingdon is not such a fan, finding the experience a little 'thin' and lacking involvement. 'I always feel a bit guilty about not liking Exiges as much as I should,' he confesses, 'but I expect more excitement for the money.'

That's not a criticism anyone would level at the 505bhp 7-litre Corvette Z06. At under £63K, it's a genuine performance bargain, even more so if, like David Yu, you spend a modest £5500 on a Lingenfelter conversion, boosting power to 570bhp. Settle yourself into the surprisingly squishy driver's seat and ahead is a superb wheel of perfect diameter and rim thickness, the effective head-up display projected onto the windscreen above the instrument binnacle. From the inside you'd never guess the Z06 was no longer than a 911, probably because it's so wide. The cockpit plastics let the side down a bit and you can't get right-hand drive, but when the engine fires-up such cares evaporate. Blip the throttle and the Vette is rocked by the snarly, throbbing V8.

Gearshifting is optional, such is the stupendous reach of this mighty engine, which is quite simply, ludicrously grunty. 'I'm not sure that as a road car the Vette benefits from the additional power,' says Hayman. 'It feels too much for the rest of the package.' The four-stage traction control keeps things in check, and once your confidence is up you can take it to a level you're happy with. 'Competitive driving mode', which allows a good few degrees of slip, is probably

as far as you should go on the road, because although the Z06 uses the bespoke chassis construction of the successful GT racers, it's not an uncompromisingly stiff road car and the ride can feel a fraction loose over undulating sections of road. The steering is quick but a fraction over-assisted, there's plenty of grip, and you can feel the rear hunker down and take attitude when you squeeze on the power mid-corner, but full throttle adventures are best saved for straight, smooth stretches of asphalt. Strangely, these seem rarer and shorter than in any other car here…

There are few more stirring sights than a GT40 in Gulf livery, and although brand new, this Hi-Tech GT40 Continuation attracts interest like an original. The attention to detail is compelling: from the additional sponsors' stickers to the Avon tyres and the cockpit trim, all appears authentic. Settle yourself into the reclined driver's seat and the large, flat Moto-Lita steering wheel, finely marked, period-look Smiths gauges and regiment of toggle switches complete the deception. Apparently real GT40 'anoraks' have looked at it and found very little to fault. The best giveaway is the air-conditioning switch tucked into the recess in the driver's door.

Originally the car had a central gearshift because that's what its makers thought the public would want. They were wrong, and a much better, direct right-hand shift, as used by the originals, has been engineered. There's room for its narrow, open gate because there's so much car either side of you it feels almost like you're centrally placed. The Roush-supplied V8 crackles and booms just behind you, the glass partition offering seemingly

'The Aston N24's acceleration is glorious, the push much more exciting and way stronger than the standard Vantage's'

minimal separation. Depress the he-man-tough clutch, slice the gearlever into first, ease up your left foot and tickle the very-long-travel throttle. Now, is it left or right to Le Mans?

It's hard to bring much objectivity to the experience because I've never driven the real thing, but the way the car drives certainly feels like it is out of the '60s – in a good way. The steering is hefty a low speeds, manageable at A-road speeds, and constantly jiggling and writhing as the front wheels traverse the road. Even on

part-throttle the V8 feels deep-chested, and when you stretch out your right leg the noise and acceleration build fantastically. It seems entirely appropriate that the Hi-Tech prefers long, sweeping curves, where you can lean on the front end's grip and play the throttle to trim its lines. It's not a car you jink and hustle; you get it to flow, guiding it gently but firmly with the steering and considered squeezes of the throttle and brakes.

Hayman, who has driven a few GT40 replicas, is impressed. 'It doesn't crash over potholes, it

doesn't tramline anywhere near as much as it could, and the steering feel is sublime. The gear linkage needs a little tweaking and toll booths would be a pain with those doors… but I still want one.' Green describes it as 'incredibly special', and young Catchpole, who is from a later decade than the original GT40, encapsulates the Hi-Tech's authenticity: 'The fact that it feels like such a huge responsibility driving it illustrates how you hardly think of it as a replica at all.'

Although the GT3 RS can trace its 911 roots back beyond the era of the original Ford GT40, apart from the location of its engine there is nothing old-fashioned about it. Having driven just about all the other contenders, within a few miles of firing-up the Porsche there's no escaping the realisation that it is the best engineered car

here; the quality and precision of its controls, the refinement of its engine's delivery, the sense of integrity it exudes and the suppleness and control of its damping are second to none. Any car from any class that demonstrated such thorough engineering would stand a very good chance of leading that class, even before it revealed the extent of its performance, efficiency and dynamic repertoire.

The GT3 RS gets better the further and harder you drive it. You feel perfectly placed to exploit its ability, sitting low in the firm but comfortable embrace of the bucket seat, the excellent poise and accuracy of the chassis evident at moderate speeds. Press the throttle to the stop and when the flat-six hits 4000rpm it seems to kick harder than this same engine does in the regular GT3, and

spins sweetly and with escalating fury towards the 8000rpm-plus red line.

Initially the steering feels a tad light, but this is soon forgotten and the feel and accuracy come to the fore, connecting you intimately with the road surface. There's so much grip from the Michelin Cup tyres and so much composure from the PASM-equipped chassis that, even going very briskly, you don't feel you're inviting understeer on turn-in or taunting the heavy tail to oversteer when you nail the throttle on the exit. The rear-engined balance is still there of course, but the RS flows like none before. It's a deeply satisfying car, both in terms of its dynamics and its engineering.

'What a car,' says Tomalin. 'When I drove the GT3, I couldn't escape the thought that it was probably the best car I'd ever driven. Hand on

heart, I can't say that the RS raises the bar that much. You've really got to want the paint job, the rear wing and the kudos of owning "the ultimate". But that doesn't diminish how great this is.'

'I want one,' says Catchpole, explaining that the RS *is* £15K better than the regular GT3 when you consider how special and distinctive it looks compared with a Gallardo or an F430, which both cost tens of thousands more. 'At which point it starts to look almost good value…'

Bovingdon isn't so sure about which one he'd have, but asks, 'The GT3 and RS are the best drivers' cars in the world right now, aren't they?'

I wouldn't argue, though I haven't yet driven the Aston Martin V8 Vantage N24. It seems rather special to be driving this one, the original, which Aston's boss Ulrich Bez and others drove in the Nürburgring 24 hours. Although brand new N24s are now being delivered, this is the only road-registered example to date.

So, strictly speaking, the N24 isn't yet a road car but, oh boy, is it a superb advert for the benefits of weight reduction. The non-fitment of most of the trim and virtually every scrap of sound-deadening helps to reduce the kerb weight of the Vantage by some 250kg. The V8 engine is enhanced a little using traditional tuning techniques, race catalysts and a re-map for an exclusive diet of 97 octane fuel to produce 409bhp, and the combination proves spectacular.

But first you've got to get in over the cross-brace of the roll-cage and strap yourself in. Flick the ignition switch, prod the glass starter button and the engine bursts into life with a much more V8-like rumble than the regular Vantage. It sounds meatier pulling gently too, and the race surroundings are enhanced by a whiff of hypoid diff oil and the sensitive, powerful and slightly grabby cold brakes.

The surprise is that the ride feels quite supple tooling along an A-road at moderate speeds. Indeed, this early in the drive you could easily imagine using one as a daily driver. I'd need the seat at least an inch higher, though, because at times the steering wheel and the wipers obscure

the vital point of an upcoming corner that you focus on to place the car precisely; when cresting brows, all you see are trees and sky. I'm often straining against the belts to be higher, and I'm 5ft 8in, which is 6in taller than Mr Meaden. He's going to have to drive Cadwell by sense of smell.

Then, when the supplementary display shows all the vitals are up to temperature, the throttle hits the stop and the N24 shows what it's made of. The acceleration is glorious, the push much more exciting and way stronger than the standard Vantage's and a match for that of the GT3 RS at all but the top end. The gearshift is nicely mechanical, the clutch is road-car easy, and knowing that the lightly-treaded Yokohamas offer more grip, you start to lean on them.

It's at this point you discover how much more of a race car the N24 is than the GT3 RS. Push the N24 and it pushes back, roll stopping when the sidewalls of the tyres have compressed. The restricted compliance of the suspension is suggested by bigger bumps, but it really hits home when you try to feel your way through a corner. No question, the N24 is hugely grippy and changes tack briskly, with a snappy agility that the road car can only dream of, but there's a much smaller window to work in and it doesn't allow for some of the lumps and bumps you can find in

the middle of corners on the road. The steering is rather light on feel in such situations, too, its weighting unchanging as the cornering force builds, and your fear is that a series of bumps will unstick the tyres and spit you off the road before you can react.

Of course, we're judging a genuine racer by its road behaviour, which is fun but not fair. I'm sure that, if it wanted to, Aston could produce an excellent suspension set-up for a road-going N24 – look at what it has managed with the Roadster. I'm also sure there are lots of people who would like to see such a car take on the GT3 RS…

Scores: road

1st	911 GT3 RS	95.0
2nd	Hi-Tech GT40	91.0
3rd	Lotus Exige S	89.7
4th	Lingenfelter Z06	88.6
5th	Aston N24	85.5

Ever had that fantasy garage conversation? You know the one: if I win the Lottery tonight what would I buy? Well, this is pretty much what my courtyard would look like. Fantastic isn't it?

Such shapes, colours, names and racing pedigrees mean none of these cars is for shrinking violets, but if you're happy to be the centre of attention then any of these five road racers can deliver trackday bliss.

Finished in a magnificent monochrome scheme, the Exige S looks better than ever. Small, pert and sinewy, the little Lotus exudes athleticism, and although clearly outgunned by the rest of this group, you just know it's going to put in an immaculate performance.

Light, precise controls, a comfortable driving position and a quick, snappy gearshift ensure your attention is focused solely on the track and how the Exige is reacting to it. There's bundles of

information flowing through the steering but, as ever with a Lotus, you also feel the limit from the way the whole car seems to squeeze itself into the tarmac as the pliant chassis progressively absorbs the lateral forces until, finally, the tyres' grip is gradually exceeded.

Such clarity and poise make the Exige S a neat and accurate car to hustle. Any understeer is easily checked with the most fractional easing of the throttle, while the supercharged engine's added torque means you can work the rear more effectively than in the normally aspirated Exige,

with a few degrees of oversteer helping especially through the nadgety Park right-hander.

With a helmet on, the blown Toyota engine's nails-down-a-blackboard soundtrack is muffled to a point where it actually sounds quite inspiring, and you become obsessed by how the note hardens under full throttle, and how you can compress the pause between coming off the brakes and getting back on the throttle to the point where it's a seamless transition.

There's still that short area of dead travel in the brake pedal, but once hard into the brakes you're left to marvel at their power, and at the reluctance of the ABS to intervene. When you hear the front tyres chirruping into Mansfield you know the brake set-up is spot-on for track work.

I've been longing to drive a 997 GT3 RS since the torment of the press passenger rides last autumn (evo 098). While Cadwell is a rather less forgiving venue than I'd hoped for my first taste

'Small pert and sinewy, the Exige exudes athleticism. You just know it's going to put in an immaculate performance'

Despite having the same engine as the GT3, Porsche asks an extra £15K for the RS version (right), but the chassis tweaks and the additional weight losses give it a distinct edge on track. Lingenfelter modifications bestow the already-potent Corvette Z06 (below right) with an additional 65bhp, giving it RS-beating straight-line performance for under £70K

of the new RS, it's somehow appropriate that the most exciting circuit in the UK should be where I get to first curl my hands around the suede-rimmed steering wheel.

It never ceases to amaze me how Porsche always manages to make a GT3 or RS feel so utterly right. You don't have to reach out to find the steering wheel, pedals and gearlever – they're right there like an extension of your body. From the moment you drop into the seat you're an integral part of the car.

It's a feeling that only gets more intense, for the power delivery, clutch bite, gearshift and steering response are united in their uniformity and immediacy. The engine has to rank as one of the greatest ever, with minimal inertia, total tractability, towering reach and a searing appetite for revs that makes every upshift an epic occasion. Mated to carbon-ceramic brakes that defy all attempts to make them wilt, the RS genuinely feels like a car bred for the racetrack.

Riding on bespoke Michelin Pilot Cups and enjoying a wider rear track that the GT3, the RS feels tighter and edgy until some heat percolates through the rubber, at which point it keys into the tarmac and becomes much more inspiring. There's something truly special about the way this 911 tackles Cadwell, the way it digs for traction out of the low-speed corners yet dances on tip-toe through the high-speed sections and, ultimately, the way you can feel how Porsche has made the unorthodox weight distribution work for you rather than against you in most circumstances.

There are times when you feel the RS begin to turn around to bite you, particularly midway through the devilish Charlies and the knife-edge Chris Curve, where you try and deploy as much power as you can while constantly turning right. The trick is to get your corrections in as early as possible using the smallest inputs. Let the moment develop and things get pretty scary very quickly.

In truth you're unlikely to push this hard when freed from the pressures of attaining a lap time, but in doing so it's clear that when you disengage PSM you need to be right on top of your game. Put the effort in, however, and your reward is an enthralling string of laps.

It's hard to imagine a more hardcore machine than the Porsche, but the acid yellow Aston is it. Built to compete in a variety of racing categories, from the VLN series on the Nordschleife to the exciting new GT4 class of international and domestic GT racing, the Vantage N24 is sold as a pure racing car, but some customers will inevitably put their cars through the SVA test.

To create the N24, Aston put the Vantage through a rigorous weight-loss programme, and it shows when you thread yourself through the full roll-cage. There's no leather and only minimal creature comforts. Plastic windows underline its competition focus.

You sit really low, almost looking up at the dashboard, which makes for some interesting lines through Hall Bends first time out, as you simply can't see where the kerbs are. A few bumps and thumps later and it's possible to drive 'blind' for subsequent laps, but it all helps to ramp-up the feeling of intimidation.

Two laps in and any apprehension has evaporated. After the edginess of the 911, the N24 feels totally planted. Agile but stable, aggressive but forgiving, it's like a big, brawny Exige. With less weight to haul down the straights the N24's V8, now tweaked to develop over 400bhp, feels more convincing than it did in the 380bhp Roadster, but it's still not savage like the Porsche's flat-six, and it's a couple of mph down on the green RS at the end of the Park Straight.

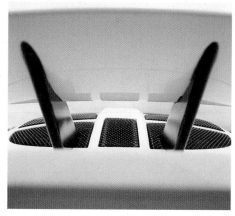

Where the N24 excels is in its ability to let you nail consistent on-limit laps, lap after lap. The GT3 RS did a best lap of 1:39.9, but when you take an average of its best three laps, that time rises to 1:40.5. Compare that with the Aston's best of 1.40.1 and its three-lap average of 1.40.5 and you can see how that consistency becomes an on-track advantage. When we bolted a set of slicks on for fun, its best time dropped to 1.37.1, and its three-lap average to 1.37.2. Now that's consistent pace!

If the Aston V8 does have a few horses missing, you only need to drive the Corvette Z06 to find out where they've gone. Now featuring a fully sorted Lingenfelter engine upgrade yielding a dyno-verified 570bhp and 535lb ft, David Yu's Vette is absolutely rampant.

Thankfully running new brake fluid and hard pad material, it has the brakes to match the grunt (just), but with stock suspension and rims, and original-spec Goodyear run-flat tyres (new ones, thanks to www.stratstonecorvette.com), ten-tenths

lapping at Cadwell in this engorged Z06 seems like a big ask.

I know the Z06 is a great road car, but I'm still half expecting it to be a horrid mix of giant grunt, huge lateral grip and absolutely no feel or finesse on track, but considering the tarmac-wrinkling poke at its disposal, it cuts a miraculous set of laps.

Yes there's wheelspin. There are some sweaty-palmed moments of profanity too, but only for as long as it takes to realise that, while this Vette

Hi-Tech GT40 Continuation (left) is one of the most impressive GT40 replicas around, and incredibly desirable. Roush-built V8 produces 420bhp, while the driving experience is authentically 1960s – and all the more enjoyable for it

corners like no other, you don't need to take your life in your hands through the turns. Just wait until the fat nose is approximately straight, then drop the bomb. The way this thing builds speed is literally breathtaking. Anything that can beat a wrung-out 911 RS by 10mph at the end of Park Straight, despite exiting Charlies with less speed, is extraordinary. When David fits his promised suspension upgrade and track-biased tyres, this Z06 will take some beating.

Catch any of the evo team in an idle moment at Cadwell and you'll find them staring like lovelorn teenagers at Nigel Hulme's Hi-Tech GT40. It really is a mesmerising sight – especially in its faithfully reproduced Le Mans livery – and so much prettier and more delicate than the modern Ford GT.

The car is literally box-fresh, with Nigel having covered just a handful of shakedown miles before swinging open the guillotine door and handing us the keys. You step unceremoniously on the seat cushion before lowering yourself into the unnervingly reclined driving position. The view is magnificent and the noise – oh, the noise – of the Roush-built 5.6-litre Ford V8 as it fires into life is pure heaven.

Having earlier witnessed Jethro absolutely murdering the R400 in a straight line, there's no doubting the Hi-Tech is going to be stunning

between the corners. What I'm worried about is just how much of a handful it's going to be through them.

The steering is heavy but not impossibly so, and once you put your shoulders into it as well as your wrists and forearms the GT40 begins to flow. Even with my Arai on, the V8 hammers at my cranium, while upshifts and downshifts trigger some magnificent pops, bangs, barks and gargles from the double-barrel exhausts.

So long as you're firm and deliberate, the right-hand gearshift (complete with dog-leg first) is co-operative, but you never punch through the gears as you do in the other cars. In deference to the car's freshness we've agreed to a self-imposed 5000-5500rpm limit instead of winding it up to the 6500rpm red line, but even so the 420bhp GT40 is a rocket-sled from Barn to Coppice and Charlies to Park. Predictably, Hayman loves it. 'Never would I tire of that fantastic engine, nor the looks, sound or chassis either. Each and every lap it gave me a bit more. It's a joy.'

Braking is an old-school affair, for while the stoppers have decent feel and power, the car squirms and wriggles on its fat Avon historic race tyres. It forces you to adopt a '60s style, braking smoothly and progressively, getting the car positioned just-so, then peeling into the corners without shedding too much speed but not over-

driving either. Wait for the front to bite, feel that the rear is with you, then turn up the heat with your right foot until you feel grunt *just* get the upper hand over grip.

It's the most physical car here, but also the one that responds best to measured inputs. It's also more benign than you'd ever think, and there's no doubt that with familiarity, full revs and a bit of fine-tuning of the suspension settings, the GT40 would knock a few seconds off its eventual 1:45.1 best. Not that the lap time really matters – we all left Cadwell wondering how we could raise the best part of £100,000, and for once we weren't thinking about the Porsche…

Scores: track

1st	Aston N24	95.0
2nd	Porsche 911 GT3 RS	94.3
3rd	Hi-Tech GT40	92.5
4th	Lotus Exige S	92.0
5th	Lingenfelter Z06	88.3

The final scores

		Road	Track	Overall	Lap time
1st	911 GT3 RS	95.0	94.3	94.7	1.39.9
2nd	Caterham R400	92.6	93.5	93.1	1.39.8
3rd	Hi-Tech GT40	91.0	92.5	91.8	1.45.1
4th	Lotus Exige S	89.7	92.0	90.9	1.42.6
5th=	Caterham R'sport	90.2	90.4	90.3	1.48.3
5th=	Aston N24	85.5	95.0	90.3	1.40.1
7th	Morgan Aero 8	90.0	90.0	90.0	1.44.7
8th	Ariel Atom 300	84.6	94.0	89.3	1.38.8
9th	Lingenfelter Z06	88.6	88.3	88.5	1.41.6
10th	Impreza RB320	87.0	89.0	88.0	1.44.9
11th	Nissan 350Z GT-S	86.8	86.7	86.8	1.46.8
12th	Aston Roadster	86.2	85.5	85.9	1.44.9
13th	Renault Mégane R26	86.7	84.5	85.6	1.48.0
14th	BMW M Coupe	84.0	86.0	85.0	1.45.4
15th	Westfield 1600	82.4	80.5	81.5	1.52.2
16th	Leon Cupra	83.4	77.5	80.5	1.49.6

Scores (above right) show how our 16 contenders fared on road, track and overall, the 911 GT3 RS (left) winning the close fight for the top spot. If you can't afford one (or the gorgeous GT40 replica), go for a Caterham or an Exige. You won't be disappointed

THE RESULTS

It's no great surprise that the practical, everyday cars occupy the lower half of the finishing order. The battle of the hatchbacks goes the Mégane R26's way, the last-placed Leon Cupra delivering a competent, rapid road performance but lacking the harder, more engaging edge of the Renault.

The characterful M Coupe is a more interesting car on road and makes its power felt on track, but in both disciplines it's most comfortable at eight-tenths, which is why the 350Z shades it – there's a greater depth of ability and more consistency to the supercharged Nissan's dynamics.

However, the car from this category that delivers the best road drive and track entertainment is the Impreza RB320. Explosive turbo power, virtually undefeatable traction and a keen chassis balance is a stimulating mix. 'What should raise eyebrows,' adds Meaden, 'is that it wasn't the four-wheel-drive saloon but the hot hatches that felt inert and unwilling to play on track.' Had it rained it might have climbed even higher up the order…

Our mixed bag of sports cars spanned the finishing order. There's a great deal of appeal in an MX-5-derived drivetrain, but until Westfield (or someone else) makes an attractive, bespoke sports car to put it in, and optimises its dynamics, it will appeal mainly on price, and most of us would prefer to spend £8K on a pristine MX-5.

Fine car that the Aston Roadster is, it shows that mass is the enemy of the truly inspiring drive. For a 1650kg car it's remarkably composed, but in this company you end up admiring it for that rather than relishing challenging sections of road.

If the Atom had a roof, windscreen and doors it would have finished higher up, but then it wouldn't have been an Atom. Manically fast and frenetic, it was the quickest car of all around Cadwell. There you can find its limits, on the road you find your own first, be they hardiness or bravery. The Caterham Roadsport 125 just pips it, proving that modest power is no bar to entertainment and involvement. It really is a gem of a sports car, with a perfect match of grip and go that is just as much fun on track as on road. It's all that you wish the Westfield was.

Seventh is a highly respectable result for the idiosyncratic Morgan, the foil to Aston's V8 Roadster. The Aero 8 ended up charming most of us with its effortless pace and engaging dynamics, and was our second-placed sports car. We'll get to the top one when we review the top three…

'The Z06 is one of the few cars I've driven that feels too fast for everywhere!' jokes Meaden. Indeed, the Lingenfelter-tuned Corvette comes very close to disproving the maxim 'you can never have too much power', its mighty 570bhp V8 dominating every drive and testing the ability of the chassis to the full. As you'd expect, the Aston N24 is fabulous on track, offering a precision that nothing else here can match and a level of urge that makes the stock V8 Vantage seem breathless. But being a race car it's uncompromisingly stiff on the road, highlighting the skill with which the chassis of the top two cars have been engineered – they both lap as quickly as the N24.

The Lotus Exige S treads the line between road suppleness and track accuracy very deftly, and its pocket-GT styling makes you want to pick it up and take it home. For some of us it's let down only by its charmless four-cylinder engine.

And so to the top three. You don't have to be an enthusiast of a certain age to be seduced by the Hi-Tech GT40. 'I felt like Steve McQueen at Le Mans,' said young Catchpole. 'It's a highly authentic experience, visually and dynamically, and although there are a whole heap of cars here that would show it the way home, that didn't make it any less desirable. Truly intoxicating.

However, the battle for the top slot was between the Caterham R400 and the 911 GT3 RS, and it was mighty close. The Seven puts you at the heart of things like no other car, connects you so directly to the action that pushing the gloriously malleable limit of grip is virtually instinctive. It's just as good on track as on road, its low inertia and natural front-engine/rear-drive balance making it fun and very fast – a tenth faster round Cadwell than the RS.

'The R400 is proof that so long as you spec your Caterham with a windscreen and doors you've got the Swiss Army knife of trackday cars,' reckons Meaden. 'No car squeezes more excitement from 200bhp.' It is, he declares, the moral victor.

The GT3 RS is irresistible, though. Yes, it's three times the cost, but the depth of its quality and breadth of its ability make it seem worth every penny. It's a perfectly habitable road car with a fine ride and wonderfully tactile steering, superb grip and a scintillating engine. It feels right at home on track too, and although it can get a little scary at the limit on a narrow track like Cadwell, it offers a challenge you'd never get bored of.

'It exceeded my expectations. A true event,' says Meaden. 'You'd simply never tire of lifting your garage door and finding the RS waiting there.' ∎

Circuit Guide: Cadwell Park

*It may be narrow and more commonly associated with motorbike racing, but Cadwell is one of the most engaging circuits in the UK. **Roger Green** has the low-down*

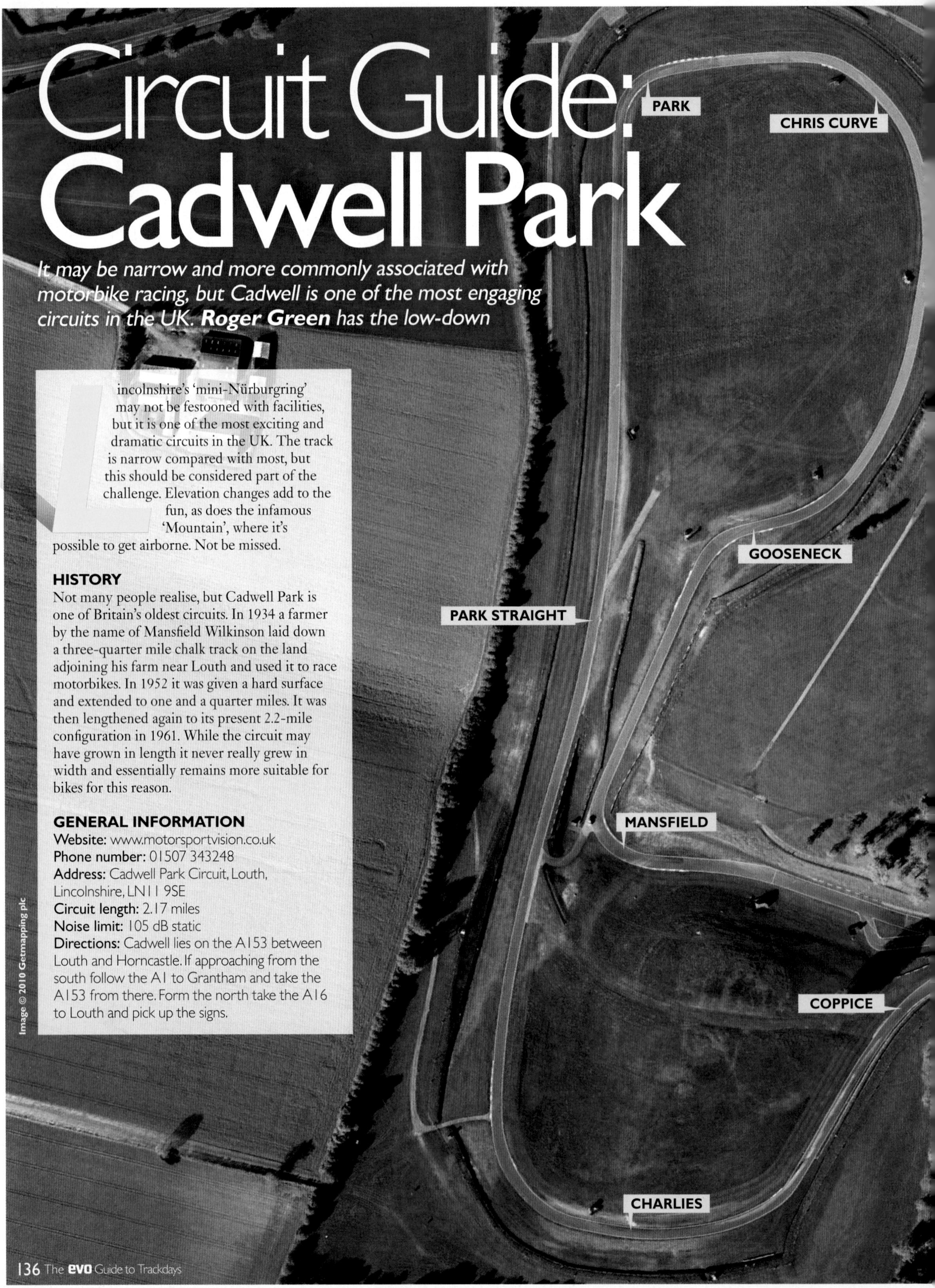

PARK

CHRIS CURVE

GOOSENECK

PARK STRAIGHT

MANSFIELD

COPPICE

CHARLIES

incolnshire's 'mini-Nürburgring' may not be festooned with facilities, but it is one of the most exciting and dramatic circuits in the UK. The track is narrow compared with most, but this should be considered part of the challenge. Elevation changes add to the fun, as does the infamous 'Mountain', where it's possible to get airborne. Not be missed.

HISTORY

Not many people realise, but Cadwell Park is one of Britain's oldest circuits. In 1934 a farmer by the name of Mansfield Wilkinson laid down a three-quarter mile chalk track on the land adjoining his farm near Louth and used it to race motorbikes. In 1952 it was given a hard surface and extended to one and a quarter miles. It was then lengthened again to its present 2.2-mile configuration in 1961. While the circuit may have grown in length it never really grew in width and essentially remains more suitable for bikes for this reason.

GENERAL INFORMATION

Website: www.motorsportvision.co.uk
Phone number: 01507 343248
Address: Cadwell Park Circuit, Louth, Lincolnshire, LN11 9SE
Circuit length: 2.17 miles
Noise limit: 105 dB static
Directions: Cadwell lies on the A153 between Louth and Horncastle. If approaching from the south follow the A1 to Grantham and take the A153 from there. Form the north take the A16 to Louth and pick up the signs.

THE HAIRPIN

HALL BENDS

THE MOUNTAIN

BARN

Google

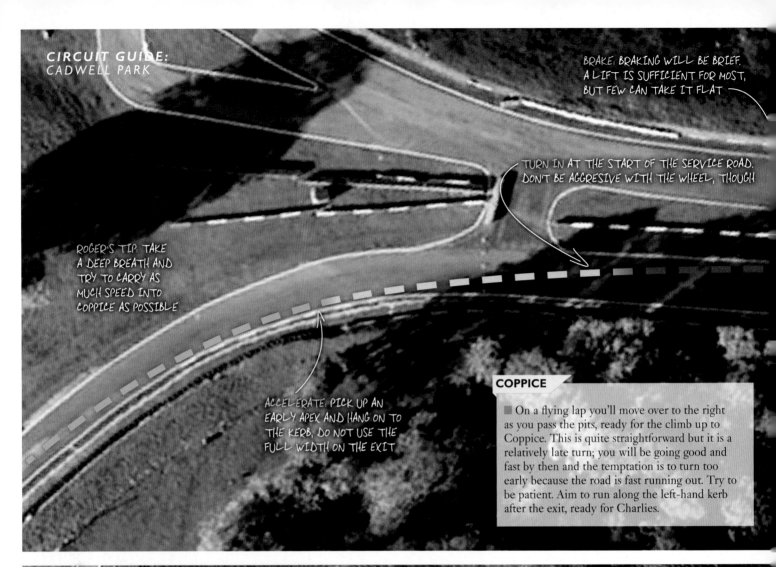

BRAKE: BRAKING WILL BE BRIEF.
A LIFT IS SUFFICIENT FOR MOST,
BUT FEW CAN TAKE IT FLAT

TURN IN AT THE START OF THE SERVICE ROAD.
DON'T BE AGGRESIVE WITH THE WHEEL, THOUGH

ROGER'S TIP: TAKE
A DEEP BREATH AND
TRY TO CARRY AS
MUCH SPEED INTO
COPPICE AS POSSIBLE

ACCELERATE: PICK UP AN
EARLY APEX AND HANG ON TO
THE KERB, DO NOT USE THE
FULL WIDTH ON THE EXIT

COPPICE

■ On a flying lap you'll move over to the right
as you pass the pits, ready for the climb up to
Coppice. This is quite straightforward but it is a
relatively late turn; you will be going good and
fast by then and the temptation is to turn too
early because the road is fast running out. Try to
be patient. Aim to run along the left-hand kerb
after the exit, ready for Charlies.

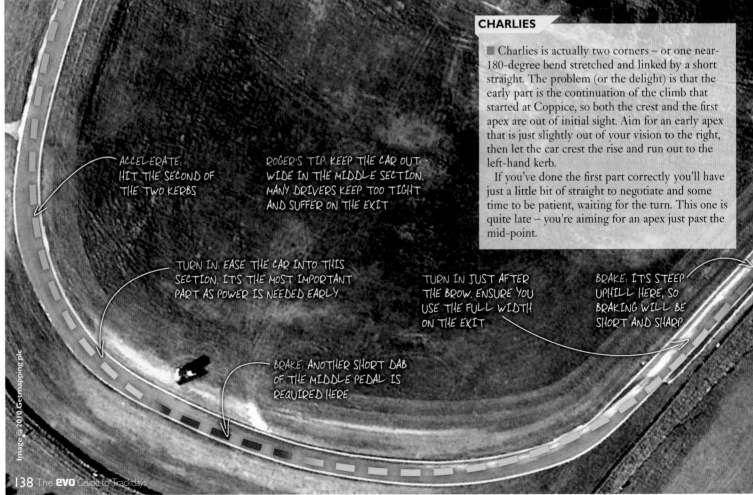

CHARLIES

■ Charlies is actually two corners – or one near-
180-degree bend stretched and linked by a short
straight. The problem (or the delight) is that the
early part is the continuation of the climb that
started at Coppice, so both the crest and the first
apex are out of initial sight. Aim for an early apex
that is just slightly out of your vision to the right,
then let the car crest the rise and run out to the
left-hand kerb.
   If you've done the first part correctly you'll have
just a little bit of straight to negotiate and some
time to be patient, waiting for the turn. This one is
quite late – you're aiming for an apex just past the
mid-point.

ACCELERATE:
HIT THE SECOND OF
THE TWO KERBS

ROGER'S TIP: KEEP THE CAR OUT
WIDE IN THE MIDDLE SECTION.
MANY DRIVERS KEEP TOO TIGHT
AND SUFFER ON THE EXIT

TURN IN: EASE THE CAR INTO THIS
SECTION. IT'S THE MOST IMPORTANT
PART AS POWER IS NEEDED EARLY

TURN IN JUST AFTER
THE BROW. ENSURE YOU
USE THE FULL WIDTH
ON THE EXIT

BRAKE: IT'S STEEP
UPHILL HERE, SO
BRAKING WILL BE
SHORT AND SHARP

BRAKE: ANOTHER SHORT DAB
OF THE MIDDLE PEDAL IS
REQUIRED HERE

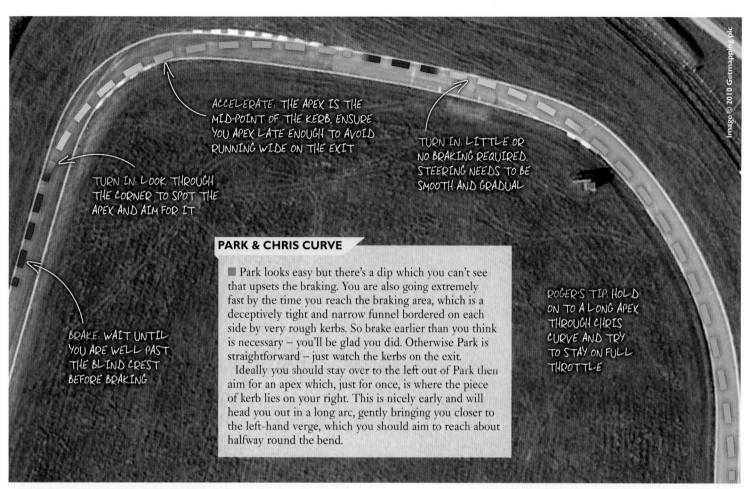

ACCELERATE: THE APEX IS THE MID-POINT OF THE KERB. ENSURE YOU APEX LATE ENOUGH TO AVOID RUNNING WIDE ON THE EXIT

TURN IN: LITTLE OR NO BRAKING REQUIRED. STEERING NEEDS TO BE SMOOTH AND GRADUAL

TURN IN: LOOK THROUGH THE CORNER TO SPOT THE APEX AND AIM FOR IT

BRAKE: WAIT UNTIL YOU ARE WELL PAST THE BLIND CREST BEFORE BRAKING

ROGER'S TIP: HOLD ON TO A LONG APEX THROUGH CHRIS CURVE AND TRY TO STAY ON FULL THROTTLE

PARK & CHRIS CURVE

Park looks easy but there's a dip which you can't see that upsets the braking. You are also going extremely fast by the time you reach the braking area, which is a deceptively tight and narrow funnel bordered on each side by very rough kerbs. So brake earlier than you think is necessary – you'll be glad you did. Otherwise Park is straightforward – just watch the kerbs on the exit.

Ideally you should stay over to the left out of Park then aim for an apex which, just for once, is where the piece of kerb lies on your right. This is nicely early and will head you out in a long arc, gently bringing you closer to the left-hand verge, which you should aim to reach about halfway round the bend.

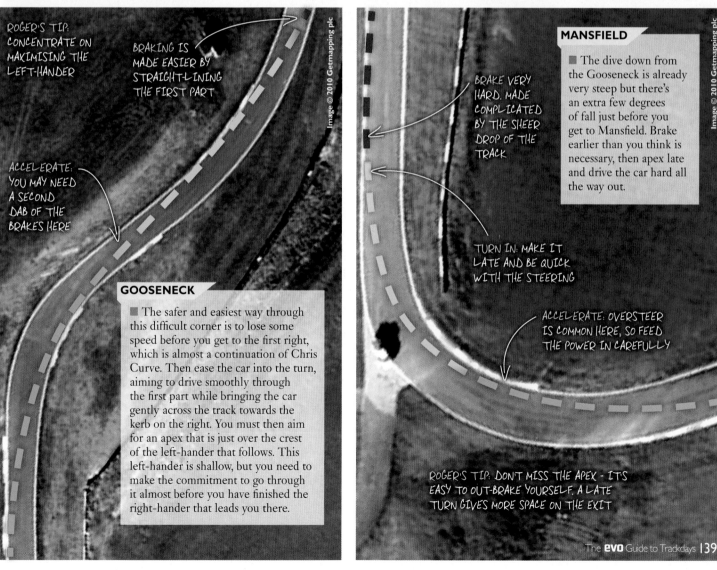

ROGER'S TIP: CONCENTRATE ON MAXIMISING THE LEFT-HANDER

BRAKING IS MADE EASIER BY STRAIGHT-LINING THE FIRST PART

ACCELERATE: YOU MAY NEED A SECOND DAB OF THE BRAKES HERE

GOOSENECK

The safer and easiest way through this difficult corner is to lose some speed before you get to the first right, which is almost a continuation of Chris Curve. Then ease the car into the turn, aiming to drive smoothly through the first part while bringing the car gently across the track towards the kerb on the right. You must then aim for an apex that is just over the crest of the left-hander that follows. This left-hander is shallow, but you need to make the commitment to go through it almost before you have finished the right-hander that leads you there.

MANSFIELD

The dive down from the Gooseneck is already very steep but there's an extra few degrees of fall just before you get to Mansfield. Brake earlier than you think is necessary, then apex late and drive the car hard all the way out.

BRAKE VERY HARD. MADE COMPLICATED BY THE SHEER DROP OF THE TRACK

TURN IN: MAKE IT LATE AND BE QUICK WITH THE STEERING

ACCELERATE: OVERSTEER IS COMMON HERE, SO FEED THE POWER IN CAREFULLY

ROGER'S TIP: DON'T MISS THE APEX - IT'S EASY TO OUT-BRAKE YOURSELF. A LATE TURN GIVES MORE SPACE ON THE EXIT

CIRCUIT GUIDE:
CADWELL PARK

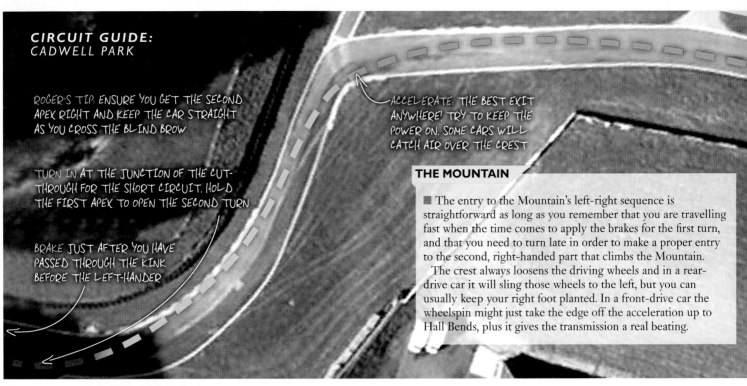

ROGER'S TIP: ENSURE YOU GET THE SECOND APEX RIGHT AND KEEP THE CAR STRAIGHT AS YOU CROSS THE BLIND BROW

TURN IN AT THE JUNCTION OF THE CUT-THROUGH FOR THE SHORT CIRCUIT. HOLD THE FIRST APEX TO OPEN THE SECOND TURN

BRAKE JUST AFTER YOU HAVE PASSED THROUGH THE KINK BEFORE THE LEFT-HANDER

ACCELERATE: THE BEST EXIT ANYWHERE! TRY TO KEEP THE POWER ON. SOME CARS WILL CATCH AIR OVER THE CREST

THE MOUNTAIN

■ The entry to the Mountain's left-right sequence is straightforward as long as you remember that you are travelling fast when the time comes to apply the brakes for the first turn, and that you need to turn late in order to make a proper entry to the second, right-handed part that climbs the Mountain.

The crest always loosens the driving wheels and in a rear-drive car it will sling those wheels to the left, but you can usually keep your right foot planted. In a front-drive car the wheelspin might just take the edge off the acceleration up to Hall Bends, plus it gives the transmission a real beating.

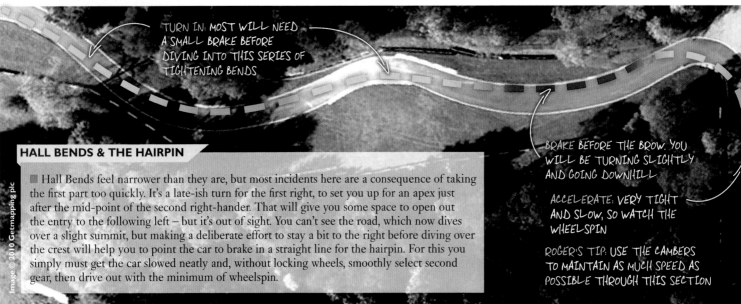

TURN IN: MOST WILL NEED A SMALL BRAKE BEFORE DIVING INTO THIS SERIES OF TIGHTENING BENDS

BRAKE BEFORE THE BROW. YOU WILL BE TURNING SLIGHTLY AND GOING DOWNHILL

ACCELERATE: VERY TIGHT AND SLOW, SO WATCH THE WHEELSPIN

ROGER'S TIP: USE THE CAMBERS TO MAINTAIN AS MUCH SPEED AS POSSIBLE THROUGH THIS SECTION

HALL BENDS & THE HAIRPIN

■ Hall Bends feel narrower than they are, but most incidents here are a consequence of taking the first part too quickly. It's a late-ish turn for the first right, to set you up for an apex just after the mid-point of the second right-hander. That will give you some space to open out the entry to the following left – but it's out of sight. You can't see the road, which now dives over a slight summit, but making a deliberate effort to stay a bit to the right before diving over the crest will help you to point the car to brake in a straight line for the hairpin. For this you simply must get the car slowed neatly and, without locking wheels, smoothly select second gear, then drive out with the minimum of wheelspin.

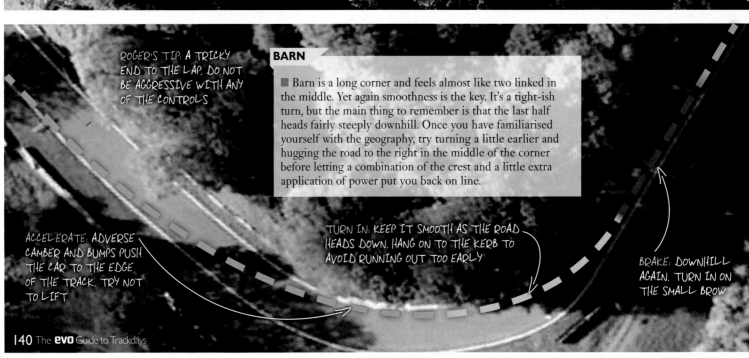

ROGER'S TIP: A TRICKY END TO THE LAP. DO NOT BE AGGRESSIVE WITH ANY OF THE CONTROLS

BARN

■ Barn is a long corner and feels almost like two linked in the middle. Yet again smoothness is the key. It's a tight-ish turn, but the main thing to remember is that the last half heads fairly steeply downhill. Once you have familiarised yourself with the geography, try turning a little earlier and hugging the road to the right in the middle of the corner before letting a combination of the crest and a little extra application of power put you back on line.

ACCELERATE: ADVERSE CAMBER AND BUMPS PUSH THE CAR TO THE EDGE OF THE TRACK. TRY NOT TO LIFT

TURN IN: KEEP IT SMOOTH AS THE ROAD HEADS DOWN. HANG ON TO THE KERB TO AVOID RUNNING OUT TOO EARLY

BRAKE: DOWNHILL AGAIN. TURN IN ON THE SMALL BROW

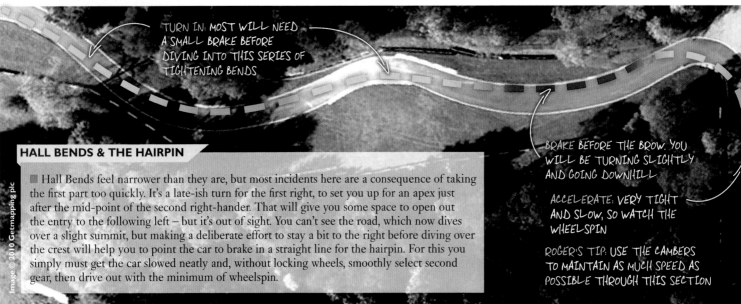Image © 2010 Getmapping plc

Masterclass

By Mark Hales

Secrets of weight transfer

Want to get an insight into weight transfer and its effects on handling? Try a Lotus Elise

The Elise is an entertaining but often tricky little beast, and it's all down to its mid/rear-engined layout. This is what happens. You drive towards the corner, brake smoothly and let the car settle before easing it into the turn. The nose responds, but not that sharply. In fact as you press on and gently squeeze on the power, you find yourself adding more lock. It's OK though, because there's no power steering to mask the feel of the road. But then the road starts to tighten. The corner is sharper than you thought and you couldn't see the exit properly because of the line of trees. You're travelling too fast and the car is now beginning to run wide towards the verge. Adding more lock doesn't seem to tighten the line and backing off the power is likely to give you a still bigger problem, but the choice is to run on to the verge and accept you will head forwards into the ditch, or back off and hope your talent will prevent a visit to the same ditch, slightly further along and going backwards.

Inevitably, you decide to rely on your talent. Lift off the power a little, gently and as progressively as time will allow. The tail begins a lazy yaw, so instinctively you whip the wheel rim in the opposite direction, but it has little effect. You start frantically to pile on more reverse lock but it's too late, the opportunity has gone. The spin continues. Once the cause is lost, you remember to straighten the wheel to stop yourself flying right or left as you come out of the gyration and get firmly on the brakes, hoping you don't hit anything in the meantime.

It's a nightmare with which Elise drivers who take their cars to the track will be familiar, and it's much, much worse in the wet – I can remember being unable to pull an Elise ahead of a well-driven Peugeot 206 at a soaking wet Anglesey. But why does it happen?

The process begins because a much larger proportion of the car's weight is resting on the rear tyres, so as you ease into the corner,

Elise's rearward weight bias
makes it trickier to balance
on the throttle when the
back starts to slide

'The tail begins a lazy yaw, so instinctively you whip the wheel rim in the opposite direction'

the fronts have less to press them to the road. The rears, meanwhile, have plenty thanks to the engine's weight, so the front end starts to nose wide. When you finally lift off because it's all going wrong, a proportion of the total is effectively transferred to the front end, so grip at the front increases but – because the total remains the same – weight pressing on the rear tyres must be less and grip there is reduced. The balance with which you initially felt comfortable is disturbed and hops the other side of a very fine line.

Much the same things can happen with a front-drive car but the big difference in the Elise is the position of the engine and gearbox. The front wheels have effectively received a slightly larger share of the total but there's still a much larger proportion remaining towards the rear which had already begun to yaw through the turn but which is now really on the move because suddenly there is less grip to restrain it. Like a dumb-bell, that mass is also a long way aft of the car's centre – or the point about which the weight is swinging – and this is what makes it less willing to stop when you

whack on the first dose of opposite lock.

You can prove the whole thing for yourself with a domestic broom. Hold the shaft close to the bristly end and move it about. It's easy and you can almost twirl it in any direction with wrist power alone. Now hold the shaft progressively further along its length – further away from the bristles - and try the same. Well before you get to the end, your wrist probably won't have the strength to arrest exactly the same weight of bristles once you have them swinging, which – as I'm sure you're aware – is a function of the polar moment of inertia.

It is also, incidentally, why tromping the accelerator when you are already in trouble doesn't necessarily make things worse as you might expect. The tail squats, weight is transferred back to the rears and you can sometimes get the balance back and stop the spin. The trouble is, when you think you're about to crash, it's always harder to give it a great bootful of power.

To counter this, Lotus have deliberately introduced bump-steer at both ends. This helps to slow down the incipient phase and gives the

driver a chance to recover the situation before it goes out of control. They've done this by arranging the Elise's geometry such that on, say, a right-hand bend, the left front wheel steers slightly more to the left as the car rolls. This effectively tugs the car's nose away from the turn and makes the steering less effective, they hope, just at the critical point when the weight transfer combined with cornering effort is dipping the nose to one side. Better known as the Elise twitch…

Meanwhile, at the back end, they use bump-steer geometry to turn the laden wheel slightly in towards the turn. Because this effect is taking place aft of the point about which the car is yawing (somewhere about the middle of the car), a rear wheel pointing in tries to turn the car away from the arc it is transcribing and makes the back less willing to follow the front into a spin.

The rate at which the whole process unfolds is also influenced by the dampers, while ride height is critical. When people lower their Elises, a proper set-up by someone who really does know their stuff is never a bad idea…

Black Art Designs Ltd
Suspension Systems

Dunmow Road
Felsted Essex
CM6 3LF
UK
Tel: 01371 856777
Email: info@blackartdesigns.com
www.blackartdesigns.com

BMW CSL

Custom made suspension for competition vehicles and motorbikes
Single adjustable units to 3 way adjustable remote canister units
Aluminium or steel
Mono tube or twin tube
Telescopic classic units (XK120's, Jaguar Mk5's etc)
1.88" I.D. Coilover (Formula Cars, Twin Shock Bikes etc)
2.25" I.D. Coilover (TVR's, Lotus Seven's, Yamaha's etc)
McPherson strut (Subaru's, Cosworth's, Lancia's etc)
Military spec (NATO approved) units
O.E.M.
Full design service
In-house dynamics software
Dyno testing service
Suspension rebuild service (most makes)

Black Art Designs Ltd custom make suspension for your requirements.
All manufacturers and models are catered for...if we've not made a particular suspension before (although our list is currently at 217 different kits) we can design a set for you working from sample units. Our attention to detail is second to none and with over 90% of our suspension systems made for race customers finishing on the podium...we can say the proof is in the driving.

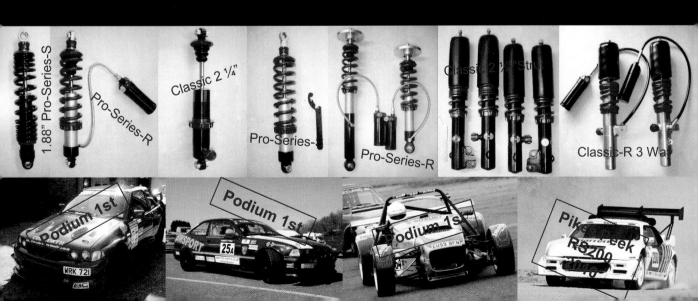

Circuit Guide: Oulton Park

*One of the finest tracks in the north of England, with a number of challenging corners and in a picturesque setting, Oulton Park is well worth a visit, as **Roger Green** relates*

As part of the MotorSport Vision empire and set in rolling Cheshire countryside, Oulton Park is another brilliantly challenging and rewarding racetrack and is also the largest venue north of Donington.

HISTORY

After being badly damaged in a WWII bombing raid, Oulton Hall and the surrounding parkland became government property. In the early 1950s a local motor club, the Mid-Cheshire Car Club, began using what was left of the original park roads as a circuit, with the first race taking place in 1953. The venue quickly established itself as real test for the drivers and many Formula 1 teams were attracted to the International Gold Cup race, which was won five times by Stirling Moss. Today it hosts some of the biggest historic meetings of the year, along with BTCC events and an F3/British GT meeting, all of which draw large crowds.

Incidentally, legend has it the Knickerbrook corner was named after some demolition experts disturbed a courting couple whilst blowing up tree stumps. After the couple in question departed in something of a hurry, an item of the young lady's underwear was discovered in a small brook close to where the track runs today.

GENERAL INFORMATION

Website: www.oultonpark.co.uk
Phone number: 0870 950 9000
Address: Oulton Park Circuit, Little Budworth, Tarporley, Cheshire, CW6 9BW
Circuit length: 2.2260 miles
Noise limit: 105 dB static
Directions: From the north take junction 19 off the M6 and follow the A556 towards Chester. From the South leave the M6 at junction 18 and follow the A54.

OLD HALL

LODGE CORNER

DRUIDS

SHELL OILS CORNER

ISLAND BEND

BRITTEN'S

CASCADES

KNICKERBROOK

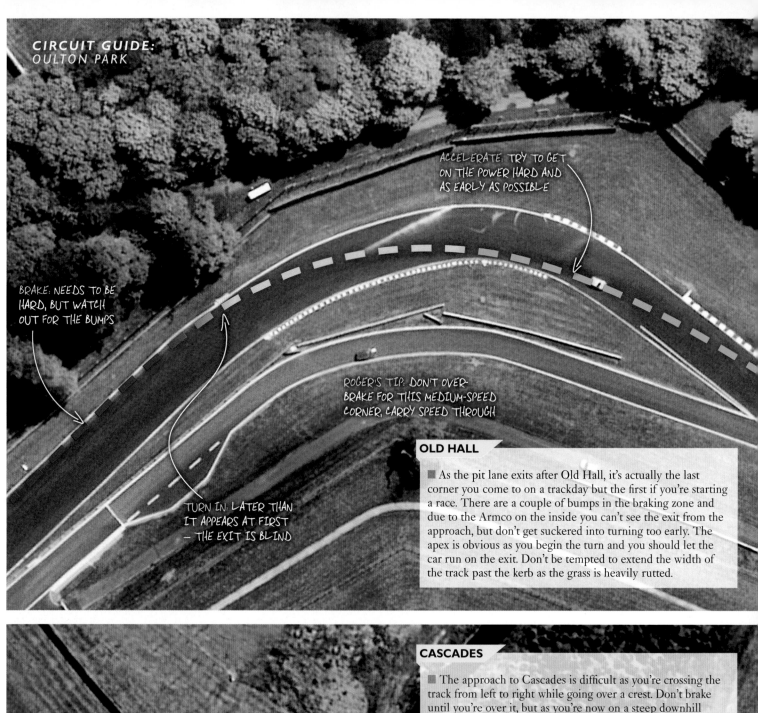

ACCELERATE: TRY TO GET ON THE POWER HARD AND AS EARLY AS POSSIBLE

BRAKE: NEEDS TO BE HARD, BUT WATCH OUT FOR THE BUMPS

ROGER'S TIP: DON'T OVER-BRAKE FOR THIS MEDIUM-SPEED CORNER, CARRY SPEED THROUGH

TURN IN: LATER THAN IT APPEARS AT FIRST — THE EXIT IS BLIND

OLD HALL

As the pit lane exits after Old Hall, it's actually the last corner you come to on a trackday but the first if you're starting a race. There are a couple of bumps in the braking zone and due to the Armco on the inside you can't see the exit from the approach, but don't get suckered into turning too early. The apex is obvious as you begin the turn and you should let the car run on the exit. Don't be tempted to extend the width of the track past the kerb as the grass is heavily rutted.

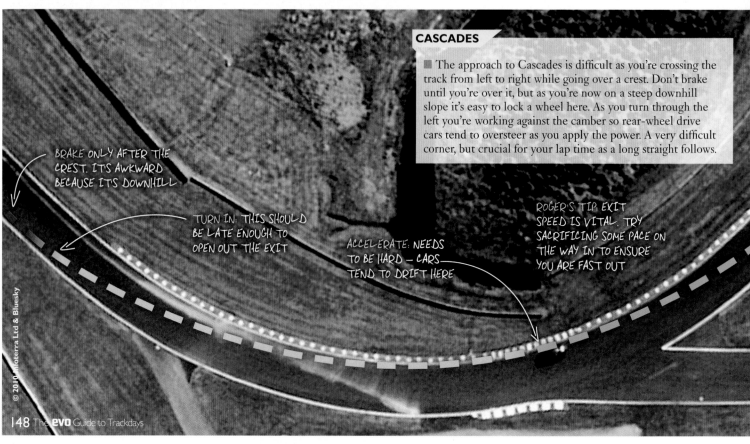

CASCADES

The approach to Cascades is difficult as you're crossing the track from left to right while going over a crest. Don't brake until you're over it, but as you're now on a steep downhill slope it's easy to lock a wheel here. As you turn through the left you're working against the camber so rear-wheel drive cars tend to oversteer as you apply the power. A very difficult corner, but crucial for your lap time as a long straight follows.

BRAKE ONLY AFTER THE CREST. ITS AWKWARD BECAUSE ITS DOWNHILL

TURN IN: THIS SHOULD BE LATE ENOUGH TO OPEN OUT THE EXIT

ACCELERATE: NEEDS TO BE HARD — CARS TEND TO DRIFT HERE

ROGER'S TIP: EXIT SPEED IS VITAL. TRY SACRIFICING SOME PACE ON THE WAY IN TO ENSURE YOU ARE FAST OUT

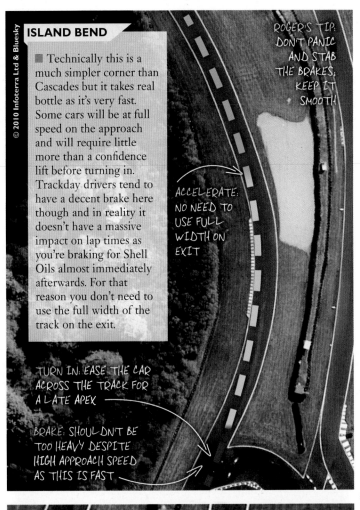

ISLAND BEND

■ Technically this is a much simpler corner than Cascades but it takes real bottle as it's very fast. Some cars will be at full speed on the approach and will require little more than a confidence lift before turning in. Trackday drivers tend to have a decent brake here though and in reality it doesn't have a massive impact on lap times as you're braking for Shell Oils almost immediately afterwards. For that reason you don't need to use the full width of the track on the exit.

ROGER'S TIP: DON'T PANIC AND STAB THE BRAKES, KEEP IT SMOOTH

ACCELERATE: NO NEED TO USE FULL WIDTH ON EXIT

TURN IN: EASE THE CAR ACROSS THE TRACK FOR A LATE APEX

BRAKE: SHOULDN'T BE TOO HEAVY DESPITE HIGH APPROACH SPEED AS THIS IS FAST

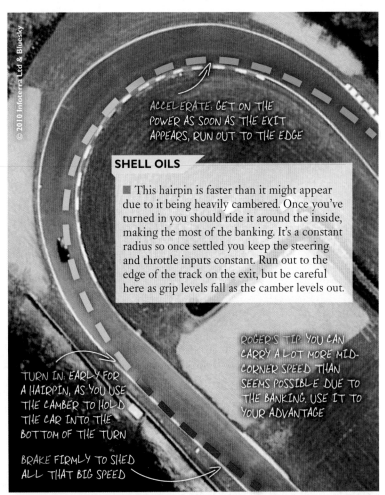

ACCELERATE: GET ON THE POWER AS SOON AS THE EXIT APPEARS, RUN OUT TO THE EDGE

SHELL OILS

■ This hairpin is faster than it might appear due to it being heavily cambered. Once you've turned in you should ride it around the inside, making the most of the banking. It's a constant radius so once settled you keep the steering and throttle inputs constant. Run out to the edge of the track on the exit, but be careful here as grip levels fall as the camber levels out.

ROGER'S TIP: YOU CAN CARRY A LOT MORE MID-CORNER SPEED THAN SEEMS POSSIBLE DUE TO THE BANKING. USE IT TO YOUR ADVANTAGE

TURN IN: EARLY FOR A HAIRPIN, AS YOU USE THE CAMBER TO HOLD THE CAR INTO THE BOTTOM OF THE TURN

BRAKE FIRMLY TO SHED ALL THAT BIG SPEED

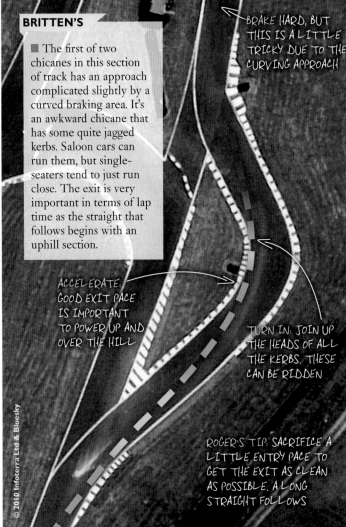

BRITTEN'S

■ The first of two chicanes in this section of track has an approach complicated slightly by a curved braking area. It's an awkward chicane that has some quite jagged kerbs. Saloon cars can run them, but single-seaters tend to just run close. The exit is very important in terms of lap time as the straight that follows begins with an uphill section.

BRAKE HARD, BUT THIS IS A LITTLE TRICKY DUE TO THE CURVING APPROACH

ACCELERATE: GOOD EXIT PACE IS IMPORTANT TO POWER UP AND OVER THE HILL

TURN IN: JOIN UP THE HEADS OF ALL THE KERBS. THESE CAN BE RIDDEN

ROGER'S TIP: SACRIFICE A LITTLE ENTRY PACE TO GET THE EXIT AS CLEAN AS POSSIBLE. A LONG STRAIGHT FOLLOWS

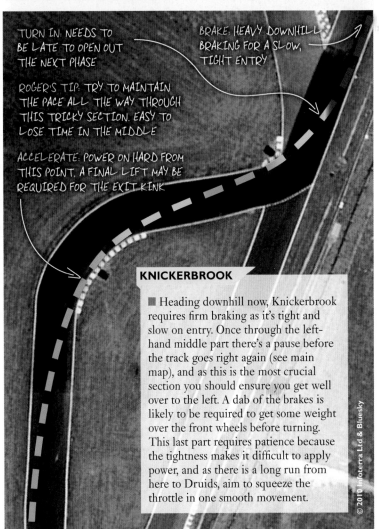

TURN IN: NEEDS TO BE LATE TO OPEN OUT THE NEXT PHASE

ROGER'S TIP: TRY TO MAINTAIN THE PACE ALL THE WAY THROUGH THIS TRICKY SECTION. EASY TO LOSE TIME IN THE MIDDLE

ACCELERATE: POWER ON HARD FROM THIS POINT, A FINAL LIFT MAY BE REQUIRED FOR THE EXIT KINK

BRAKE: HEAVY DOWNHILL BRAKING FOR A SLOW, TIGHT ENTRY

KNICKERBROOK

■ Heading downhill now, Knickerbrook requires firm braking as it's tight and slow on entry. Once through the left-hand middle part there's a pause before the track goes right again (see main map), and as this is the most crucial section you should ensure you get well over to the left. A dab of the brakes is likely to be required to get some weight over the front wheels before turning. This last part requires patience because the tightness makes it difficult to apply power, and as there is a long run from here to Druids, aim to squeeze the throttle in one smooth movement.

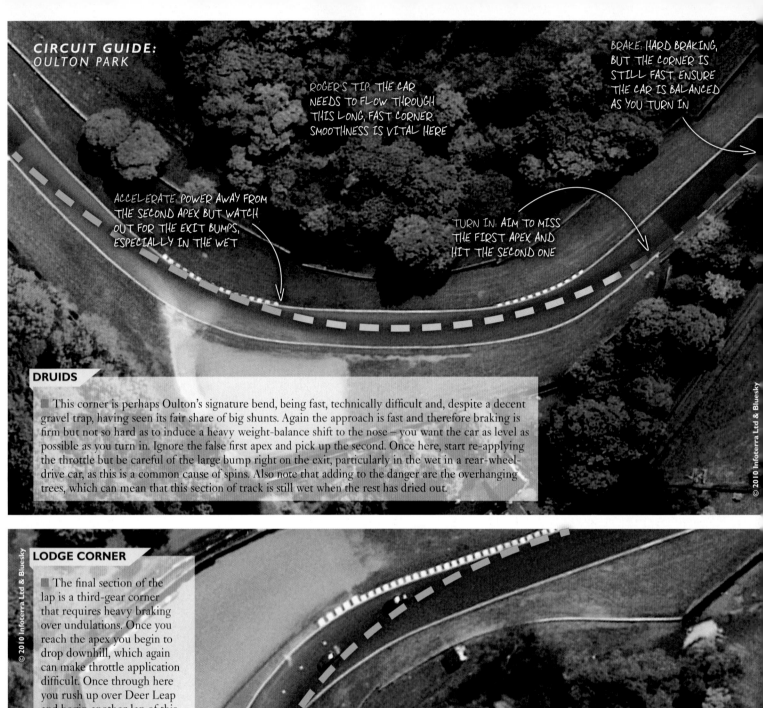

ROGER'S TIP: THE CAR NEEDS TO FLOW THROUGH THIS LONG, FAST CORNER. SMOOTHNESS IS VITAL HERE

BRAKE: HARD BRAKING, BUT THE CORNER IS STILL FAST. ENSURE THE CAR IS BALANCED AS YOU TURN IN

ACCELERATE: POWER AWAY FROM THE SECOND APEX BUT WATCH OUT FOR THE EXIT BUMPS, ESPECIALLY IN THE WET

TURN IN: AIM TO MISS THE FIRST APEX AND HIT THE SECOND ONE

DRUIDS

This corner is perhaps Oulton's signature bend, being fast, technically difficult and, despite a decent gravel trap, having seen its fair share of big shunts. Again the approach is fast and therefore braking is firm but not so hard as to induce a heavy weight-balance shift to the nose – you want the car as level as possible as you turn in. Ignore the false first apex and pick up the second. Once here, start re-applying the throttle but be careful of the large bump right on the exit, particularly in the wet in a rear-wheel-drive car, as this is a common cause of spins. Also note that adding to the danger are the overhanging trees, which can mean that this section of track is still wet when the rest has dried out.

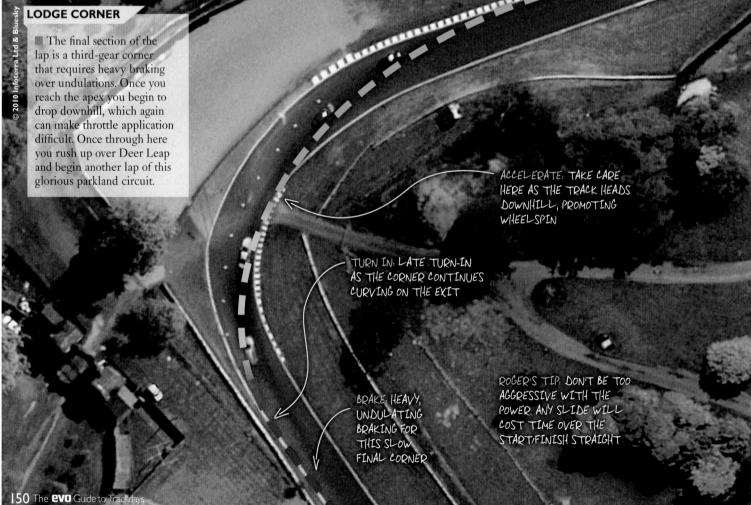

LODGE CORNER

The final section of the lap is a third-gear corner that requires heavy braking over undulations. Once you reach the apex you begin to drop downhill, which again can make throttle application difficult. Once through here you rush up over Deer Leap and begin another lap of this glorious parkland circuit.

ACCELERATE: TAKE CARE HERE AS THE TRACK HEADS DOWNHILL, PROMOTING WHEELSPIN

TURN IN: LATE TURN-IN AS THE CORNER CONTINUES CURVING ON THE EXIT

BRAKE: HEAVY, UNDULATING BRAKING FOR THIS SLOW FINAL CORNER

ROGER'S TIP: DON'T BE TOO AGGRESSIVE WITH THE POWER. ANY SLIDE WILL COST TIME OVER THE START/FINISH STRAIGHT

evo

TRACK CAR OF THE YEAR 2009

For our 2009 contest to find the best trackday car, we headed for the Bedford Autodrome.
Twelve contenders, from affordable hatchbacks to the most extreme lightweights
yet devised, battled it out for the title of evo Track Car of the Year

Pictures Matt Howell & Matt Vosper

The specs

	LAYOUT	ENGINE	MAX POWER	MAX TORQUE	WEIGHT	POWER-TO-WEIGHT	0-60MPH	TOP SPEED	BASIC PRICE (2009 PRICES)
RENAULT CLIO 200 CUP	Front engine, front-wheel drive	In-line 4-cyl, 1998cc	197bhp @ 7100rpm	159lb ft @ 5400rpm	1204kg	166bhp/ton	6.6sec	141mph (claimed)	£15,750
FORD FOCUS RS	Front engine, front-wheel drive	In-line 5-cyl, 2522cc, turbo	300bhp @ 6500rpm	324lb ft @ 2300rpm	1467kg	208bhp/ton	5.9sec	163mph (claimed)	£25,745
HONDA CIVIC TYPE-R MUGEN	Front engine, front-wheel drive	In-line 4-cyl, 1998cc	237bhp @ 8300rpm	157lb ft @ 6250rpm	1233kg	195bhp/ton	5.9sec (est)	155mph (est)	£38,599
MITSUBISHI EVO X FQ-400	Front engine, four-wheel drive	In-line 4-cyl, 1998cc, turbo	403bhp @ 6500rpm	387lb ft @ 3500rpm	1560kg	262bhp/ton	3.8sec (claimed)	155mph (claimed)	£49,999
LAMBORGHINI LP550-2 BALBONI	Mid engine, rear-wheel drive	V10, 5204cc	542bhp @ 8000rpm	398lb ft @ 6500rpm	1380kg	399bhp/ton	3.9sec (claimed)	199mph (claimed)	£157,550
PORSCHE 911 GT3	Rear engine, rear-wheel drive	Flat-six, 3797cc	429bhp @ 7600rpm	317lb ft @ 6250rpm	1395kg	312bhp/ton	4.2sec (claimed)	194mph (claimed)	£81,914
CATERHAM SUPERLIGHT R300	Front engine, rear-wheel drive	In-line 4-cyl, 1999cc	175bhp @ 7000rpm	139lb ft @ 6000rpm	515kg	345bhp/ton	4.5sec (claimed)	140mph (claimed)	£27,500
ARIEL ATOM 3 SUPERCHARGED	Mid engine, rear-wheel drive	In-line 4-cyl, 1998cc, s'charger	300bhp @ 8200rpm	162lb ft @ 7200rpm	550kg	554bhp/ton	3.3sec	155mph (claimed)	£42,000
LOTUS SPORT 2-ELEVEN GT4	Mid engine, rear-wheel drive	In-line 4-cyl, 1800cc, s'charger	266bhp @ 8200rpm	179lb ft @ 7200rpm	670kg	403bhp/ton	3.7sec (est)	155mph (est)	£76,590
KTM X-BOW	Mid engine, rear-wheel drive	In-line 4-cyl, 1984cc, turbo	296bhp @ 5500-5600rpm	295lb ft @ 3000-5000rpm	790kg	381bhp/ton	3.5sec (claimed)	147mph (claimed)	£67,206
RADICAL SR8LM	Mid engine, rear-wheel drive	V8, 2800cc	460bhp @ 10,500rpm	260lb ft @ 8000rpm	680kg	687bhp/ton	3.2sec (est)	168mph	£88,000
CAPARO T1	Mid engine, rear-wheel drive	V8, 3499cc	610bhp @ 10,500rpm	310lb ft @ 9000rpm	689kg	899bhp/ton	3.8sec	205mph (claimed)	£225,500

Left: specs shows what a diverse bunch the contenders are, from hot hatches to trackdays specials (including the R300, above) to supercars (like the Balboni, left)

Finding our Track Car of the Year requires a whole new set of priorities to a regular car of the year test. The recipe for success here needs different ingredients. Yes, the cars are more extreme, though they shouldn't be so wild that they can't be driven to and from a circuit or enjoyed on the road every time the urge for a full-on blast takes hold. The exposed and edgy nature of an Ariel Atom, for example, might pall on a long run.

That's not to say you wouldn't have fun in it, but it's so intense that after 20 minutes most drivers would probably have cried enough. The sensory overload combined with the physical bashing from the elements mean it is best enjoyed in short doses. At the other end of the spectrum, for all a Lotus Evora's ride and handling brilliance on the road, if you used it regularly on a racetrack you'd probably wish you had bought one of Lotus's more focused products, something a little more aggressive, lighter, more responsive and faster. Something like the 2-Eleven GT4.

John Barker, one of our four referees for this test, says he's looking for entertainment, reward and a challenge. I agree. The winner of this test will be a car you can grow with and learn something from at every trackday you attend, and trackday specials like the Atom and 2-Eleven are perfect for that.

They're not alone here, though. KTM may have had a tough time with its X-Bow, but the 300bhp version we tested last month has the power that the chassis has been crying out for, so it has earned a place. Caterham's new-this-year R300 is here too. The Dartford factory may have been churning out similar products for decades now, but you'd be a fool to discount them – Caterhams have won three previous Track Car of the Year contests.

You don't need a bespoke toy to enjoy your circuit driving, though. Go to virtually any trackday and you'll find Porsches out in force, particularly the kind wearing bright paintwork and the letters G, T and 3 scribed on their high-winged rumps. We've had some of our most memorable drives in the indomitable 911 and it's likely to put in an equally strong showing at the Bedford Autodrome.

But it won't have things all its own way. The rear-wheel-drive Balboni-spec Gallardo should be rapid, beautifully sonorous and, with its manual gearbox, involving too. We reckon it's the first Lamborghini that can be used as a true trackday tool. However, in an effort to keep both it and the GT3 honest, we've also lobbed a rally-rocket into the mix, and the FQ-400 Evo X has the all-wheel-drive hardware, the aero tricks and the kind of turbocharged punch that brings supercar owners out in a cold sweat.

The Clio 200 Cup has claimed a number of big-money scalps, and its chuckable nature should be well suited to the demands of the West Circuit. Meanwhile, Fords that wear RS badges have always made great trackday companions and we see no reason why the RevoKnuckled Focus should buck that trend. The final contender to slot into the hot hatch group is the Mugen version of the Civic Type-R. With more power, less weight, better brakes, uprated suspension and numerous racy details, it was a hit when we featured it previously and it should score well here.

If, however, you want to go really fast – and I mean eye-poppingly, trousers-on-fire fast – then there are a couple of companies ready to help. Radical smashed its own production-car lap record at the Nürburgring in August 2009 with the SR8LM, and when we recently lapped the car here at Bedford it came within a smidge of our outright lap record. It achieved this despite running the ultra-long gearing from the Ring, but now it returns with a more conventional set of ratios to take on the defending champ, the Caparo T1. This car may have endured a difficult birth but it still reigns supreme at the top of our charts. Can it hold on to its crown? This will be the gloves-off decider – Nürburgring lap record holder versus West Circuit record holder. It should be quite a fight.

The **Hot Hatches**

Focus RS v Clio 200 Cup v Civic Type-R Mugen

HAVING seen the line-up, it wouldn't have taken the brain power of Stephen Hawking to predict where the slowest lap time of the day was going to come from, but as we know, the Clio can stand tall in any performance-car gathering. You certainly sit quite high in the excellent (optional) Recaro seats, but the Cup chassis'd Clio 200 remains flat through the turns, and its adjustability means it can be driven in a number of different styles. Chris Harris describes it as 'a little crackerjack' before explaining his reasoning. 'It has a top-notch chassis and an engaging powertrain,' he says. 'It tips into turns well and likes to punish any throttle hesitation with big oversteer. Just the way it should be.' For something comfortably the right side of £20K, there's little to match it for verve.

Unfortunately the Focus RS doesn't display quite the same enthusiasm for track work. Its five-cylinder engine may have 50 per cent more power, but the additional weight virtually nullifies the extra straight-line performance and that extra mass is felt through the turns, where the RS fails to respond quite so eagerly. Henry Catchpole agrees: 'It's really too big and heavy for a track car, but if you don't bully it and don't overload the front tyres then there is a very enjoyable balance to it. You need to judge the entry speed just right so it doesn't understeer. If you can get the front tyres to cling on, the tail gets nicely involved and an inside rear wheel can be found dangling in the breeze.'

'Mugen has turned the Civic Type-R into a proper little Touring car'

Above: Focus RS needs careful handling in the corners to get the best from it; Mugen Civic feels race-car sharp in comparison. Far right: Clio proves you don't need big power to have big fun. Left: VBOX used to record lap times

You have a small window in which to work, though, and because of this the Focus fails to inspire or entertain like the Clio. At least the brakes are strong – Bedford is tough on stoppers but the 336mm vented front discs remain fade-free on the timed laps. Pity the engine feels strangely flat across the mid-range, never quite hitting the full stride we've experienced in other RSs we've tried. This in part probably explains why it only eclipses the Clio's time by 0.6sec, netting a 1:31.3.

Neither Clio nor Focus is a match for the Mugen Civic. When we first tested this car a couple of months ago it comprehensively outclassed the regular Type-R. A limited run of 20 hand-built examples has now been

confirmed, and at £38,599 it's very expensive for a hot hatch, but Mugen has created a proper little touring car. Every single part of this Type-R's make-up has been optimised to make it faster, more precise, more responsive, more intense. It's the Japanese R26.R (although it was designed and will be built in Northampton).

Getting 237bhp from a normally aspirated 2-litre engine is an astonishing achievement and at the top end of its rev-range it sounds far more exotic than a four-pot has any right to be. However, you do need to keep it on the boil, and that means you need to think about what you're doing behind the wheel. JB concurs. 'You have to get your head around it,' he says. 'You warm the tyres up and it then takes a couple

of laps to work out when to get on the power in the corners to hook the diff up without pushing wide. But get it flowing, keep it in the power- band and it's very satisfying and not too energy-sapping.' It's also fast. The 1:28.0 it nails makes it the fastest front-wheel-drive car we've ever tested around the West Circuit.

'Your average family car can't dispatch the 0-60mph dash

The **Road Racers**

Porsche 911 GT3 v Lambo LP550-2 Balboni v Mitsubishi Evo X FQ-400

HERE we have two of the cars from eCoty 09 slugging it out again, which will be interesting, and with the added twist of the hottest of the current generation of Mitsubishi Evos to keep both of the supercars on their toes.

It takes a while to get the best from the GT3. The weight distribution means you have to learn to interpret the flow of information being fed back from the front wheels to decipher the level of bite on offer before you begin to lean on them and work the rear. Once you've mastered it, the poise is wonderful and the overall grip and the traction exiting tight turns is deeply impressive. The engine feels as magnificent out on a vast featureless racetrack as it did in Scotland, but you do have to watch how you use its performance in the faster corners because when the tail starts arcing wide you need to be on top of your game to hang with it. Once you're in the groove, though, it's immensely satisfying.

The LP550-2 Valentino Balboni is very different to earlier Gallardos. Removing the front driveshafts has resulted in a chassis that feels like it has had extra purity dialled into it. It's more predictable too. I guessed that it would oversteer wildly, and taming the tail is indeed the biggest job the driver faces when aiming for a lap time. You have to treat the throttle pedal as if it were a champagne glass, gently squeezing the power on rather than just stomping on it. Get the slip angles just so and it feels sublime, but get greedy and you have to work hard and fast to regain the balance.

The ceramic brakes that felt grabby on the road are right at home here and the manual gearbox is such a delight to use you'd never miss the time you might have saved with the e-gear paddle-shift transmission. At the end of our laps the Balboni's best time, a 1:23.4, is just a tenth of a second behind the GT3's.

And so we come to the outsider. What is a practical four-door saloon with Isofix points and a proper boot doing in such exalted company? Well, your average family car probably can't dispatch the 0-60mph dash in a supercar-like 3.8sec (the Balboni needs 3.9sec to get there and the GT3 a comparatively yawning 4.2), and although at £50K the FQ-400 is hardly cheap, if it can keep tabs with the elite then you could perhaps make a case for it offering value for money.

The previous incarnation, the IX, was an Evo with attitude. In fact you could corner it at whatever attitude, or yaw angle, you liked. It was as natural as it was thrilling. This incarnation doesn't quite do that. As with the IX, its nose still hunts out apexes as enthusiastically as a boar snuffles truffles, but the adjustability and aggression has gone, and with it a big chunk of what made the old FQ-400 such a giant killer. The power all arrives at the top of the rev-range so there's not the thumping mid-range kick you might expect from a high-output turbo. In fact the whole thing feels a little flat, and that's a disappointment. It can't keep up with the Porsche and Lambo either, its best lap of 1:25.9 being a good 2.5sec off the pace.

'in a supercar-like 3.8 seconds'

Above: 911 GT3's 3.8-litre flat-six is good for 429bhp, while its location at the rear of the car helps generate impressive traction out of corners. Below, from top: in Evo X form the FQ-400 lacks the attitude and the natural adjustability of the previous-generation version, and is less thrilling as a result; Catchpole mulls over the steering feel of the first rear-wheel-drive Gallardo; Green finds the limit of the GT3's rear-end grip

'The 2-Eleven's pace is blistering. It laps faster than the supercharged Ariel Atom'

The *Trackday Specials*
Lotus 2-Eleven v KTM X-Bow 300bhp v Caterham R300 v Ariel Atom 3

YES, we've seen plenty of Caterhams before, but they are the original trackday toy, and in terms of performance and entertainment per pound they've yet to be knocked off their perch. The R300 will further enhance the Seven's reputation. After a run in this 175bhp, 2-litre Duratec-powered car, John Barker jumps out with a broad grin. 'This will be pretty hard to beat with its brilliant combo of pace, feel, handling and over-the-limit catchability,' he says. This particular example is a tad soft at the front, but that's because we like Sevens that slide. Everything is adjustable, though, so you can tailor the car to suit your own experience, which means it will be ridiculously involving whether you're a novice or a circuit god.

Ariel and the **evo** Track Car of the Year test have grown up together. A youthful Atom took part in our inaugural 2001 test, but back then it was yet to get the supercharger and LSD, and the eight years of continuous development. This season's revisions include some subtle damper tweaks and a remapped ECU to smooth out the throttle response, but don't for one minute think that the smallest fraction of the madness has been ironed out – it's still as unhinged as it looks. Chris Harris reckons that as an experience it's right up there. 'Forced-induction torque and a lack of mass makes for inertia-free acceleration,' he says. 'Even the Radical pauses for breath, but this just bungs you down the track. There's a lot for the driver to manage.'

Very true, and the badly timed gentle drizzle falling during the timed lap probably costs it half a second. Setting a time is a buzzy, frenetic, all-action affair, arguably the antithesis of what an efficient racer should be, but it's still fast, recording a 1:22.9 (1.4sec faster than the Caterham), and boy is it fun.

The road-legal GT4 version of the 2-Eleven has been launched quietly by Lotus Sport, but a few laps are all you need to realise that it's a serious contender for this year's prize. The lever for the sequential gearbox may look like it was designed by Gustave Eiffel but it's brilliant to use and allows incredibly fast upshifts. Once the front tyres have some heat in them, the grip is

astonishing too. There's downforce at work here, but also race-spec two-way Öhlins adjustable dampers, maximising the high lateral G loadings the Yokohama AO48 tyres can generate.

The brakes are equally impressive and they come with ABS tuned for the track so you can trail-brake impossibly late with no fuss at all, and when you pick up the throttle there are no traction issues despite the engine upgrade. The supercharged Toyota four-pot now has 266bhp (up from 252bhp) and the resulting pace is blistering, the 2-Eleven lapping 2.8sec faster than the Ariel. Just when I think it will be difficult to find anything wrong with the GT4, I discover the price. £76,590. Gulp.

Speaking of pricey, the £67K 300bhp KTM

X-Bow has the weak pound working against it, but there's much to commend. It still looks incredible and the stiff carbon tub and downforce-inducing body certainly work. The lap time it achieves – a 1:21.5, exactly halfway between the 2-Eleven and the Atom – is very impressive. It never feels that quick, though, because you can't turn in as fast or as hard as you might want to since it's very easy to tip the car into momentum oversteer. If that happens you have to wait for rear grip to return before getting back on the throttle. It's fun but it costs time, and the vagueness of the gearbox draws further criticism. Shame, because the X-Bow concept is terrific and there's plenty of entertainment to be had.

Green prepares to set a time in the 554bhp-per-ton Ariel Atom. As always, all the timed laps are recorded with a passenger on board, which staff writer Stephen Dobie looks well chuffed about

Opposite page, top: 2-Eleven impresses from the moment you climb aboard – its seats are the best in this group, feeling secure and comfortable; Caterham can be set up as the driver prefers (oversteery in this case). Above: 300bhp X-Bow is closer to being the car we always hoped it would be, but it still has some frustrating niggles

'The corners rush towards you like you're watching a video at double speed'

Both Radical (right) and Caparo (below) have been modified since their last West Circuit apperances, the Radical with more suitable shorter gearing and the Caparo with new silencers intended to keep it below the Autodrome's noise limit

The **Extreme Sports**

Caparo T1
v Radical SR8LM

HERE it is then, the dust-up we've been waiting for, and it's the on-paper underdog up first. When I lapped the Radical SR8LM here a few weeks ago with its intergalactic gear ratios it still knuckled down to an extraordinary 1:15.9. There was obviously more to come, but would it be enough to edge its way past the faintly absurd 1:14.8 previously posted by the Caparo T1? Time to slide into the moulded seats and find out.

The first thing that strikes you about the SR8LM is just how user-friendly it is, particularly for a racer. The driving position is perfect. You sit low, tucked in behind the screen, just high enough to see everything but low enough to be out of the buffeting air. It moves away cleanly and easily. There's no awkward, heavy clutch, no jerky low-speed lumpiness from the 460bhp 2.8-litre Powertec V8. It immediately feels highly developed, honed and completely sorted, giving you the confidence to really lean on the car from the off. You don't feel like you need to learn it, to

get to know it, you just get on with the driving. And wow, is it rapid.

Harris will later remark that it is 'amazingly benign when it lets go, especially when you consider the terrifying on-paper stats'. And he's right. You don't expect to be able to drift something that offers proper levels of downforce, but you can, and as long as you have an average level of track-driving competence you can really work it hard.

So what did it do? A 1:13.5, making it 1.3sec faster than the existing Caparo mark. That T1 time was set by Barker earlier in the year, but he was stopped by the noise police before he really got a handle on the car. This time we're hoping the repacked silencers will avoid that.

Getting into the T1 is a complicated task, particularly for my passenger (and possibly our maddest office member), Stephen Dobie, who has to wriggle himself into a space that looks like it would be tight for Mick Jagger. I hope he won't have to get out in a hurry.

The Caparo is pure race-car. The cogs in the gearbox clunk together as first gear engages when I tug the (unnervingly bendy) right-hand carbonfibre paddle towards me, and the transmission chunters and whines

as I ease the car up the pitlane. The engine needs revs before it feels happy and I notice the limited steering lock too. Hope it's not too oversteery… I gun the 3.5-litre V8 engine and 610bhp instantly lights up the rears tyres. It sounds loud back there. The scream penetrates my Arai and embeds itself deep into my eardrums. It must be even more extreme for Stephen as he's right next to the air intake. If he wasn't so firmly strapped in he'd be in danger of being sucked in. If I look down I can see his feet next to my knees, but there's no time to glance away from the view ahead. Corners rush towards you like you're watching a video at double speed, even after the Radical.

Thankfully the brakes are monumental. Stamp on the middle pedal and the G-forces feel strong enough to splatter water from your tearducts onto the inside of your visor. I peel into the turns with care at first, feeling the grip from the tyres as the downforce crushes them into the tarmac. They're not hot enough yet… and alas they never get the chance to warm up because we're called in for smashing the noise limit to smithereens. A new pair of silencers are fitted, but it makes little difference. There will be no record run from the Caparo today.

The **Lap Times**

Radical sets a new West Circuit record, knocking 1.2sec off the Caparo's previous best. The 2-Eleven is 6.5sec behind the SR8LM, but speed isn't everything...

CLUB CHICANE

HANGAR HAIRPIN

PALMER CURVES

TOWER

NEW PIF-PAF

BedfordAutodrome
THE WEST CIRCUIT

O'ROUGE

BANK COMPLEX

BECKHAM ESSES

Radical SR8LM
Lap time **1:13.6**
Peak speed **127.8mph**

Lotus 2-Eleven GT4
Lap time **1:20.1**
Peak speed **113.2mph**

KTM X-Bow 300bhp
Lap time **1:21.5**
Peak speed **112.7mph**

Ariel Atom 3 Supercharged
Lap time **1:22.9**
Peak speed **114.6mph**

Porsche 911 GT3
Lap time **1:23.3**
Peak speed **114.5mph**

Lamborghini LP550-2 Balboni
Lap time **1:23.4**
Peak speed **116.8mph**

Caterham Superlight R300
Lap time **1:24.3**
Peak speed **101.5mph**

Mitsubishi Evo X FQ-400
Lap time **1:25.9** Peak speed **107.5mph**

Renaultsport Clio 200 Cup
Lap time **1:31.9**
Peak speed **97.2mph**

Ford Focus RS
Lap time **1:31.3**
Peak speed **104.2mph**

Civic Type-R Mugen
Lap time **1:28.0**
Peak speed **104.3mph**

The **Verdict**

NO QUESTION, you would enjoy a trackday in any of our contenders, but two of them failed to instil a deep desire in our judging panel. Neither the Focus RS nor the Evo X quite lived up to the hype their bodywork addenda promised. The Focus was quick and unflappable but lacked true driver interaction, while the FQ-400 was efficient but a shadow of its former self in terms of the aggressive attack angles that it used to carry in its armoury.

Finding a place for the Caparo in the final ranking proved tricky due to the lack of running, but then finding a trackday where you could use it would be a problem for the same reason.

It would be allowed on the Nürburgring and we understand Caparo will be taking one there next spring. The driver will need nads of steel, though, for this is not a toy to be taken lightly. Oversteer, limited lock and monster grunt in a waif-like body should be enough for the T1 to come with a government health warning. But what a buzz. It makes the Noble M600 feel sane, and virtually everything else pedestrian.

The Clio can hold its head high even though it doesn't quite shade the Balboni this time. It's a cracking little all-rounder but it can't quite see off the drama of 542 of the finest Italian horses smearing a racetrack with molten rubber.

Seventh place is where we find the first of the trackday specials, and it's the KTM X-Bow, which surprised us with its pace and its propensity for tail-out action but was marked down for the on/off nature of the torque delivery and the vagueness of its gearbox.

Ariel's Atom just misses out on a top-five berth, but don't think for a minute that it disgraced itself. It's deranged, but in a good way. Don't buy one if you want a relaxing day out, but do buy one if you want a windy blast up your trouser legs and the thrill of controlling a car with more power than grip. Mugen's Civic just shades it, though, as once you've coaxed

'It's a road car that became a race car that's now
a trackday car. Sounds like a horribly
confusing mix, but it's fabulous'

some heat into its tyres the chassis wakes up and turns you into Fabrizio Giovanardi.

Caterham is a master of the trackday breed, so it's no wonder its cars change so little year-on-year. If it ain't broke, why fix it? If price was a major factor in our selection criteria then the R300 would win hands down. It only misses the podium because there are three cars that gave us more of a thrill than the 175bhp Duratec engine could manage.

The Radical is an extraordinary machine and is thoroughly deserving of a place on the dais. It is the fastest road-legal car we've ever lapped at the West Circuit and I could have driven it

that hard all day. The only thing preventing it from taking the top-step laurels is the nagging thought that it's actually too fast for trackdays. You'd be permanently held up by slow stuff. Like supercars.

Two to go and it's a top pairing that has a very familiar ring to it from our earlier Car of the Year contest: Porsche GT3 versus Lotus. The result is a repeat too, the little car from Hethel winning by the tiniest of margins. Porsche can console itself with the knowledge that in the GT3 it has created the greatest all-rounder of the year, and were we to combine both eCoty and TCoty 09 it would comfortably have come

top. It's nothing short of brilliant and I reckon it actually performs even better on track than road. The lap time stands as a testament to that.

Its only problem was that it came up against a car that every single judge described as 'superb' in their assessment notes. Henry summed it up best when he said: 'It's a road car that became a race car that's now a trackday car. Sounds like a horribly confusing mix, but it's fabulous. It takes the habitability, finish and dimensions of the road car and adds in the dynamics and awesome gearbox of a race car.' A sweet victory for Lotus, then, because the 2-Eleven GT4 is our Track Car of the Year.

Circuit Guide: Bedford Autodrome

No racing takes place on this former WWII airbase, which means there's plenty of run-off. **Roger Green** *is your guide for an on-the-limit lap*

It's not been with us long and no racing takes place at the Autodrome, but it is already well established on the trackday scene. It may be flat and featureless, but it contains a huge variety of corners and has plenty of run-off, so if you want to really push the envelope, this is the place to do it. There are four individual circuits that can be run simultaneously or linked together in various combinations. Most popular for trackdays is the South-West layout, which combines the South and West circuits, so that's the one featured here, although the extra turns for the West Circuit (indicated by the dashed line) – as used by evo for all its track tests – are also covered.

HISTORY

The site of the Bedford Autodrome was originally an American airbase during World War II and later a Royal Aerospace development centre. Since August 1999 its main role has been as a corporate and private-individual entertainment venue run by Palmersport, where customers can get behind the wheel of a multitude of machines from Caterhams to Formula Palmer Audi single-seaters.

The four circuits (named after their appropriate compass orientations) are often hired by trackday companies, but Palmersport also runs its own trackdays.

GENERAL INFORMATION

Website: www.palmersport.com
Phone number: 01234 332 400
Address: Bedford Autodrome, Thurleigh Airfield Business Park, Thurleigh, Bedford, MK44 2YP
Circuit length (South-West): 2.8 miles
Circuit length (West): 1.85 miles
Noise limit: 101 dB static
Directions: Bedford Autodrome is located approximately 10 miles north of Bedford town centre and 20 miles east of Northampton, just off the A6 near Thurleigh.

PALMER CURVES

TOWER

O'ROUGE LEFT

PIF–PAF

BECKHAM ESSES

BANK

HANGAR HAIRPIN

CRAB

HARRIER 2

HARRIER 1

HARRIER I

THE FLICK

O'ROUGE RIGHT

Google

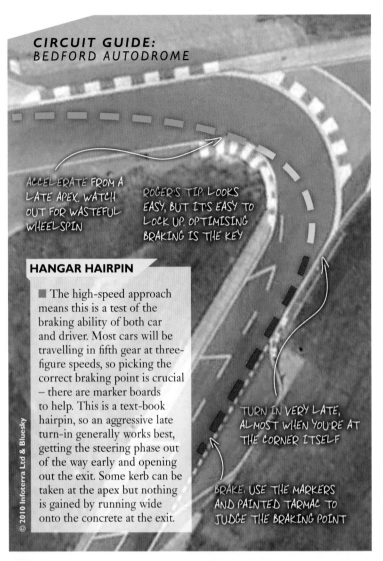

ACCELERATE FROM A LATE APEX. WATCH OUT FOR WASTEFUL WHEELSPIN

ROGER'S TIP: LOOKS EASY, BUT IT'S EASY TO LOCK UP. OPTIMISING BRAKING IS THE KEY

TURN IN VERY LATE, ALMOST WHEN YOU'RE AT THE CORNER ITSELF

BRAKE: USE THE MARKERS AND PAINTED TARMAC TO JUDGE THE BRAKING POINT

HANGAR HAIRPIN

■ The high-speed approach means this is a test of the braking ability of both car and driver. Most cars will be travelling in fifth gear at three-figure speeds, so picking the correct braking point is crucial – there are marker boards to help. This is a text-book hairpin, so an aggressive late turn-in generally works best, getting the steering phase out of the way early and opening out the exit. Some kerb can be taken at the apex but nothing is gained by running wide onto the concrete at the exit.

© 2010 Infoterra Ltd & Bluesky

PALMER CURVES

■ This is a technical sequence that puts the emphasis on both lateral grip and traction. A poor-handling car will struggle here. Turn left from the edge of the track and brake in a straight line right up to the first clipping point. If not coned it's possible to cut the corner a little as there's no kerb and this will help to open out the second part.

Bring the car over to the right slightly to open out the left section a little, but don't go too wide. Once on the second apex try to hug the white line for as long as possible to open out the final right-hander. You should be accelerating hard from the first apex, so don't worry if you can't hold the white line for long – it's better to let the car run wide than excessively scrub off speed.

By now the speed is really fast and it's often worth short-shifting into fourth before making the transition to the final right-hander. If you have the first parts right the line through the final section is obvious as the corner opens out. Get as close to the gutter as possible at both the apex and exit, but avoid the drain covers. And don't hold the car too tightly on the exit – this is the cause of many high-speed spins.

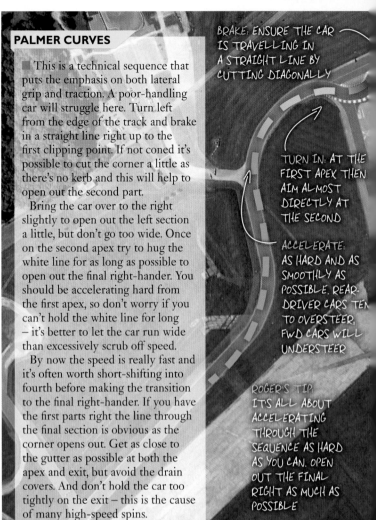

BRAKE: ENSURE THE CAR IS TRAVELLING IN A STRAIGHT LINE BY CUTTING DIAGONALLY

TURN IN: AT THE FIRST APEX THEN AIM ALMOST DIRECTLY AT THE SECOND

ACCELERATE: AS HARD AND AS SMOOTHLY AS POSSIBLE. REAR-DRIVER CARS TEND TO OVERSTEER, FWD CARS WILL UNDERSTEER

ROGER'S TIP: IT'S ALL ABOUT ACCELERATING THROUGH THE SEQUENCE AS HARD AS YOU CAN. OPEN OUT THE FINAL RIGHT AS MUCH AS POSSIBLE

PIF-PAF

■ This comes up fast after the exit of Palmer Curves and requires heavy braking and a two-gear drop. Formula cars and some lightweight specials can brake all the way through the left, but for most Pif-Paf should be taken in two parts. Ensure the pitch angle of the car is not too extreme on entry or the car will oversteer as you turn left. If you avoid that you can actually accelerate a little before braking again for the right, and it's possible to open things out by using some of the painted sections of track (don't go near them in the wet). The exit is a little bumpy and curves left. In anything but a big-power rear-wheel-drive machine you should be hard on the throttle here.

© 2010 Infoterra Ltd & Bluesky

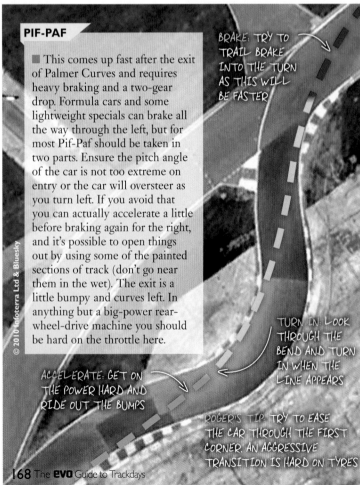

BRAKE: TRY TO TRAIL BRAKE INTO THE TURN AS THIS WILL BE FASTER

TURN IN: LOOK THROUGH THE BEND AND TURN IN WHEN THE LINE APPEARS

ACCELERATE: GET ON THE POWER HARD AND RIDE OUT THE BUMPS

ROGER'S TIP: TRY TO EASE THE CAR THROUGH THE FIRST CORNER. AN AGGRESSIVE TRANSITION IS HARD ON TYRES

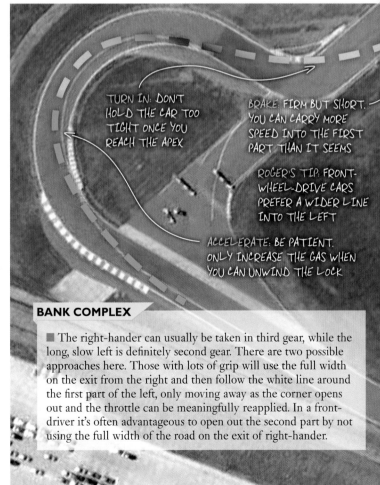

TURN IN: DON'T HOLD THE CAR TOO TIGHT ONCE YOU REACH THE APEX

BRAKE: FIRM BUT SHORT. YOU CAN CARRY MORE SPEED INTO THE FIRST PART THAN IT SEEMS

ROGER'S TIP: FRONT-WHEEL-DRIVE CARS PREFER A WIDER LINE INTO THE LEFT

ACCELERATE: BE PATIENT. ONLY INCREASE THE GAS WHEN YOU CAN UNWIND THE LOCK

BANK COMPLEX

■ The right-hander can usually be taken in third gear, while the long, slow left is definitely second gear. There are two possible approaches here. Those with lots of grip will use the full width on the exit from the right and then follow the white line around the first part of the left, only moving away as the corner opens out and the throttle can be meaningfully reapplied. In a front-driver it's often advantageous to open out the second part by not using the full width of the road on the exit of right-hander.

BECKHAM ESSES (WEST CIRCUIT ONLY)

■ Another big stop, but the line is quite simple and obvious. The throttle should be hard on from the first apex so you are gaining speed past the second.

ACCELERATE: YOU SHOULD BE ON FULL POWER FROM THE FIRST APEX

ROGER'S TIP: ENTRY SPEED IS CRUCIAL. EASY TO BE TOO SLOW OR TOO FAST

TURN IN ONCE YOU CAN SEE THE FIRST APEX

BRAKE: HARD BRAKING. USE THE 'BRAKE' BOARD AS A GUIDE

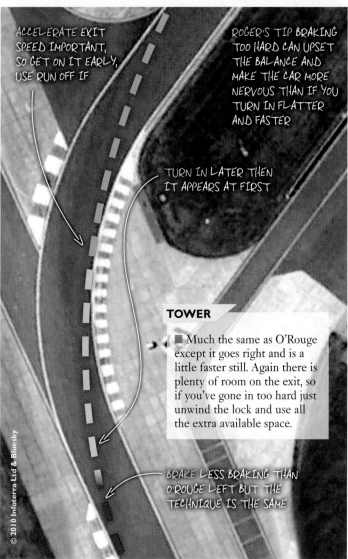

ACCELERATE EXIT SPEED IMPORTANT, SO GET ON IT EARLY, USE RUN OFF IF

ROGER'S TIP: BRAKING TOO HARD CAN UPSET THE BALANCE AND MAKE THE CAR MORE NERVOUS THAN IF YOU TURN IN FLATTER AND FASTER

TURN IN LATER THEN IT APPEARS AT FIRST

TOWER

■ Much the same as O'Rouge except it goes right and is a little faster still. Again there is plenty of room on the exit, so if you've gone in too hard just unwind the lock and use all the extra available space.

BRAKE: LESS BRAKING THAN O'ROUGE LEFT BUT THE TECHNIQUE IS THE SAME

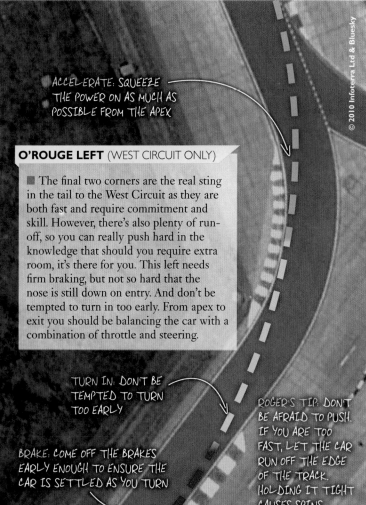

ACCELERATE: SQUEEZE THE POWER ON AS MUCH AS POSSIBLE FROM THE APEX

O'ROUGE LEFT (WEST CIRCUIT ONLY)

■ The final two corners are the real sting in the tail to the West Circuit as they are both fast and require commitment and skill. However, there's also plenty of run-off, so you can really push hard in the knowledge that should you require extra room, it's there for you. This left needs firm braking, but not so hard that the nose is still down on entry. And don't be tempted to turn in too early. From apex to exit you should be balancing the car with a combination of throttle and steering.

TURN IN: DON'T BE TEMPTED TO TURN TOO EARLY

BRAKE: COME OFF THE BRAKES EARLY ENOUGH TO ENSURE THE CAR IS SETTLED AS YOU TURN

ROGER'S TIP: DON'T BE AFRAID TO PUSH. IF YOU ARE TOO FAST, LET THE CAR RUN OFF THE EDGE OF THE TRACK. HOLDING IT TIGHT CAUSES SPINS

THE FLICK (SOUTH-WEST CIRCUIT ONLY)

■ A very fast approach into a very fast chicane. Use the marker boards as a braking reference and ensure you're off the brakes by the turn-in point. There is space to make errors, but ensure you use all the road on the exit before moving back to the right for Harrier 1.

ROGER'S TIP: TRY USING THE KERBS IF THEY DON'T UNSETTLE YOUR CAR

TURN IN: DON'T STEER TOO HARD. EASE THE CAR IN

ACCELERATE FROM THE FIRST APEX. USE FULL WIDTH ON EXIT

BRAKE: NEEDS TO BE FIRM, BUT SPEED STILL HIGH

CIRCUIT GUIDE:
BEDFORD AUTODROME

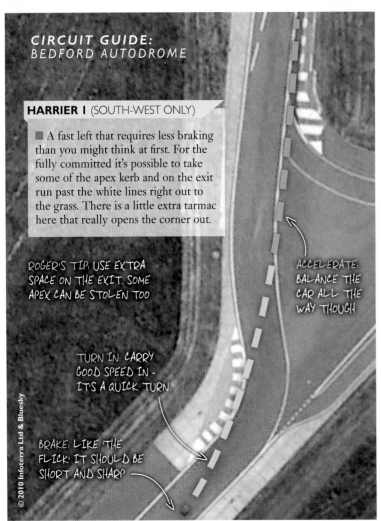

HARRIER 1 (SOUTH-WEST ONLY)

■ A fast left that requires less braking than you might think at first. For the fully committed it's possible to take some of the apex kerb and on the exit run past the white lines right out to the grass. There is a little extra tarmac here that really opens the corner out.

ROGER'S TIP: USE EXTRA SPACE ON THE EXIT. SOME APEX CAN BE STOLEN TOO

ACCELERATE: BALANCE THE CAR ALL THE WAY THOUGH

TURN IN: CARRY GOOD SPEED IN - ITS A QUICK TURN

BRAKE: LIKE THE FLICK IT SHOULD BE SHORT AND SHARP

© 2010 Infoterra Ltd & Bluesky

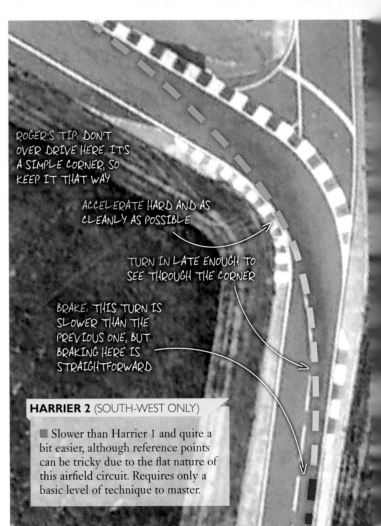

ROGER'S TIP: DON'T OVER DRIVE HERE. ITS A SIMPLE CORNER, SO KEEP IT THAT WAY

ACCELERATE HARD AND AS CLEANLY AS POSSIBLE

TURN IN LATE ENOUGH TO SEE THROUGH THE CORNER

BRAKE: THIS TURN IS SLOWER THAN THE PREVIOUS ONE, BUT BRAKING HERE IS STRAIGHTFORWARD

HARRIER 2 (SOUTH-WEST ONLY)

■ Slower than Harrier 1 and quite a bit easier, although reference points can be tricky due to the flat nature of this airfield circuit. Requires only a basic level of technique to master.

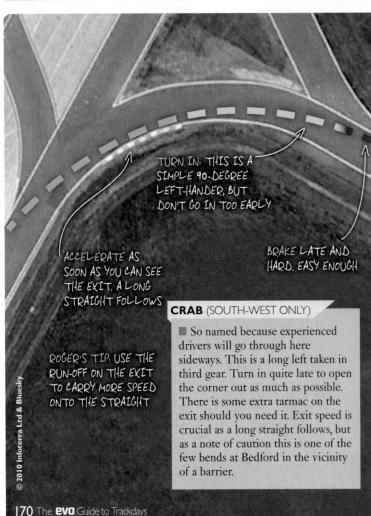

TURN IN: THIS IS A SIMPLE 90-DEGREE LEFT-HANDER, BUT DON'T GO IN TOO EARLY

ACCELERATE AS SOON AS YOU CAN SEE THE EXIT. A LONG STRAIGHT FOLLOWS

BRAKE LATE AND HARD. EASY ENOUGH

ROGER'S TIP: USE THE RUN-OFF ON THE EXIT TO CARRY MORE SPEED ONTO THE STRAIGHT

CRAB (SOUTH-WEST ONLY)

■ So named because experienced drivers will go through here sideways. This is a long left taken in third gear. Turn in quite late to open the corner out as much as possible. There is some extra tarmac on the exit should you need it. Exit speed is crucial as a long straight follows, but as a note of caution this is one of the few bends at Bedford in the vicinity of a barrier.

© 2010 Infoterra Ltd & Bluesky

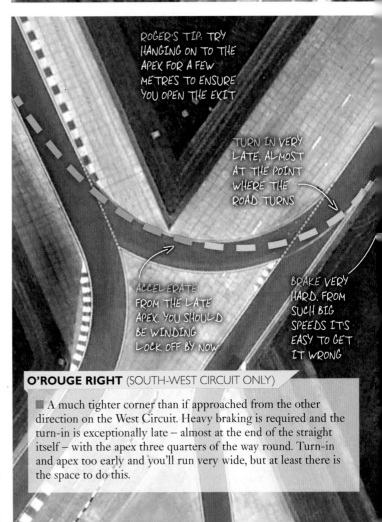

ROGER'S TIP: TRY HANGING ON TO THE APEX FOR A FEW METRES TO ENSURE YOU OPEN THE EXIT

TURN IN VERY LATE, ALMOST AT THE POINT WHERE THE ROAD TURNS

ACCELERATE FROM THE LATE APEX. YOU SHOULD BE WINDING LOCK OFF BY NOW

BRAKE VERY HARD. FROM SUCH BIG SPEEDS ITS EASY TO GET IT WRONG

O'ROUGE RIGHT (SOUTH-WEST CIRCUIT ONLY)

■ A much tighter corner than if approached from the other direction on the West Circuit. Heavy braking is required and the turn-in is exceptionally late – almost at the end of the straight itself – with the apex three quarters of the way round. Turn-in and apex too early and you'll run very wide, but at least there is the space to do this.

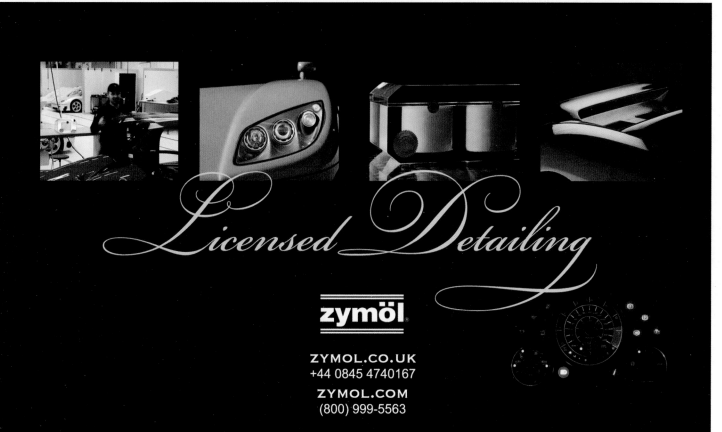

3 steps to trackday heaven

*Thinking about optimising your car for trackdays? There are plenty of ways to go about it, and it needn't cost a fortune. In fact there are modifications to suit any budget, and you might even like to get stuck in yourself. **Ralph Hosier** explains how to prep your car for a successful trackday*

STEP 1 ESSENTIAL PREPARATION

Of course you don't have to spend a fortune on modifications to run your car round a track – many cars have more than enough performance straight out of the box – but the fact that it will spend much of the day flat-out means that there are a few essential jobs to do to stop it melting or falling apart.

The first piece of preparation work is a thorough service, including gearbox, differential, brakes and the cooling system, using fluids more tuned to harsh use (for example, Castrol Edge engine oil).

Depending on the car it may be best to run the oil level towards the low mark on the dipstick to prevent 'pull over' (where oil gets into the inlet manifold at high revs), or towards the top end if the engine is prone to surge (where the oil in the sump sloshes away from the pick-up pipe). Find out from a specialist or look on an owners' club forum. Either way, check the level after each run, as consumption will be higher than in normal road use.

Every critical component should be inspected, because even on modern cars bolts and clips can become loose. Older cars, including popular trackday-car choices such as the BMW E30 and original Golf GTI, need a very thorough check over because the twin demons of time and vibration will have reached deep into the car's bowels and tried to loosen everything. It's essential to check the tightness of brake caliper bolts, engine mounts, gearbox mounts, the exhaust, subframe mountings, the steering rack and all the suspension fixings.

Sometimes when you get a new (to you) car you start to discover that parts have been repaired incorrectly, bolts mis-threaded or fixings broken off. If a job has been botched in the past the best course of action is often to completely remove the part and check it over before re-fitting it properly.

Make sure the tyres are in good condition. If it's your first trackday then the chances are you won't wear them down very much, but it's still important to have some tread left at the end of the day. Tyre pressures are critical to the way a car handles, and a lot of fine tuning can be done to suit your style, for example changing the amount of under or oversteer by adjusting the relative traction front and rear. The front suspension 'toe' angle can also be tweaked to adjust the turn-in (the initial reaction to a steering input). Again, ask the experts. Most road cars are set to be slightly slow to react – a bit safer for the average driver. A smidgeon of toe-in usually sharpens up the response but can make the car a bit more twitchy.

Initially there's no need to take the spare wheel out – the weight penalty is usually negligible anyway – but make sure the wheel, jack and any tools are very securely strapped in.

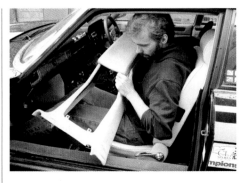

Below left: a thorough service should be your starting point. Above: removing extraneous trim will reduce weight! Below right: be particularly thorough when checking components such as brakes on older cars

STEP 2 BASIC MODIFICATIONS

A few tweaks can make the world of difference to a car's on-track performance, and for £500 to £1000 there is quite a lot than can be done without breaking the bank.

Without doubt the first modification is to fit new track-biased tyres. You might not need the stickiest rubber in the world, just something consistent and reliable so you can have fun sliding the car all day long. Remember that tyres harden with age, so avoid using any that are more than about three years old.

Before going any further the best thing to do is to try the car on track as it is. Then you will end up with a list of things to change that are tailored to your own needs rather than those of a random collection of forum users or someone competing in a race series that you aren't in. Remember there is no point changing things that have no effect on your driving pleasure.

The next thing to note – and this may surprise you – is that there is absolutely no point tuning the engine. The unique selling point of a trackday is that it is safe (relatively) for everyone to drive fast all day long. This is achieved by having very strict rules that prevent cars coming together, and racing other cars is forbidden. So getting more power out of the engine gives you no advantage and only serves to reduce reliability and cost money that would be better spent elsewhere.

Stripping out unnecessary weight is the next step, as this will improve performance and give

the brakes and suspension an easier time too. But don't get too hung up on it at this stage. As a rough guide removing less than 10 per cent of the car's original weight is not noticeable, so what's the point? For instance, most door cards weigh next to nothing, but many folk remove them and then find they have no way of shutting the door. Another frequent casualty are the door mirrors, but even motorised ones weigh less than 2kg and removing them will make no appreciable difference to performance but will make it more difficult to see cars coming up to overtake. So just remove things you really don't need, like the back seat, spare wheel, carpet and sound-deadening material. Some people swap to a smaller battery, saving several kilos (the standard one will start the car in Arctic conditions, but that's not relevant to a trackday).

Various things can be done to improve reliability, such as modifying the fan and cooling system. Engine-driven fans can become unreliable at constant high engine speeds, so they can be removed and a good quality electric fan used instead. This also helps when you come into the pits, as all the heat that has soaked into the engine and exhaust requires extra cooling at low speed. Sometimes heat builds up under the bonnet as there is nowhere for the hot air to escape. In this case a few well-placed vents or simply securely propping the bonnet open can save the day.

Brakes take a hammering on track and heat is their biggest enemy. The easiest modification is to fit race-spec brake pads (such as EBC Red or Yellow) and just as importantly racing brake fluid (such as Motul RBF600), which will really help prevent fade. But remember,

'Any engine modifications should be checked and tuned at a reputable rolling road to optimise performance and reliability'

racing fluid has to be changed more often than ordinary road fluid, possibly twice a year. It is also common to remove any stone guards and other obstructions to free airflow around the brake discs. If after that you still have fade then ducting fresh air from the front of the car using heat-resistant tubing pointing at the middle of the discs may help; some people get fresh air in by removing the foglights from the front spoiler and ducting the tube into the hole.

You might consider fitting a good seat and harnesses to hold you in securely as you throw the car about the track. Being more directly connected to the car gives a better feel, but seats are a very personal thing so it's worth trying a few out before buying.

Lowering the car will make a big difference to handling, but different suspension designs respond in different ways. For instance, semi-trailing arms (as fitted on the rear of most

BMWs) increase wheel camber as they move up. At extreme travel this can reduce traction because the tyre is running on its inside edge all the time. It's worth trawling the forums and specialist websites to get a feel for what is a good ride height for your car. Firmer springs can reduce roll, but going too hard will make the car skittish over rougher tarmac. Good adjustable dampers are more useful as they can be tuned to suit different circuits.

Top: uprated oil cooler (here fitted externally) will improve reliability; also note air intake in place of headlight. Below: heavy standard seats can be replaced with lighter, more supportive race-style items (left)

Although I have suggested the engine should not be tuned, there is something to be said for fitting a sporty exhaust and air intake. This may make a very small improvement to power but a single-box exhaust will weigh less and a cold-air intake kit can improve power slightly and tidy up the engine bay a bit. And, of course, if nothing else will make your car *sound* faster! But watch those noise limits – there's nothing more frustrating than being turned away for noise.

STEP 3. THE ULTIMATE TRACKDAY WEAPON

The next stage for the suspension is to build in more adjustment. Adapting the camber, for instance, changes the way the tyre tread is presented to the ground when cornering. For drivers pushing harder into corners, stiffer springs and dampers will be needed. Taking even more of the compliance out, by replacing soft rubber bushes with harder polyurethane or metal spherical joints, will control the wheels more accurately.

Tyre choices can also be expanded once the suspension control is improved. Full race compounds have substantially more grip than sports road tyres but wear out faster. You might even consider slicks, but be warned that the grip they offer is phenomenal and so the cornering forces transmitted through the suspension are much higher and every component must be up to the job. Slicks also show up your brakes and engine too…

Bigger brakes not only provide greater stopping force but also improve pedal feel and controllability. The key factors are the piston area and the distance between caliper and hub, so larger calipers and bigger diameter discs are the order of the day. Grooves on the disc can improve bite but only a few are needed. Cross drilling aids cooling but can cause cracking. As the braking force is improved the balance between front and rear may need to be adjusted, so a bias valve or adjustable pedal box can restore the balance and allow you to tune it to suit the conditions on the day.

For the ultimate trackday monster you will need a suitably monstrous engine, either by tuning the existing engine or by transplanting in something considerably bigger. Turbo engines can be tuned fairly easy by increasing boost, but the engine may need major surgery to cope with the extra forces. Any mods should be checked and tuned at a reputable rolling road to optimise performance and reliability.

As acceleration increases so does the speed of gearchanges, so a tougher and slicker gearbox becomes a necessity, as does a more durable race clutch. More power and less weight means the tyres are more likely to spin up. A limited-slip differential can solve this. A torque-biasing differential puts the most force on the wheel with the most grip, but viscous or plate type diffs work very well too.

The weight loss programme now becomes more important, so door innards and even

Above: quality tyres will help give consistent handling, but make sure they're still legal if you're driving home

things like the boot floor can be cut out and glass replaced with polycarbonate. The dashboard can be replaced by a simple set of race clocks set in a small pod. The interior heater unit can be ditched in favour of anti-mist treatment on the windscreen and a small electric fan to cool your adrenalin. Even the wiring can be stripped of unused cables, saving several kilos. These steps can add up to nearly a third of the car's weight.

Collisions are very rare on trackdays but

many people fit a full roll cage. However, this in itself brings new dangers. Hard steel bars next to your head can result in severe injuries unless you are very tightly secured in the seat and wearing a good helmet. If the car is going to be used on the road without a helmet then a cage should be avoided. Tubes near the driver's head must be fitted with proper motorsport cage padding – soft foam or pipe lagging is utterly useless. Cheap aluminium 'show' cages offer no crash protection and can fold into lethal razor-sharp edges. If you are going to fit a cage then make it an FIA-approved one.

Tube-work also helps stiffen the chassis. The higher forces experienced on track twist a car much more than it was designed for and sometimes suspension mounting points can move slightly, upsetting the handling. Cars with strut-type suspension can benefit from strut braces to sharpen up the response. Connecting a roll cage to the suspension pick-up points makes for a very stiff structure.

Whatever modifications you choose, make sure the work is to the highest standard – it could be a matter of life and death. But also make sure the car you end up with makes you happy. This is all about having fun, after all.

Left: fitting harder polyurethane suspension bushes will improve wheel control. Below: a roll cage can stiffen your car's bodyshell and improve handling as well as safety – but it may not be wise to go this far if you regularly use your car on the road

Circuit Guide: Rockingham

*The UK's newest major racetrack offers more than just its high-speed oval — trackday-goers get to enjoy its involving infield circuit, as **Roger Green** explains*

Built originally for IndyCar racing, Rockingham is dominated by the oval track and the huge grandstands that surround it, but the infield circuit (which runs anti-clockwise) has plenty of challenging turns for the keen trackday driver.

HISTORY

Constructed on industrial wasteland left from a steel works, the Rockingham Motor Speedway opened in January 2001 and was the first ground-up, purpose-built new racetrack in the UK since Brooklands almost a century earlier.

Rockingham soon earned the title of the fastest circuit in Europe when, in September of its first year, Tony Kanaan lapped the 1.5-mile oval course in his Champ Car in 24.719 seconds – that's an average lap speed of 215.4mph!

The infield circuit (known as the International Circuit) is nowhere near as fast, despite using Turn 1 of the oval. Formula Three, BTCC and British GT all hold rounds of their championships at Rockingham and trackdays are run here regularly.

GENERAL INFORMATION

Website: www.rockingham.co.uk
Phone number: 01536 500500
Address: Rockingham Motor Speedway, Mitchell Road, Corby, Northamptonshire, NN17 5AF
Circuit length: 1.94 miles
Noise limit: 105 dB static
Directions: Being just outside Corby, Rockingham is centrally located and signposted all the way from the A14 midway between the M1 and A1

TURN 4 CHICANE

TURN 1

GRACELANDS

PIF PAF

CHAPMAN CURVE

DEENE

TARZAN

YENTWOOD

Google

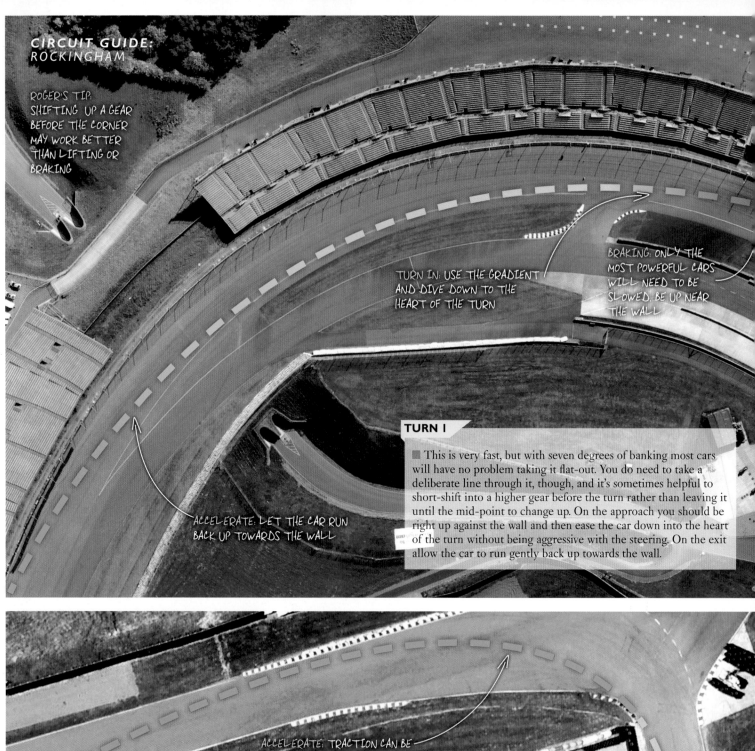

ROGER'S TIP:
SHIFTING UP A GEAR
BEFORE THE CORNER
MAY WORK BETTER
THAN LIFTING OR
BRAKING

TURN IN: USE THE GRADIENT
AND DIVE DOWN TO THE
HEART OF THE TURN

BRAKING: ONLY THE
MOST POWERFUL CARS
WILL NEED TO BE
SLOWED. BE UP NEAR
THE WALL

ACCELERATE: LET THE CAR RUN
BACK UP TOWARDS THE WALL

TURN 1

■ This is very fast, but with seven degrees of banking most cars will have no problem taking it flat-out. You do need to take a deliberate line through it, though, and it's sometimes helpful to short-shift into a higher gear before the turn rather than leaving it until the mid-point to change up. On the approach you should be right up against the wall and then ease the car down into the heart of the turn without being aggressive with the steering. On the exit allow the car to run gently back up towards the wall.

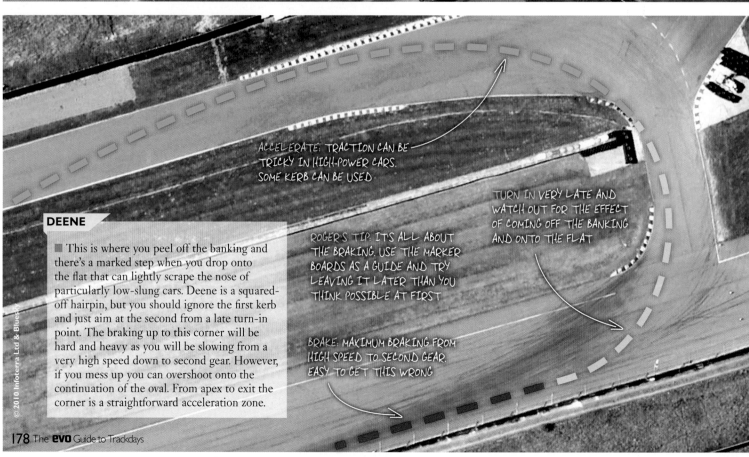

ACCELERATE: TRACTION CAN BE
TRICKY IN HIGH-POWER CARS.
SOME KERB CAN BE USED

TURN IN VERY LATE AND
WATCH OUT FOR THE EFFECT
OF COMING OFF THE BANKING
AND ONTO THE FLAT

DEENE

■ This is where you peel off the banking and there's a marked step when you drop onto the flat that can lightly scrape the nose of particularly low-slung cars. Deene is a squared-off hairpin, but you should ignore the first kerb and just aim at the second from a late turn-in point. The braking up to this corner will be hard and heavy as you will be slowing from a very high speed down to second gear. However, if you mess up you can overshoot onto the continuation of the oval. From apex to exit the corner is a straightforward acceleration zone.

ROGER'S TIP: IT'S ALL ABOUT
THE BRAKING. USE THE MARKER
BOARDS AS A GUIDE AND TRY
LEAVING IT LATER THAN YOU
THINK POSSIBLE AT FIRST

BRAKE: MAXIMUM BRAKING FROM
HIGH SPEED TO SECOND GEAR.
EASY TO GET THIS WRONG

ACCELERATE: THE KERB ON THE OUTSIDE CAN BE USED TO OPEN OUT THE EXIT

TURN IN: THE LINE IS QUITE OBVIOUS FOR THIS 90-DEGREE RIGHT HANDER

YENTWOOD

■ It's easy to remember the corner names at Rockingham because they're written on large signs on the tyre walls. On paper this looks like a simple 90-degree right, but the road drops a little on the approach adding a small twist. However, the late turn and tight apex will see you right. Let the car run wide on the exit; use all of the road.

ROGER'S TIP: ITS ONLY A SHORT RUN TO THE NEXT TURN BUT THE EXIT IS IMPORTANT AS ITS UPHILL

BRAKING: LOCKING UP IS EASY HERE AS THE TRACK HEADS DOWNHILL

© 2010 Infoterra Ltd & Bluesky

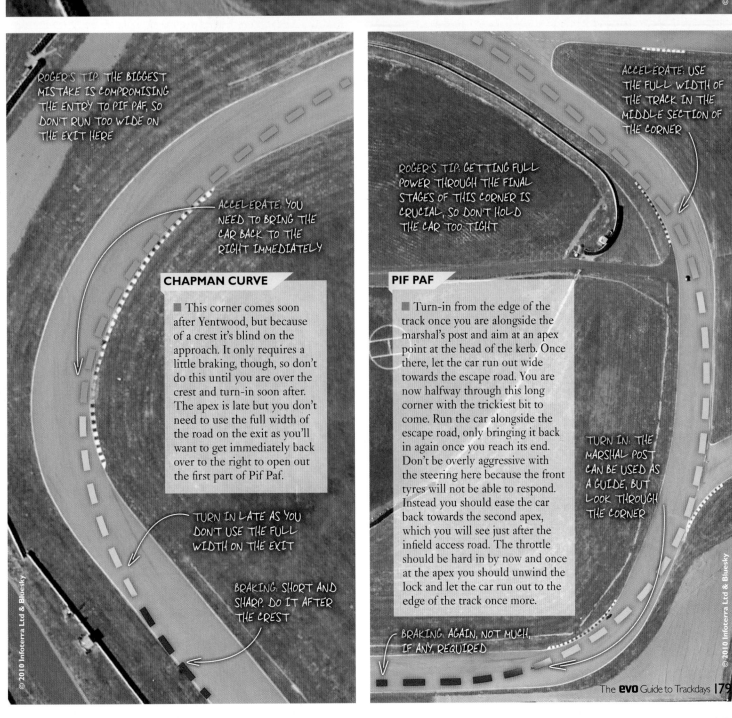

ROGER'S TIP: THE BIGGEST MISTAKE IS COMPROMISING THE ENTRY TO PIF PAF, SO DON'T RUN TOO WIDE ON THE EXIT HERE

ACCELERATE: YOU NEED TO BRING THE CAR BACK TO THE RIGHT IMMEDIATELY

ACCELERATE: USE THE FULL WIDTH OF THE TRACK IN THE MIDDLE SECTION OF THE CORNER

ROGER'S TIP: GETTING FULL POWER THROUGH THE FINAL STAGES OF THIS CORNER IS CRUCIAL, SO DON'T HOLD THE CAR TOO TIGHT

CHAPMAN CURVE

■ This corner comes soon after Yentwood, but because of a crest it's blind on the approach. It only requires a little braking, though, so don't do this until you are over the crest and turn-in soon after. The apex is late but you don't need to use the full width of the road on the exit as you'll want to get immediately back over to the right to open out the first part of Pif Paf.

PIF PAF

■ Turn-in from the edge of the track once you are alongside the marshal's post and aim at an apex point at the head of the kerb. Once there, let the car run out wide towards the escape road. You are now halfway through this long corner with the trickiest bit to come. Run the car alongside the escape road, only bringing it back in again once you reach its end. Don't be overly aggressive with the steering here because the front tyres will not be able to respond. Instead you should ease the car back towards the second apex, which you will see just after the infield access road. The throttle should be hard in by now and once at the apex you should unwind the lock and let the car run out to the edge of the track once more.

TURN IN: THE MARSHAL POST CAN BE USED AS A GUIDE, BUT LOOK THROUGH THE CORNER

TURN IN LATE AS YOU DON'T USE THE FULL WIDTH ON THE EXIT

BRAKING: SHORT AND SHARP. DO IT AFTER THE CREST

BRAKING: AGAIN, NOT MUCH, IF ANY, REQUIRED

© 2010 Infoterra Ltd & Bluesky

© 2010 Infoterra Ltd & Bluesky

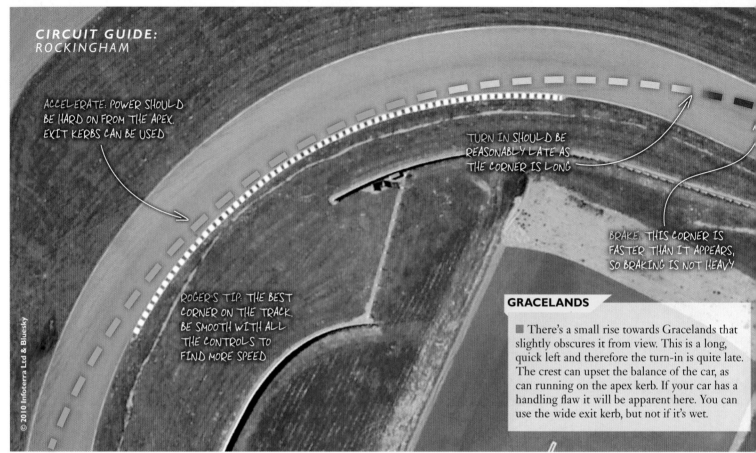

ACCELERATE: POWER SHOULD BE HARD ON FROM THE APEX. EXIT KERBS CAN BE USED

TURN IN SHOULD BE REASONABLY LATE AS THE CORNER IS LONG

BRAKE: THIS CORNER IS FASTER THAN IT APPEARS, SO BRAKING IS NOT HEAVY

ROGER'S TIP: THE BEST CORNER ON THE TRACK. BE SMOOTH WITH ALL THE CONTROLS TO FIND MORE SPEED

GRACELANDS

■ There's a small rise towards Gracelands that slightly obscures it from view. This is a long, quick left and therefore the turn-in is quite late. The crest can upset the balance of the car, as can running on the apex kerb. If your car has a handling flaw it will be apparent here. You can use the wide exit kerb, but not if it's wet.

© 2010 Infoterra Ltd & Bluesky

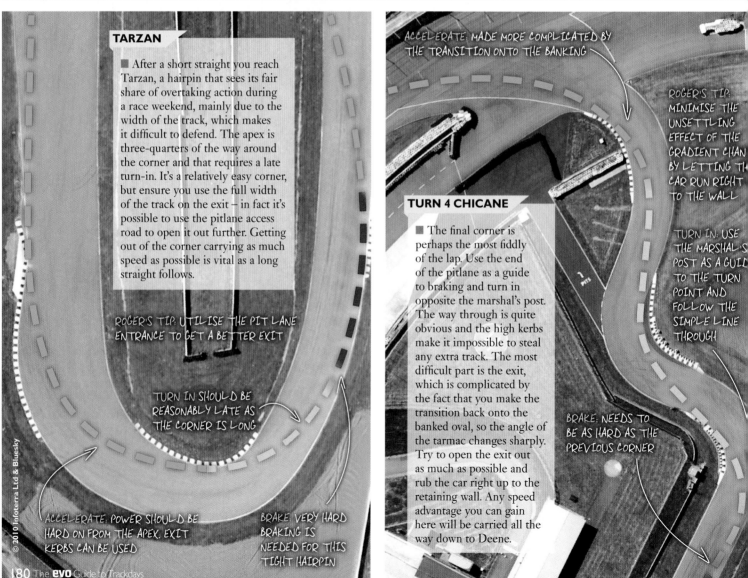

TARZAN

■ After a short straight you reach Tarzan, a hairpin that sees its fair share of overtaking action during a race weekend, mainly due to the width of the track, which makes it difficult to defend. The apex is three-quarters of the way around the corner and that requires a late turn-in. It's a relatively easy corner, but ensure you use the full width of the track on the exit – in fact it's possible to use the pitlane access road to open it out further. Getting out of the corner carrying as much speed as possible is vital as a long straight follows.

ROGER'S TIP: UTILISE THE PIT LANE ENTRANCE TO GET A BETTER EXIT

TURN IN SHOULD BE REASONABLY LATE AS THE CORNER IS LONG

ACCELERATE: POWER SHOULD BE HARD ON FROM THE APEX. EXIT KERBS CAN BE USED

BRAKE: VERY HARD BRAKING IS NEEDED FOR THIS TIGHT HAIRPIN

ACCELERATE: MADE MORE COMPLICATED BY THE TRANSITION ONTO THE BANKING

ROGER'S TIP: MINIMISE THE UNSETTLING EFFECT OF THE GRADIENT CHAN BY LETTING TH CAR RUN RIGHT TO THE WALL

TURN IN: USE THE MARSHAL'S POST AS A GUID TO THE TURN POINT AND FOLLOW THE SIMPLE LINE THROUGH

TURN 4 CHICANE

■ The final corner is perhaps the most fiddly of the lap. Use the end of the pitlane as a guide to braking and turn in opposite the marshal's post. The way through is quite obvious and the high kerbs make it impossible to steal any extra track. The most difficult part is the exit, which is complicated by the fact that you make the transition back onto the banked oval, so the angle of the tarmac changes sharply. Try to open the exit out as much as possible and rub the car right up to the retaining wall. Any speed advantage you can gain here will be carried all the way down to Deene.

BRAKE: NEEDS TO BE AS HARD AS THE PREVIOUS CORNER

© 2010 Infoterra Ltd & Bluesky

Circuit Guide: Best of the rest

The venues covered in our full circuit guides aren't the only places in the UK where you can push your car to the limit. **Roger Green** *looks at some alternatives*

PEMBREY

■ It may be located right off the end of the M4 and it may not look particularly glamorous when you arrive at this bleak-looking former airfield, but don't let that you put you off. Pembrey is a high-speed, action-packed buzz with a couple of hairpins thrown in for good measure. Its short, 1.5-mile loop makes it ideal for both novices and experts alike and trackdays are run there on a regular basis.

GENERAL INFORMATION
Website: www.barc.net/venues/pembrey
Phone number: 01554 891042
Address: Pembrey Motor Racing Circuit, Pembrey, Llanelli, Carmarthenshire, South Wales, SA16 0HX

KNOCKHILL

■ Scotland's National Motorsport Centre is a rare thing in that it isn't formed from a former airbase. Instead it was built in the '70s by a sheep farmer who loved motorcycling around one of his fields, so unlike many of the circuits in the UK, Knockhill is heavily undulating. Someone once described it as being like a normal circuit screwed up and thrown against a mountainside, and that pretty much sums it up.

It's short – a lap is just 1.3 miles – but what it lacks in length it more than makes up for in action. Being the only true circuit in Scotland, it's packed with events and in the summer months track evenings are run as well as full trackdays.

GENERAL INFORMATION
Website: www.knockhill.com
Phone number: 01383 723337
Address: Knockhill Racing Circuit, by Dunfermline, Fife, Scotland, KY12 9TF

MALLORY PARK

■ Originally a pony trotting track, Mallory has had a varied life, and although it doesn't have the high profile of other UK circuits, it makes a great venue for a trackday. In fact its short, simple layout is ideal for novices, while there's plenty of technical bits to keep experienced drivers absorbed too.

Tarmac was first laid in 1955 by Clive Wormleighton, a local builder who had dreams of seeing racing in his back yard. Situated in a natural amphitheatre, it soon became popular with spectators, attracting crowds in excess of 50,000 people for motorbike meetings. The layout has barely changed since, and its 1.35-mile lap includes one of the longest corners you'll find anywhere.

Website: www.mallorypark.co.uk
Phone number: 01455 842931
Address: Mallory Park Racing Circuit, Kirkby Mallory, Leicestershire, LE9 7QE

ANGLESEY

■ Also known as Trac Mon and Ty Croes, Anglesey was completely redeveloped in 2007 and the new 2.1-mile circuit is completely different to the original mile-long course, although it still sits on top of cliffs overlooking the sea and the hills of Snowdonia.

Using the access roads of a former army radar and missile base, Anglesey can run in four different configurations, but it is the full International layout that is most commonly used for the 50 trackdays that are now held here every year. In addition to these, Anglesey also hosts around a dozen race meetings for cars and a similar number for bikes.

GENERAL INFORMATION
Website: www.angleseycircuit.com
Phone number: 01407 811 400
Address: Anglesey Circuit, Ty Croes, Anglesey, Wales, LL63 5TF

SNETTERTON

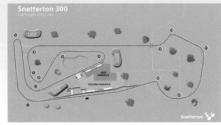

■ Currently undergoing redevelopment, Snetterton will be relaunched in 2011 as an international-standard venue with a track length increased to almost three miles. There will be three layouts, but we are told that all will retain Snetterton's current character, and that's good news, because although the track is predominately flat, it has a great mix of fast and technical turns. The two long straights remain, as does the nerve-jangling first turn, Riches, and the Esses, while Coram is being extended – but they will all be given new names by the time the circuit re-opens in the spring.

GENERAL INFORMATION
Website: www.motorsportvision.co.uk
Phone number: 01953 887303
Address: Snetterton Circuit, Norwich, Norfolk, NR16 2JU

AIRFIELDS

■ The beauty of airfield events is that there is usually a huge amount of run-off space, so it makes them ideal for novices who are worried about making mistakes. However, experienced drivers won't find them as rewarding, particularly as the course is often marked out by cones. Other common issues are increased tyre wear from the more abrasive surface and a higher likelihood of stone-chips to bodywork. That said, they're cheap and provide a great place to explore the handling limits of your car in safety.

AIRFIELD VENUES
Bruntingthorpe, Leicestershire
Abingdon, Oxfordshire
Crail, Scotland
Elvington, York
Woodbridge, Suffolk
Barkston Heath, Lincolnshire
Blyton Park, Lincolnshire
Keevil, Wiltshire
Colerne, Bath
Hullavington, Wiltshire

Track Car
of the
Year

We return to Cadwell Park to find out which of these
five new trackday cars from 2010 is most worthy
of your attention. Roger Green reports

SPECIFICATION

Ginetta G40
Engine In-line 4-cyl, 1800cc
Power 150bhp @ 6000rpm
Torque 130lb ft @ 4500rpm
Weight 850kg
Power-to-weight 179bhp/ton
0-60mph 6.5sec (est)
Top speed 135mph (est)
Price as tested £29,400

Pictures Matt Howell

SPECIFICATION

Caterham Superlight R400
Engine In-line 4-cyl, 1999cc
Power 210bhp @ 7800rpm
Torque 152lb ft @ 5750rpm
Weight 525kg
Power-to-weight 406bhp/ton
0-60mph 3.8sec (est)
Top speed 140mph (est)
Price as tested £37,140

SPECIFICATION

Lotus Exige S RGB Special Edition
Engine In-line 4-cyl, 1796cc, supercharger
Power 257bhp @ 8000rpm
Torque 174lb ft @ 6000rpm
Weight 890kg
Power-to-weight 293bhp/ton
0-60mph 4.0sec (claimed)
Top speed 152mph (claimed)
Price as tested £41,950

SPECIFICATION

Westfield Sport Turbo UK225
Engine In-line 4-cyl, 1598cc, turbocharged
Power 225bhp @ 6250rpm
Torque 251lb ft @ 3600rpm
Weight 620kg
Power-to-weight 369bhp/ton
0-60mph 3.8sec (est)
Top speed 150mph (est)
Price as tested £25,649

SPECIFICATION

Chevron GR8
Engine In-line 4-cyl, 1996cc
Power 255bhp @ 7500rpm
Torque 200lb ft @ 6200rpm
Weight 635kg
Power-to weight 408bhp/ton
0-60mph 3.6sec (est)
Top speed 160mph (est)
Price as tested £64,625

The gods appear to be smiling on us. An eye-squintingly bright yellow blob has clambered its way above the horizon and the heavy overnight clouds have finally lifted to reveal a promisingly azure colour scheme. Long, autumnal shadows are now being thrown over Cadwell Park's small upper paddock, and on this leaf-strewn tarmac strip a motley collection of transporters are slowly disgorging their contents.

The captivating mix of emerging shapes dispels any lingering sleepiness. Laid out in front of us are the best new trackday machines of the year, while the UK's 'mini Nürburgring' is all ours until the sun completes its arc and

the Wolds become cloaked in darkness once more. Welcome to Track Car of the Year 2010. This should be fun.

Some of the shapes are completely new, some as familiar as your favourite pair of old race boots, but all are pure trackday machines. In past years we've included everything from hot hatches to supercars in our annual round-up, but we're breaking from tradition and keeping things pure this time.

This new format has effectively turned this test into a battle of the Brits, for no other country has such a large industry based around the thrill of circuit driving. All these machines are affordable, lightweight and way faster than road cars costing at least twice as much. They

are all produced with the sole aim of providing joy and entertainment by the bucket-load, irrespective of driver ability.

And speaking of ability, this year's judging panel can lay claim to victories in the 24-hour races at Le Mans and Daytona, race wins in the BTCC and a Nürburgring lap record. Sadly none of those achievements is mine, though I did once nearly win a race at Cadwell in a Radical SR8, so at least I know which way the track goes.

Which gives me some sort of advantage over Andy Wallace. He says he'll need a couple of sighting laps to refresh the memory banks as he hasn't been here since 1984. Mind you, the 1988 Le Mans winner did score his first

'All of these machines are affordable, lightweight

ever race win here in '81. 'This paddock was all grass back then, and I think I pitched my tent just there,' he says, pointing at where Phil Bennett is standing. 'Flat-out Phil' has more recent experience of Cadwell's twists and sharp elevation changes – in between his racing and Ring-record duties he used to treat **evo** trackday attendees to the fastest passenger rides of their life here.

We won't be setting any lap times today. Instead we'll be judging the cars purely on how entertaining they are to drive. Despite their vast experience, both Andy and Phil are looking forward to getting stuck in as much as I am, and the Chevron GR8 catches Phil's eye as it's lowered on the tail-lift. At close quarters

and way faster than road cars costing at least twice as much'

Top: Ginetta interior has an impressive finish. Above: Westfield's 1.6-litre turbocharged VXR engine. Right: Exige making its last TCOTY appearance. Below: Caterham and Westfield

it's smaller than I expected it to be – like it's been built to 7/8ths scale – but it looks every inch the hardcore racer. It is perhaps the most extreme of our group, although the equally diminutive Ginetta G40 alongside could well have something to say about that, particularly as it can also be raced by anyone in the Ginetta Junior Championship. As long as you're between 14 and 17 years of age, that is.

That pair look like they were designed with Cadwell's narrow track in mind, and our third contender won't have any problem with the lack of width either. The Lotus Exige is one of only two cars that were actually driven to the track this morning, and its highway useability is something we should exploit while we still can, for production of the Exige is about to come to an end (same goes for the Elise R and SC). Euro 5 emissions regulations are to blame. This Roger Becker special edition – named after the recently retired director of vehicle engineering who was instrumental in the development of the Exige and effectively defined the Lotus ride and handling we know and love today – is a final hurrah for the Series 2 car that has been part of these yearly tear-ups since 2004.

Lurking behind the Becker Special are two machines that have been winding up supercar owners since what seems like the dawn of time. Caterham has introduced R500 suspension and detailing to the R400, and since the 400 offers perhaps the best mix of power and handling of all the R cars, it should be in with a shot of top honours. Westfield may have something to say about that, however, and its latest contender, the Sport Turbo UK255, comes with turbocharged Vauxhall VXR power. Expect no punches to be pulled.

With the cars ready, it's time to put a lid on. The track is drying, but it's a slow process at this time of year and the greasy section under the shedding trees of Hall Bends and Barn looks particularly treacherous, so I plump for the only car here with ABS and traction control: the RB Exige. It's also fitted with the

'The Ginetta's grip is merciless. You end
up diving harder and harder into the
corners until the car starts to move'

fastest of the Toyota 1.8-litre options, the 257bhp supercharged 2ZZ unit, and comes fully specced-up with the Sport Pack, the Touring Pack and the Performance Pack (bringing, respectively, sharper handling, extra comfort and increased power), plus lightweight forged alloys and the structural shear panel fitted to the Cup car that increases the lateral stiffness of the rear subframe by 30 per cent.

I've made the right choice, for this Exige finds grip everywhere, even on the slippery bits. It's just soft enough to find bite through Hall Bends but doesn't roll or pitch excessively on the high-speed dry section of Coppice and Charlies. It's an intimate experience, with a superb level of feedback that soon gives you the confidence to wind the adjustable traction control off completely and drive right up to (and over) the limits – even in the quick, scary sections. It'll generally understeer first, but a well-timed lift will pivot the rear around the nose and then it can be balanced with a decent whack of supercharged power.

The real kick from the engine is towards the top end of the rev-range, but the power-band is wide enough to allow you to run a higher gear through a corner should you wish – a technique occasionally employed by Wallace. 'The shift from second to third is particularly vague and awkward,' he says after his laps, 'so in the end I left it in third for the tight stuff.' Other than that he is mainly very impressed. 'Despite being totally road-legal, with impressive fit and finish, it becomes a proper trackday car when you leave the pit lane,' he says. 'You can chuck it around and carry good speed into all the corners, and it's easy to adjust your line if you get too greedy. It's a shame the brake pedal is over-servoed, though.'

He's right. Modulation of the brakes is tricky and the ABS cuts in too early, partly due to the oversensitive nature of that servo. Bennett reckons the Exige is at its most compromised on the wet sections, which is where it should shine. In fact Phil has a bit of a downer on the Lotus. 'I know many are going to disagree, but the Exige isn't enough for me on track,' he says.

Above, from top: Exige's supercharged 1.8 has 257bhp; Green gets lidded up; Bennett checks out the R400's pedal box; Chevron's Cosworth 2-litre. Below: Wallace in the Exige. Right: Bennett enjoying the Caterham

'The Westfield's 225bhp is enough to turn this 620kg machine into something of a dragster'

'Its road ability may make it a good all-rounder, but out here it loses focus. I would prefer something that's more extreme, even if that means it's more uncomfortable on the road. The 260 Cup is closer to what I'm after.'

The Westfield Sport Turbo has also been designed predominantly for road use, with the odd trackday thrown in, so its set-up is a little softer than ideal, but perhaps surprisingly it still finds a friend in Phil – mainly because of the way its engine dominates proceedings. 'The motor is very strong but still driveable,' he says, 'and the noise reminds me of an old BTCC RS500! It'd be great to drive at night because there are flames on the overrun.'

The Sport Turbo's engine is a 1.6-litre Vauxhall VXR unit running 1.5bar of boost and producing 225bhp – enough to turn a 620kg

machine into something of a dragster. You fly through the gears so fast you often have to enter a corner a gear higher than you would in anything else, because otherwise you'd run out of revs before the exit. Unfortunately those corners can't be attacked quite as hard as you want, as the slack in the suspension has to be absorbed and the nose has to settle before you can get heavy with the throttle. Understeer is the order of the day, and getting aggressive with the power eventually results in an uncomfortably violent snap into oversteer. The set-up can be modified, though, because the car has fully independent, adjustable rose-jointed suspension, so it shouldn't be dismissed.

The Sport 225 does a different job to its Caterham counterpart – it's significantly cheaper and would leave the R400 for dead

in a straight line. But not over a lap. The Caterham is another old-stager but it has never stopped evolving. Originally the 400 had a Rover K-series motor, but today it comes with a 2-litre Duratec lump with more power (210bhp) and plenty of guts all the way across the rev-range. It now gets a dry sump as standard too, and this car is even fitted with keyless ignition, proving that Caterham will go to any length to save a gram or two. It also has the carbon dash and, more significantly, the dampers from the R500. The R400 was the other car driven to the track, although the hardy crew did have a windscreen and doors for the trip. Those have now been left in the paddock and replaced by a small aero screen.

Perfecting the set-up is crucial on a Caterham as it's so easy to alter the balance, and this one is just about spot-on. It means you can attack corners any way you like: fast and smooth, or for more fun just lob it into the turn and steer it on the ultra-keen throttle. Drive the R400 in a less outrageous manner and it'll turn in with the usual crispness and sit there in a state of neutrality as if waiting for you to decide what you want to do next. The common trait of high-speed understeer is evident through Coppice, but with warm tyres and a slug of nerve this fifth-gear climbing left-hander can be taken completely flat-out.

Phil seems to spend whole laps sideways, but that doesn't stop him finding some irritations. 'The pedal box could do with some work,' he reckons. 'The throttle and brake pedals have to be perfect as with this high state of engine tune the initial stab in heel-and-toe downchanges can choke the motor.' Andy didn't find the R400 quite as fluid as the Exige and also observes that it 'wouldn't be much fun in the rain unless you like getting drenched!'

You'd be okay inside the Ginetta in the rain, although unless you're pint-sized like Andy, clambering aboard the G40 is a tricky business. But it's worth it. There's a tangible sense of

integrity that was missing from the earlier G20. Like the bigger, more powerful G50, it feels like a bona fide race machine.

The driving position is perfect, the detailing and ergonomics impressive, particularly for a 'junior' car. It has a large brake pedal that's very firm underfoot, a sequential five-speed Quaife gearbox and is the only car of the group that arrived on slicks. At £29,400 as tested it's good value, but it won't be setting any outright lap records, for its motivational force comes from the ageing 1800cc Ford Zetec motor that's good for only 150bhp. That in itself wouldn't be a problem if the level of grip matched the power, but the Ginetta's hold is merciless. You end up diving harder and harder into the corners until the car starts to move, and then things get interesting because, as Andy says, 'without the power under your right foot you can get into a bit of a mess mid-corner if you need a stab of throttle to correct.' And he should know: our three-time Daytona winner spun it!

I'm convinced there's a very good chassis underneath it all, though. The overall balance is right, the steering is accurate and as a training tool it does a very good job – it's an easy

machine in which to perfect left-foot braking and it promotes smooth driving. However, as a trackday driver you feel restrained when you want to cut loose. You can have it with more power (Ginetta reckons it can handle 300bhp), but as it is even novice track drivers would soon want more. If you don't go for extra grunt, we'd recommend forgetting the slicks and fitting it with low-grip fuel-saving tyres instead.

The Chevron doesn't have a power issue, for in the middle of its steel-tube frame sits a Cosworth-tuned 2-litre Duratec lump pushing out 255bhp through a five-speed sequential Hewland transaxle. Created by Vin Malkie, the

'You're at the heart of the action in the Chevron. There's no

Top: Westfield is fast, but too soft for regular track work. Above: Bennett completes a hard day's driving (mostly sideways). Far left: Green, Wallace and Bennett discuss the finishing order. Bottom left: Chevron GR8 made a real impression. Left: GR8 interior is as basic as they come

slack and its engine envelopes you in its angry, rip-snorting bark'

aim with the GR8 was to produce a modern version of Chevron's iconic B8, and sitting aboard this similar-scale machine I think he's achieved it. I drove a B8 a few years back and from the driving seat the GR8 does feel very similar. Your backside is an inch from the deck and the view through the low-raked screen is almost identical. In fact the main difference is that your surroundings feel more substantial – where the delicate B8 felt about as robust as thin cardboard, the GR8 offers modern levels of security.

It's very bare inside, with nothing that adds weight, not even air-con or a heater; you get the feeling they'd have done away with the steering wheel too if they could have found another way of turning the car. The GR8 is comfortably the quickest of our group but it's also the most intense. You really are at the heart of the action – there's no slack in anything it does – and while the engine doesn't produce the most cultured soundtrack, it envelopes you in its angry, rip-snorting bark.

With a career built in Sportscars, Wallace feels at home in the GR8. 'It's very stable in the quick stuff,' he says. 'It feels like it's producing some useful downforce and there's good turn-in, excellent traction and it's very stable under braking.' Any negatives? 'On the wish list would be a flat-shift sensor.' (This would automatically ease the power on full-throttle clutchless upshifts for a smooth gearchange.)

Bennett concurs, but adds that the front end is so sharp that the rear occasionally has trouble keeping up. He'd prefer more linearity in the

throttle travel too. These are things that can be tailored to suit each individual driver, and the fact that our judges are getting picky is a sure sign that they're impressed.

It's time to choose a winner. The overall view is that this is a strong group of cars offering markedly different ways of scratching that trackday itch. Ultimately the Westfield and Lotus find themselves towards the bottom of the order, mainly due to the road compromise diluting the final level of detail and interaction. The Exige shades the Sport 225 because of the way it flows around a lap – its precision soon becomes addictive. However, if you want a cost-effective ballistic speed rush, look no further than the Westie. The Ginetta G40, meanwhile, is a frustrating experience, as a potentially great little car is being held back by a listless engine.

Up at the sharp end are the Caterham

and the Chevron, and while the R400 is the definitive expression of front-engine rear-drive entertainment, it doesn't offer anything new or significantly move the marque forward.

The Chevron does, though. It may be the most focused, the most expensive and perhaps a touch exuberant for trackdays, but the GR8 delivers on every level, from the way it looks to the way it sounds and goes. It's individual and manages to mix '60s retro with the demands of today's trackday driver. It was the most compelling contender in this year's test from the moment it was lowered onto the Cadwell tarmac, and it's our Track Car of the Year.

SEE VIDEO FROM TCOTY AT EVO.CO.UK

Circuit Guide:
Spa-Francorchamps

The Belgian circuit of Spa-Francorchamps is as challenging as it is spectacular and guaranteed to give you a memorable trackday. **Roger Green** *talks you through its famous turns*

A t around three hours from Calais, Spa is readily accessible for the UK track driver (often combined with a visit to the Ring), and it's well worth the effort. Widely viewed as one of the best circuits in the world, it's a high-speed challenge for F1 drivers and trackdayers alike.

HISTORY

One of the most revered circuits on the F1 calendar, Spa returned to prominence in 1983 after a 13-year sabbatical and was very different to the former 15km public road iteration previously raced on. In terms of distance, the new layout was less than half the length of the original, and yet the designers managed to retain the magic.

Today it's one of the fastest circuits you can drive on, but thanks to the addition of large areas of run-off tarmac it's far safer than it ever has been. Some say that has reduced the challenge, but the trackday driver visiting the circuit for the first time will still be blown away by the size of the place, the dramatic changes in gradient, and the legendary top-speed turns.

GENERAL INFORMATION

Website: www.spa-francorchamps.be/en/
Phone number: +32 87 293700
Address: Circuit of Spa Francorchamps, Route du Circuit, 55, B-4970 Francorchamps
Circuit length: 4.35 miles
Car rental: www.rsrnurburg.com
Directions: Take the Channel Tunnel. In France follow the A16/A18/A18 towards Brussels, then towards Aachen on the A3, then A27 for Trier/Verviers, taking exit 10 for Francorchamps.

STAVELOT

BLANCHIMONT

FAGNES

POUHO

RIVAGE

NO NAME

LES COOMBES

MALMEDY

LA SOURCE

BUS STOP

EAU ROUGE

Google

LA SOURCE

■ Use the 100m board as a guide to braking – the slight uphill nature helps to slow things down. Turn in late and follow the wall before running out wide and getting the power on as early as possible to maximise the run to Eau Rouge.

TURN IN VERY LATE.
AIM TOWARDS THE APEX
WALL ON THE INSIDE

BRAKE HARD AND
LATE. SLIGHTLY
UPHILL NATURE
ASSISTS

ACCELERATE. LET THE CAR
RUN OUT RIGHT TO THE EDGE.
MANAGE THE WHEELSPIN

ROGER'S TIP: TIME IS USUALLY LOST BY
BRAKING TOO EARLY OR IMPATIENCE WITH
THE THROTTLE ON EXIT. AVOID BOTH

Image © 2010 Aerodata International Surveys

Image © 2010 Aerodata International Surveys

EAU ROUGE

■ One of the greatest corners in the world with an epic approach. You accelerate steeply downhill out of La Source so that speed builds very quickly, and as you hug the pitwall the sequence looms large in front of you. Very few cars can take it flat and high-powered road cars require a firm brake, although very few require slowing before the initial left turn, which you make opposite the 50m board. You can use a little of the kerb on the left to open out the crucial right-hand section – begin to turn right here just after the road starts to climb.

The apex is a little later than you might imagine – if you clip too early you will run off the track as you crest the brow. This is less of an issue now there is a large tarmac run-off, unless it's raining (which it often is). Once you reach the correct apex you should straighten the car as you cross the brow – you cannot see where the track goes until you have crossed it, but you will soon get used to this. Exit halfway along the kerb on the right – you can run over this if you need to. Remember, the speed at which you reach this point is vital as the very long uphill Kemmel straight follows.

BRAKE: MAKE A
STRAIGHT LINE
AFTER THE LEFT
TURN AND DO ALL
THE BRAKING HERE

ACCELERATE: POWER ON OVER
THE CREST AND USE THE
FULL WIDTH OF THE TRACK

TURN IN: DON'T APEX
TOO EARLY. TAKE TIME
BEFORE BUILDING UP
SPEED AS ITS BLIND

ROGER'S TIP:
MAXIMISING SPEED THROUGH
AND OUT OF EAU ROUGE IS
CRUCIAL AS A VERY LONG
UPHILL RUN FOLLOWS. BE
BRAVE BUT NOT AGGRESSIVE

ROGER'S TIP: EXPERIMENT WITH HOW WIDE YOU CAN RUN IN THE MID SECTION AS IT VARIES DEPENDING ON THE CAR

BRAKE: YOU'LL HAVE BRAKED HARD ON THE UPHILL APPROACH. A SECOND DAB MAY BE NEEDED BETWEEN THE TURNS

TURN IN: TURN FIRST AT THE END OF THE KERB. NOT NECESSARY TO USE FULL WIDTH IN THE MIDDLE AS GETTING BACK TO THE LEFT IS MORE IMPORTANT

ACCELERATE: THE CAR MAY MOVE AROUND ON THE EXIT. KERB CAN BE USED

LES COOMBES AND MALMEDY

■ Use the left-hand kerb as a braking marker and turn-in at the end of the kerbing. Try to straight-line as much as possible between the two apex points but don't use too much kerb as it upsets the balance. Once the car is at the exit of the first part it needs to be brought back immediately to open out Malmedy (you may need to dab the brakes here too). You can use the kerbs on the exit here.

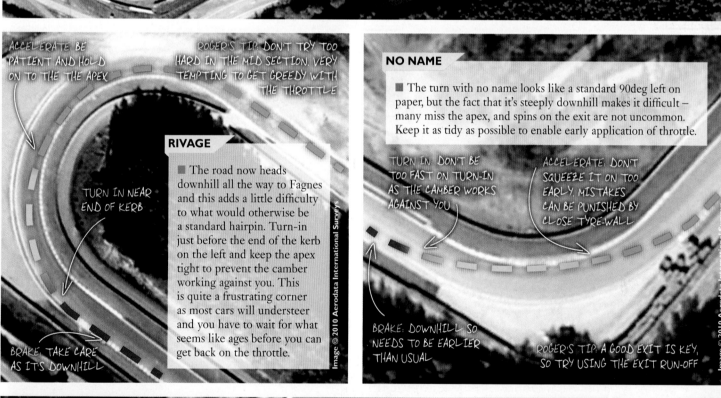

ACCELERATE: BE PATIENT AND HOLD ON TO THE THE APEX

ROGER'S TIP: DON'T TRY TOO HARD IN THE MID SECTION. VERY TEMPTING TO GET GREEDY WITH THE THROTTLE

TURN IN NEAR END OF KERB

RIVAGE

■ The road now heads downhill all the way to Fagnes and this adds a little difficulty to what would otherwise be a standard hairpin. Turn-in just before the end of the kerb on the left and keep the apex tight to prevent the camber working against you. This is quite a frustrating corner as most cars will understeer and you have to wait for what seems like ages before you can get back on the throttle.

BRAKE: TAKE CARE AS IT'S DOWNHILL

NO NAME

■ The turn with no name looks like a standard 90deg left on paper, but the fact that it's steeply downhill makes it difficult – many miss the apex, and spins on the exit are not uncommon. Keep it as tidy as possible to enable early application of throttle.

TURN IN: DON'T BE TOO FAST ON TURN-IN AS THE CAMBER WORKS AGAINST YOU

ACCELERATE: DON'T SQUEEZE IT ON TOO EARLY. MISTAKES CAN BE PUNISHED BY CLOSE TYRE-WALL

BRAKE: DOWNHILL SO NEEDS TO BE EARLIER THAN USUAL

ROGER'S TIP: A GOOD EXIT IS KEY, SO TRY USING THE EXIT RUN-OFF

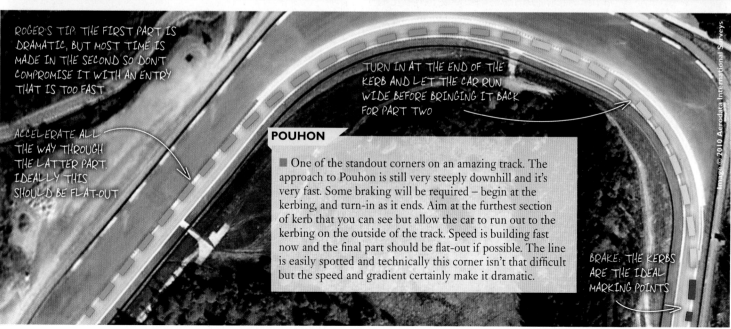

ROGER'S TIP: THE FIRST PART IS DRAMATIC, BUT MOST TIME IS MADE IN THE SECOND SO DON'T COMPROMISE IT WITH AN ENTRY THAT IS TOO FAST

TURN IN AT THE END OF THE KERB AND LET THE CAR RUN WIDE BEFORE BRINGING IT BACK FOR PART TWO

ACCELERATE ALL THE WAY THROUGH THE LATTER PART. IDEALLY THIS SHOULD BE FLAT-OUT

POUHON

■ One of the standout corners on an amazing track. The approach to Pouhon is still very steeply downhill and it's very fast. Some braking will be required – begin at the kerbing, and turn-in as it ends. Aim at the furthest section of kerb that you can see but allow the car to run out to the kerbing on the outside of the track. Speed is building fast now and the final part should be flat-out if possible. The line is easily spotted and technically this corner isn't that difficult but the speed and gradient certainly make it dramatic.

BRAKE: THE KERBS ARE THE IDEAL MARKING POINTS

FAGNES

■ The road finally levels out, making braking easier, and again you should turn in at the end of the kerb markings. This is late but it keeps you tight on the right past the first apex and this opens out the following left. Hold on to both apexes and exit half way along the outside kerb, which can be used if required.

Image © 2010 Aerodata International Surveys

ROGER'S TIP: THE LEFT IS MORE IMPORTANT THAN THE RIGHT, AND YOU CAN USE A LITTLE EXIT KERB IF REQUIRED

ACCELERATE: OPEN THE SECOND PART TO MAXIMISE ACCELERATION

TURN IN AT THE END OF THE KERBING

BRAKE: NEEDS TO BE FIRM BUT THIS IS EASY AFTER THE LAST FEW CORNERS

BLANCHIMONT

■ Another corner that looks innocent on the page – and would be if weren't for the fact that it's approached at maximum speed and can almost be taken flat-out. Gentle steering is required and make sure you don't start to turn too early; you want to run alongside the kerb on the exit but not over it. The exit can't be seen at the entry point so it will take time before you're ready to take it at top speed.

Image © 2010 Aerodata International Surveys

ACCELERATE: RUN RIGHT OUT TO THE KERBS. WHEN YOU GET THERE YOU CAN BREATHE AGAIN!

BRAKE: ANY BRAKING SHOULD BE LIGHT TO KEEP THE CAR LEVEL

TURN IN: GENTLE WITH THE STEERING. NO AGGRESSIVE MOVES

ROGER'S TIP: THERE'S A LARGE TARMAC RUN-OFF ON THE EXIT SO YOU CAN PUSH. IF YOU OVERDO IT, LET THE CAR RUN OUT WIDE. DON'T HOLD IT IN

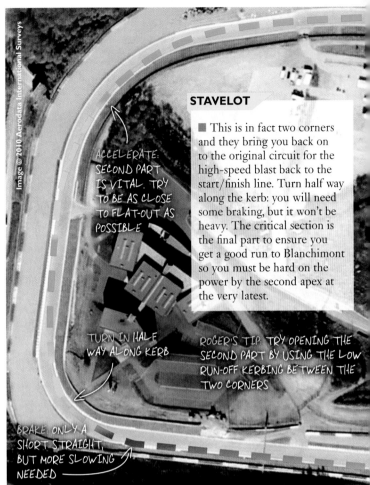

STAVELOT

■ This is in fact two corners and they bring you back on to the original circuit for the high-speed blast back to the start/finish line. Turn half way along the kerb: you will need some braking, but it won't be heavy. The critical section is the final part to ensure you get a good run to Blanchimont so you must be hard on the power by the second apex at the very latest.

Image © 2010 Aerodata International Surveys

ACCELERATE: SECOND PART IS VITAL. TRY TO BE AS CLOSE TO FLAT-OUT AS POSSIBLE

TURN IN HALF WAY ALONG KERB

ROGER'S TIP: TRY OPENING THE SECOND PART BY USING THE LOW RUN-OFF KERBING BETWEEN THE TWO CORNERS

BRAKE: ONLY A SHORT STRAIGHT, BUT MORE SLOWING NEEDED

BUS STOP

■ So-named because the layout used to look like a bus layby, but circuit revisions have now completely changed it. This is a slightly frustrating end to what has been an adrenalin-fuelled lap because it is very slow and fiddly. Heavy braking is required as you need to slow the car from maximum speed down to second gear. Turn in very late because the corner turns slightly back on itself and you want to get the best possible run onto the start/finish straight. It's not helpful to use the kerbs here.

TURN IN LATE AS IT'S MORE THAN 90 DEGREES

BRAKE VERY HARD FROM MAXIMUM SPEED DOWN TO SECOND GEAR

ROGER'S TIP: MAXIMISING THE BRAKING AND THE EXIT ARE THE TRICKS HERE. THE MID SECTION IS FAR LESS IMPORTANT

ACCELERATE: THE EXIT REQUIRES SOME PATIENCE AS WHEELSPIN IS COMMON

Based at the Nürburgring
& Spa Francorchamps

RSRNürburg
car rentals • driver instruction • trackdays • tour rallies •

RSR, specialised in car rentals, driver instruction and trackdays, is located at 300 metres from the Nordschleife entrance. We go the extra mile to make sure your days at the Nürburgring and Spa Francorchamps will be unforgettable. This is why we have a high return rate of customers and this is why you should look no further and book with us.

Why RSRNürburg?
- we're in existence for over 15 year
- great location right next to the Nordschleife entrance (300 metres)
- exclusive bespoke packages to suit you, your budget or your group
- we organise trackdays at the Nürburgring and Spa Francorchamps
- local knowledge, also for non track related activities
- specialised in driver instruction and all-inclusive packages
- international orientated company with a global customers base
- experienced staff; all with a race background
- always lots of new cars in our fleet
- largest selection of cars to choose from
- almost all cars are available in RHD as well
- we supply VBOX recording hardware and software (rent or buy)
- we know all the great hotels
- English & German staff
- seating area in front of the shop
- great guest lounge
- watch F1 on our big screen HD- TV
- we serve drinks, hot and cold
- car storage both inside and outside
- always a lot of special and rare cars on display
- emergency car-repair service
- we supply an airport-shuttle

RSR is also your supplier of trackdays at Spa Francorchamps; the second most beautiful track in the world. Spa and de Nürburgring are only 100km or an hours drive apart.

RSR organises Tour Rallies where you drive the worlds super-cars or old timers on a great tour through the beautiful Eifel region. A great escape from the often dangerous race track or simply the best way to discover and enjoy the phenomenon Nürburgring without the stress of negotiating corners and traffic.

RSRNürburg
Antoniusweg 1a
53520 Nürburg
DEUTSCHLAND

Tel: +49 2691 931952
Fax: + 49 2691 931666

RSRNurburg.com
ron@rsrnurburg.com

RSRNürburg • Antoniusweg 1a • 53520 Nürburg • Deutschland • +49 2691 931952 • RSRNurburg.com • ron@rsrnurburg.com

Showdown

To celebrate 100 issues of **evo**, back in 2006 we brought together everything from an Atom to a McLaren F1 for the ultimate circuit shootout. This is what happened

BRAKE!

'**W**ouldn't it be great,' said associate editor Tomalin, 'if for the 100th issue we could get the fastest group of road cars we could possibly muster, together, on the same day, and see which is quickest around the West Circuit.'

It was during our 'Science of Speed' cover story back in issue 094 that the seed of this compelling idea was sown. As ever, the West Circuit was an element of the test, and, to our genuine surprise, the Carrera GT came within 8/100ths of a second of our fastest ever recorded lap, 1.19.62, set by the rabid Caterham R500 Evo in issue 069.

Having compiled a wish-list of staggering optimism, we set about making the shootout happen, embarking on a charm offensive of unprecedented, er, charm. Ford was happy to stump-up a GT, the habitually generous Paul Bailey was positively bursting to see his Enzo and Carrera GT slug it out, while Iain Litchfield was only too pleased to see his ballistic Type-25 Impreza have a pop at some exotica. Caterham would bring a CSR 260 and the R500 Evo (kindly provided by its owner, Steve Moffat), while Ariel, Radical, Lotus and Dax would also be coming to the party, the latter with the positively scary Rush MC. Oh, and we'd also have a late-20th-century BMW-engined supercar called the McLaren F1. Some of you may know it.

The scale of what we're doing hits home when I arrive at the Autodrome. There are cars everywhere. Some emerging from transporters,

some buzzing impatiently on fast idle, struggling to warm their vital fluids on this chilly morning. Others sit in menacing silence: an unmistakable wedge of scarlet and a fizzing slice of acid yellow marking Paul Bailey's spectacular brace of supercars, while brooding at the far end of the pitlane is a magnificent blue McLaren F1. Gulp.

With eleven cars to lap in just over half a day, it seems sensible to start with the most familiar and, to be brutally honest, least scary cars first. Kicking off with Iain Litchfield's all-wheel-drive Type-25 Impreza, it's my intention to then get stuck into the lightweights, gradually ramping-up the power, and fear, until we reach the supercars, ending with The Big One: the daunting, £1million McLaren.

With Cosworth engine internals, AST suspension, Porsche 'Big Red' brakes and Dunlop Direzza rubber, it's no wonder the 415bhp Type-25 feels little like the UK-spec STi you'll find in your local Subaru showroom. We've said it before, but the statement bears repeating: this is as close to a four-door, four-seat 911 RS as you're ever likely to drive.

After a lap, the tyres are 'in' like a set of fresh, hot slicks, and the turbocharged 2.5-litre engine is hungrily gulping in the damp, cold air. Time to start the first attacking laps of the day. It's a violent, exciting process, all scrabbling tyres, tumescent rushes of torque and brickwall braking. It keeps you busy, not because it's a handful, but because you always need to be ready to throw another gear at the acceleration and to play with the balance to bring the tail into play. It's a fabulous, frenzied machine.

Time constraints mean we have a total of only six or seven laps in each car. With cold track temperatures, that means three flying laps, perhaps four at a push, plus warm-up and cool-down laps. Not long, in other words. Nevertheless, when we return to the pitlane and interrogate the V-Box data, the flying Impreza has laid down an impressive 1.22.25 marker, some 5/100ths quicker than a Koenigsegg CCX. Game on.

Next up is the Lotus Exige S, looking every inch the road-racer in brilliant white with black magnesium wheels. Dropping through the narrow door opening and into the hard driver's seat, it feels tiny after the boxy Subaru saloon, an impression enhanced by the snickety gearshift, beautifully tactile unassisted steering and buzzy, small-capacity engine.

ARIEL ATOM	
Layout	Mid engine, rear-wheel drive
Engine	In-line 4-cyl, 1998cc, s/c
Max power	300bhp @ 8200rpm
Max torque	162lb ft @ 7200rpm
Weight	550kg
Power/weight	554bhp/ton
0-60mph	3.3sec
Max speed	155mph (claimed)
Price as tested	£37,500

Supercharged Atom, we know, will be one of the fiercest challengers, as will the bike-engined road-racer Radical. The R500 Evo is back to fight to retain its crown, but it'll have to see off the turbo'd Dax Rush MC (far right), Exige S, Type-25 and current Caterham CSR (top right)

Again it takes a good lap and a half to get some heat into the tyres, but once warmed the Exige begins to work. Precise and fluid, it also feels surprisingly soft, with more body-roll than you'd expect. It doesn't hamper progress too much, though, even through the rapid direction changes at Pif-Paf and Beckham. True to type, the Exige S is tidy, consistent and so easily placed on every apex. It isn't powerful enough to feel truly fast, but it's clearly efficient, delivering an easily achieved 1.22.40: a few tenths down on the bombastic Type-25's best effort, but still one of the quicker cars we've ever lapped here.

After the relative sanity of the Subaru and Lotus we're straight into the more focused, single-minded machinery. First is the Caterham CSR 260 Superlight. Bigger and heavier than the record-holding 'old-school' R500 but more

sophisticated and more powerful, the new-generation Caterham posted a 1.21.85 earlier this year, so we're not expecting it to threaten the R500 Evo, but it certainly has the means to mount a challenge.

Subjectively the CSR isn't a patch on the old-school screamer. Neater, grippier and torquier, it lacks the sheer excitement and fighting spirit. It doesn't feel as instinctive either, nor as fierce down the straights, but when we check the times there's a 1.19.60 staring us in the face! Two-hundredths quicker than the R500's current record. Blimey.

Next up is the Ariel Atom. Still as barmy-looking as ever, in supercharged form the Atom is a unique and uniquely rapid machine. We've long been fans of the concept, but only recently has the chassis become a match for

the banzai powertrain. This, then, is a chance to fulfil its ample promise.

For the first lap or two, the intensity of the experience is almost overwhelming. The demented shriek from the engine, the gearing that feels like Ariel has fitted a 'box full of second gears, the neck-straining slipstream and the tremendous fast-twitch response from steering and throttle combine to explosive effect.

Where this Atom differs from previous examples I've tested is that it has a level of progression and precision earlier cars simply didn't have. Consequently, where you'd fight and ultimately fail to tame the spiky stabs of oversteer, you can now drive through them. Likewise the brakes, which, though still more willing to lock than a Caterham's, can now be modulated to better effect.

'Lightweights first, gradually ramping up the power – and the fear'

RADICAL SR3 1300	
Layout	Mid engine, rear-wheel drive
Engine	In-line 4-cyl, 1300cc
Max power	205bhp @ 9500rpm
Max torque	120lb ft @ 6500rpm
Weight	490kg
Power/weight	366bhp/ton
0-60mph	3.5sec (claimed)
Max speed	145mph (claimed)
Price as tested	£40,000

CATERHAM R500 EVO	
Layout	Front engine, rear-wheel drive
Engine	In-line 4-cyl, 1998cc
Max power	250bhp @ 8000rpm
Max torque	190lb ft @ 4000rpm
Weight	460kg
Power/weight	552bhp/ton
0-60mph	3.9sec
Max speed	150mph
Price when new	£42,000

DAX RUSH MC	
Layout	Front engine, rear wheel drive
Engine	In-line 4, 1299cc, turbo
Max power	300bhp @ 9400rpm
Max torque	220lb ft @ 7200rpm
Weight	520kg
Power/weight	586bhp/ton
0-60mph	3.2sec (claimed)
Max speed	150mph+ (claimed)
Price as tested	£24,500

PORSCHE
CARRERA GT

Layout	Mid engine, rear-wheel drive
Engine	V10, 5773cc
Max power	604bhp @ 8000rpm
Max torque	435lb ft @ 5700rpm
Weight	1380kg
Power/weight	445bhp/ton
0-60mph	3.8sec
Max speed	206mph (claimed)
Price as tested	c£323,000

CATERHAM CSR
SUPERLIGHT

Layout	Front engine, rear-wheel drive
Engine	In-line 4-cyl, 2261cc
Max power	256bhp @ 7500rpm
Max torque	200lb ft @ 6200rpm
Weight	565kg
Power/weight	460bhp/ton
0-60mph	3.8sec
Max speed	155mph (claimed)
Price as tested	£41,500

LOTUS EXIGE S

Layout	Mid engine, rear-wheel drive
Engine	In-line 4-cyl, 1796cc, s/c
Max power	218bhp @ 7800rpm
Max torque	159lb ft @ 5500rpm
Weight	935kg
Power/weight	237bhp/ton
0-62mph	4.3sec (claimed)
Max speed	148mph (claimed)
Price as tested	£41,740

FORD GT

Layout	Mid engine, rear-wheel drive
Engine	V8, 5409cc, s/c
Max power	550bhp @ 6500rpm
Max torque	500lb ft @ 3750rpm
Weight	1583kg
Power/weight	353bhp/ton
0-60mph	3.7sec (claimed)
Max speed	205mph (claimed)
Price as tested	£125,000

It's always fascinating to pitch traditional supercars against lightweight sports cars. Carrera GT is one of the quickest we've ever figured around the West Circuit, so should be in with a shout here. Ford GT, on the other hand, is a Bedford virgin

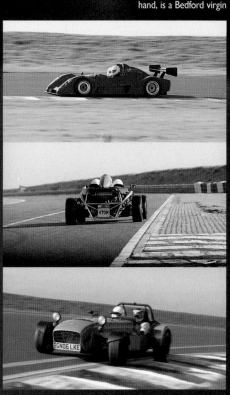

From the driver's seat you'd swear it was by far the quickest yet. In fact an identical time to the CSR is impressive, though the fact that it looks, sounds and feels so spectacular means we're expecting more. However, a look at our lap time archive reveals it's gone 1.8sec quicker than it did in the summer. It's a great result for the innovative and committed Somerset concern.

Calling the Radical SR3 a road car is stretching the description to the limit. Even Radical admits as much. Still, with a number-plate, tax disc and SVA certificate, it qualifies. Just.

While you could be forgiven for thinking the others needn't have bothered turning up, this SR3 is powered by a 1300cc Powertec motor, rather than the full-on 1500cc we've sampled previously. Reclined in the cockpit with sack-of-spuds Catchpole crammed in next to me, it feels every inch the racer it is. The bike-derived motor and sequential six-speed transmission gnash and chunter like a sleeping John Hayman after four pints of Stella, and the sheer cornering ability generated by the Dunlop Direzza tyres and generous aerodynamic addenda completely change the complexion of the West Circuit.

The Palmer Curves are now a seamless head-lolling sequence of flat-shifts through second-third-fourth-fifth, while the normally tricky Pif-Paf chicane is a dab-and-downshift jink at almost 70mph. And as for the mighty Tower, you don't even so much as lift.

With a few more laps to fully recalibrate my driving style, it might have gone even quicker. Even so, the Radical posts a quite sensational 1.17.10. Two and a half seconds inside our current record. It may stretch the definition of road car to breaking point, but it's still awe-inspiring.

From the sublime to the downright ballistic. Rather like the fire-snorting, petrol-spraying madness that was the original Westfield SEight, the Dax Rush MC is one of those fringe cars with such compelling performance even the most dyed-in-the-wool car snob can't ignore it. Yes, it's easy to have preconceived ideas about cars like the Dax, especially when you've got a McLaren F1 parked down the pitlane. However, ten minutes chatting to its owner, Duncan Cowper, and you see beyond the Rush MC's ugly Seven-clone looks and appreciate its intriguing engineering.

Beneath, or rather poking through the bonnet is a turbocharged Suzuki Hayabusa engine, good for 350bhp+ on its day. A pair of curved metal levers behind the steering wheel reveals a paddle-shift gear system, while the front-end features Dax's extraordinary camber-

Above: an awful lot of cars to get through in one day. Meaden leaps from GT and heads for Carrera GT, which proves as snappy as ever. Dax (top) is pretty hairy, too. Below: Enzo v McLaren F1

compensation front suspension, which maintains the front tyres' contact patch by keeping the wheels upright even under the highest cornering load.

The car's only here thanks to Cowper putting in a week's worth of all-nighters to re-assemble the car; when Henry Catchpole had phoned him, the motor was in pieces on his kitchen table. Consequently it's not running full boost but should still be good for 300bhp. Enough in a car that weighs just 520kg.

Sticking to our tight quota of laps is hard in a car like the Rush, for it takes some getting used to. Cowper says upshifts are clutchless, and the paddles work well, but as paddle-shift normally means no clutch pedal at all, it's tricky synchronising your left leg with each pull of the left-hand paddle for downshifts.

The engine is explosively powerful at high revs, but it also thumps out plenty of torque, which makes it more tractable than you'd think through the tighter corners. However, all of this pales into insignificance compared with getting used to the camber compensation front-end. Though it allows the body to roll, the suspension loading remains even, so you don't have the same tactile reference points to judge when you're at or over the limit. It's clever and effective, but a bit spooky to try and master in a few flat-out laps, as the front remains nailed while the tail can be snappier than a Jack Russell puppy and just as hard to catch.

Almost inevitably we end the session on the grass at the exit of Tower, a stab of turn-in

oversteer and two attempts at correcting it taking us off the tarmac. It's a suitably hairy end to a visceral few laps, the best of which yielded a 1.19.70, just a tenth behind the CSR and Atom.

And now it's the turn of our reigning West Circuit champ, the Caterham R500 Evo, still resplendent in its dazzling Rizla livery.

As ever, sliding down behind the sideplate-sized steering wheel is the perfect way to focus your mind on the job in hand. You don't so much get in a Caterham as put it on, and it's this snug, tailored fit that breeds such intimacy between you and the car, and what gives you such confidence to drive out of your skin.

In deference to the owner, Caterham asks us to use 8000rpm or so as a maximum; with the 2-litre K-series motor literally £15K a pop, it's a perfectly reasonable request, and as its maximum 250bhp arrives at 8000rpm we're not sacrificing any power. All the slightly restricted rev-limit means is a few extra gearshifts during the lap.

A glance at the rims reveals Caterham may have missed a trick by fitting the R500 Evo with the same type of Avon CR500 tyres it was shod with for our 'Fast Club 2004' feature. Stickier ACB10 tyres would surely steal a second or so from the lap time. We'll know whether it needs the help in just over ten minutes from now.

There's something extraordinary about driving this Caterham in anger. It fizzes, sparks and jolts like a raw nerve, your hands, feet and butt cheeks wired to the chassis, sensing the limit, twitching inputs through the steering wheel and pedals almost without conscious effort. Better still, it's

LITCHFIELD TYPE-25

Layout	Front engine, four-wheel drive
Engine	Flat 4-cyl, 2457cc, turbo
Max power	415bhp @ 6500rpm
Max torque	420lb ft @ 3800rpm
Weight	1385kg
Power/weight	304bhp/ton
0-60mph	3.7sec (est)
Max speed	175mph (claimed)
Price as tested	£39,995

FERRARI ENZO

Layout	Mid engine, rear-wheel drive
Engine	V12, 5998cc
Max power	650bhp @ 7800rpm
Max torque	485lb ft @ 4000rpm
Weight	1365kg
Power/weight	484bhp/ton
0-60mph	3.5sec
Max speed	217mph (claimed)
Price when new	c£450,000

one of those cars that thrive on aggression. You don't stroke a time out of it like the Lotus, you get stuck right in, catching slides, j-u-s-t locking a wheel here and there, driving on instinct and adrenalin.

A massive buzz, then, but is it quick? You betcha. A best of 1.19 dead, over half a second inside its old record. Aside from the Radical, it's the quickest yet. But will anything go faster?

With all the lightweights done, it's time to try the supercars for size. It's the stage I've been looking forward to and dreading in equal measure, for while huge power always equates to big fun at Bedford, the prospect of binning one of these babies has magazine-closing consequences, thanks to an insurance excess that would make your eyes water.

I climb into the Ford GT first. It feels vast after the skeletal flyweights. Soft too, and quiet, while the power-assisted steering feels all too light for

the task ahead. It does its best to reassure me, though, with a slick gearshift, strong brakes and so much grunt I could probably do the whole lap in fourth.

What it lacks is ultimate grip, for while it turns-in keenly it soon begins to wash wide of the apex. It's also a bit lively on the entry to the chicanes, requiring some correction to keep the tail in line. Through direction changes you can feel the delayed weight transfer, which manifests itself as oversteer once you get back on the throttle, and although it can be balanced relatively easily, you can feel the time slipping away like sand through your fingers. If that's the penalty for the sublime on-road set-up that seduced us at last year's eCoty, then so be it. Here and now, though, the Ford GT is fighting with one hand tied, as a 1.22.75 testifies.

There's nothing remotely soft-edged about the Carrera GT, as I well know, but it decides

to remind me by snapping into evil turn-in oversteer three times during the first warm-up lap. On cold tyres the Porsche takes no prisoners.

Even when sufficient temperature is in the tyres, you don't *attack* the lap, rather you methodically, meticulously zero yourself in on the Carrera GT's limits like a marksman adjusts the sight on his rifle. Only by girding your skill and courage and nudging ever closer to the point where you feel your inputs harmonise with the chassis' behaviour can you begin to extract the best from the GT, and even then it feels like you're dancing on a knife edge.

The engine, gearbox and brakes are a sensational combination, the tortured V10 yowl interrupted only momentarily with every punchy up or downshift, the ceramic brakes soaking up the speed without once waking the ABS sensors.

Perhaps it's the hairy warm-up lap. Perhaps it's the low track temperature. Perhaps it's the fact

MCLAREN F1	
Layout	Mid engine, rear-wheel drive
Engine	V12, 6064cc
Max power	627bhp @ 7500rpm
Max torque	480lb ft @ 5600rpm
Weight	1140kg
Power/weight	559bhp/ton
0-60mph	3.2sec
Max speed	240mph
Price when new	£630,000

that the tyres, by owner Bailey's own admission, are past their best. Perhaps I'm just not feeling as brave today. Whatever, the Carrera GT fails to match its previous best, managing a still impressive 1.20.20. The R500 can breathe again.

Who'd be Paul Bailey? 'Me!!!' I hear you cry. Okay, so it's hard to deny he's a jammy sod, but ask yourself this. Would you allow me to drive both of your prized supercars, worth a combined total of £800,000, flat-out at Bedford? Hmm, thought not.

So, you can imagine the scene on the pit-wall when, on the last of my flying laps, the Enzo kicks sideways at the best part of 100mph, and 'poor' Paul clutches his chest in what onlookers hope is a feigned seizure.

Inside the Enzo things are calmer. Yes, it's hairy (good job Paul didn't see his pride and joy snap into oversteer at a V-Box-recorded 105.3mph on the exit of the Palmer Curves), but it's also happier to adopt bigger angles of slide than the tidier but less forgiving Porsche. If you're comfortable with oversteer (and don't own the car), it's the more enjoyable to hustle.

Like the Porsche, the brakes are awesome, but the paddle-shift transmission feels hesitant in a post-599 Fiorano world, and the high-speed oversteer makes you wonder about the Enzo's much-vaunted underfloor aerodynamics. Even so, it's a tough call to make a subjective decision on whether the Porsche or Ferrari is quickest, for it's hard to gauge whether nudging towards the Carrera GT's limits leaves more time untapped than you waste in the process of exceeding the limits in the Enzo. By displaying a best of 1.21.30 for the Ferrari, the V-Box hands honours dispassionately to Stuttgart.

We've got one more roll of the dice left, and it's the one that I, Harry and doubtless our insurers have been dreading: the McLaren F1.

In truth we're not expecting even the combined genius of Gordon Murray's vision, BMW's peerless power, Peter Stevens's timeless design and McLaren's obsessive attention to detail to scare the pointy end of the order, for it's a decade

Flame-spitting Dax (right) makes the top five. Ford GT (above, centre) just misses out on a place in the final top ten. Above: Enzo had its Tubi Style exhaust replaced with standard system by Graypaul Ferrari to pass Bedford's strict noise limits

and a half since the F1 altered our perception of performance, packaging and price tag. Hell, when the McLaren F1 was new I had a 28in waist.

As with many of the cars here, six or seven laps are barely enough to scratch the surface, but thanks to the generosity of this particular F1's owner (Pistonheaders amongst you will know him as 'Flemke') I've got the opportunity to throw myself in at the deepest of deep ends. Oh yes, and he's sitting just behind my left shoulder.

A man of sharp wit and rare comedic timing, as the driver's door is pushed shut, Flemke decides to give me his unique brand of pre-flight briefing. 'Err, I think this is a good time to remind you that the chassis stinks, there's no downforce and the brakes are terrible. But it's got a great engine!' Err, thanks, you've been a big help.

This is the point at which the day gets serious. The central driving position, the convoluted start procedure, the overwhelming value and the legendary reputation (good and bad) are oppressive. The fact that everyone, and I mean everyone, has gathered on the pit-wall to watch twists my guts into knots. Most of all, I don't want to let the F1 down.

Once again, the cold manifests itself with the impression that the West Circuit has been surreptitiously smeared with butter. I decide to

take a couple of laps to put some heat into the tyres, resorting to race-style zig-zagging down the straights.

When the time comes to get on with it, my heart's punching a hole in my chest, but strangely the all-encompassing, jagged induction roar of that amazing V12 has a soothing effect on my nerves. This, I decide, is a once-in-a-lifetime experience, and nothing's going to stop me from savouring every last moment. Well, nothing except the pant-soiling moment on the exit of O'Rouge that has me reaching for several armfuls of right lock in a desperate effort to save the car, the magazine and, ultimately, my skin. Flemke, to his credit, doesn't even whimper.

During the three laps that follow I make many major discoveries. The first is that the brakes are indeed terrible. In fact, they're shite. The second is that the absence of a rear anti-roll bar means you're always chasing the F1's tail, be it under power through a corner or under braking into a corner. The third is that the steering really is as heavy as contemporary road tests would have you

believe, the fourth that BMW built the finest, sharpest, most beautifully responsive engine ever to grace a road car. The fifth, and frankly unexpected revelation is that despite the obvious and at times unnerving flaws, the F1 remains an intoxicating challenge, a car you could dedicate your whole life to learning.

The sixth is the lap time – a highly creditable 1.21.20 – which eclipses the Enzo, a cutting-edge supercar benefiting from 15 years of engine, chassis and brake development. True, Flemke's car has had some subtle development of its own, most obviously the bigger wheels and modern rubber (the same type and size as the Enzo), but it's by no means a complete reworking. To my great relief, the F1's honour is upheld.

It's been an unforgettable day with so many memorable moments. The Radical has triumphed overall, but the moral victory belongs to the tiny, cycle-winged Caterham R500 Evo. A hundred issues after another minnow faced the big bad world head-on, it's a timely reminder never to underestimate the underdog.

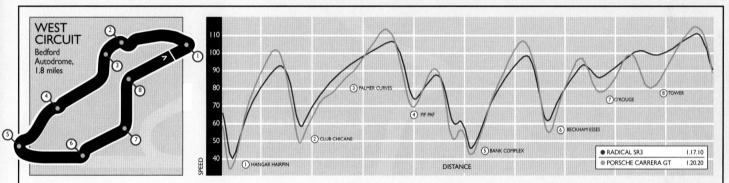

WEST CIRCUIT
Bedford Autodrome, 1.8 miles

▲ Traces (above) show where the ultra-lightweight bike-engined Radical steals more than 3sec a lap from the V10-engined Carrera GT. The Porsche accelerates far more strongly at high speed and reaches much higher peaks, but the Radical carries so much more speed through the corners, particularly the faster corners at the end of the lap, where downforce takes effect

WEST CIRCUIT TOP TEN

1	Radical SR3 1300	1.17.10
2	Caterham R500 Evo	1:19.00
3=	Ariel Atom	1:19.60
3=	Caterham CSR 260	1:19.60
5	Dax Rush MC	1:19.70
6	Porsche Carrera GT	1:20.20
7	McLaren F1	1:21.20
8	Ferrari Enzo	1:21.30
9	Litchfield Type-25	1:22.25
10	Lotus Exige S	1:22.40

NOTE: These figures stood until 2008, when the West Circuit was slightly revamped. evo's current record holder is the Radical SR8LM

MASTERING
THE 'RING

The Nürburgring Nordschleife is arguably the world's greatest circuit. Here's how to get the best from a visit

The Nordschleife is like no other track on earth; 73 corners (many of them blind and all lined with unyielding Armco) mixed with massive elevation changes, bumps, jumps, compressions and flat-out blasts as the 12.9-mile ribbon of tarmac winds its way up and down the forested Eifel valleys. How, then, do you go about learning your way around the circuit once described by Jackie Stewart as 'the ultimate driver challenge'?

The short answer is to take your time. Computer games, books and magazine guides will help you feel familiar with the trial that lies ahead, but nothing can fully prepare you for the real thing; you simply have to go there and drive it. The common myth is that it takes 100 laps before you really feel you know the complex details of the bends, cambers, elevation changes, and the various grip levels of the many surface changes.

The simplest way to get to know the Ring is to divide the lap into three main sections; Hatzenbach to Adenauer-Forst, Metzgesfeld to Karussell and then the most difficult section of all, from there through Wippermann to the end of the lap. Approached this way, your brain thinks of it as learning three circuits simultaneously. Okay, they are all complicated and your first lap will blow your mind, but if you spend a complete day on track we reckon you'll be confident of what lies over each crest by late afternoon.

It may sound boring, but the obvious advice is best: you have to start slowly, driving it just like a road you don't know. Soak in the history, take plenty of breaks (a single lap requires intense concentration), take your time and always give yourself a margin for error.

The Ring is unique, and to help you round it we've highlighted the main corners, with tips from race driver and good friend of **evo** Phil Bennett, who holds the fastest road-legal lap-time, and additional info from Ring trackday expert Ron Simons of RSR Nurburg (rsrnurburg.com), who can supply both track car rentals and driver coaching.

8. Kallenhard to Exmühle

7. Metzgesfeld

6. Adenauer-Forst

5. Fuchsröhre

4. Schwedenkreuz

3. Flugplatz

2. Hatzenbach

1. Turn One

Circuit stats

Length: 20.8km (12.9 miles)
Corners: 33 left-handers, 40 right-handers
Steepest climb: 17 per cent
Steepest drop: 11 per cent
Highest point: 620m above sea level (start/finish straight)
Lowest point: 320m above sea level (Breidscheid)

Race lap records over the years

1927 Christian Werner . . . 15:51.6
1932 Tazio Nuvolari 10:49.4
1936 Bernd Rosemeyer . . . 9:56.6
1958 Stirling Moss 9:09.2
1969 Jacky Ickx 7:43.8
1975 Clay Regazzoni 7:06.4

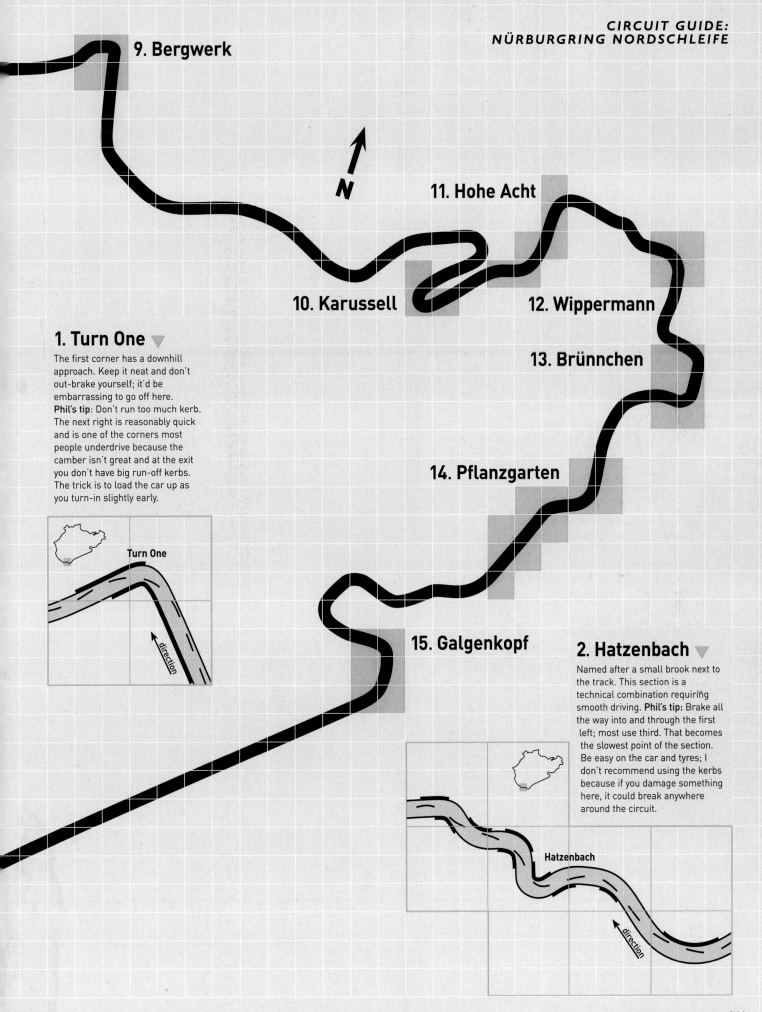

9. Bergwerk

11. Hohe Acht

10. Karussell

12. Wippermann

13. Brünnchen

14. Pflanzgarten

1. Turn One ▼

The first corner has a downhill approach. Keep it neat and don't out-brake yourself; it'd be embarrassing to go off here. **Phil's tip:** Don't run too much kerb. The next right is reasonably quick and is one of the corners most people underdrive because the camber isn't great and at the exit you don't have big run-off kerbs. The trick is to load the car up as you turn-in slightly early.

Turn One

direction

15. Galgenkopf

2. Hatzenbach ▼

Named after a small brook next to the track. This section is a technical combination requiring smooth driving. **Phil's tip:** Brake all the way into and through the first left; most use third. That becomes the slowest point of the section. Be easy on the car and tyres; I don't recommend using the kerbs because if you damage something here, it could break anywhere around the circuit.

Hatzenbach

direction

3. Flugplatz

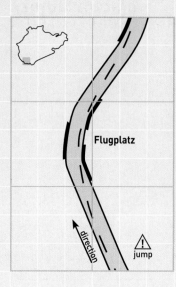

One of the infamous named curves, it has a literal translation of 'flying place', which is appropriate as the crest on the approach feels like a launch pad. **Phil's tip:** The run through Quiddelbacher Hohe is flat-out – simply make as straight a line as possible before the crest prior to Flugplatz. In a Porsche 997 road car I'd brake gently enough to get back to fourth and stay left before the crest. Then off the brakes at the crest and brake again to get the car turned for the double right, which will be in fourth at around 100mph.

4. Schwedenkreuz

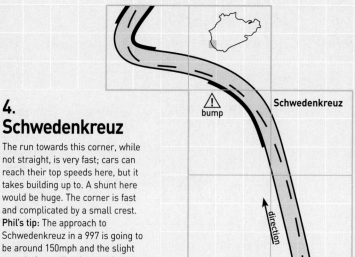

The run towards this corner, while not straight, is very fast; cars can reach their top speeds here, but it takes building up to. A shunt here would be huge. The corner is fast and complicated by a small crest. **Phil's tip:** The approach to Schwedenkreuz in a 997 is going to be around 150mph and the slight crest before will ultimately be easy flat, although the car gets airborne. Schwedenkreuz itself will be in fifth and it's important to get the line right as you don't want big steering inputs here. Then hard on the brakes and back into third for Aremberg (watch the greasy surface in the wet); you can sneak a little exit kerb here.

7. Metzgesfeld

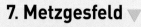

Phil's tip: Quicker than most are prepared to go, and you need to be careful of the small bump that unsettles the car before corner entry.

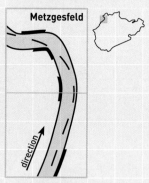

5. Fuchsröhre

Or Foxhole. Named after a fox seen here during construction, it's steeply downhill inside a tunnel of over-hanging trees. **Phil's tip:** The downhill bit is easy. Keep the car as straight as possible between the small kinks. Speed builds quickly and you'll be in fifth and over 140mph before the compression. I don't brake because the car has no suspension travel left.

6. Adenauer-Forst

Tight second-gear section that can arrive as a surprise after travelling so fast. **Phil's tip:** Stay left as the road will open up at the final left/right, and it's important to carry a good approach speed.

8. Kallenhard to Exmühle

A steep, technical downhill section that requires experience to make the most of. Greasy in the wet, too. **Phil's tip:** Thankfully, until Exmühle it's hard to fall off and do major damage! The approach to Exmühle is downhill, slightly off-camber with a nice hard concrete wall to catch the over-brave – you have been warned!

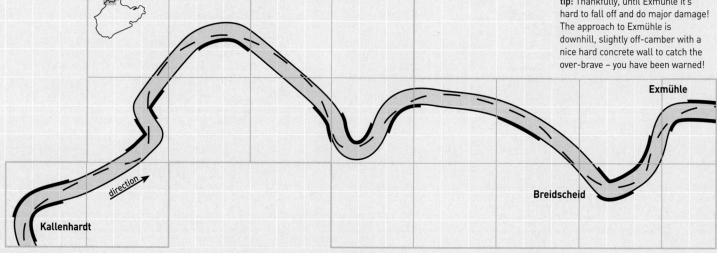

How to get there

From Calais, pick up the E40 and follow it past Brussels and on to Liège (or Luik, as the Belgians call it). From Liège pick up the E42 passing by Spa-Francorchamps before taking the 410 past Prüm and Gerolstein and all the way to Kelberg. Once there take the 257, which takes you to the bottom end of the Grand Prix circuit. Total journey time from Calais is around four and a half hours.

Where to stay

Dorint Hotel – overlooks the GP circuit and has secure underground parking. www.dorint.com

Hotel An Der Nordschleife – secure parking and balconies overlooking the track. www.hotel-an-der-nordschleife.de

Agnesen-Hof – space for trailers, small but good rooms and fine food. www.agnesen-hof.de

Hotel Am Tiergarten – popular with 'Ring regulars, attached to Pistenklause restaurant. Owned by Schmitz family. www.am-tiergarten.de

Car rentals and driver training

RSR Nurburg
These guys offer the complete package – rentals, trackdays, and training. Based just 300m from the Nordschleife entrance, they can supply everything from Renault hot hatches to Lotuses, M3s and GT3s, and cater for beginners as well as seasoned trackday goers. Boss Ron Simons clocks an amazing 1200 laps a year so he knows the track backwards. www.rsrnurburg.com

BMW Driver Training
A three-day course which includes track-walks, driving the wrong way up the track and uniquely - the chance to try a brake-failure drill in a BMW-provided car: stopping the car by rubbing it along the Armco! www.fahrerlehrgang.info

Rent Race Car
Hire anything from a Suzuki Swift Sport to a Porsche 911 GT3 RS. First-timers get a free introductory lap of the Ring with an experienced racer/instructor. www.rent-racecar.de

Rent 4 Ring
More Suzuki Swifts. www.rent4ring.de

Other attractions

There is a museum on site with a collection of cars and bikes that have competed on the great track, and next door is an indoor kart track. Helicopter flights over the circuit are also available – details can be found on the main circuit website, www.nuerburgring.de

Fuel

The closest petrol station is situated on the 258 towards Döttingen, alongside the main straight, and as well as fuel and oil it has a model shop that also sells the all-important car stickers.

Food

For lunch the restaurant next to the public pay-tolls serves bratwurst and chips and there's another small café next to the petrol station.

By far the most famous restaurant in the area is the Pistenklause, situated underneath the Tiergarten hotel. The walls and ceilings are plastered with posters, photos and autographs from some of the world's greatest drivers.

Fuchsrohre: situated near the BMW showroom, this small pasta and pizza restaurant is run by 'Ring Taxi driver Sabine Schmitz.

Websites

http://www.nuerburgring.de/
Official site for both GP and Nordschleife.

http://www.nurburgring.org.uk/
Ben Lovejoy's absolutely excellent site – everything you could ever need.

http://www.24h-rennen.de/
24hr race site.

http://www.youtube.com/
Type in 'Ferrari 599XX record' and watch in awe

History

Even before the First World War, Germany had emerged as a force to be reckoned with in the new and rapidly developing sport of motor racing, despite not having a purpose-built circuit of its own. After the war, Eifel District Council member Dr Otto Cruz got together with Konrad Adenauer, the Mayor of Cologne, and persuaded the government to invest in the economically depressed Eifel region. The plan was for a race track and test facility, the like of which the world had never seen.

Construction commenced on April 27, 1925, and the circuit was cut into the hills over the next two years by 3000 workers. Initially there were two separate loops that could be combined into one huge 19-mile track, although now only the longest remains. The Sudschleife made way for the current Grand Prix track, although if you look hard enough you can still find some remaining sections hidden by overgrown trees and bushes.

The original pit garages can be found next to the Dorint Hotel and can still be hired today.

The first race was run here on June 19, 1927, and won by Rudolf Caracciola in a Mercedes. A month later the Nürburgring hosted its first Grand Prix, which was won by Otto Merz (former chauffeur to Archduke Franz Ferdinand!). Through the Thirties there were some great drives including legendary performances by Nuvolari and Rosemeyer. In 1938 British driver Richard Seaman won in front of a crowd of 350,000 but caused great controversy back home by saluting Hitler.

After the Second World War, the 'Ring enjoyed arguably its greatest period, with Alberto Ascari and then Juan-Manuel Fangio proving the new stars. Fangio's win in 1957 is regarded by many as the greatest performance seen in grand prix racing. His Maserati 250F was not as quick as the Ferraris of Mike Hawthorn and Peter Collins and a bungled pit stop left him a minute behind with eight laps to go. However, driving in a style he later said he never wanted to repeat again, he worked his way to the front and won the race by a scant three seconds.

Through the '60s, wins were taken by heroes such as Hill, Surtees, Clark and Ickx, but the issue of safety was beginning to loom large and in 1970 the GP was held at Hockenheim to allow the 'Ring to have barriers fitted – until then trees and hedges marked the edge of the track for much of its lap. With speeds increasing rapidly, fears remained despite the work and in 1976 they came to a head with Nicki Lauda's fiery crash. In qualifying he'd produced the first sub-seven-minute lap, taking pole in 6:58.6, which will probably stand as the fastest F1 lap for eternity.

Sports car racing continued until the '80s, by which time Steffan Bellof screamed his Porsche 956 round in a scarcely believable 6:11.1 and set an outright race lap record of 6:25.9 (which still stands) before suffering a massive crash at the end of the long straight. Racing continues today with the VLN series for Touring car and GT machines, the highlight being the 24-hour race, still one of the largest sporting events in Germany.

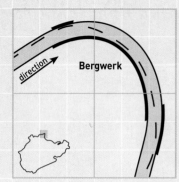

9. Bergwerk

Bergwerk is vital to a good lap time and difficult to master. Be patient with the throttle and concentrate on your line. If the track's wet take particular care here - from apex to exit there's little grip. **Phil's tip:** From Bergwerk to the Karussell is something first-time visitors to the circuit will simply not get their teeth into. After all, we are now around six miles into the circuit and your memory won't retain the detail. Plus, you'll be looking in the mirrors at the faster traffic! It's made worse because unless you're in a car with 300bhp+, the run up through Kesselchen to Klostertal is going to be slower than you think. In something like a Porsche 997 you might touch 140mph.

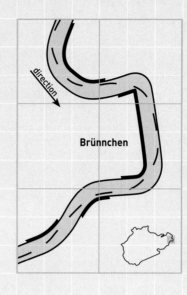

13. Brünnchen

Brunnchen is quite friendly and, as it's where the spectators will be hanging over the fence, it's a must to showboat through here!

15. Galgenkopf

Final corner if you're on a public session and one of the most important because of the straight that follows. **Phil's tip:** This is fourth gear in a 997 and once you've got the car turned in it's the slowest point; even though we have a double apex, the corner doesn't get any tighter.

10. Karussell

The heavily cambered banking of the inside line is very bumpy. To enter look for the tallest pine tree on the uphill approach – that's your line. Brake, snatch third and drop in. Don't allow the car to come out too early or you'll be acquainting yourself with the barriers. Concrete surface particularly slippery when wet. **Phil's tip:** Remember whose car it is and that you may want to drive home in it – the Karussell is so rough that unless you take care, it can destroy your suspension and drivetrain.

12. Wippermann

Again we're under the trees and this section is technical with constant directional changes. **Phil's tip:** This is real fun. It's a right, long left/right combination that allows you to bang over the kerbs like a Touring car hero. The initial right is miles quicker than most go and on slicks in a race car is actually flat. In a 997 it will be fourth gear and an ease- back simply to retain a balance and allow the car to grip. Then we take the flat apex kerb on the left and right, which is necessary in order to carry the speed through.

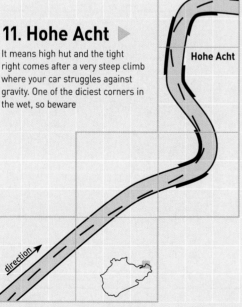

11. Hohe Acht

It means high hut and the tight right comes after a very steep climb where your car struggles against gravity. One of the diciest corners in the wet, so beware

14. Pflanzgarten

1. From Pflanzgarten to Galgenkopf is where the speed builds again. The trick is to brake before the crest and drop a gear. Then off the brakes at the crest and back to the throttle before turning into the long right.
2. Very important to get the car pointing straight as you go over the crest otherwise you'll spin. **Phil's tip:** In a racer with slicks this is flat all the way to Schwalbenschwanz. But in a road car you're having to manage the weight on tyres which have had enough by now. You'll be in fourth moving to fifth but nice and easy with the power, balancing the car through the direction changes.

Public days

The easiest way of getting on the 'Ring is to visit on one of the public lapping sessions. It's relatively cheap, but there are a number of vagaries you should be aware of. It's certainly not like taking your car on a UK trackday; for a start, anything goes in terms of what vehicles are allowed on track, so you will be mixing it with bikes and even buses! Your car needs to be road legal and there is a noise limit of 95 db(A) – there's occasionally random noise testing in the collecting area.

It's worth checking your insurance to ensure your car is covered while on the circuit, and you should also be aware that any damage caused to the track or barriers will have to be paid for. If you have to be towed in after breaking down, you will be charged several hundred euros for the privilege. You can only do a single lap at a time and the car park cum paddock is sited halfway along the main straight; access to it is gained from the road that runs through Nürburg.

The days available for public lapping are numerous. For schedules and weather info, log on to www.nuerburgring.de

Price per single lap (car) – €22.00
4-lap ticket – €75.00
8-lap ticket – €145.00
15-lap ticket – €250.00
25-lap ticket – €390.00
Season ticket valid one year €1075

Trackday organisers

Companies who regularly run trackdays at the Nordschleife include:
RMA (www.rma-limited.com),
Circuit Days (www.circuit-days.co.uk)
Destination Nürburgring (www.destination-nurburgring.com).
Bookatrack (www.bookatrack.com)
Ringweekends (www.ringweekends.com)

The Ring Taxi

Ride in a 500bhp BMW M5 alongside a professional racer like Andy Priaulx or Claudia Hürtgen. The cost is a steep 195 euros, but it's an unforgettable experience. Book a place at www.bmw-motorsport.com/ringtaxi

Road car lap records

As racing began to decline at the 'Ring through the '80s and '90s, so it began to be used increasingly for road car development. BMW development engineer Klaus Schmidt described working at the 'Ring as 'accelerated development', reckoning it to be about 20 times more effective than driving on regular roads. Never ones to miss a trick, car makers began using their fastest lap times in press releases and it quickly became competitive.

There are no official records and most of the timing is done with little or no independent ratification, but in Germany a car's 'Ring time is as important as the 0-60mph sprint is to UK magazine readers. Anything under eight minutes can be regarded as seriously rapid. Some of these records are widely accepted, while others are viewed with scepticism and doubt, but there are a number of cars and drivers who have passed into legend for their exploits here. Here are some of the highlights over the years:

Dirk Schoysman set the first recognised road car record in 1996 with a 7min 59sec lap in a Nissan GT-R R33 V-spec. He was soon outrun by Röhrl in a 911 GT3, before Robert Nearn pitched up in a Caterham R500 and lopped another three seconds off the time, dropping it to 7:56.

By 2005 the record had been lowered to 7:18.01 by Horst von Saurma, editor of Sport Auto magazine, in a Donkervoort D8 RS. That eclipsed the time set by Phil Bennett two years earlier in a Radical SR3 Turbo by just a second. Both the Radical and the Donkervoort were road legal, but many (usually the German press) argue that they are not true road cars. The fastest of this breed so far has been the Radical SR8 LM, which went round in an astonishing 6min 48sec in 2009.

Of the full production cars, Ferrari's Enzo has posted a lap of 7:25.21 in the hands of racer Marc

Basseng, who lapped its Maserati sister, the MC12, in 7:24.29. On the same day in 2008 he took a Pagani Zonda F round in 7:24.65.

More recently, the Corvette ZR1 has recorded a stunning 7:26.4, and Porsche's formidable GT2 RS is reported to have turned in a 7min 18sec lap, which is going to take some beating...

However, there are two other times that have been forgotten by many. The first was set in the early 90s by Danish sports car ace John Nielsen, who lapped an XJ220 around the course in 7:43. Then there was Hans Stuck, who bludgeoned an extraordinary McLaren F1-engined 750bhp BMW X5 to a kerb-hopping 7:50 lap. Both must stand as some of the bravest lappers of all.

Radical SR3 Turbo (below), driven by Phil Bennett, held the road car lap record in the mid-2000s. Jaguar XJ220 (bottom) a little-known previous record holder

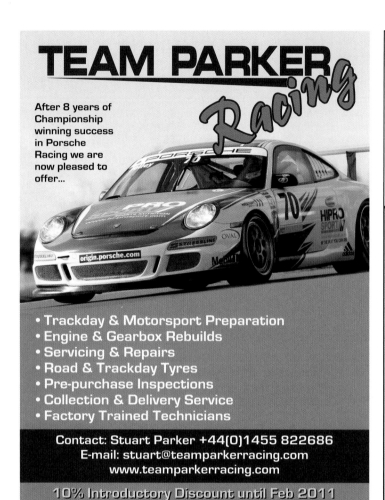
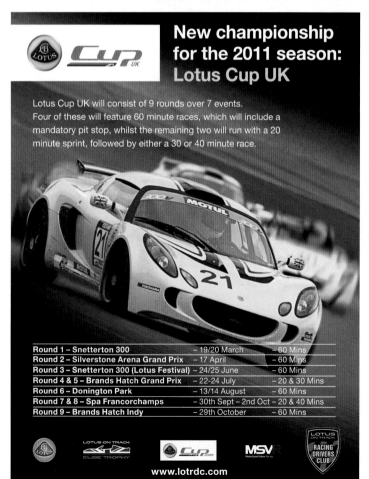

THE KNOWLEDGE

ALL THE FIGURES AND **evo**'S VERDICT ON EVERY POTENTIAL TRACKDAY CAR, FROM £10K HATCHBACKS TO £1M SUPERCARS

KEY: The first column shows the issue number of evo featuring our most recent major test of the car. You can order back issues of some issues where still available – call 0844 8440039 for details. (R = Road test or group test with our own performance figures, D = Driven, F = Feature article). The price is on-the-road including VAT and delivery charges. Entries in *italics* are no longer on sale (where the car is off sale, you can see the years of manufacture). Weight is the car's kerb weight as quoted by the manufacturer. Bhp/ton is the power-to-weight ratio based on manufacturer's kerb weight. 0-60 and 0-100 figures in **bold** are independently recorded, all other performance figures are manufacturers' claims. CO2 is the official EC figure and EC mpg is the official 'Combined' figure or equivalent. * = grey import.
STAR RATINGS: ★ Thrill-free zone ★★ Tepid ★★★ Interesting ★★★★ Seriously good ★★★★★ A truly great car

SUPERMINIS & HOT HATCHES

OUR CHOICE Renaultsport Clio 200 Cup. All Renaultsport Clios make cracking little trackday cars, and the current Clio 200 Cup is right up there with the very best of them. If you're buying secondhand, look for a 182 Cup or, even better, a 182 Trophy.

Best of the Rest: The Ford Focus RS (right) is rabidly quick and totally involving, while VW's grown-up Golf GTI and Mini's mad JCW also appeal. Further down the ladder, the Fiat Panda 100HP, Renault Twingo 133 Cup and Suzuki Swift Sport are all evo favourites.

	Issue no.	Price	Engine cyl/cc	Bhp/rpm	Lb ft/rpm	Weight	Bhp/ton	0-60mph	0-100mph	Max mph	CO2 g/km	EC mpg	evo rating	
Abarth 500 Esseesse	129 R	£16,100	4/1368	158/5750	170/3000	1035kg	155	**7.2**	**20.4**	131	155	-	+ A properly fun, old-school hot hatch - Limited numbers being imported	★★★★
Alfa Romeo Mito Cloverleaf	149 F	£17,895	4/1368	168/5500	184/2500	1145kg	149	7.5	-	136	139	47.1	+ Great MultiAir engine, impressive ride - Not as feisty as we hoped	★★★½
Alfa Romeo Giulietta Cloverleaf	144 D	£24,495	4/1742	232/5500	251/1900	1320kg	179	6.8	-	150	177	37.2	+ Shows signs of deep talent... - ...but should be more exciting	★★★½
Alfa Romeo 147 GTA	053 F	'03-'06	6/3179	247/6200	221/4800	1360kg	185	**6.0**	**15.5**	153	-	23.3	+ Focus RS pace without the histrionics - Slightly nose-heavy	★★★★
BMW 130i M Sport (3dr)	106 R	'05-'10	6/2996	261/6650	232/2750	1450kg	183	**6.1**	**15.3**	155	-	34.0	+ Fantastic engine - Suspension can still get a little boingy	★★★★
BMW 325ti Compact	031 D	'01-'05	6/2494	189/6000	181/3500	1480kg	130	7.1	-	147	-	31.7	+ Terrific engine, chassis, price - Looks a bit geeky	★★★★
Citroën C2 GT	064 R	'04-'05	4/1587	108/5750	108/4000	1027kg	107	8.7	-	121	-	-	+ Appealing and affordable homologation special - Inert steering	★★★★
Citroën Saxo VTR	013 R	'97-'03	4/1587	100/5700	100/3500	920kg	99	**9.3**	-	116	-	36.7	+ VTS poise, half the insurance group - Cramped pedals	★★★★
Citroën Saxo VTS	020 R	'97-'03	4/1587	120/6600	107/5200	935kg	130	**7.6**	**22.6**	127		34.9	+ Chunky, chuckable charger - Can catch out the unwary	★★★★½
Citroën Xsara VTS		'98-'04	4/1997	167/7000	142/4750	1190kg	143	8.0	-	137		33.6	+ Citroën's GTI-6 - Missing one gear and a bit of handling polish	★★★½
Fiat Panda 100HP	132 F	£11,005	4/1368	99/6000	97/4250	975kg	103	9.5	-	115	154	43.5	+ Most fun per pound on the market - Optional ESP can't be turned off	★★★★½
Ford Fiesta Zetec S	123 D	£13,995	4/1596	118/6000	112/4050	1045kg	115	9.9	-	120	134	47.9	+ Genuinely entertaining supermini - Grown up compared to Twingo/Swift	★★★★
Ford Fiesta Zetec S Mountune	132 F	c£16,150	4/1596	138/6750	125/4250	1080kg	130	7.9	-	120	134	-	+ As above, with a fantastically loud exhaust... - ...if you're 12 years old	★★★★
Ford Fiesta Zetec S	020 R	'00-'02	4/1596	102/6000	107/4000	976kg	106	**10.2**	-	113	-	38.2	+ Better than you'd ever believe - No-one else will believe it	★★★★
Ford Fiesta ST185 Mountune	115 R	'08	4/1999	185/6700	147/3500	1137kg	165	6.9	-	129	-	-	+ Fiesta ST gets the power it always needed - OTT exhaust note	★★★★
Ford Focus ST	119 R	£22,895	5/2522	222/6000	236/1600	1392kg	162	**6.7**	**16.8**	150	224	30.4	+ Value, performance, integrity - Big engine compromises handling	★★★★
Ford Focus ST Mountune	137 R	c£23,595	5/2522	256/5500	295/2500	1392kg	187	**5.8**	**14.3**	155	224	-	+ ST takes extra power in its stride - You probably still want an RS	★★★★½
Ford Focus RS (Mk2)	139 R	£27,895	5/2522	300/6500	324/2300	1467kg	208	**5.9**	**14.2**	163	225	30.5	+ Huge performance, highly capable fwd chassis - It could be the last RS...	★★★★★
Ford Focus RS500	146 R	£35,750	5/2522	345/6000	339/2500	1467kg	239	**5.6**	**12.7**	165	225	-	+ More power and presence than above - Pricey (and all sold!)	★★★★★
Ford Focus RS (Mk1)	053 R	'02-'03	4/1998	212/5500	229/3500	1278kg	169	**5.9**	**14.9**	144	-	-	+ Some are great - Some are awful (so make sure you drive plenty)	★★★
Ford Escort RS Cosworth	011 F	'92-'96	4/1993	227/6250	224/3500	1304kg	176	5.8	-	143	-	24.5	+ The ultimate Essex hot hatch - Ultimate trophy for tea leaves	★★★★
Ford Puma 1.7	095 F	'97-'02	4/1679	123/6300	116/4500	1041kg	120	**8.6**	**27.6**	122	-	38.2	+ Everything - Nothing. The 1.4 is worth a look too	★★★★★
Ford Racing Puma	016 F	'00-'01	4/1679	153/7000	119/4500	1174kg	132	**7.8**	**23.2**	137	-	34.7	+ Exclusivity - Expense. Standard Puma does it so well	★★★★
Honda Civic Type-R	102 R	£20,620	4/1998	198/7800	142/5600	1267kg	158	**6.8**	**17.5**	146	215	31.0	+ Looks great, VTEC more accessible - Steering lacks feel, inert balance	★★★½
Honda Civic Type-R Mugen	144 F	£38,599	4/1998	237/8300	157/6250	1233kg	195	5.9	-	155	-	-	+ Fantastic on road and track - There'll only be 20, and it's a tad pricey...	★★★★★
Honda Civic T-R C'ship White	126 D	'09-'10	4/1998	198/7800	142/5600	1267kg	158	6.6	-	146	-	31.0	+ Limited-slip diff a welcome addition - It's not available on standard car...	★★★★
Honda Civic Type-R	075 R	'01-'05	4/1998	197/7400	145/5900	1204kg	166	**6.8**	**16.9**	146	-	31.7	+ Potent and great value - Looks divide opinion, duff steering	★★★★
Lancia Delta Integrale	011 F	'88-'93	4/1995	210/5750	220/3500	1350kg	158	5.7	-	137	-	23.9	+ One of the finest cars ever built - Demands love, LHD only	★★★★★
Mini Cooper S	149 F	£17,640	4/1598	181/5500	177/1600	1205kg	153	**7.0**	-	142	136	48.7	+ New engine, Mini quality - Lacks old car's direct front end	★★★★½
Mini John Cooper Works	137 F	£21,670	4/1598	208/6000	206/1850	1205kg	175	6.5	-	148	165	40.9	+ Most exciting new Mini yet - Occasionally just a little *too* exciting	★★★★
Mini Cooper S Works (Mk2)	111 F	'07-'08	4/1598	189/6000	199/1750	1130kg	170	**7.6**	**18.0**	145	-	-	+ Cracking hot Mini, until the JCW - Expensive with option packs included	★★★★½
Mini Cooper S Works GP	144 F	'06	4/1598	218/7100	184/4600	1090kg	203	6.5	-	149	-	32.8	+ Storming engine, agility - Tacky styling 'enhancements'	★★★★★
Mini Cooper S (Mk1)	077 R	'02-'06	4/1598	168/6000	155/4000	1140kg	143	**7.8**	**19.9**	135	-	33.6	+ Strong performance, quality feel - Over-long gearing	★★★★½
Mini Cooper S Works (Mk1)	074 D	'03-'06	4/1598	210/6950	181/4500	1140kg	187	6.6	-	143		-	+ Even more power and pace than the 197bhp version - Even pricier, too	★★★★★
Nissan Sunny GTi-R		'92-'93	4/1998	220/6400	197/4800	1269kg	176	6.1	-	134	-	25.1	+ Nissan's Escort Cossie - Make sure it's a good one	★★★★
Peugeot 106 Rallye (Series 2)		'97-'98	4/1587	103/6200	97/3500	865kg	121	8.8	-	121	-	34.0	+ Bargain no-frills thrills - Not as much fizz as original 1.3	★★★★
Peugeot 106 Rallye (Series 1)	095 F	'94-'96	4/1294	100/7200	80/5400	826kg	123	9.3	-	118	-	35.6	+ Frantic, thrashy fun - Needs caning to extract full potential	★★★★★
Peugeot 106 GTI 16v	034 R	'97-'04	4/1587	120/6600	107/5200	950kg	128	**7.4**	**22.2**	127	-	34.9	+ Fine handling supermini - Looks its age	★★★★½
Peugeot 205 GTI 1.9	095 F	'88-'91	4/1905	130/6000	119/4750	910kg	145	7.9	-	124	-	36.7	+ Still scintillating after all these years - Brittle build quality	★★★★★
Peugeot 306 GTI-6	020 R	'93-'01	4/1998	167/6500	142/5500	1215kg	139	**7.2**	**20.1**	140	-	30.1	+ One of the great GTIs - They don't make them like this any more	★★★★★
Peugeot 306 Rallye	095 F	'98-'99	4/1998	167/6500	142/5500	1199kg	141	**6.9**	**19.2**	137	-	30.1	+ Essentially a GTI-6 for less dosh - Limited choice of colours	★★★★★
Peugeot 309 GTI		'89-'92	4/1905	130/6000	119/4750	985kg	134	8.3	-	124	-	28.2	+ 205 GTI in drag, cheap - Who wants a cheap drag queen?	★★★★
Renaultsport Twingo 133 Cup	132 F	£12,100	4/1598	131/6750	118/4400	1049kg	127	8.7	-	125	159	40.4	+ Renaultsport experience for pocket money - Could handle extra 30bhp	★★★★½
Renault 5GT Turbo	123 F	'87-'91	4/1397	120/5750	122/3750	831kg	146	7.8	-	120	-	28.4	+ Clio Williams' grand-daddy - Most have been thrashed	★★★★★
Renaultsport Clio 200 Cup	139 R	£16,710	4/1998	197/7100	159/5400	1204kg	166	**6.6**	**16.7**	141	190	34.4	+ The hot Clio is back to its best - Why the long face?	★★★★★
Renaultsport Clio 197 Cup	115 R	'07-'09	4/1998	194/7250	158/5550	1240kg	161	6.9	-	134	-	33.6	+ Quick, polished and capable - Not as much sheer fun as 182 Cup	★★★★
Renaultsport Clio 182	066 R	'04-'06	4/1998	180/6500	148/5250	1110kg	165	**6.6**	**17.5**	139	-	34.9	+ Took hot hatches to a new level - Flawed driving position	★★★★★
Renaultsport Clio 182 Cup	074 D	'04-'06	4/1998	180/6500	148/5250	1090kg	168	6.5	-	139	-	34.9	+ Full of beans, fantastic value - Sunday market upholstery	★★★★★
Renaultsport Clio Trophy	095 F	'05-'06	4/1998	180/6500	148/5250	1090kg	168	**6.6**	**17.3**	140	-	34.9	+ Most fun you can have on three wheels - Just 500 were built	★★★★★
Renaultsport Clio 172 Cup	048 R	'02-'04	4/1998	170/6250	147/5400	1011kg	171	**6.5**	**17.7**	138	--	-	+ Bargain old-school hot hatch - Nervous in the wet, no ABS	★★★★
Renaultsport Clio V6 255	057 R	'03-'05	6/2946	255/7150	221/4650	1400kg	182	5.8	-	153	-	23.0	+ Revised Clio V6 is a winner - Uninspired interior	★★★★★
Renaultsport Clio V6	029 F	'99-'02	6/2946	230/6000	221/3750	1335kg	175	**5.8**	**17.0**	145	-	23.0	+ Pocket supercar - Mid-engined handling can be tricky	★★★★
Renault Clio Williams	095 F	'93-'96	4/1988	150/6100	126/4500	981kg	155	**7.6**	**20.8**	121	-	26.0	+ One of the best hot hatches ever - Can be fragile like an Integrale	★★★★★
Renaultsport Mégane 250 Cup	139 R	£23,160	4/1998	247/5500	251/3000	1387kg	181	**6.1**	**14.6**	156	195	33.6	+ Fantastic chassis... - ...partially obscured by new-found maturity	★★★★½
Renaultsport Mégane R26.R	125 F	'08-'09	4/1998	227/5500	229/3000	1220kg	189	**5.8**	**15.1**	147	-	-	+ One of the true hot hatch heroes - Two seats, plastic rear windows	★★★★★
Renaultsport Mégane 230 R26	102 R	'07-'09	4/1998	227/5500	229/3000	1345kg	171	**6.2**	**16.0**	147	-	-	+ Best hot Mégane... until the R26.R - F1 Team stickers in dubious taste	★★★★★
Renaultsport Mégane 225 Cup	087 F	'05-'09	4/1998	222/5500	221/3000	1345kg	167	6.5	-	147	-	32.1	+ Good value and plentiful - You gotta like big backsides	★★★★½
Renaultsport Mégane Trophy	087 F	'05	4/1998	222/5500	221/3000	1355kg	166	**6.7**	**17.3**	147	-	32.1	+ Mega grip and traction - Steering needs a touch more feel	★★★★
SEAT Ibiza FR	134 D	£15,670	4/1390	148/5800	162/1250	1167kg	129	7.7	-	130	146	44.8	+ Fun and frugal - You're forced to have the DSG automatic 'box	★★★★
SEAT Ibiza Cupra	139 R	£17,020	4/1390	178/6200	184/2000	1172kg	154	**6.9**	-	140	148	44.1	+ Funky (especially in Bocanegra trim), economical - The FR's a better drive	★★★½
SEAT Leon FR	131 D	£19,900	4/1984	208/5300	206/1700	1334kg	158	7.2	-	145	170	35.8	+ As quick as a Golf GTI but £4K cheaper - Misses the VW's completeness	★★★★
SEAT Leon Cupra	105 F	£21,500	4/1984	237/5700	221/2200	1375kg	175	6.3	-	153	190	34.0	+ Great engine, composure - Doesn't have adjustability of old Cupra R	★★★★
SEAT Leon Cupra R	139 R	£25,205	4/1984	261/6000	258/2500	1375kg	193	**6.1**	**14.0**	155	190	-	+ Bold car, blinding engine - Lacks the character of its rival mega-hatches	★★★½
SEAT Leon Cupra R 225	067 R	'03-'06	4/1781	222/5900	206/2200	1376kg	164	6.9	-	150	-	32.1	+ Cross-country pace, practicality, value - Not as thrilling as some	★★★★
Skoda Octavia vRS (Mk2)	085 D	£19,380	4/1998	197/5100	206/1700	1395kg	143	7.3	-	149	175	37.7	+ Drives like a GTI but costs much less - Green brake callipers?	★★★★
Skoda Octavia vRS (Mk1)	032 D	'01-'05	4/1781	180/5500	173/1950	1354kg	135	7.9	-	146	-	35.3	+ Remarkably fun and capable - Cabin quality	★★★★
Subaru WRX STI	151 D	£32,995	4/2457	296/6000	300/4000	1505kg	200	5.1	-	155	243	26.9	+ Spec C suspension makes a better drive - No blue paint or gold wheels	★★★★½
Subaru Impreza STI CS400	146 R	£49,995	4/2457	395/5750	400/3950	1505kg	267	**4.6**	**10.7**	155	-	-	+ Cosworth kudos. Fastest hatch we've tested - Pricey. Lifeless steering	★★★½
Subaru Impreza STI 330S	124 F	'08-'10	4/2457	325/5400	347/3400	1505kg	219	4.4	-	155	-	-	+ A bit quicker than the STI... - ...but not better	★★★★
Suzuki Swift Sport	132 F	£12,740	4/1586	123/6800	109/4800	1105kg	113	8.9	-	124	165	39.8	+ Entertaining handling, well built - Lacking in steering feedback	★★★★½
Vauxhall Astra VXR	102 R	£22,875	4/1998	237/5600	236/2400	1393kg	173	**6.7**	**16.7**	152	221	30.7	+ Fast and furious - Lacks a little composure and precision	★★★★
Vauxhall Astra VXR 888	127 D	£26,573	4/1998	295/4650	317/4250	1393kg	215	5.1	-	160	221	-	+ Crazy power, chassis copes admirably - Lacks exploitability of Mégane R26	★★★★
VW Golf GTI (Mk6)	139 R	£24,295	4/1984	207/5300	207/1700	1318kg	160	**6.4**	**16.5**	149	170	38.7	+ Still a very accomplished hot hatch - 207bhp isn't a lot any more	★★★★
VW Golf R (Mk6)	140 D	£30,345	4/1984	266/6000	258/2500	1521kg	178	5.5	-	155	199	33.6	+ Great engine, tremendous pace and poise - High price, ACC only optional	★★★★½
VW Golf GTI (Mk5)	102 R	'05-'09	4/1984	197/5100	207/1800	1336kg	150	**6.7**	**17.9**	145	-	-	+ Character and ability: the original GTI is back - Lacking firepower?	★★★★★
VW Golf R32 (Mk5)	087 F	'06-'09	6/3189	246/6300	236/2500	1510kg	165	**5.8**	**15.2**	155	-	26.4	+ Traction's great and you'll love the soundtrack - We'd still have a GTI	★★★★
VW Golf GTI 16v (Mk2)		'88-'92	4/1781	139/6100	124/4600	1111kg	127	8.0	-	124	-	28.8	+ Arguably the best all-round Golf GTI ever - We'd be splitting hairs	★★★★★
VW Golf GTI (Mk1)	095 F	'82-'84	4/1781	112/5800	109/3500	840kg	135	8.1	-	112	-	36.0	+ The car that started it all - Tricky to find an unmolested one	★★★★

Buying a new car?
Don't make the wrong choice!

The website that helps you decide which new car to buy

Expert reviews in plain English
New cars rated for practicality, performance, comfort, reliability, safety, value for money and running costs

Detailed specifications
Facts and figures for every new car on sale in the UK, plus photos inside and out

Easy-to-use search engine
Find your perfect car with our powerful matching engine

Video test drives
We show you what each car is really like to drive and to own

Tips & advice
Essential guides that help you save time and money

Helping you decide which car to buy

THE KNOWLEDGE | | | Showroom

☆ OUR VERDICT ON NEW AND SECONDHAND TRACKDAY CARS

SALOONS

OUR CHOICE BMW M3. It's got two more doors than the coupe version but the M3 saloon costs nearly £1500 less. OK, it does without the carbon roof, but everything else that makes the two-door great is present and correct. What's not to like?

Best of the Rest: Most BMW M-cars are trackable, and most RS Audis too. We also rate the Lexus IS-F with its glorious high-revving V8 and playful rear-wheel drive. Moving up a size, we've been impressed by the Jaguar XFR (right) with its supercharged V8.

	Issue no.	Price	Engine cyl/cc	Bhp/rpm	Lb ft/rpm	Weight	Bhp/ton	0-60mph	0-100mph	Max mph	CO2 g/km	EC mpg	evo rating
Alfa Romeo 156 GTA	045 F	'02-'06	6/3179	247/6200	221/4800	1410kg	180	6.3	-	155	-	23.3	+ Noise, pace and individuality - Front-drive chassis can't keep up ★★★
Alpina D3		£30,950	4/1995	211/4000	332/2000	1495kg	143	6.9	-	152	-	52.3	+ Excellent chassis, turbodiesel oomph - Rather narrow powerband ★★★★½
Alpina B5 Biturbo	149 D	£69,995	8/4395	500/5500	516/3000	2040kg	265	4.7	-	191	-	-	+ Big performance and top-line luxury - Driver not really involved ★★★½
Alpina B5 S	118 D	'07-'10	8/4398	523/5500	535/4750	1720kg	309	4.5	-	197	-	23.0	+ Quicker and more exclusive than the E60 M5 - Suspension has its limits ★★★★½
Audi S4 (Mk3)	134 F	£36,530	6/2995	328/5500	325/2900	1650kg	202	5.1	-	155	234	29.1	+ More fun than you'd believe possible - When's the new RS4 coming? ★★★★
Audi S4 (Mk2)	073 D	'05-'08	8/4163	339/7000	302/3500	1700kg	206	5.4	-	155	-	-	+ Effortless V8, agile handling - Lacks ultimate finesse of class leaders ★★★½
Audi RS4	088 F	'06-'08	8/4163	414/7800	317/5500	1650kg	255	**4.5**	**10.9**	155	-	-	+ A leap on for fast Audis, superb engine - Busy under braking ★★★★★
Audi RS4	024 R	'00-'02	6/2671	375/6100	325/2500	1620kg	236	**4.8**	**12.1**	170	-	17.0	+ Effortless pace - Lacks finesse. Bends wheel rims ★★★★
Audi RS2		'94-'95	5/2226	315/6500	302/3000	1595kg	201	**4.8**	**13.1**	162	-	18.0	+ Storming performance (thanks to Porsche) - Try finding one ★★★★
Audi RS6	124 D	£76,715	10/4991	572/6250	479/1500	1985kg	293	4.5	-	155	331	20.3	+ Looks and drives better than estate version - M5 is ten grand cheaper... ★★★★½
Audi RS6	052 R	'02-'04	8/4172	444/5700	413/1950	1840kg	245	**4.8**	**11.6**	155	-	19.3	+ Huge real-world performance - Inert steering ★★★★
BMW 330d SE	123 D	£31,775	6/2993	241/4000	384/1750	1610kg	150	6.1	-	155	152	49.6	+ More power, refinement and mpg - Electric power steering lets side down ★★★★
BMW 325i M Sport		£30,540	6/2996	215/6700	199/2400	1505kg	145	6.6	-	155	168	39.2	+ Stunning drivetrain, controlled chassis - Looks a bit steady ★★★★
BMW 335i M Sport	134 F	£36,045	6/2979	302/5800	295/1300	1610kg	190	5.6	-	155	196	31.0	+ As above, with added wallop - Still looks a bit steady ★★★★
BMW M3 (E90)	123 R	£51,805	8/3999	414/8300	295/3900	1680kg	250	**4.9**	**10.7**	**165**	290	22.8	+ Every bit as good as the M3 coupe - No carbon roof ★★★★★
BMW 325i SE		'99-'05	6/2494	192/6000	181/3500	1485kg	131	7.1	-	149	-	31.4	+ Loses little to 330i - Steering not the best ★★★★
BMW 330i Sport	028 R	'99-'05	6/2979	231/5900	221/3500	1510kg	153	**5.9**	**17.0**	155	-	30.0	+ Clean, classy and confident - Too smooth for its own good? ★★★★
BMW 535i SE	141 D	£37,300	6/2979	302/5800	295/1200	1760kg	174	6.1	-	155	199	33.2	+ New 5-series impresses... - But only with all the chassis options ticked ★★★
BMW M5 (E60)	129 F	'04-'10	10/4999	500/7750	384/6100	1855kg	276	4.7	10.4	155	-	19.6	+ Close to being the ultimate supersaloon - SMG gearbox feels old-tech ★★★★½
BMW M5 (E39)	110 F	'99-'03	8/4941	400/6600	369/3800	1720kg	236	**4.9**	**11.5**	155	-	-	+ Magnificent V8-engined supersaloon - We'd be nit-picking ★★★★★
BMW M5 (E34)	110 F	'92-'96	6/3795	340/6900	295/4750	1653kg	209	**5.9**	**13.6**	155	-	-	+ The Godfather of supersaloons - The family can come too ★★★★★
BMW M5 (E28)	110 F	'86-'88	6/3453	286/6500	250/4500	1431kg	203	6.2	-	151	-	-	+ The original storming saloon - Two handfuls in the wet ★★★★★
Brabus Bullit	119 F	c£300,000	12/6233	720/5100	811/2100	1850kg	395	3.8	-	217	-	-	+ Seven hundred and twenty bhp - Three hundred thousand pounds ★★★★★
Ford Mondeo ST220	043 D	'02-'07	6/2967	223/6150	204/4900	1550kg	146	6.8	-	151	-	27.7	+ Muscular engine, fine chassis - Hotted-up repmobile image ★★★½
Ford Sierra RS Cosworth 4x4		'90-'93	4/1993	220/6250	214/3500	1305kg	159	6.6	-	144	-	24.4	+ Fast and furious - Try finding a straight one ★★★★½
Ford Sierra RS Cosworth		'86-'90	4/1993	204/6000	204/4500	1220kg	169	6.2	-	143	-	-	+ Roadgoing Group A racecar - Don't shout about the power output! ★★★★★
Holden HSV GTS S'charger	041 D	'02	8/5665	502/6050	457/5100	1799kg	283	4.5	-	180	-	-	+ Massive linear power, great chassis - Slow 'shift, cheap interior ★★★½
Honda Civic Type-R *	108 D	'07-'10	4/1998	222/8000	158/6100	1252kg	180	5.9	-	150	-	-	+ Screaming engine, razor-sharp chassis - Specialist import only ★★★★★
Honda Accord Type-R	012 R	'99-'03	4/2157	209/7200	158/6700	1306kg	163	**6.1**	**17.4**	142	-	29.4	+ One of the finest front-drivers of all time - Lack of image ★★★★½
Infiniti G37S		£34,470	6/3696	316/7000	265/5200	1709kg	188	5.8	-	155	248	26.7	+ Credible alternative to its German rivals - Lacks their looks and kudos ★★★½
Infiniti M37S	150 D	£39,650	6/3696	316/7000	265/5200	1765kg	182	6.2	-	155	235	27.7	+ Stands out from the crowd - Not as involving as some rivals ★★★½
Jaguar XFR	138 F	£62,600	8/5000	503/6000	461/2500	1891kg	270	**4.8**	**10.2**	155	292	22.5	+ Brilliant blend of pace and refinement - Looks too discreet? ★★★★½
Jaguar XF SV8	116 F	'08-'09	8/4196	410/6250	413/3500	1842kg	226	5.1	-	155	-	22.4	+ Convincing driving experience - Overshadowed by XFR ★★★★½
Lexus IS-F	151 R	£56,540	8/4969	417/6600	372/5200	1714kg	247	**4.7**	**10.9**	**173**	270	24.8	+ Shockingly good Lexus - The M3's available as a four-door too ★★★★½
Lotus Carlton	035 F	'91-'93	6/3615	377/5200	419/4200	1658kg	231	**4.8**	**10.6**	176	-	17.0	+ The Millennium Falcon of saloon cars - Every drive a work-out ★★★★★
Maserati Quattroporte S	137 R	£85,550	8/4691	425/7000	361/4750	1990kg	216	**5.1**	**12.1**	174	365	18.0	+ Finally, a QP with more bhp - New grille a bit Hannibal Lecter ★★★★½
Maserati Q'porte Sport GTS	141 F	£92,355	8/4691	433/7000	361/4750	1990kg	221	5.1	-	177	365	17.9	+ The most stylish supersaloon - Slightly wooden brakes, unforgiving ride ★★★★
Maserati Quattroporte	085 F	'04-'08	8/4244	394/7000	333/4500	1930kg	207	5.1	-	171	-	17.9	+ Redefines big-car dynamics - Don't use auto mode ★★★★½
Maserati Q'porte Sport GTS	113 D	'07-'08	8/4244	396/7000	339/4250	1930kg	208	5.5	-	167	-	-	+ Best Quattroporte chassis so far - More power wouldn't go amiss ★★★★½
Mazda 6 MPS	093 F	'06-'07	4/2261	256/5500	280/3000	1665kg	156	6.5	-	149	-	27.7	+ Agility, effective 4wd system, price - Inconsistent steering ★★★½
Mercedes-Benz 190E 2.5 16		'89-'92	4/2498	197/6750	177/5500	1360kg	147	7.2	-	142	-	24.4	+ M-B's M3 alternative - Not as nimble as the Beemer ★★★★
Mercedes-Benz C63 AMG	151 R	£52,435	8/6208	451/6800	442/5000	1730kg	264	**4.4**	**9.7**	**160**	312	21.1	+ Monstrous pace and extremely engaging - M3's just a little better... ★★★★★
Mercedes-Benz DR520	148 D	£62,430	8/6208	513/6800	479/5000	1730kg	301	4.1	-	187	-	-	+ C63 AMG goes feral - For an extra ten grand, though ★★★★★
Mercedes-Benz C55 AMG	088 R	'04-'08	8/5439	367/5250	376/4000	1635kg	228	5.2	-	155	-	23.7	+ Furiously fast, commendably discreet - Overshadowed by M3 and RS4 ★★★★
Mercedes-Benz E63 AMG	134 D	£71,900	8/6208	518/6800	464/5200	1840kg	286	4.5	-	155	295	-	+ Sounds good, drives very well - Not as lazily grunty as its rivals ★★★★
Mercedes-Benz E63 AMG	096 D	'06-'09	8/6208	507/6800	464/5200	1840kg	280	4.5	-	155	-	19.8	+ Brilliant engine, indulgent chassis - Vague steering, speed limits ★★★★
Mercedes-Benz E55 AMG	052 R	'03-'06	8/5439	476/6100	516/2650	1760kg	271	**4.8**	**10.2**	155	-	21.9	+ M5-humbling grunt, cosseting ride - Speed limits ★★★★
Mercedes-Benz E55 AMG		'98-'02	8/5439	354/5500	390/3000	1642kg	219	5.5	-	155	-	23.0	+ Dragster disguised as a limo - Tyre bills ★★★½
Mercedes-Benz CLS63 AMG	099 F	£77,960	8/6208	507/6100	464/2650	1905kg	270	4.5	-	155	345	19.5	+ Beauty, comfort, awesome performance - M5 has the edge on B-roads ★★★★½
MG ZS 180	071 D	'01-'05	6/2497	175/6500	177/4000	1235kg	144	7.3	-	139	-	29.7	+ Sweet V6 engine, pace, tidy handling - Image ★★★½
MG ZT 260 V8	068 F	'03-'05	8/4601	256/5000	302/4000	1680kg	155	**6.5**	**16.3**	155	-	21.5	+ Lovely woofly V8, well-sorted rear-drive chassis - Thirst ★★★★
Mitsubishi Evo X FQ-300		£30,299	4/1998	290/6500	300/3500	1560kg	189	4.7	-	155	246	27.4	+ The Evo grows up - Perhaps just a little too sensible? ★★★★
Mitsubishi Evo X FQ-300 SST	118 F	£33,799	4/1998	290/6500	300/3500	1590kg	185	**5.2**	**13.9**	155	256	26.2	+ As above with twin-clutch transmission - As above, with paddles on ★★★½
Mitsubishi Evo X FQ-330 SST	134 F	£36,799	4/1998	324/6500	322/3500	1590kg	207	4.4	-	155	256	-	+ Great engine and gearbox combo - It still lives in the shadow of the Evo IX ★★★★
Mitsubishi Evo X FQ-360	122 D	£38,229	4/1998	354/6500	363/3500	1560kg	230	4.1	-	155	328	19.9	+ Ridiculously rapid new Evo - A five speed gearbox?! ★★★★
Mitsubishi Evo X FQ-400	138 F	£50,799	4/1998	403/6500	387/3500	1560kg	262	3.8	-	155	328	-	+ The best Evo X so far... - ...is about X grand too much ★★★★
Mitsubishi Evo IX FQ-340	088 F	'05-'07	4/1997	345/6800	321/4600	1400kg	250	**4.3**	**10.9**	157	-	-	+ Gives Porsche drivers nightmares - Points. Lots of ★★★★★
Mitsubishi Evo IX MR FQ-360	103 F	'05-'07	4/1997	366/6887	363/3200	1400kg	266	3.9	-	157	-	-	+ Well-executed engine upgrades - Prison food ★★★★★
Mitsubishi Evo VIII	055 F	'03-'04	4/1997	276/6500	289/3500	1410kg	199	5.1	-	157	-	-	+ The Evo grows up - Brakes need beefing up ★★★★½
Mitsubishi Evo VIII MR FQ-300	057 R	'03-'05	4/1997	305/6800	289/3500	1400kg	221	4.8	-	157	-	20.5	+ Extra pace, extra attitude - Price premium ★★★★½
Mitsubishi Evo VII	031 F	'02-'03	4/1997	276/6500	282/3500	1360kg	206	**5.0**	**13.0**	140	-	20.4	+ Terrific all-rounder - You tell us ★★★★★
Mitsubishi Evo VII RS Sprint	041 D	'02-'03	4/1997	320/6500	327/6200	1260kg	258	4.4	-	150	-	-	+ Ruthlessly focused road weapon - For the truly committed ★★★★★
Mitsubishi Evo VI RS Sprint	011 F	'99	4/1997	330/6500	323/3000	1255kg	267	**4.5**	**11.8**	145	-	-	+ Lighter, keener, quicker than regular Evo - A little uncompromising ★★★★½
Mitsubishi Evo VI Makinen Ed.	128 F	'00-'01	4/1997	276/6500	275/2750	1365kg	205	4.6	-	150	-	-	+ Still one of our favourite Evos. Exclusive, too - Import only ★★★★★
Porsche Panamera Turbo	137 R	£97,358	8/4806	493/6000	516/2250	1970kg	254	**3.6**	**8.9**	188	286	23.2	+ Fast, refined and dynamically sound - It still leaves us cold ★★★½
Saab 9-5 2.8T XWD Aero	146 D	£37,795	6/2792	296/5500	295/2000	2065kg	146	6.9	-	155	244	26.6	+ Brilliant start to new Saab era - Steering and transmission could be better ★★★★
Subaru WRX STI	151 D	£32,995	4/2457	296/6000	300/4000	1505kg	200	5.1	-	158	243	26.9	+ The fast Subaru saloon is back - Blue paint and gold wheels aren't ★★★★½
Subaru Impreza WRX GB270	109 D	'07	4/2457	266/5700	310/3000	1410kg	192	5.2	-	143	-	-	+ Fitting final fling for 'classic' Impreza - End of an era ★★★★½
Subaru Impreza WRX	087 F	'05-'07	4/2457	227/5600	236/3600	1410kg	163	5.4	-	143	-	27.4	+ 2.5 litres gives even greater thump - Slightly light steering ★★★★
Subaru Impreza STI	090 R	'05-'07	4/2457	276/6000	289/4000	1495kg	188	5.3	-	158	-	25.9	+ Stunning to drive - Not so stunning to look at ★★★★
Subaru Impreza STI Spec C *	084 D	'05-'07	4/1994	320/6730	311/3500	1350kg	240	4.3	-	157	-	-	+ Lighter, faster, fiercer - The need for self-restraint ★★★★★
Subaru Impreza RB320	105 F	'07	4/2457	316/6000	332/3750	1495kg	215	4.8	-	155	-	-	+ Fitting tribute to a rallying legend - Too hardcore for some? ★★★★½
Subaru Imp'a WRX STI PPP	073 F	'03-'05	4/1994	300/6000	299/4000	1470kg	207	**5.2**	**12.9**	148	-	-	+ A Subaru with real edge - Bit too edgy in the wet ★★★★½
Subaru STi Type RA Spec C *	067 F	'03-'05	4/1994	335/7000	280/3750	1380kg	247	**4.3**	**11.1**	160	-	-	+ Best Impreza since the P1 - Has lost its throbby flat-four voice ★★★★★
Subaru Impreza WR1	067 R	'04-'05	4/1994	316/5800	310/4000	1470kg	218	**5.3**	**13.1**	155	-	-	+ Most powerful official UK Impreza until RB320 - Spec C is better ★★★★½
Subaru Impreza Turbo	011 F	'98-'00	4/1994	215/5600	214/4000	1235kg	177	**5.4**	**14.6**	144	-	27.2	+ Destined for classic status - Thirsty ★★★★★
Subaru Impreza P1	067 F	'00-'01	4/1994	276/6500	260/4000	1283kg	219	**4.9**	**13.3**	150	-	25.0	+ Ultimate old-shape Impreza - Prices reflect this ★★★★★
Subaru Impreza RB5 (PPP)	011 F	'99	4/1994	237/6000	258/3500	1235kg	195	**5.0**	**14.1**	143	-	-	+ Perfect blend of poise and power - Limited numbers ★★★★★
Subaru Impreza 22B	011 F	'98-'99	4/2212	276/6000	265/3200	1270kg	220	**5.0**	**13.1**	150	-	-	+ On paper, the ultimate - On the road, too uncompromising ★★★★
Subaru Forester STi *	087 F	'05-'08	4/2457	320/5800	330/3500	-	-	4.8	-	150+	-	-	+ Undercover fun, gutsy engine - Lacks ultimate edge of an Impreza ★★★★
Vauxhall Insignia VXR	134 D	£32,290	6/2792	321/5250	321/5250	1810kg	180	5.6	-	155	249	24.7	+ Highly able and very likeable - It's a £31K Vauxhall... ★★★★
Vauxhall Vectra VXR	102 D	'06-'09	6/2792	276/5500	262/1800	1580kg	177	6.1	-	161	-	27.4	+ Great engine, effortless pace, good value - Numb steering, lumpy ride ★★★★
Vauxhall VXR8	122 D	£35,275	8/6162	425/6000	405/4400	1831kg	236	4.9	-	155	-	18.6	+ Oversteer, price, oversteer, practicality - Suspension can get befuddled ★★★★
Vauxhall VXR8 Supercharged	113 R	£42,095	8/5967	533/6000	568/4400	1831kg	296	4.5	-	180	-	-	+ The Lotus Carlton reinvented - Doesn't have polish of best Europeans ★★★★
Vauxhall VXR8 Bathurst S	148 F	£44,995	8/6162	564/6000	527/4000	1866kg	307	**4.6**	**10.7**	155	-	-	+ A tauter VXR8. Bonkers pace, brilliant noise - Gearchange still rubbish ★★★★½
VW Passat R36	120 D	£34,375	6/3597	296/6600	258/2400	1689kg	178	5.6	-	155	227	26.9	+ On paper a poor man's RS4 - You'd rather have a secondhand RS4 ★★★½

GET 3 ISSUES OF **evo** FOR £1

Experience the **thrill of driving** every month with **evo**, the magazine devoted exclusively to the sexiest cars in the world. If you're passionate about performance cars then **evo** is your ultimate monthly read.

WHY NOT TRY EVO FOR YOURSELF?

Claim 3 issues of evo for just £1 today, and you'll receive the best performance car features hot-off-the-press for 3 months with **NO OBLIGATION**. If you enjoy reading it after the introductory period your subscription will automatically continue at the low rate of just £21.30 every 6 issues – saving you 19% on the shop price too, so order yours today!

CALL NOW
0844 844 0039

Or order online at: **www.dennismags.co.uk/evo**
quoting offer code G1011TRACK

Your susbscription will continue at the **LOW RATE of £21.30** every 6 issues, **saving 19% on the shop price.**

If **evo** isn't for you, simply write to cancel within your trial period and no more than £1 will be debited from your account.

☆ OUR VERDICT ON NEW AND SECONDHAND TRACKDAY CARS

SPORTS CARS & CONVERTIBLES

OUR CHOICE Porsche Boxster. OK, it's become a bit of a cliché and it's got all the visual tension of a bar of soap, but the Boxster's still a great drive and the latest version boasts fresher, more powerful engines. New Spyder iteration (left) is even more driver-focused.

Best of the Rest: The back-to-basics Lotus Elise is a joy, with sublime handling and just enough power, while the revamped Mazda MX-5 handles like it should again. For the ultimate road and track thrills, though, buy a Caterham R300 (right) or an Ariel Atom.

	Issue no.	Price	Engine cyl/cc	Bhp/rpm	Lb ft/rpm	Weight	Bhp/ton	0-60mph	0-100mph	Max mph	CO2 g/km	EC mpg	evo rating	
Ariel Atom 3 245	113 D	£29,954	4/1998	245/8200	155/5200	500kg	498	3.2	-	150	-	33.0	+ The Atom just got a little bit better - Can still be a bit draughty...	★★★★½
Ariel Atom 3 Supercharged	138 F	£42,000	4/1998	300/8200	162/7200	550kg	554	3.3	-	155	-	-	+ It's brilliant - It's mental	★★★★★
Ariel Atom V8 500	150 R	£146,699	8/3000	475/10,500	284/7750	550kg	877	3.0	5.8	170	-	-	+ An experience unlike anything else on Planet Car - £150K for an Atom	★★★★★
Ariel Atom 2 300 Supercharged	123 R	'03-'09	4/1998	300/8200	162/7200	550kg	554	3.3	-	155	-	28.0	+ Makes your face ripple - ...like Clarkson's	★★★★★
Ariel Atom 2 275	068 D	'03-'08	4/1998	275/8400	192/7650	500kg	559	3.4	-	150	-	-	+ Supercharged engine is a scream - One for the brave	★★★★
Ariel Atom 1	015 F	'99-'03	4/1796	125/5500	122/3000	496kg	256	5.6	18.0	115	-	-	+ Amazing styling, huge fun - As practical as a chocolate teapot	★★★★
Audi TTS Roadster	122 D	£36,825	4/1984	268/6000	258/2500	1455kg	187	5.6	-	155	189	34.4	+ Effortlessly quick - Long-term appeal open to question; not cheap either	★★★★
Audi TT RS Roadster	133 D	£46,715	5/2480	335/5400	332/1600	1510kg	225	4.7	-	155	221	29.7	+ Terrific engine... - ...is the best thing about it	★★★½
Audi R8 5.2 V10 quattro Spyder	143 F	£112,500	10/5204	518/8000	391/6500	1720kg	306	4.1	-	194	356	19.0	+ Looks and sounds sensational - It's the most expensive Audi ever	★★★★★
BMW Z4 sDrive 35i (Mk2)	130 D	£38,480	6/2979	302/5800	295/1300	1600kg	213	5.2	-	155	219	30.1	+ As above, with more power - Not as much fun as it used to be	★★★½
BMW Z4 3.0si (Mk1)	094 D	'06-'09	6/2996	265/6600	232/2750	1385kg	194	5.7	-	155	-	32.9	+ Terrific straight-six - Handling not as playful as we'd like	★★★★
BMW Z4 M Roadster	091 R	'06-'09	6/3246	338/7900	269/4900	1485kg	231	4.8	-	155	-	23.3	+ Exhilarating and characterful, that engine - Stiff suspension	★★★★½
BMW M Roadster	002 F	'98-'02	6/3246	325/7400	258/4900	1450kg	228	5.3	-	155	-	25.4	+ Fresh-air M3, that motor, hunky looks - M Coupe drives better	★★★½
BMW M3 Convertible (E93)	119 D	£57,285	8/3999	414/8300	295/3900	1885kg	223	5.3	-	155	269	21.9	+ M DCT transmission, pace, slick roof - Extra weight blunts the edge	★★★★
Brooke 260 Double R	094 F	£32,995	4/2261	260/7500	200/6100	550kg	480	3.9	-	155+	-	-	+ Fast, dynamic, well built - No roof, looks not for everyone	★★★½
Caterham 7 Classic	068 F	£16,300	4/1397	105/6000	95/5000	540kg	198	6.5	-	110	-	-	+ The Caterham experience starts here - It's pretty raw	★★★½
Caterham 7 Roadsport 125	105 F	£21,200	4/1595	125/6100	120/5350	539kg	235	5.9	-	112	-	-	+ New Ford-engined model is just great - Bigger drivers need SV model	★★★★½
Caterham 7 Roadsport SV 175	140 D	£28,300	4/1999	175/7000	139/6000	555kg	321	4.8	-	138	-	-	+ The Caterham for everyday use, R300 engine - Loses intensity of R300	★★★★½
Caterham 7 Superlight R300	150 F	£29,500	4/1999	175/7000	139/6000	515kg	345	4.5	-	140	-	-	+ Possibly all the Caterham you need - Factory-built cars can top £30K	★★★★★
Caterham 7 Superlight R400	105 F	£33,600	4/1999	210/7800	152/5750	525kg	406	3.8	-	140	-	-	+ R400 reborn with (lots of) Ford power - Slightly hesitant low-rev pick-up	★★★★
Caterham 7 Superlight R500	123 R	£40,200	4/1999	263/8500	177/7200	506kg	528	2.9	-	150	-	-	+ Better power-to-weight ratio than a Veyron - Until you add the driver	★★★★★
Caterham CSR 260 Superlight	094 F	£42,900	4/2261	256/7500	200/6200	565kg	460	3.8	-	155	-	-	+ Brilliant for high days, holidays and trackdays - Wet Wednesdays	★★★★½
Caterham Levante	131 F	£115,000	8/2398	550/10000	300/8500	520kg	1074	4.8	8.2	150	-	-	+ Twice the power-to-weight ratio of a Veyron! - Not easy to drive slowly	★★★★½
Caterham 7 R300	068 F	'02-'06	4/1796	160/7000	130/5000	500kg	325	4.7	-	130	-	-	+ Our 2002 Trackday Car of the Year - Not for wimps	★★★★★
Caterham 7 R400	068 F	'03-'06	4/1796	200/7500	150/5750	490kg	415	3.9	-	140	-	-	+ Race-car with a number plate - Your missus will leave you	★★★★★
Caterham 7 R500	068 F	'99-'06	4/1796	230/8600	155/7200	460kg	510	3.6	8.8	146	-	-	+ Fine for the Nürburgring - Hard work around the Bullring	★★★★½
Caterham 7 R500 Evolution	069 F	'04	4/1998	250/8000	190/4000	460kg	552	3.9	8.1	150	-	-	+ Madder than Mad Jack McMad - Er, it's a bit mad	★★★★½
Chevrolet Corvette C6	083 D	£56,186	8/6162	430/5900	424/4600	1460kg	300	4.3	-	186	-	21.2	+ Corvette performance - Convertible dynamics, electronics	★★★½
Fiat Barchetta	061 D	'95-'05	4/1747	130/6300	117/4300	1060kg	125	8.7	-	124	-	33.2	+ Out-chics the MX-5, great fun and terrific value, too - LHD only	★★★½
Ginetta G20		£15,995	4/1796	140/5800	101/3500	660kg	341	6.3	-	126	-	-	+ Classic looks, old-fashioned value - Vintage driving experience	★★★
Honda S2000	118 D	'99-'09	4/1997	237/8300	153/7500	1260kg	191	6.2	-	150	-	28.2	+ An alternative and rev-happy roadster - The Boxster's better	★★★★
Jaguar XKR	130 F	£81,500	8/5000	503/6000	461/2500	1800kg	284	4.8	-	155	292	23.0	+ Gains Jag's fantastic new V8 - Loses sporting ground to its main foes	★★★★
Jaguar XKR		'06-'09	8/4196	414/6250	413/4000	1705kg	247	5.0	-	155	-	-	+ First Jag sports car for years - Overwrought detailing	★★★★½
KTM X-Bow	138 F	£49,482	4/1984	237/5500	229/2000	790kg	305	3.8	-	137	-	-	+ Mad looks; real quality feel - Heavier and pricier than we'd hoped	★★★★
Light Car Company Rocket	104 F	£46,000	4/1002	143/10500	77/8500	406kg	358	4.4	-	145	-	35.0	+ Single-seater style, speed - Old Formula Fords cost £5K	★★★★
Lotus Elise S 1.6	144 D	£27,450	4/1598	134/6800	118/4400	876kg	155	6.0	-	127	149	45.0	+ New 1.6-litre Elise is light and fantastic - Very slightly slower than 1.8	★★★★★
Lotus Elise R	068 F	£31,450	4/1796	189/7800	133/6800	860kg	223	5.6	13.9	150	196	34.4	+ Most thrillsome Elise yet - Blaring engine note	★★★★★
Lotus Elise SC	131 F	£34,450	4/1794	218/8000	156/5000	870kg	254	4.5	11.4	148	199	33.2	+ All the usual Elise magic - Supercharged engine lacks sparkle	★★★★½
Lotus 2-Eleven	126 F	£32,440	4/1796	189/7800	133/6800	720kg	267	4.3	-	140	-	-	+ Not far off supercharged car's pace - Pricey once it's made road-legal	★★★★½
Lotus 2-Eleven Supercharged	123 R	£40,945	4/1796	252/8000	179/7000	670kg	382	3.8	-	150	-	-	+ Impressive on road and track - Not hardcore enough for some	★★★★★
Lotus 2-Eleven GT4	138 F	£76,590	4/1796	266/8200	179/7200	670kg	403	3.7	-	155	-	-	+ evo Track Car of the Year 2009 - It's a 76-grand Lotus with no roof	★★★★★
Lotus Elise S 1.8	104 F	'06-'10	4/1794	134/6200	127/4200	860kg	158	6.3	18.7	127	-	37.2	+ Brilliant entry-level Elise - Precious little	★★★★★
Lotus Elise S2 111S	049 F	'02-'04	4/1796	156/7000	129/4650	860kg	197	5.1	-	131	-	40.9	+ A genuinely useable Elise - Air-con? In an Elise?	★★★★★
Lotus Elise S2 Sport 135	040 D	'03	4/1796	135/6200	129/4850	726kg	189	5.4	-	129	-	-	+ One of our fave S2 Elises - Brakes need more bite and pedal feel	★★★★★
Lotus Elise S2 Sport 190	044 F	'03	4/1796	190/7800	128/5000	710kg	272	4.7	12.1	135	-	-	+ Fabulous trackday tool - Pricey	★★★★½
Lotus Elise S1	126 F	'96-'00	4/1796	118/5500	122/3000	731kg	164	6.1	18.5	126	-	39.4	+ A modern classic - A tad impractical?	★★★★★
Lotus 340R	126 F	'00	4/1796	190/7800	146/5000	658kg	293	4.5	12.5	126	-	-	+ Hardcore road-racer... - ...that looks like a dune buggy from Mars	★★★★★
Lotus Elan SE	095 F	'89-'95	4/1588	165/6600	148/4200	1022kg	164	6.7	-	137	-	21.0	+ Awesome front-drive chassis - Rather uninvolving	★★★★
Lotus Elan Sprint	126 F	'71-'73	4/1558	126/6500	113/5500	720kg	178	6.6	-	122	-	-	+ Sensational chassis, properly quick - Affording a mint one	★★★★★
Mazda MX-5 1.8i SE		£17,245	4/1798	124/6500	123/4500	1155kg	109	9.9	-	121	167	40.4	+ Basic MX-5 offers ESP-less fun - But you'll probably want the 2.0's power	★★★★
Mazda MX-5 2.0i Sport Tech	138 F	£20,645	4/1999	158/7000	139/5000	1173kg	144	7.6	-	132	181	37.2	+ Handles brilliantly again - Less than macho image	★★★★½
Mazda MX-5 1.8i (Mk3 v1)	091 F	'05-'09	4/1798	124/6500	123/4500	1155kg	108	9.3	-	122	-	-	+ Gearchange, interior - Lost a lot of the charm of old MX-5s	★★★
Mazda MX-5 1.8i (Mk2)	017 R	'98-'05	4/1839	146/7000	124/5000	1065kg	140	8.6	-	123	-	32.5	+ Affordable ragtops don't get much better - Cheap cabin	★★★★★
Mazda MX-5 1.6 (Mk1)	131 F	'89-'97	4/1597	115/6500	100/5500	971kg	120	9.0	-	114	-	-	+ The original and still (pretty much) the best - Less than rigid	★★★★★
Mercedes-Benz SLK350	120 R	£38,260	6/3498	301/6500	266/4900	1485kg	206	5.5	13.5	155	227	29.1	+ Best non-AMG SLK yet - Still no Boxster-beater	★★★½
Mercedes-Benz SLK55 AMG	087 F	£53,790	8/5439	355/5750	376/4000	1575kg	229	4.9	-	155	-	23.5	+ Superb engine, responsive chassis - No manual option, ESP spoils fun	★★★★
Mercedes SLK55 AMG Black	110 F	'07-'08	8/5439	394/5750	383/3750	1495kg	268	4.9	11.2	174	-	-	+ AMG gets serious - Dull-witted 7G-Tronic auto box, uneven dynamics	★★★½
MG TF LE500		£16,399	4/1796	133/6750	122/5000	1185kg	114	8.4	-	127	185	35.8	+ It's not bad to drive - But it can't be recommended at this price	★★★
Morgan Roadster V6	073 D	£39,038	6/2967	202/6000	206/4900	950kg	216	4.9	-	134	225	28.8	+ Lusty V6, romantic atmosphere - Bygone dynamics	★★★
Morgan Aero SuperSports	145 F	£126,900	8/4799	362/6300	370/3600	1180kg	312	4.2	-	170	-	-	+ As above, with a targa top - It's proper supercar money	★★★★
Morgan Aero 8	105 F	'02-'08	8/4799	362/6300	361/3400	1100kg	334	4.5	-	170	-	25.2	+ Glorious sound, view over bonnet, dynamics - Awkward-looking rear	★★★★
Porsche Boxster		£34,726	6/2893	252/6400	214/4400	1335kg	192	5.9	-	163	221	30.1	+ Still as impressive as ever - It's a typically Porsche facelift	★★★★★
Porsche Boxster S	128 F	£41,724	6/3436	306/6400	265/5500	1355kg	229	5.3	-	170	223	29.7	+ As above, but with more power - Lighter steering than before	★★★★★
Porsche Boxster Spyder	140 F	£45,603	6/3436	316/7200	273/4750	1275kg	252	5.0	-	166	221	-	+ Lighter, more driver-centric Boxster - Collapsed-brolly roof not practical	★★★★★
Porsche Boxster (Mk2)		'05-'09	6/2687	241/6500	201/4600	1305kg	188	6.0	-	160	-	29.4	+ Mk2 Boxster is even better than the Mk1 - Ubiquity?	★★★★★
Porsche Boxster S (Mk2)	101 D	'07-'09	6/3387	291/6250	251/4400	1355kg	218	5.3	-	169	-	27.2	+ Real drop-top alternative to a 911 - It ain't cheap	★★★★★
Porsche Boxster (Mk1)	049 F	'99-'04	6/2687	228/6300	192/4700	1275kg	182	6.3	-	155	-	29.1	+ Still an impeccable sports car - Very little	★★★★★
Porsche Boxster S (Mk1)	070 F	'99-'04	6/3179	260/6200	228/4700	1320kg	200	5.5	-	164	-	26.9	+ Added power is seductive - As above	
Radical SR4 Tracksport	070 F	£28,995	4/1500	250/9000	130/8000	462kg	550	3.5	-	160	-	-	+ 2004 Trackday Car of the Year - You may want a trailer	★★★★½
Radical SR8LM	138 F	£88,000	8/2800	460/10,500	260/8000	680kg	687	3.2	-	168	-	-	+ Fastest car around the Nordschleife - Convincing people it's road legal	★★★★★
Toyota MR2	078 F	'00-'06	4/1794	138/6400	125/4400	975kg	141	7.2	21.2	130	-	38.2	+ Tight lines, taut dynamics - Minimal luggage space	★★★★½
TVR T350T	067 D	'04-'07	6/3605	350/7200	290/5500	1100kg	318	4.4	-	175+	-	-	+ Targa top roof, grunty engine - Lacks polish	★★★½
TVR Tamora	070 F	'01-'07	6/3605	350/7200	290/5500	1050kg	338	4.5	-	160	-	-	+ Well-sorted soft-top TVR - Awkward styling	★★★★
TVR Tuscan Convertible	091 R	'05-'07	6/3996	365/6800	315/6000	1100kg	337	3.8	8.1	195+	-	-	+ Spirit of the Griff reborn - Over 195mph? Really?	★★★★½
TVR Chimaera 5.0	007 R	'93-'03	8/4988	320/5500	320/3750	1060kg	307	4.6	-	167	-	26.4	+ Gorgeous noise, tarmac-rippling grunt - Details	★★★★
TVR Griffith 4.3	068 F	'92-'93	8/4280	280/5500	305/4000	1060kg	268	4.8	11.2	148	-	-	+ The car that made TVR. Cult status - Mere details	★★★★½
TVR Griffith 500	009 R	'93-'01	8/4988	320/5500	320/3750	1060kg	307	4.8	11.2	167	-	22.1	+ Gruff diamond - A few rough edges	★★★★½
Ultima GTR	017 R	£45,500	8/6300	534/5800	528/4800	990kg	548	3.9	8.2	204	-	-	+ Turns the M1 into the Mulsanne - You'll have to build it yourself	★★★★
Vauxhall VX220	023 R	'00-'04	4/2198	145/5800	150/4000	875kg	168	5.6	-	136	-	34.4	+ Absurdly good Vauxhall - The badge?	★★★★½
Vauxhall VX220 Turbo	066 R	'03-'05	4/1998	197/5500	184/1950	930kg	215	4.7	-	151	-	-	+ Nothing comes close for the money - Marginal everyday usability	★★★★★
Westfield Megabusa	036 F	£24,450	4/1298	175/9800	102/9000	430kg	413	3.7	-	140	-	-	+ Bike-engined road-rocket - Not big on practicality...	★★★½
Westfield 1600 Sport Turbo	140 D	£27,499	4/1598	195/5850	170/2000	650kg	305	4.7	-	142	-	-	+ Very quick and composed - Expensive, and a little on the heavy side	★★★★
Westfield XI	078 D	£16,950	4/1275	65/6000	72/3000	498kg	132	8.5	-	120	-	-	+ Old-school charm - Old-school power	★★★★½
Westfield XTR4	068 D	£33,995	4/1781	220/5500	184/5000	542kg	413	3.6	-	160	-	-	+ Mini-Le Mans racer - You wouldn't want to drive it there	★★★½
Westfield SEiGHT	068 F	'92-'94	8/3900	270/6000	-	622kg	441	4.4	9.4	144	-	-	+ Snarling, fire-breathing V8, ferocious pace - Spits fuel at you	★★★★

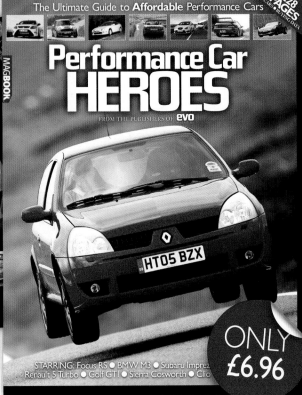

COUPES/GTs

OUR CHOICE Porsche 997.2 GT3 RS. From its gloriously vocal flat-six to its race-car aero addenda, the latest RS is a machine optimised for the circuit, yet it also works extraordinarily well on the road. Simply intoxicating, and our 2010 Car of the Year.

Best of the Rest: Lotus's Evora (right) was our 2009 eCoty, offering Elise fun and tactility in a baby-supercar package. Nissan's GT-R (our 2008 eCoty) is supercar-quick, while Audi's R8s are sublime and BMW's M3 is mega, especially with the Competition Pack.

	Issue no.	Price	Engine cyl/cc	Bhp/rpm	Lb ft/rpm	Weight	Bhp/ton	0-60mph	0-100mph	Max mph	CO2 g/km	EC mpg	**evo** rating	
Aston Martin V8 Vantage 4.7	120 F	£88,995	8/4735	420/7000	346/5750	1630kg	262	4.7	-	180	328	20.4	More power lifts Vantage to a new level - Ride is unremittingly firm	★★★★
Aston Martin V8 Vantage N420	147 F	£96,995	8/4735	420/7000	346/5750	1603kg	266	4.7	-	180	-	20.4	Aston's best V8 Vantage yet... - ...is by far the most expensive	★★★★★
Aston Martin V8 Vantage 4.3	*109 F*	*'05-'08*	*8/4281*	*380/7300*	*302/5000*	*1630kg*	*237*	**5.2**	**12.0**	*175*	-	-	*Gorgeous, awesome soundtrack - Can't quite match 911 dynamically*	★★★★
Aston Martin V8 Vantage N400	*114 F*	*'07-'08*	*8/4281*	*400/7300*	*309/5000*	*1630kg*	*249*	*4.9*	-	*177*	-	-	*Brilliant limited edition Vantage - They should have built more like this*	★★★★★
Audi TT RS	135 R	£44,775	5/2480	335/5400	332/1600	1450kg	235	**4.4**	**11.1**	155	214	31.0	Sublime 5-cylinder turbo engine - Rest of package can't quite match it	★★★★
Audi TT Sport (Mk1)	*081 D*	*'05-'06*	*4/1781*	*237/5700*	*236/2300*	*1390kg*	*173*	*5.7*	-	*155*	-	*30.3*	*Deliciously purposeful interior, crisp chassis - Numb steering*	★★★★
Audi RS5	151 R	£57,480	8/4163	444/8250	317/4000	1725kg	261	**4.3**	**10.6**	155	-	-	Brilliant engine and accomplished chassis... - ...don't gel together	★★★
Audi R8 4.2 V8 quattro	106 R	£85,100	8/4163	414/7800	317/4500	1560kg	270	**4.1**	**9.9**	187	332	20.3	Finally, a true 911 alternative - Exclusivity comes at a price	★★★★★
Audi R8 5.2 V10 quattro	146 R	£105,810	10/5204	518/8000	391/6500	1620kg	325	**3.9**	**8.4**	196	351	19.2	The fabulous R8 gets a supercar engine - Looks a lot like the V8	★★★★★
Audi R8 GT	151 D	£142,585	10/5204	552/8000	398/6500	1520kg	369	3.6	-	199	-	-	Everything we love about the R8 - Not as hardcore as we wanted	★★★★★
Audi Quattro 20V	*019 F*	*'90-'91*	*5/2226*	*220/5900*	*228/1950*	*1329kg*	*146*	**6.2**	**18.2**	*143*	-	*19.1*	*Modern classic - Buy wisely to avoid big bills*	★★★★★
BMW 135i M Sport	113 F	£30,675	6/2979	302/5800	295/1300	1560kg	197	5.3	-	155	198	30.7	Fast, fun, £20K cheaper than an M3 - Not as wild as we'd hoped	★★★★
BMW 330Ci	*071 R*	*'00-'06*	*6/2979*	*231/5900*	*221/3500*	*1522kg*	*154*	**6.4**	**16.6**	*155*	-	*31.0*	*Not much slower than a contemporary M3 - Coupés should be bolder*	★★★★
BMW 335i M Sport	095 D	£38,215	6/2979	302/5800	295/1300	1600kg	192	**5.2**	**12.2**	155	196	31.0	Eager engine, exploitable chassis - Slightly unadventurous styling	★★★★½
BMW M3 (E92)	151 R	£53,275	8/3999	414/8300	295/3900	1655kg	254	**4.3**	**10.3**	155	290	22.8	Fends off all of its talented new rivals - Priced very close to 911 territory	★★★★★
BMW M3 GTS (E92)	150 F	£115,215	8/4361	444/8300	324/3750	1530kg	295	4.3	-	155	-	-	Highly exclusive, feels special - Highly priced, too. And it's no GT3 RS	★★★★½
BMW M3 (E46)	*066 F*	*'00-'07*	*6/3246*	*338/7900*	*269/5000*	*1570kg*	*219*	**5.1**	**12.3**	*155*	-	*23.7*	*One of the best BMWs ever - Slightly artificial steering feel*	★★★★½
BMW M3 CS (E46)	*088 F*	*'05-'07*	*6/3246*	*338/7900*	*269/5000*	*1570kg*	*219*	*5.1*	-	*155*	-	*23.7*	*CSL dynamics without CSL price - Looks like the standard car*	★★★★★
BMW M3 CSL (E46)	*060 R*	*'03-'04*	*6/3246*	*355/7900*	*273/4900*	*1385kg*	*255*	**5.3**	**12.0**	*155*	-	-	*Stripped-down road-race M3 - Standard brakes barely adequate*	★★★★★
BMW M3 (E36)		*'93-'98*	*6/3201*	*321/7400*	*258/3250*	*1515kg*	*215*	**5.4**	**12.8**	*157*	-	*25.7*	*Performance, image - Never quite as good as the original*	★★★★
BMW M3 (E30)	*019 F*	*'86-'90*	*4/2302*	*220/6750*	*180/4750*	*1257kg*	*178*	**6.7**	**17.8**	*144*	-	*20.3*	*Best M-car ever! Race-car dynamics for the road - LHD only*	★★★★★
BMW Z4 M Coupe	*097 F*	*'06-'09*	*6/3246*	*338/7900*	*269/4900*	*1424kg*	*241*	*5.0*	-	*155*	-	*23.3*	*A real drivers' car - You've got to be prepared to get stuck in*	★★★★½
BMW M Coupe	*005 R*	*'98-'03*	*6/3246*	*325/7400*	*258/3250*	*1450kg*	*228*	*5.1*	-	*155*	-	*25.0*	*Quick and characterful - Lacks finesse*	★★★★
BMW M6	106 R	£87,335	10/4999	500/7750	384/6100	1785kg	285	**4.8**	**10.0**	155	342	19.8	Awesome GT, awesome sports car - SMG gearbox now off the pace	★★★★½
Chevrolet Corvette Z06	099 F	£66,403	8/7011	505/6300	469/4800	1418kg	363	**3.9**	**8.5**	198	-	19.2	8.5 to 100, brakes, price - Not quite the road-racer we expected	★★★★½
Honda Integra Type-R (DC2)	*095 F*	*'96-'00*	*4/1797*	*187/8000*	*131/7300*	*1101kg*	*173*	**6.2**	**17.9**	*145*	-	*28.9*	*Arguably the greatest front-drive car ever - Too raw for some*	★★★★★
*Honda Integra Type-R (DC5) **	*037 F*	*'01-'06*	*4/1998*	*217/8000*	*152/7000*	*1250kg*	*176*	*7.1*	*16.7*	*140*	-	-	*Sharp looks, massive grip - Lost a little of the DC2's magic*	★★★★
Honda NSX	*043 F*	*'90-'05*	*6/3179*	*270/7300*	*220/5300*	*1410kg*	*196*	*5.5*	-	*168*	-	*22.8*	*'The useable supercar' - 270bhp sounds a bit weedy today*	★★★★½
*Honda NSX-R **	*051 F*	*'02-'03*	*6/3179*	*276/7100*	*224/5300*	*1270kg*	*221*	*4.4*	-	*168*	-	-	***evo** Car of the Year 2002 - Honda never brought it to the UK*	★★★★★
Jaguar XKR	129 D	£75,500	8/5000	503/6000	461/2500	1753kg	292	4.6	-	155	292	23.0	Fast and incredibly rewarding Jag - The kids will have to stay at home	★★★★½
Jaguar XKR 75	150 F	£85,500	8/5000	523/6000	488/2500	1762kg	302	4.4	-	174	-	-	Fastest and most involving Jag - They're only making 75 of them	★★★★½
Lotus Exige S	105 F	£35,550	4/1796	218/7800	158/5500	930kg	238	4.5	-	148	199	33.2	Non-limited edition of the Exige 240R - Uninspiring soundtrack	★★★★★
Lotus Exige Cup 260	139 D	£45,950	4/1796	256/8000	174/6000	890kg	293	4.0	-	152	199	31.1	Feels like a race car, yet works on the road - Costs the best part of £50K	★★★★½
Lotus Exige (series 2)	*068 R*	*'04-'08*	*4/1796*	*189/7800*	*133/6800*	*875kg*	*219*	*4.9*	-	*147*	-	*32.1*	*Highly focused road and track tool - Lacks visual impact of S1*	★★★★★
Lotus Exige 240R	*087 F*	*'05*	*4/1796*	*243/8000*	*174/7000*	*930kg*	*264*	*3.9*	*9.9*	*155*	-	-	*Lightweight with a hefty punch - Instantly sold out*	★★★★★
Lotus Exige (series 1)	*067 D*	*'00-'01*	*4/1796*	*192/7800*	*146/5000*	*780kg*	*247*	*4.6*	-	*136*	-	-	*Looks and goes like Elise racer - A tad lacking in refinement*	★★★★★
Lotus Evora	138 F	£48,550	6/3456	276/6400	258/4700	1382kg	203	**5.6**	**13.6**	162	205	32.5	Sublime ride and handling. Our 2009 car of the year - Pricey options	★★★★★
Lotus Evora S	151 D	£57,550	6/3456	345/7000	295/4500	1430kg	245	4.6	-	172	239	-	A faster and better Evora - But one which spars with the Porsche 911...	★★★★★
Lotus Esprit Sport 350	*005 R*	*'99-'00*	*8/3506*	*350/6500*	*295/4250*	*1299kg*	*274*	**4.3**	**9.9**	*175*	-	*22.0*	*Designed for track work but brilliant on the road - Limited edition*	★★★★
Maserati Coupe	*064 F*	*'03-'07*	*8/4244*	*390/7000*	*333/4500*	*1680kg*	*237*	*4.8*	-	*177*	-	*17.6*	*Glorious engine, improved chassis - Overly sharp steering*	★★★★
Maserati GranSport	*073 F*	*'04-'07*	*8/4244*	*400/7000*	*333/4500*	*1680kg*	*239*	*4.8*	-	*180*	-	-	*Maser Coupe realises its full potential - Very little*	★★★★½
Mercedes-B CLK63 AMG Black	*106 F*	*'07-'09*	*8/6208*	*500/6800*	*464/5250*	*1760kg*	*289*	*4.2*	-	*186*	-	-	*AMG goes Porsche-hunting - Dull-witted gearshift spoils the party*	★★★★½
Nissan 370Z	131 F	£28,345	6/3696	326/7000	269/5200	1520kg	218	5.4	-	155	248	-	Quicker, leaner, keener than 350Z - Not quite a Cayman-killer	★★★★½
Nissan 350Z (309bhp)	*107 R*	*'07-'09*	*6/3498*	*309/6800*	*264/4800*	*1532kg*	*205*	**5.5**	**13.0**	*155*	-	*24.1*	*Huge fun, and great value too - Honestly, we're struggling*	★★★★½
Nissan 350Z (276bhp)	*059 D*	*'03-'06*	*6/3498*	*276/6200*	*268/4800*	*1525kg*	*184*	**6.1**	**14.8**	*155*	-	*24.8*	*Original 350Z makes a great used buy - Slightly low-rent interior*	★★★★½
Nissan 200SX		*'94-'02*	*4/1998*	*197/6400*	*195/4800*	*1267kg*	*158*	*6.5*	-	*142*	-	*29.1*	*Fast, cheap and rwd - Looks, image*	★★★½
Nissan GT-R	150 D	£69,950	6/3799	520/6400	475/3200	1740kg	304	3.5	-	194	295	-	Our 2008 Car of the Year. Now even better - Pricier than before	★★★★★
Nissan GT-R Spec V	150 F	£124,950	6/3799	478/6400	447/3500	1680kg	289	3.4	-	193	295	-	Phenomenal brakes and handling - Not really worth the extra £55K	★★★★
Nissan Skyline GT-R (R34)	*009 R*	*'99-'02*	*6/2568*	*276/7000*	*289/4400*	*1560kg*	*180*	**4.7**	**12.5**	*165*	-	*20.1*	*Big, brutal, and great fun - Very firm ride*	★★★★
Noble M400	*089 F*	*'04-'06*	*6/2968*	*425/6500*	*390/5000*	*1060kg*	*407*	*3.5*	-	*185*	-	-	*Devilishly fast - Demon Tweeks interior*	★★★★½
Noble M12 GTO-3R	*070 F*	*'03-'06*	*6/2968*	*352/6200*	*350/3500*	*1080kg*	*332*	*3.8*	-	*170*	-	-	*The ability to humble exotica - Flawed driving position*	★★★★
Noble M12 GTO	*023 R*	*'00-'03*	*6/2544*	*310/6000*	*320/3500*	*980kg*	*321*	**4.1**	**10.2**	*165*	-	-	*Gives GT3 drivers a fright - Styling could be more cohesive*	★★★★
Porsche Cayman	131 F	£37,261	6/2893	261/7200	221/4400	1330kg	199	5.8	-	165	221	30.1	Extra power, just as involving - Still lacks desirability of other Porsches	★★★★½
Porsche Cayman S	132 F	£45,449	6/3436	315/7200	273/4750	1350kg	237	5.2	-	172	223	29.7	Still want that 911? - Yeah, us too (even though it's the best Cayman yet)	★★★★½
Porsche Cayman S	*097 F*	*'06-'09*	*6/3387*	*291/6250*	*251/4400*	*1350kg*	*219*	**5.3**	**12.2**	*171*	-	*26.6*	*Pure and rewarding - If they'd just move the engine back a bit...*	★★★★½
Porsche 911 Carrera S (997.2)	121 F	£72,894	6/3800	380/6500	310/4400	1425kg	271	4.6	-	188	242	27.4	Poise, precision, blinding pace - Feels a bit clinical	★★★★½
Porsche 911 GT3 (997.2)	138 F	£85,564	6/3797	429/7600	317/6250	1395kg	312	**4.2**	**9.2**	194	303	22.1	Even better than the car it replaces - Give us a minute...	★★★★★
Porsche 911 GT3 RS (997.2)	150 F	£106,870	6/3797	444/7900	317/6750	1370kg	329	4.0	-	193	314	-	Our 2010 car of the year - Looks and noise are slightly OTT	★★★★★
Porsche 911 GT3 (997.1)	*103 R*	*'07-'09*	*6/3600*	*409/7600*	*298/5500*	*1395kg*	*298*	**4.3**	**9.4**	*192*	-	-	*Runner-up **evo** Car of the Year 2006 - Ferrari 599 GTBs*	★★★★★
Porsche 911 GT3 RS (997.1)	*105 F*	*'07-'09*	*6/3600*	*409/7600*	*298/5500*	*1375kg*	*302*	*4.2*	-	*193*	-	-	***evo** Car of the Year 2007 - £15K more than the brilliant GT3*	★★★★★
Porsche 911 GT3 (996.2)	*066 F*	*'03-'05*	*6/3600*	*375/7400*	*284/5000*	*1380kg*	*272*	**4.3**	**9.2**	*190*	-	-	***evo** Car of the Year 2003 - Looks softer than previous GT3*	★★★★★

EXPERIENCE AN **evo** TRACKDAY!

Drive your car on some of the most exciting circuits in the UK with **evo**'s 2011 Trackdays

FIND OUT HOW YOUR CAR PERFORMS ON TRACK, MEET MEMBERS OF THE EVO TEAM AND GET UP CLOSE TO THE CARS FROM THE MAGAZINE'S FAST FLEET

For dates, venues, prices and more information
go to www.evo.co.uk/trackdays

	Issue no.	Price	Engine cyl/cc	Bhp/rpm	Lb ft/rpm	Weight	Bhp/ton	0-60mph	0-100mph	Max mph	CO2 g/km	EC mpg	evo rating	
Porsche 911 GT3 RS (996.2)	068 R	'03-'05	6/3600	375/7400	284/5000	1330kg	286	4.2	9.2	190	-	-	+ Track-biased version of above - Limited supply	★★★★★
Porsche 911 RS (993)	036 R	'95	6/3746	300/6500	262/5400	1270kg	240	4.7	11.2	172	-	-	+ Barking engine note, gearchange - Not quite hardcore enough	★★★★½
Porsche 911 GT3 (996.1)	066 F	'99	6/3600	360/7200	273/5000	1350kg	271	**4.5**	**10.3**	187	-	21.9	+ Our Car of the Year 1999 - Porsche didn't build enough	★★★★★
Porsche 911 Carrera S (997.1)	070 F	'04-'08	6/3824	350/6600	295/4600	1420kg	246	**4.6**	**10.9**	182	-	24.5	+ 'S' is like a junior GT3 - Tech overload?	★★★★★
Porsche 911 Carrera 4S (996)	051 F	'02-'05	6/3596	316/6800	273/4250	1470kg	218	5.1	-	174	-	-	+ Second best 996 only to the GT3 - Very little	★★★★★
Porsche 911 Carrera (996 3.4)	008 R	'98-'01	6/3387	300/6800	258/4600	1320kg	230	4.6	-	173	-	28.0	+ Beautifully polished 911 - Some like a bit of rough	★★★★★
Porsche 911 Carrera (993)		'94-'97	6/3600	285/6100	251/5250	1372kg	211	5.2	-	168	-	25.0	+ More character than 996 - Harder work at speed	★★★★½
Porsche 968 Club Sport	019 F	'93-'95	4/2990	240/6200	225/4100	1335kg	183	**6.1**	**15.7**	149	-	-	+ One of the all-time greats - Lots have been driven very hard	★★★★★
Porsche 928 GTS		'92-'95	8/5396	350/5700	317/4250	1790kg	199	5.2	-	171	-	17.0	+ Big-hearted and beautiful - Be sure to buy a good one	★★★★
Renault Alpine A610		'92-'96	6/2975	250/5750	258/2900	1420kg	179	**5.4**	**13.8**	160	-	21.0	+ Overlooked, bargain-price French 911. Try one - R5 interior	★★★★
Superformance Daytona Coupe	149 D	£102,225	8/6162	437/5900	424/4600	1300kg	342	3.9	-	200+	-	-	+ Awesome engine, awesome looks - Damp roads equal moist palms	★★★★
TVR T350C	057 R	'03-'07	6/3605	350/7200	290/5500	1100kg	318	**4.7**	**10.0**	175	-	-	+ Looks, engine - Unsupportive seats; chassis lacks ultimate polish	★★★★
TVR Sagaris	099 D	'05-'07	6/3996	406/7500	349/5000	1078kg	383	3.7	-	185	-	-	+ Looks outrageous - 406bhp feels a touch optimistic	★★★★½
TVR Tuscan S (Mk2)	076 R	'05-'07	6/3996	400/7000	315/5250	1100kg	369	4.0	-	185	-	-	+ Possibly TVR's best ever car - Aerodynamic 'enhancements'	★★★★½
TVR Typhon	102 F	'06	6/3996	400/7000	330/5250	1060kg	383	3.9	-	180+	-	-	+ Carbon body, exclusivity - Interesting damping, no supercharger	★★★★
TVR Cerbera Speed Six	004 R	'98-'04	6/3966	350/6800	330/5000	1130kg	315	**5.0**	**11.4**	160+	-	-	+ Accomplished and desirable - Check chassis for corrosion	★★★★½
TVR Cerbera 4.5	014 F	'97-'04	8/4578	420/6750	380/5500	1100kg	388	3.9	-	180+	-	-	+ Genuine supercar pace - Integrity?	★★★★
Vauxhall Monaro VXR 6.0	079 D	'05-'07	8/5967	398/6000	391/4400	1677kg	241	5.1	-	180+	-	-	+ Improved chassis and steering, 180mph - Looks a bit snouty	★★★★
VW Scirocco 2.0 TSI	122 R	£23,615	4/1984	207/5300	207/1700	1298kg	162	6.9	-	149	172	38.2	+ Golf GTI price and performance - Interior lacks flair	★★★★½
VW Scirocco R	138 F	£28,505	4/1984	261/6000	258/2500	1352kg	196	5.8	-	155	189	35.3	+ Great engine, grown-up dynamics - Looks very grown-up, too	★★★★
VW Corrado VR6	095 F	'92-'96	6/2861	190/5800	180/4200	1237kg	156	6.2	-	143	-	29.5	+ One of the great all-rounders - A little nose-heavy	★★★★½
Wiesmann GT MF4	117 D	£108,000	8/4799	362/6300	361/3400	1250kg	294	4.5	-	174	-	-	+ Old-school looks with new-school go - Big-school price	★★★★½
Wiesmann GT MF5	127 D	£150,000	10/4999	500/7750	383/6100	1380kg	368	3.9	-	193	-	-	+ Striking coupe mated to BMW M5's V10 - Steering a little light	★★★★★

SUPERCARS

OUR CHOICE Ferrari 599 GTO. You can argue about the use of the Gran Turismo Omologato tag (one thing it isn't is an homologation car), but everything else about the GTO just feels so right, from its 661bhp V12 to its racecar-sharp chassis. A legend in the making.

Best of the Rest: You don't see many supercars on the average trackday, but most Porsches perform consistently well. If you really want to show off, go for a Murciélago LP670-4 SV (right). To impress those in the know, turn up in the V10-engined Lexus LFA.

	Issue no.	Price	Engine cyl/cc	Bhp/rpm	Lb ft/rpm	Weight	Bhp/ton	0-60mph	0-100mph	Max mph	CO2 g/km	EC mpg	evo rating	
9ff GT9R	127 D	c£450,000	6/4000	1120/7850	774/5970	1346kg	845	2.9	-	260	-	-	+ Above 100mph eats Veyrons for breakfast - Eats M3 dust at traffic lights	★★★★★
Aston Martin V12 Vantage	146 R	£135,000	12/5935	510/6500	420/5750	1680kg	308	**4.4**	**9.7**	190	388	17.3	+ The best car that Aston Martin makes - Erm, a tad thirsty?	★★★★★
Aston Martin Vanquish S	110 F	'05-'07	12/5935	520/7000	425/5800	1875kg	282	**4.9**	**10.1**	200	-	-	+ Vanquish joins supercar greats - A tad intimidating at the limit	★★★★★
Bugatti Veyron 16.4	134 F	c£925,000	16/7993	1000/6000	922/2200	1950kg	521	**2.8**	**5.8**	253	-	-	+ Superbly engineered 4wd quad-turbo rocket - Er, lacks luggage space?	★★★★★
Bugatti Veyron Super Sport	151 F	c£2.0m	16/7993	1183/6400	1106/3000	1838kg	654	2.5	-	268	539	-	+ The world's fastest supercar - Limited to 258mph for us mere mortals	★★★★★
Caparo T1	138 F	£301,975	8/3499	575/10,500	310/9000	689kg	848	**3.8**	**6.2**	205	-	-	+ Absolutely staggering performance - Absolutely staggering price tag	★★★★½
Chevrolet Corvette ZR1	133 R	£106,605	8/6162	638/6500	603/3800	1528kg	424	**3.8**	**7.6**	205	-	18.8	+ Huge pace and character - Take plenty of brave pills if there's rain	★★★½
Ferrari 458 Italia	149 F	£169,545	8/4499	562/9000	398/6000	1485kg	384	3.4	-	202	307	21.2	+ An astounding achievement, looks fantastic - There'll never be a manual	★★★★★
Ferrari 599 GTB Fiorano	101 R	£207,620	12/5999	611/7600	448/5600	1688kg	368	**3.5**	**7.4**	205	415	15.8	+ evo Car of the Year 2006 - Banks are getting harder to rob	★★★★★
Ferrari 599 GTB Fiorano HGTE	146 R	£221,884	12/5999	611/7600	448/5600	1688kg	368	**3.5**	**7.4**	205	415	-	+ As above, with a bit more edge - Can be a little too edgy in the wet	★★★★½
Ferrari 599 GTO	149 F	£299,300	12/5999	661/8250	457/6500	1605kg	418	3.4	-	208	-	-	+ One of the truly great Ferraris - Erm, the air con isn't very good	★★★★★
Ferrari F430	087 F	'04-'10	8/4308	483/8500	343/5250	1450kg	342	4.0	-	196	-	18.6	+ Just brilliant - Didn't you read the plus point?	★★★★★
Ferrari 430 Scuderia	121 R	'07-'10	8/4308	503/8500	347/5250	1350kg	378	**3.5**	**7.7**	198	-	15.7	+ Successful F1 technology transplant - Likes to shout about it	★★★★★
Ferrari 360 Modena	008 R	'99-'04	8/3586	400/8500	275/4750	1390kg	292	4.5	9.0	180+	-	17.0	+ Worthy successor to 355 - Not quite as involving as it should be	★★★★½
Ferrari 360 Challenge Stradale	068 R	'03-'04	8/3586	420/8500	275/4750	1280kg	333	4.1	-	186	-	-	+ Totally exhilarating road-racer. It's loud - It's very, very loud	★★★★★
Ferrari F355 F1 Berlinetta	003 F	'97-'99	8/3496	375/8250	268/6000	1332kg	286	4.7	-	183	-	16.7	+ Looks terrific, sounds even better - Are you kidding?	★★★★★
Ferrari 575M 'Fiorano'	050 D	'02-'06	12/5748	508/7250	434/5250	1730kg	298	**4.2**	**9.6**	202	-	12.3	+ 'Fiorano pack' makes 575 truly great - It should have been standard	★★★★★
Ferrari 550 Maranello	066 F	'97-'02	12/5474	485/7000	415/5000	1716kg	287	4.3	10.0	199	-	12.3	+ Everything - Nothing	★★★★★
Ferrari Enzo	149 F	'02-'04	12/5998	650/7800	485/5500	1365kg	484	**3.5**	**6.7**	217+	-	-	+ Intoxicating, exploitable - Cabin detailing falls short of Zonda or F1	★★★★★
Ferrari F50	064 F	'96-'97	12/4968	513/8000	347/6500	1229kg	424	3.7	-	202	-	-	+ The best drivers' Ferrari - Lines lack tension	★★★★★
Ferrari F40	064 F	'87-'92	8/2936	478/7000	425/4000	1100kg	441	3.7	-	201	-	-	+ The shape that launched a thousand posters - Er...	★★★★★
Ford GT	087 F	'04-'06	8/5409	550/6500	500/3750	1583kg	353	3.7	-	205	-	-	+ Our 2005 Car of the Year - JC had one. Reckoned it didn't handle...	★★★★★
Gumpert Apollo	110 F	£275,000	8/4163	690/6300	675/4000	1200kg	584	3.0	-	220+	-	-	+ Stupendous perfomance, 'Apollo' - High price, 'Gumpert'	★★★★½
Jaguar XJ220	131 F	'92-'94	6/3498	542/7200	475/4500	1470kg	375	3.7	-	213	-	-	+ Britain's greatest supercar... - ...until McLaren built the F1	★★★★
Koenigsegg CCX	094 F	c£500,000	8/4700	806/6900	678/5700	1180kg	694	**3.9**	**7.7**	241	-	-	+ Sweden's greatest supercar - Sweden's *only* supercar	★★★★★
Koenigsegg CCXR Edition	118 F	c£1.5m	8/4800	1004/7000	796/5600	1280kg	797	2.8	-	254+	-	-	+ The world's fastest car. Probably - Spikey power delivery	★★★★★
Lamborghini Gallardo LP550-2	138 F	£166,784	10/5204	542/8000	398/6500	1380kg	399	3.9	-	199	-	-	+ The mad rear-driven Lambo is back! - For a limited period only...	★★★★★
Lamborghini Gallardo LP560-4	122 R	£149,107	10/5204	552/8000	398/6500	1410kg	398	**3.7**	**7.8**	202	327	20.0	+ Great car gets quicker and cleaner - Rocky ride; grabby carbon brakes	★★★★½
Lamborghini LP570-4 S'leggera	150 F	£174,840	10/5204	562/8000	398/6500	1340kg	426	**3.5**	**-**	202	325	-	+ A reminder of how great the Gallardo is - LP560-4 does as good a job	★★★★½
Lamborghini Gallardo	094 F	'06-'08	10/4961	513/8000	376/4250	1520kg	343	**4.3**	**9.4**	196	-	-	+ On a full-bore start it spins all four wheels, cool - Slightly clunky e-gear	★★★★½
Lamborghini G'ardo S'leggera	104 F	'07-'08	10/4961	522/8000	376/4250	1420kg	373	3.8	-	196	-	-	+ Lighter, more agile - Grabby carbon brakes, clunky e-gear	★★★★
Lamborghini Murciélago LP640	093 F	£212,750	12/6496	631/8000	487/6000	1665kg	385	3.3	-	211	-	21.3	+ Compelling old-school supercar - You'd better be on your toes	★★★★★
Lambo M'lago LP670-4 SV	138 F	£270,038	12/6946	661/8000	487/6500	1565kg	429	**3.2**	**7.3**	212	-	-	+ A supercar in its truest, wildest sense - Be prepared for stares	★★★★★
Lamborghini Murciélago	089 D	'01-'06	12/6192	570/7500	479/5400	1650kg	351	4.0	-	205	-	-	+ Gorgeous, capable and incredibly friendly - V12 feels stressed	★★★★★
Lamborghini Diablo 6.0	019 F	'00-'02	12/5992	550/7100	457/5500	1625kg	343	3.8	-	200+	-	-	+ Best-built, best-looking Diablo of all - People's perceptions	★★★★½
Lamborghini Diablo GT	016 F	'99-'00	12/5992	575/7300	465/5500	1490kg	392	**4.1**	**8.3**	211	-	12.5	+ Briefly the world's fastest production car - They made only 80	★★★★★
Lexus LFA	141 F	£336,000	10/4805	552/8700	354/6800	1480kg	379	3.7	-	202	-	-	+ Absurd and compelling supercar - Badge and price don't quite match	★★★★½
Maserati MC12	079 R	'04-'05	12/5998	621/7500	481/5500	1445kg	437	3.8	-	205	-	-	+ Rarer than an Enzo - The Ferrari's better	★★★★
McLaren F1	145 F	'94-'98	12/6064	627/7500	479/4000	1137kg	560	3.2	6.3	240+	-	19.0	+ Still the most single-minded supercar ever - There'll never be another	★★★★★
Mercedes SL65 AMG Black	131 F	£250,000	12/5980	661/5400	737/2200	1876kg	358	**4.0**	**8.1**	199	-	-	+ Bonkers looks, bonkers speed - Bonkers price	★★★★
Mercedes SLS AMG	146 R	£157,500	8/6208	563/6800	479/4750	1620kg	335	**4.1**	**8.4**	197	308	-	+ Great engine and chassis (gullwing doors too!) - Slightly tardy gearbox	★★★★★
Mercedes SLR McLaren	073 F	'04-'07	8/5439	617/6500	575/3250	1618kg	387	3.7	-	208	-	-	+ Zonda-pace, 575-style drivability - Dreadful brake feel	★★★★
Noble M600	138 F	c£200,000	8/4439	650/6800	604/3800	1250kg	528	3.0	-	225	-	-	+ Noble's unbelievably good attack on the supercar class - It's a bit pricey	★★★★★
Pagani Zonda F	082 F	'05-'06	12/7291	602/6150	575/4000	1230kg	497	3.6	-	214	-	-	+ Everything an Italian supercar ought to be - Choose interior carefully	★★★★★
Pagani Zonda C12S	096 F	'01-'05	12/7291	555/5900	553/4050	1250kg	451	3.6	-	197	-	-	+ Set a new supercar benchmark - Harry won't let us use his long-termer	★★★★★
Porsche 911 Turbo (997.2)	140 R	£105,927	6/3800	493/6000	479/1950	1570kg	319	**3.2**	**7.3**	193	272	24.8	+ The Turbo at the very top of its game - The GT3's cheaper...	★★★★★
Porsche 911 Turbo S (997.2)	146 R	£123,263	6/3800	523/6250	516/2100	1570kg	339	**2.9**	**6.8**	196	268	-	+ As above, with more power - The GT3's even cheaper...	★★★★½
Porsche 911 GT2 RS (997.2)	149 F	£164,107	6/3600	611/6500	516/2250	1370kg	453	3.5	-	205	284	-	+ More powerful than a Carrera GT. Handles, too - Erm...	★★★★★
Porsche 911 Turbo (997.1)	094 F	'06-'09	6/3600	472/6000	457/1950	1585kg	303	**4.0**	**8.7**	193	-	22.1	+ Monster cornering ability - A bit woolly on its standard settings	★★★★★
Porsche 911 Turbo (996)	017 F	'00-'06	6/3600	420/6000	413/4600	1540kg	272	**4.1**	**10.0**	189	-	21.0	+ The 911 for all seasons - We can't find any reasons	★★★★★
Porsche 911 GT2 (996)	072 F	'04-'06	6/3600	475/5700	457/3500	1420kg	339	4.0	-	198	-	-	+ Later revisions made it even more of a star - Care still required	★★★★★
Porsche 911 Turbo (993)	066 F	'95-'98	6/3600	408/5750	398/4500	1502kg	276	4.3	9.2	180	-	19.4	+ Stupendous all-weather supercar - It doesn't rain enough	★★★★★
Porsche 911 GT2 (993)	003 F	'96-'99	6/3600	430/5700	398/4500	1290kg	339	3.9	-	184	-	-	+ Hairy-arsed homologation special - Our publisher won't buy one	★★★★★
Porsche Carrera GT	149 F	'04-'06	10/5733	604/8000	435/5750	1380kg	445	**3.8**	**7.6**	205	-	-	+ Probably the greatest modern supercar - Can bite	★★★★★
Ruf Rt 12	097 F	c£155,000	6/3600	641/7000	641/3500	1530kg	426	3.3	-	219	-	-	+ Beautifully executed car with truly immense power - Needs care	★★★★★
Ruf CTR3	126 F	c£357,000	6/3746	691/7600	656/4000	1400kg	501	3.2	-	235	-	-	+ The best 911 that Porsche never made - But not the best looking...	★★★★★
Ruf CTR 'Yellow Bird'	097 F	'87-'89	6/3366	469/5950	408/5100	1170kg	345	4.1	-	211	-	-	+ A true legend - We can't all drive like Stefan Roser	★★★★★
Ultima GTR640	080 F	£68,000	8/6277	640/6500	560/4800	980kg	666	2.7	5.5	231	-	-	+ Awesomely rapid, and capable too - Race-car compromises	★★★★

2011 Trackday Calendar

Key trackday dates for the 2011 season

More events will be announced as the season progresses. Check websites for details. (Dates correct at time of going to press but may be subject to change.) And look out for the 2011 evo trackday dates, coming soon – visit evo.co.uk for the latest news

JANUARY
Fri 21st Cadwell Park javelintrackdays.co.uk
Sat 22nd Bedford (taster) clubmsv.com
Sat 22nd Brands (Indy) (taster) clubmsv.com
Tues 25th Oulton Park clubmsv.com
Weds 26th Brands (Indy) javelintrackdays.co.uk
Sat 29th Bedford easytrack.co.uk
Sat 29th Brands (Indy) clubmsv.com
Sat 29th Oulton Park javelintrackdays.co.uk
Sat 29th Silverstone circuit-days.co.uk
Sun 30th Cadwell Park easytrack.co.uk

FEBRUARY
Fri 4th Brands (Indy) clubmsv.com
Fri 4th Oulton Park clubmsv.com
Sat 5th Anglesey javelintrackdays.co.uk
Sat 5th Silverstone easytrack.co.uk
Sat 5th Cadwell Park clubmsv.com
Tues 8th Oulton Park clubmsv.com
Fri 11th Oulton Park easytrack.co.uk
Sat 12th Silverstone goldtrack.co.uk
Sat 12th Castle Combe bookatrack.com
Sat 12th Elvington javelintrackdays.co.uk
Sat 12th Brands (Indy) easytrack.co.uk
Sun 13th Mallory Park javelintrackdays.co.uk
Mon 14th Brands (Indy) (taster) clubmsv.com
Thurs 17th Brands (Indy) clubmsv.com
Fri 18th Oulton Park bookatrack.com
Sat 19th Castle Combe bhptrackdays.co.uk
Sat 19th Oulton Park javelintrackdays.co.uk
Sat 19th Anglesey bookatrack.com
Sun 20th Cadwell Park javelintrackdays.co.uk
Sun 20th Snetterton javelintrackdays.co.uk
Fri 25th Oulton Park circuit-days.co.uk
Sat 26th Snetterton (new) bookatrack.com
Sat 26th Castle Combe circuit-days.co.uk
Sat 26th Cadwell Park easytrack.co.uk
Sat 26th Bedford clubmsv.com
Sun 27th Silverstone goldtrack.co.uk
Mon 28th Bedford javelintrackdays.co.uk

MARCH
Weds 2nd Donington (national) goldtrack.co.uk
Fri 4th Cadwell Park clubmsv.com
Fri 11th Oulton Park clubmsv.com
Fri 11th Cadwell (novices) clubmsv.com

Sat 5th Donington bookatrack.com
Sat 5th Oulton Park (tbc) easytrack.co.uk
Sat 5th Rockingham circuit-days.co.uk
Sun 6th Snetterton circuit-days.co.uk
Sat 12th Cadwell Park circuit-days.co.uk
Sun 13th Silverstone (national) goldtrack.co.uk
Tues 15th Brands (Indy) clubmsv.com
Sun 20th Silverstone goldtrack.co.uk
Mon 21st Castle Combe bhptrackdays.co.uk
Thurs 24th Silverstone circuit-days.co.uk
Fri 25th Castle Combe javelintrackdays.co.uk
Sat 26th Cadwell bhptrackdays.co.uk
Sat 26th Spa bookatrack.com
Sat 26th Anglesey circuit-days.co.uk
Sun 27th Spa bookatrack.com
Mon 28th Bedford javelintrackdays.co.uk
Weds 30th Cadwell Park javelintrackdays.co.uk
Thurs 31st Thruxton goldtrack.co.uk

APRIL
Sat 2nd Mallory Park javelintrackdays.co.uk
Mon 4th Spa circuit-days.co.uk
Tues 5th Oulton Park goldtrack.co.uk
Sun 17th Anglesey bookatrack.com
Mon 18th Silverstone goldtrack.co.uk
Mon 18th Spa javelintrackdays.co.uk
Tues 26th Castle Combe bhptrackdays.co.uk
Weds 27th Cadwell javelintrackdays.co.uk
Weds 27th Oulton Park circuit-days.co.uk
Fri 29th Anglesey bookatrack.com
Sat 30th Mallory Park circuit-days.co.uk

MAY
Mon 2nd Croft javelintrackdays.co.uk
Mon 2nd Anglesey circuit-days.co.uk
Tues 3rd Silverstone goldtrack.co.uk
Fri 6th Castle Combe javelintrackdays.co.uk
Fri 6th Silverstone circuit-days.co.uk
Tues 10th Silverstone goldtrack.co.uk
Sat 14th Mallory javelintrackdays.co.uk
Mon 16th Castle Combe bhptrackdays.co.uk
Mon 16th Silverstone goldtrack.co.uk
Thurs 19th Snetterton javelintrackdays.co.uk
Mon 23rd Silverstone goldtrack.co.uk
Weds 25th Cadwell javelintrackdays.co.uk
Weds 25th Oulton Park bhptrackdays.co.uk

Thurs 26th Snetterton (new) goldtrack.co.uk
Mon 30th Silverstone goldtrack.co.uk

JUNE
Tues 7th Castle Combe bookatrack.com
Tues 7th Cadwell Park circuit-days.co.uk
Weds 8th Brands Hatch (GP) goldtrack.co.uk
Weds 8th Oulton Park circuit-days.co.uk
Fri 10th Anglesey bookatrack.com
Sat 11th Mallory Park javelintrackdays.co.uk
Sat 11th Croft circuit-days.co.uk
Tues 14th Snetterton circuit-days.co.uk
Mon 20th Silverstone goldtrack.co.uk
Mon 20th Snetterton bhptrackdays.co.uk
Tues 21st Silverstone (eve) goldtrack.co.uk
Weds 22nd Cadwell Park javelintrackdays.co.uk
Fri 24th Rockingham circuit-days.co.uk
Mon 27th Castel Combe bhptrackdays.co.uk
Tues 28th Spa goldtrack.co.uk
Weds 29th Spa goldtrack.co.uk

JULY
Fri 1st Castle Combe javelintrackdays.co.uk
Weds 6th Cadwell Park bhptrackdays.co.uk
Thurs 7th Snetterton javelintrackdays.co.uk
Tues 19th Cadwell Park javelintrackdays.co.uk
Mon 25th Castle Combe bhptrackdays.co.uk

AUGUST
Tues 9th Cadwell Park javelintrackdays.co.uk
Weds 10th Oulton Park bhptrackdays.co.uk
Mon 15th Snetterton javelintrackdays.co.uk
Mon 22nd Castle Combe bhptrackdays.co.uk
Mon 29th Croft bookatrack.com
Tues 30th Knockhill bookatrack.com

SEPTEMBER
Fri 2nd Anglesey bookatrack.com
Tues 13th Cadwell Park javelintrackdays.co.uk

OCTOBER
Mon 3rd Castle Combe bhptrackdays.co.uk
Weds 5th Cadwell Park javelintrackdays.co.uk
Fri 7th Castle Combe javelintrackdays.co.uk
Mon 10th Spa goldtrack.co.uk
Tues 11th Spa goldtrack.co.uk